Mosaics of Meaning: Enhancing the Intellectual Life of Young Adults through Story

❖ ❖ ❖ ❖ ❖

edited by

Kay E. Vandergrift

The Scarecrow Press, Inc.
Lanham, Md., & London

SCARECROW PRESS, INC.

Published in the United States of America
by Scarecrow Press, Inc.
4720 Boston Way
Lanham, Maryland 20706

4 Pleydell Gardens, Folkestone
Kent CT20 2DN, England

British Cataloguing-in-Publication Information Available

Library of Congress Cataloging-in-Publication Data

Vandergrift, Kay E.
Mosaics of meaning : enhancing the intellectual life of young adults through
story / edited by Kay E. Vandergrift.
p. cm.
Includes bibliographical references and index.
1. Young adult fiction, American—History and criticism. 2. Young adults—
Books and reading. I. Vandergrift, Kay E.
PS374.C454M67   1996   813.009'9283—dc20   95-51386   CIP

ISBN 0-8108-3110-4 (cloth : alk. paper)

⊖™ The paper used in this publication meets the minimum requirements of
American National Standard for Information Sciences—Permanence of
Paper for Printed Library Materials, ANSI Z39.48–1984.
Manufactured in the United States of America.

For

Lillian, My Mother,

Jane,

Betty Jean,

and

Kimberly, the Youngest Author Here,

Who, With Me in the Middle,

Represent Almost a Century of Women

Making Mosaics of Meaning of Their Lives

Table of Contents

Introduction

Mosaics are made of many fragments, often broken and irregular, arranged into unified, even beautiful, patterns or pictures. Thus, the mosaic is an appropriate metaphor for both the content and the creation of this book. Young adults today live in a world of immediacy, of fragmentation, of uncertainty. At a time when their greatest anxiety should be about which of a multitude of possibilities they will pursue for the future, many young people are not even certain there will be a future. Rather than asking "What will I be when I grow up?" they see hate, fear, pollution, and random violence in the world and ask "Will I grow up?" Even for many of our brightest young adults, the intellectual life pales in comparison to life in the streets.

One of the best means of combating the disassociation and depersonalization of young lives is through story, either fictional or informational narratives. Engagement with story is life-affirming; it puts us in touch with the world, with one another, and with our essential selves. Story also empowers readers to create wholeness, to make meanings that unify our own fragmented experiences and ideas with those expressed in story. Story helps us shape and reshape life, to give it importance and to reflect on who we are and who we might become.

The perspectives represented here are inclusive, interdisciplinary, and representative of topics not often dealt with and of common topics dealt with in unique ways. Many of the authors write from a standpoint in feminist theory, and all have a belief in the power of story to help young adults find and create deeper and more secure meanings in their lives. Several chapters focus on coming of age novels because it is these stories that most directly and most closely connect with the lives of young adults. The other arts are also important means of sharing both unique, personal perspectives and the commonalty of human experiences. Curricular subjects and concerns are examined and extended to encourage more thoughtful approaches as well as personal involvement and responsibility.

Each of the authors of these chapters contributes to this mosaic, this picture of young adults and story, in an effort to help other professionals interpret materials and engage in a dialogue among themselves and with young people. Most of these authors are children's or young adult librarians who interact with young people on a daily basis. Their reflections on young adults and literature are thought-provoking and demonstrate that theory follows practice as well as leading it. The four academics come from different disciplines, reinforcing the underpinnings of inclusiveness and diversity that unite this work. Although multiple approaches and points of view are represented, there is a commonality of spirit that brings these authors and their works together.

It was important to begin this book with the voice of a young adult. Even the strongest advocates for young people too often forget to stop and really listen to those we wish to serve. Kimberly Leanne Collins' portrait of herself as a young reader not only reaffirms our belief in the power of literature; it reminds us of the curiosity, the eclecticism, and the appetite for all forms of story that can enhance both the intellectual and aesthetic lives of youth.

My own "Journey or Destination: Female Voices in Youth Literature" presents a theoretical framework for examining the feminist ideas and approaches of many of the chapters that follow. Pamela E. Groves' "Coming-of-Rage: Young, Black and Female in America" begins with the personal pain of a young woman of color in an otherwise all-white graduate class discussing young adult literature. Like other authors, however, she looks within and beyond her own experience to help others understand that experience and to appreciate alternative approaches to the selection and discussion of literature representing the full range of human experience. In chapter four, Mary K. Lewis elaborates on literary examples that reveal the loss of voice now commonly identified by researchers as silencing young women in their early adolescence and demonstrates that this silencing has long been reflected in story.

Chapter five by Daughter/Woman is a powerful prose poem exposing the effects of incest—even on those a generation removed from the abuse—and comparing real-life coping strategies with those revealed in coming of age novels.

Hilary S. Crew's "The Making of a Heroine" focuses attention on female voices as revealed in historical novels, enabling readers to recognize that the lives of women have counted when the stories of history are told from a female perspective. In "A Lesson in Activism for Young Adults," Karen Toron Cooper uses novels of the Danish resistance during World War II to look at the holocaust from a different perspective. Her discussion of these stories engages readers in understanding the relationship between caring and taking a stand, putting care into action in the world.

Carol Jones Collins' "Finding the Way" looks more broadly at morality and ethics and uses young adult literature as a way of examining moral dilemmas faced by young adults. In "Graybeards and Grannies" B. Elizabeth Mina looks at the role of the elderly in society and shows the conflicting messages we send to young people through the literature created for them.

In "Catching the Shape of Their Dreams," Tess Beck Stuhlmann looks at the art of quilting as one of the ways people—most often women—tell their stories and shows the direct relationship to the metaphor of the mosaic. It is particularly important for young people to see that an art form such as quilting is a valid means of expression for deep feelings. Farris J. Parker discusses painting as another way of telling stories. In "Establishing Roots" he looks at African American paintings as a means of developing self-esteem and respect for others in a culturally diverse world.

Janet Kleinberg and Lynn Cockett report on their research examining the responses of young people to humor in "Why Angels Fly." This reader-response study helps us understand some of the things that evoke much needed laughter in the lives of young adults. In "Foul Play, Fair Play-Gender Awareness in Movement Education" Linda A. Catelli traces the history of gender bias in movement education and offers a framework for change. She provides a new way for professionals to look at sports stories for young women. An analysis of ninth grade health education textbooks in "Sex Education in an Age of Sexual Epidemic" by Nancy L. Roth teaches us to read carefully what these books tell young people about their own sexuality. In so doing, she heightens our awareness to the danger of faulty messages and language that distances sexual behavior from human emotions.

"To Boldly Go. . . Science Fiction (A Personal Odyssey)" by Bonnie Kunzel is a companion chapter to Kimberly Leanne Collins' in that it shows the extension of an interest in story from the young adult years through adulthood. The rich resource of titles discussed here is reflective of the many futures young adults may find as readers of science fiction. Marlyn Kemper Littman's "Alternative Meanings Through the World of Virtual Reality" introduces us to new forms of story, the beginnings of which young adults are now exploring on MOO (Multiuser Object-Oriented spaces) sites and the World Wide Web. Her work reminds us that stories have always presented virtual realities and that these alternative meanings are powerful means of enhancing the intellectual lives of young adults.

I am grateful to all of the authors not only for what they have written here, but for the many ways they have enriched my life. As friends and colleagues, they have jarred my mind, enlarged my horizons, and gladdened my heart. I am pleased and proud to be a part of this network of caring professionals. Two other friends whose care and concern are reflected on every page deserve more gratitude than I can express. Without the continuing efforts of Jane Anne Hannigan and Betty Jean Parks, this book would not have come to be. Finally, I wish to thank Julie Kuzneski and Shirley Lambert of Scarecrow Press for their encouragement and their help in bringing the project to fruition.

CHAPTER
ONE

Litanies of a Literature Lover, or Confessions of a Young Adult Reader

Kimberly Leanne Collins

Read (verb). 1. to examine and grasp the meaning of written or printed characters, words, or sentences. 2. to interpret the nature or meaning of through close examination or observation. Synonyms found in a thesaurus are "to apprehend, understand, construe, comprehend, discern, perceive, make meaning of, translate, analyze, and pore over." Of all these various meanings and synonyms, I love the meaning "to pore over." I have been known to sit and pore over a book for hours. It doesn't matter if the book is school related or not, I'm happy just as long as I'm reading. My passion is reading. I love to read, anything and anywhere. Ever since I can remember, I've had a book in my hand. I'm seventeen now and a senior in high school. When I'm not reading for course requirements, I read what I like. I've loved books that have taken me on some glorious adventure. The varieties have been and continue to be endless.

I truly believe that the major influences on how well and how often a child reads is the parent and the teacher. If a child is read to nightly, as I was by my mother, then that child will take a healthy interest in books. And up until the time I reached fourth grade, my teachers always scheduled story reading days. In second grade, we were faithfully read to. My classmates and I had books read to us written by Carolyn Haywood, such as *Little Eddie, Eddie's Menagerie, B Is For Betsy*, and *Betsy's Little Star*. We thrilled to the books of Robert McCloskey. *Homer Price* and *Centerburg Tales* are still unforgettable to me. For several years after second grade, I got *The Canterbury Tales* and *Centerburg Tales* confused with each other. Geoffrey Chaucer must have rolled over in his grave several times. My third grade class enjoyed such books as *The BFG, James and the Giant Peach, Bunnicula,* and *The Phantom Tollbooth.* Later, when these story sessions had stopped, I remember eagerly awaiting the S.S.R. (Silent Sustained Reading) periods in the school day. I was more than content to read any book of my choice on my own.

Between second and fifth grade, favorite authors of mine included Beverly Cleary, Lois Lowry, Lois Duncan, and Judy Blume. My first love was definitely Beverly Cleary. Her Ramona books were a way for me to forget about me, and to step into the shoes of another little girl my age. To me, Ramona Quimby was a real kid with real problems. She had to deal with her older sister, Beezus, not to mention a mean after-school babysitter. Then there was always the problem of not getting enough attention from her family. Ramona had it rough. Beverly Cleary told me about this child's problems and adventures with a definite comic flair, and I loved everything she wrote. When I watched a horror movie, which I loved doing, and couldn't sleep, I whipped out a Ramona book. When I wanted to laugh, Ramona was there. But don't think for a minute that the Ramona collection was the only work of Beverly Cleary's that I read. Before I moved from the Cleary phase, I had gone through thirteen of her books.

Another series that I faithfully read was the brainchild of Lois Lowry, none other than Anastasia Krupnik. The first thing I noticed about this character was her name. The names Anastasia and Krupnik certainly make for an interesting combination. The character herself has the same opinion and spends the entire book, *Anastasia Krupnik,* contemplating her name, her parents, and life in general. To make matters more interesting, her parents announce that after ten years they're having another child. What adolescent could ask for anything more? After reading the first of the Anastasia books, I was hooked. I couldn't get enough of the character and snatched up one book after another. Now, although I've long since left my Anastasia phase, occasionally I see a book about her that I haven't read and get this feeling that I'm missing out on something wonderful. Because I loved Anastasia Krupnik so much, I read other books by Lois Lowry, in some cases more than once or twice. I loved *A Summer to Die*. I devoured *Find a Stranger, Say Goodbye*. I thought that *Switcharound* was sensational.

A third favorite author of mine (because good things come in three's) was Judy Blume. *Superfudge* was the first Judy Blume book that I read, and by the second page I was laughing hysterically. Thus began my love affair with Judy Blume books. Aside from *Superfudge*; *Are You There, God? It's Me, Margaret*; *Tales of a Fourth Grade Nothing*; *Then Again, Maybe I Won't*; and *Otherwise Known As Sheila the Great* were all read and loved by me.

By the time I reached fifth grade, I had decided it was time for me, as an African American, to dip into the world of African American literature. I figured that since it was never assigned or discussed in school, I would have to read it on my own. Mildred Taylor's *Roll of Thunder, Hear My Cry*; *Song of the Trees*; and *Let the Circle Be Unbroken* were books I read and wrote book reports on. I also made an attempt to read Alice Walker's *The Color Purple*, but was forced to stop due to parental pressure (my mother believed that ten was too young to read this particular piece of literature). Fifth grade also found me exploring the realms of young adult literature. Years later, *Sorrow's Kitchen*, a biography of Zora Neale Hurston by Mary Lyons, was included on my reading list.

Up until this point I had been reading young adult literature sporadically, beginning with Francine Pascal's *Sweet Valley High* series in third grade. These books star the dazzling identical twins, Elizabeth and Jessica Wakefield. Elizabeth is smart, beautiful, and studious. She will do anything for anyone in need. On the other hand, Jessica is beautiful, boy crazy, adventurous, conniving, and comes and goes as she pleases. The twins have a good looking older brother, Steven, as well as wonderful parents. In short, they are all living a basically utopian life in sun drenched southern California. I bought approximately thirty-five to forty of these books. My goal was to have possession of all one hundred or so that were then in existence. I lasted through about twenty-six. At the time, I believed these books were both romantic and realistic. I'm sorry to say this, but occasionally I even wondered what it would be like to have a twin sister and to live the marvelous lives they lived. Fortunately, I finally came to the opinion that these books lacked substance quite some time before I actually stopped reading them. Nevertheless, I was determined to reach my goal of reading them all.

Because I had always been a fan of horror and thrillers, Lois Duncan fit in nicely with my collection of authors. *Summer of Fear* is the quintessential tale of unwanted house guests. In this case, the heroine's cousin stays for the summer and turns out to be a bad witch (as opposed to a good witch, such as Glinda, the Good Witch of the East). *Killing Mr. Griffin* is a story that many high school students may fantasize about, if only briefly. For all you high school students, be honest—hasn't killing your most hated teacher crossed your mind? In this book, the students do more than just think about it. *I Know What You Did Last Summer* is a book that was written in the style of a nightmare that never ends. In the book, several teens are directly involved in a hit-and-run car accident and try to keep it a secret. Months later, they are threatened by an unknown person who apparently knows about the accident. *Down a Dark Hall* is a book that could make any young adult think twice before going off to boarding school.

Along with Lois Duncan, Christopher Pike was on my list of favorite writers of horror. *Spellbound* was the first book of his that I read. It really scared me, most likely because I was able to see the scenes so vividly in my head. While this happens with almost all the books I read, the imagery is formed more clearly in some than in others. If the writing is particularly descriptive, a clear picture is formed. This is the style of writing I found in Pike's writing. Most of the time, I was scared to death reading his books.

My reading of *Spellbound* sparked the beginning of a beautiful relationship. I read *Slumber Party* and for years thought of that book when I went to sleepovers. *Chain Letter* was a book that kept me eagerly turning pages, waiting to see how long those teenagers would be terrorized. The last book I read by Pike was *Gimme A Kiss*. It was from this book that I learned what a Molotov cocktail is. One was used in an attempt to kill the heroine. This was heavy reading! I did start *Remember Me*, having been attracted by its cover. The cover was luridly illustrated with a girl's body sprawled out on the sidewalk to which she had just been hurled. This was a little too much. It was time to move on.

Two of the last young adult horror books I read were *The Seance* and *The Other Side of Dark* by Joan Lowery Nixon. In the first book, when several young people in a small town get together to have a seance, events more horrifying than they could have imagined occur. *The Other Side of Dark* deals with a girl who wakes up from a coma to find that years have passed and that the person who tried to kill her is still at large. Both were satisfyingly haunting.

The works of Cynthia Voigt came into my life at age eleven. I read *Homecoming* for a book report. *Homecoming* was heart wrenching. Several children, all siblings, are abandoned by their mother in a shopping center parking lot. After hours of waiting for her return, they realize that she isn't coming back, thus beginning a very long walk to the only person who might take them in. I liked this book so much that I got my mom to read it. Later, I read *Dicey's Song*, *Homecoming*'s sequel.

Sometimes I read books that were given to me as gifts and not because I chose them. This was the case when I became involved with the books of Paul Zindel. *The Pigman* left me horribly depressed. It is a story about two teenagers who befriend a lonely old man who lives alone in a large house. The book covers everything from love and friendship to death and betrayal. The Pigman himself dies at the end of the story. *The Pigman* had a sequel, *The Pigman's Legacy*. I began reading it, but never finished, thinking that it too would be sad. But this didn't stop me from reading Zindel altogether. *I Never Loved Your Mind* is a very funny book in its own unique way. I read it more than once. It put an interesting twist on teenage romance. The same is true for *Pardon Me, You're Stepping on my Eyeball*. I suppose I needed laughter more than I needed sadness at this time in my life.

As I got older, I found myself reading less upbeat books and switching to ones with more sobering topics. During this period, I stumbled upon Norma Klein. *Give Me One Good Reason* was a book I had seen in a bookstore, forgotten about, and then decided I just had to read. The book is about a financially stable, single woman who has a career and a basically good life.

However, she decides that the one thing missing from her life is a child. She decides to have one on her own and wants to know one good reason why she shouldn't. The book follows the course of her pregnancy and ends with the birth of her son.

Sunshine was the second and last Norma Klein book I read. It is a true story about a young mother who is diagnosed with incurable cancer. She spends the last few months of her life compiling a tape as a way to say goodbye to her baby. Needless to say, I was not made too happy by reading this book. This might be the reason that I read no more Norma Klein.

The *Anne of Green Gables* chronicles were a birthday gift to me one year. I enjoyed the first of the series, *Anne of Green Gables*, and thought the second, *Anne of Avonlea*, was an interesting sequel. However, I never got past the second book in that series. Maybe the fact that I felt unable to identify with Anne explains why I quickly lost interest in her. I decided to read other books by L. M. Montgomery. I chose *Emily of New Moon*. Since it was a quick and good read, I moved on to *Emily Climbs*. Once again, I couldn't finish this second book. I decided to leave L. M. Montgomery forever. I just could not relate to the characters and the situations.

While still in elementary school, I began to stray from young adult literature and move into adult literature. I was finding it hard to relate to the characters, the plots, and the settings in books for young adults. I felt removed from that fare. I yearned for something different. But before I finally left that literature, I made one last stab at it. Ever since I could remember, *Cracker Jackson* by Betsy Byars had sat in the Wyoming School library ready to read, but prohibited to those students below the sixth grade. It actually had a little sign on its cover saying, **YOU MUST BE IN SIXTH GRADE TO CHECK OUT THIS BOOK.** The mere thought that the book had been censored made me desperate to read it. I vowed to read *Cracker Jackson* the second I became a sixth grader. I waited years to read it and expected blood, gore, and sex on every page. Instead, the book was about spousal abuse. This didn't seem to me to be a topic that needed to be censored. The book managed to be both informative and disappointing at the same time.

Finally, I read two books which were written about the

African American experience. *Iggie's House* by my old favorite author Judy Blume is about a black family that moves into a white neighborhood. The book describes how the family is accepted by their new neighbors. Although not thoroughly captivated by the book, I could relate to it because I live in a predominately white neighborhood, as well as in a predominately white town. *Freedom Crossing* by Margaret Goff-Clark is about a young white girl who helps a young runaway slave to freedom. The book was interesting, and I liked, but didn't love it. But by the time I had finished reading these books I was already moving on up to the big leagues.

I was now reading books not only written by, but for adults. The book that actually started me on this path was *The Nurse's Story* by Carol Gino. I think what I liked most about it was its graphic and gory detail about disease and injury. This kind of book led me naturally to the next level. For years an uncle of mine had several Stephen King books on clear display in a bookcase in his family room. For years I tried reading one when my family came to visit, but there was always something distracting going on. Rarely was I able to read more than a few pages. Eventually and much to my surprise, my uncle gave me all of his Stephen King books. Included in the collection was the hard cover copy of *It*. The book in its entirety was over one thousand one hundred pages long. I had never tackled such a long book before. But tackle it I did.

I basically became the talk of the fifth grade, as I carried that book to and from school every day, reading it whenever I could. The other kids would say, "There goes Kim with her Stephen King book." Soon I began to see them come to school with King books. I was, for a very brief moment, a trendsetter. After I read *It*, other King books followed. *The Dark Half*, *Pet Sematary*, and *Thinner* were all much to my liking. Fairly recently, however, I've sworn off of King because more and more his books involve a great deal of cruelty to animals, and I love animals of all kinds. *Needful Things* was the book that finally pushed me over the edge. I was never able to finish it. My fellow students, however, still seem to be reading the master of the macabre with gusto.

Don't think that all I read at this time was fiction. I also read non-fiction. My favorites were on the mysterious and the disconcerting. I was most interested in books on the Loch Ness monster. My elementary school library had only two books on "Nessie," but this in no way stopped me. I merely read the same two books over and over. How neat, I thought, that an actual monster possibly lived in the murky depths of the Loch. The dark, freezing, unfathomable depths of the Loch, the old castle overlooking it, and the reported sightings of the monster all made Scotland seem like the ideal country to visit.

I loved to read "true" ghost stories, books about witches, and those about natural disasters. But by now, I definitely needed a change—a bit of fluff. Thus, 1991 began the age of the romance novel for me. I actually went to the bookstore and stood in the romance novels section for a full fifteen minutes, trying to find the perfect book to feast my eyes on. There were such interesting authors: Shirl Henke, Amanda Quick, and Johanna Lindsey. It was all so very exciting. Romance novels have classic lines in them like, "Her voluptuous breasts heaved as her blood raced, and she arched her back to receive his kiss." I finally chose a Johanna Lindsey book, entitled *Savage Thunder*. Lindsey specializes in historical romances, and this particular one is about a rough and rugged western outlaw and the upper class woman whose heart he eventually wins. Although I gave up romance novels soon after this, I must have subconsciously liked the genre, because about a year later I was back in the romance section looking for another book. It was right before midterm exams, and I needed to unwind. Johanna Lindsey became my favorite romance novelist. In fact, she is the only romance novelist I've read.

Although it began with *Savage Thunder*, my collection increased significantly after that. *Prisoner of My Desire* is probably my favorite. It tells a tale set in feudal England. The heroine, Rowena, is of royal blood, but is forced by her evil stepbrother to bear an heir and if she doesn't, he will have her mother killed. Rowena does the logical thing. She has her servants capture a serf, whom she rapes, apologizing the entire time. The serf is released after his forced service to her, and Rowena becomes pregnant. The serf, however, turns out to be a knight who is very, very angry at her. He, in turn, captures her and makes her his slave. After many trials and tribulations, they fall in love, and Rowena bears their child. What adventure! What romance! The other Lindsey books I've read and gotten a great kick out of reading are *A Gentle Feuding*, *Heart of Thunder*, *Tender Is the Storm*, and *Love Only Once*. After my then best friend became interested in Lindsey's books, the novelty wore off.

While it may seem that I've read romances for a long time, the phase only lasted for a year. One day I abandoned Johanna Lindsey, just abandoned her, and stepped up to Jackie Collins. I think her last name had something to do with my fascination. Jackie Collins has never been classified as a full-fledged romance novelist. Since she is found in the "plain" fiction section, I felt more respectable. Collins' books have a lot of sex in them, but her books are not formulaic in the same way that the romance novels are. Books such as *Hollywood Wives*, *Sinners*, *Rock Star*, *The World Is Full of Married Men*, and *Lovers and Gamblers* have many different characters, all of them being fairly well developed, physically, emotionally, and sexually. Yet, if you've read one, you've read them all. Each falls into a certain pattern that is not difficult to predict. Alas, I haven't read a Jackie Collins book in a year. But I am always open to reading any new Collins book that seems interesting.

I believe that mystery loves company. I love a good mystery. It all began in elementary school with the *Choose Your Own Adventure* series, and my interest in mysteries has never left me. Currently, all of the authors I have read regularly are women. I hadn't exactly planned that my favorite authors would be women, but I'm definitely not complaining.

Sara Paretsky—V. I. Warshawski—Chicago—private investigator—heaven! Out of all the mystery series and all the investigators and all the mystery writers, Sara Paretsky is my favorite author, and V. I. Warshawski is my favorite female private investigator, brainchild of Paretsky. I was prompted to read the V. I. Warshawski series after seeing the movie starring Kathleen Turner. Although the movie was not a huge success, it did give me great pleasure. For me, Kathleen Turner was perfect as Warshawski. She played her the way I thought she should be played. Warshawski is intellectual, extremely independent, with a very fashionable wardrobe. What's more, she is tough as nails. Who could ask for anything more? I certainly couldn't.

After the movie was over, I didn't want the story to end, so I rushed out and bought the first book in the V. I. Warshawski series. I now think that it was one of the best purchases I have ever made. *Indemnity Only* is the name of that book. It was rapidly followed by over six more. After reading the last and most recent book, *Tunnel Vision*, I've been experiencing withdrawal symptoms. I can't wait for Paretsky's next book.

The second mystery writer I read was none other than Dame Agatha Christie. However, I am very particular about which Christie books I read. I've always stuck strictly to Hercule Poirot. I began reading his series after becoming addicted to the *Mystery!* television series on PBS, starring David Suchet. His Poirot is so perfect. Out of all the actors who have played Poirot, I like Suchet the best. Now when I read any Poirot mystery, I always envision Suchet as Poirot. I can't envision any other Poirot.

The third female mystery writer I have discovered is Lynda LaPlante, and I've just done that recently. *Prime Suspect* is the only book of hers that I've read. The television series that began my fascination with Jane Tennison, the protagonist in the show, was actually three separate programs, *Prime Suspect, Prime Suspect 2,* and *Prime Suspect 3.* Only the first *Prime Suspect* is in book form to my knowledge. My interest in this book and in the British police officer, Jane Tennison, flow naturally from my seeing the television series.

Beginning in 1991, Helen Mirren has played the role of Detective Chief Inspector Jane Tennison. In the first of the three programs filmed so far, Tennison is up against a myriad of incredible obstacles, including extremely sexist and uncooperative colleagues, an impossible murder case, and a chaotic personal life. Mirren played the role to such perfection that I've watched some of her scenes so often that I have memorized whole segments of dialogue. It was due to Mirren's performance that I decided to read the actual book. Needless to say, I loved it.

After reading about my interest in mysteries, it is obvious that movies or television have played a role in what I read. But plays have also played a role. Several years ago I saw the Broadway play *Gypsy,* starring Tyne Daly as Mama Rose. I was so impressed that I ran to the library and got everything I could find on Gypsy Rose Lee. I read *Gypsy, A Memoir*, the work that made the play possible. I also read *Gypsy and Me*, by Gypsy Rose Lee's son, Erik Lee Preminger. After a failed attempt at finding *The G-String Murders*, a mystery written by Gypsy Rose Lee herself, I saw the movie based on the book, starring Barbara Stanwyck.

Another Broadway play I saw recently that made quite an impact on me was *Medea*, starring Dame Diana Rigg. The first thing that made me want to see *Medea* was Diana Rigg. She is elegant, refined, husky voiced (I like husky voices), and British. So off I went to the theater. The play was wonderful, the set was stunning, and Rigg was a breathtaking Medea. Never in my life had I seen a play so powerful. I wanted to see it over and over again. Since I couldn't, I bought and read Euripides' tragedy to relive the magic. I was not disappointed.

Since I've always been a big fan of the movies, old movies, that is, it was only natural that I became interested in the lives of the actresses and actors I'd become so accustomed to watching. I was raised seeing the *African Queen* from the time I was five or six. It is my mother's favorite film. She knows it backwards and forwards. While I don't know it as well as that, I do know it well. As a result, Katharine Hepburn and Humphrey Bogart have always been favorites of mine. However, the first celebrity life I read was Ava Gardner's autobiography, entitled *Ava: My Story*. After seeing *55 Days at Peking*, not even her most famous movie, I became intrigued with Ava Gardner. I absolutely loved the book. It was fabulous and funny. I've read the book more than once, and might read it again. She wrote about her three rocky marriages, her incessant battles with her husbands, her on again, off again relationship with third husband Frank Sinatra, her movie roles, and her bi-continental lifestyle with a light touch and a comic flair.

The second celebrity that I latched onto was Susan Hayward. This Susan Hayward kick has gone on for several years and is still going strong. The first Hayward movie I ever saw was *A Woman Obsessed*, actually a pretty bad movie. The picture was in color and took place in the country. To make matters worse, Hayward had an accent that never did sound quite right. Nevertheless, I was flipping television channels and stopped at the American Movie Classics channel. When I saw this woman with flaming red hair, I couldn't figure out who she was. Every time I heard the name Susan Hayward, I pictured Rita Hayworth. I actually knew they weren't the same person, but was merely confused about them. So the next time I saw her, this time in the movie *I'll Cry Tomorrow*, I was hooked. I rushed out to my nearest library and got a biography on her. In all, I've read three, some good, some bad. Whenever I go to the library now, I still look for biographies on her I haven't read.

While none of my other "kicks" have been quite as strong as Hayward and Gardner, they still were significant. I've not read any biographies lately, but ones I have read have included those on Rosalind Russell, Ginger Rogers, Lauren Bacall, Vivien Leigh, Barbara Stanwyck, Natalie Wood, and Robert Wagner. I also managed to include a biography on Zora Neale Hurston. With the exception of Hurston's, all the other biographies were prompted by my seeing an old movie I liked.

I'm now in the midst of reading feminist literature. My interest and ultimate involvement with feminism actually began with Gloria Steinem. After having problems with low self-esteem and low self-confidence, I chose to read a self-help book. I read *Revolution from Within*, a book by Steinem on self-esteem. It is an understatement to say that I loved the book. It helped me to see that many other women, including Gloria Steinem, have suffered from this malady. The book made me feel better. I felt so much better that I wrote Gloria Steinem to tell her how I felt. She wrote me back! Gloria Steinem actually wrote me back! The letter was on her personal stationery, written in her own hand, and signed "Gloria." I was on cloud nine. Furthermore, a few months later, Steinem's assistant wrote and then later called me about participating in a young women's feminist group. I joined the group. Today, I have more than my share of books by Susan Winters, bell hooks, Naomi Wolf, Dorothy Dinnerstein, Katie Roiphe, Alice Walker, and Gloria Steinem.

Looking back and seeing many of the books I've read over the years down on paper, I think it's quite a collection. I suppose I have what might be called eclectic taste. I've gone from Johanna Lindsey and Jackie Collins to *Medea* and *Prime Suspect*. Although the connections might be strange, there are still connections. One thing seemed to flow from the other. One book seemed to naturally lead to another on the same topic or by the same author. And there were definite phases. I had my humor stage, my "kid like me" stage, my Black stage, my horror stage, and my romance stage, to name a few. All were extremely interesting and filled a need I had at that moment. And I like the way my reading seems to dovetail with television and the movies.

Some people might wonder why I stopped reading young adult literature so early. My first thought was that I don't have the slightest clue. But on giving it further thought, I think that I wanted to be different from all the other kids I knew. I wanted to read different things and to know different things. In many ways, my interests were already quite different. I loved old movies in elementary school, and I was nuts about horror movies—still am. It seems natural that my reading habits would also be different. So I quickly moved to books that were more in line with my interests. Young adult literature didn't seem to be dealing with the breadth of things I was interested in. Perhaps that has changed to some degree now. In any case, most of the books I read were unique, whether I liked them or not. People may come and go, relationships may change, the sky may fall in, but I'm certain of one thing: it's going to take a lot to stop me from reading. I love books, and I love to read. Who could ask for anything more?

WORKS CITED

Bachman, Richard. *Thinner*. New York: New American Library, 1984.
Blume, Judy. *Are You There, God? It's Me, Margaret*. Englewood Cliffs: Bradbury, 1970.
_____. *Iggie's House*. Englewood Cliffs: Bradbury, 1970.
_____. *Otherwise Known as Sheila the Great*. New York: Dutton, 1972.
_____. *Superfudge*. New York: Dutton, 1980.
_____. *Tales of a Fourth Grade Nothing*. New York: Dutton, 1972.
_____. *Then Again, Maybe I Won't*. Scarsdale: Bradbury, 1971.
Byars, Betsy. *Cracker Jackson*. New York: Viking, 1985.
Collins, Jackie. *Hollywood Wives*. New York: Pocket, 1983.
_____. *Lovers and Gamblers*. New York: Warner, 1977.
_____. *Rock Star*. New York: Pocket, 1988.
_____. *Sinners*. New York: Pocket, 1971.
_____. *The World Is Full of Married Men*. New York: Pocket, 1968.

Dahl, Roald. *The BFG*. New York: Puffin, 1982.

_____. *James and the Giant Peach*. New York: Knopf, 1961.

Duncan, Lois. *Down a Dark Hall*. Boston: Little, 1973.

_____. *I Know What You Did Last Summer*. Boston: Little, 1973.

_____. *Killing Mr. Griffin*. New York: Dell, 1978.

_____. *Summer of Fear*. New York: Dell, 1976.

Euripides. *Medea and Other Plays*. Trans. Philip Vellacott. New York: Penguin, 1963.

Gardner, Ava. *Ava: My Story*. New York: Bantam, 1990.

Gino, Carol. *The Nurse's Story*. New York: Linden, 1982.

Goff-Clark, Margaret. *Freedom Crossing*. New York: Scholastic, 1980.

Haywood, Carolyn. *B is for Betsy*. New York: Brace, 1939.

_____. *Betsy's Little Star*. New York: Morrow, 1950.

_____. *Eddie's Menagerie*. New York: Morrow, 1978.

_____. *Little Eddie*. New York: Morrow, 1947.

Howe, James. *Bunnicula: A Rabbit Tale of Mystery*. New York: Atheneum, 1979.

King, Stephen. *The Dark Half*. New York: Viking, 1989.

_____. *It*. New York: Viking, 1986.

_____. *Needful Things*. New York: Viking, 1991.

_____. *Pet Sematary*. Garden City: Doubleday, 1983.

Klein, Norma. *Give Me One Good Reason*. New York: Putnam, 1973.

_____. *Sunshine*. New York: Avon, 1976.

LaPlante, Lynda. *Prime Suspect*. New York: Dell, 1991.

Lee, Gypsy Rose. *The G-String Murders*. Matituck: Amereon, 1941.

_____. *Gypsy, A Memoir*. New York: Harper, 1957.

Lindsey, Johanna. *A Gentle Feuding*. New York: Avon, 1984.

_____. *Heart of Thunder*. New York: Avon, 1983.

_____. *Love Only Once*. New York: Avon, 1985.

_____. *Prisoner of My Desire*. New York: Avon, 1991.

_____. *Savage Thunder*. New York: Avon, 1989.

_____. *Tender Is the Storm*. New York: Avon, 1985.

Lowry, Lois. *Anastasia Krupnik*. New York: Bantam, 1981.

_____. *Find a Stranger, Say Goodbye*. Boston: Houghton, 1978.

_____. *A Summer to Die*. Boston: Houghton, 1977.

_____. *Switcharound*. Boston: Houghton, 1985.

Lyons, Mary. *Sorrow's Kitchen: The Life and Folklore of Zora Neale Hurston*. New York: Scribner's, 1990.

McCloskey, Robert. *Centerburg Tales*. New York: Viking, 1951.

_____. *Homer Price*. New York: Viking, 1943.

Montgomery, L. M. *Anne of Avonlea*. New York: Grosset, 1936.

_____. *Anne of Green Gables*. New York: Grosset, 1935.

_____. *Emily Climbs*. New York: Bantam, 1983.

_____. *Emily of New Moon*. New York: Bantam, 1983.

Nixon, Joan Lowery. *The Other Side of Dark*. New York: Delacorte, 1986.

_____. *The Seance*. New York: Dell, 1981.

Norton, Juster. *The Phantom Tollbooth*. New York: Random, 1964.

Paretsky, Sara. *Indemnity Only*. New York: Dell, 1982.

_____. *Tunnel Vision*. New York: Bantam, 1994.

Pike, Christopher. *Chain Letter*. New York: Avon, 1986.

_____. *Gimme A Kiss*. New York: Pocket, 1988.

_____. *Remember Me*. New York: Pocket, 1989.

_____. *Spellbound*. New York: Pocket, 1988.

_____. *Slumber Party*. New York: Scholastic, 1985.

Preminger, Erik Lee. *Gypsy and Me*. New York: Thorndike, 1985.

Steinem, Gloria. *Revolution from Within*. New York: Little, 1992.

Taylor, Mildred. *Let the Circle Be Unbroken*. New York: Bantam, 1981.

_____. *Roll of Thunder, Hear My Cry*. New York: Bantam, 1976.

_____. *Song of the Trees*. New York: Bantam, 1975.

Voight, Cynthia. *Homecoming*. New York: Atheneum, 1981.

_____. *Dicey's Song*. New York: Atheneum, 1982.

Walker, Alice. *The Color Purple*. New York: Harcourt, 1982.

Zindel, Paul. *I Never Loved Your Mind*. New York: Harper, 1970.

_____. *Pardon Me, You're Stepping on My Eyeball*. New York: Bantam, 1983.

_____. *The Pigman*. New York: Harper, 1968.

_____. *The Pigman's Legacy*. New York: Harper, 1980.

CHAPTER TWO

Journey or Destination: Female Voices in Youth Literature

Kay E. Vandergrift

All of living is a process of coming of age, of reconciling the essence of the inner self with one's outer being, with the world, and with the changing expectations for that self in the world. The teen years, when young people are perched precariously on the brink between childhood and adult responsibilities, are, of course, when the coming of age process is most obvious. It is then that most young adults are making decisions which will have tremendous influence on the shape of their lives to come. Although the male coming of age story has been well documented, both in literature and in developmental theories, only lately have we realized that neither the authorized views of human development nor traditional coming of age novels really represent female lives.

A number of recent research studies document the fact that girls and young women are regularly thwarted in their coming of age process in our society.[1] Obviously, we need to be involved in changing all those societal factors that impede the development of young women, but we also need to actively present a wide variety of positive female images for them to emulate. Identifying strong female voices in children's and young adult literature and sharing that literature with young people is one way to present such positive images.

As Carolyn Heilbrun said in *Writing a Woman's Life*, "lives do not serve as models; only stories do that. And it is a hard thing to make up stories to live by. We can only retell and live by the stories we have read or heard." (37) Those of us who believe this know how important it is for young women to encounter the kinds of stories that will provide them with a rich variety of strong female characters, both young protagonists and older women, to serve as role models at critical stages in their development. These stories help to shape the lives of young women and also help to shape the ways females are perceived by young males.

THE RESEARCH DESIGN

In an attempt to maximize the power of stories to shape the lives and the perceptions of young women, I have initiated a research study based on my Model of Female Voices in Youth Literature (See Figure 1). The research design consists of four phases, the first two of which are complete. The third, represented in this chapter, is well under way; but the final phase, and ultimately the most important one, is yet to be realized.

The four phases of this research design are:

1. The extrapolation of feminist themes from the theoretical literature in three basic disciplines—general feminist theory, feminist literary theory, and feminist theories of child and adolescent development. Of course, each of these areas of study has many subsets, and there is some overlapping of the three. All have a strong historical component as feminist scholars in many fields work to uncover and reclaim female versions of the past. There is also a strong multicultural strand throughout in an attempt to include all those *others* who have been marginalized by dominant white, male perspectives.

2. The development of the Model of Female Voices in Youth Literature as a graphic representation of themes extrapolated from the above literature. The form of the model went through several stages in an attempt to avoid forms of representation commonly perceived to be either linear or hierarchical. The difficulty in achieving this visualization reminded me of how firmly ingrained such patterns of thinking are in the consciousness of all of us who grew up and

FIGURE 1. MODEL OF FEMALE VOICES IN YOUTH LITERATURE

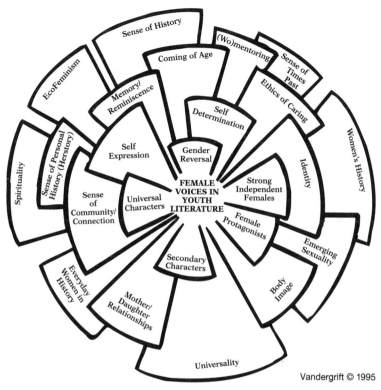

Vandergrift © 1995

General feminist theory, feminist literary theory, and theories of child and adolescent development provide the scholarly underpinnings from which this model is drawn. Since minority women have too often been excluded from the primarily eurocentric work of feminists, parallel strands of work by women of color attempt to assure the inclusion of all female voices. Of particular importance in general feminist theory are those texts that present alternative historical perspectives. Gerda Lerner's work, including *The Creation of Patriarchy* and *The Creation of Feminist Consciousness*, provide an overall theoretical standpoint for the study of women's history. Judith Zinsser's *History and Feminism*; Ann-Louise Shapiro's *Feminists Revision History*; Bonnie Anderson and Judith Zinsser's *A History of Their Own*; Patricia Morton's *Disfigured Images*; Sara M. Evans' *Born for Liberty*; Linda K. Kerber, Alice Kessler-Harris, and Kathryn Kish Sklar's *U.S. History As Women's History*; and Flora Davis' *Moving the Mountain* examine specific historical events from a feminist perspective. The body of work by bell hooks, Patricia Hill Collins' *Black Feminist Thought*, Alice Walker's *In Search of Our Mothers' Gardens*, Audre Lorde's *Sister Outsider*, Cherríe Moraga and Gloria Anzaldúa's *This Bridge Called My Back*, and Vicki Ruiz and Ellen Carol Du Bois' *Unequal Sisters* all help me see beyond my own privileged white perspective to consider the positions of women marginalized even by the feminist movement. Robyn R. Warhol and Diane Price Herndt's *Feminisms* presents a valuable introduction to literary theory and criticism as do Mary Jacobus' *Reading Women*, Sara Mills' *Gendering the Reader*, Molly Hite's *The Other Side of the Story*, Elizabeth A. Flynn and Patrocinio P. Schweickart's *Gender and Reading*, Anne Cranny-Francis' *Feminist Fiction*, Elaine Showalter's *The New Feminist Criticism*, and Carolyn Heilbrun's *Writing a Woman's Life*. Leigh Gilmore's *Autobiographics*, Joanne Braxon's *Black Women Writing Autobiography*, and Jill Ker Conway's *Written By Herself* offer insight into ways women represent themselves in their writing, often giving credit to others or to good fortune for their hard-earned accomplishments. *Women's Ways of Knowing* by Mary Field Belenky, Emily Hancock's *The Girl Within*, Carol Gilligan's *In a Different Voice*, and Lyn Brown and Carol Gilligan's *Meeting at the Crossroads* are exemplars of the many studies focusing on psychological development and the female coming of age process; and *The Female Adolescent* by Katherine Dalsimer explores this theme in the canonical literature. All of these works touch upon many of the themes represented in this model. There are, however, many additional sources that elucidate particular themes. For example, Greta Gaard's *Ecofeminism*; the work of Carol Christ, Judith Plaskow, Mary Daly and Cynthia Eller on spirituality; Terri Apter on mother/daughter relationships; and, of course, Carol Gilligan and Nel Noddings on the ethics of caring.

were educated in a world dominated by male paradigms. My first attempt to visualize these concepts took the form of a spiral; but, although that circular form is characteristic of female images, it also seemed to represent a logical and linear progression from the center to the outside. I then tried to design a kind of exploding circle with various pieces that would come together to make a complete geometric whole. That image appeared too regular, too sharp, and too angular to represent these often overlapping themes. The version of the model included here is more organic in nature, almost as petals of a stylized flower from which individual elements can be removed for independent study without destroying the totality of the organic form. As an organic form, it is expected that this model will be modified by those who use it, growing and changing as young people and adult intermediaries find their own connections between literature and feminist theory.

3. The identification of youth literature that includes the themes represented in the model and the validation of those themes in relation to the original theories from which they were drawn. It is important to include a sample of story with a strong female protagonist as a universal character in which gender is not a critical issue, just as it is important for racial and ethnic minorities to appear in universal childhood stories as well as those imbedded in race or ethnicity. The majority of the works included here, however, do have definite feminist subtexts that can be validated against feminist scholarship. This is not to say that such subtexts were deliberately, or even consciously, included in the literary composition or that they would necessarily be recognized by all readers. Nor am I positing that feminist themes should always be highlighted as we share these stories with children, believing that implicit messages of the media are often as powerful as explicit ones. What I am advocating is that feminist teachers and scholars join me in identifying and validating feminist themes in youth literature and make sound teaching judgments about when to focus on them in their work.

4. Reader-response studies with young adults, both male and

female, to determine whether or not these themes are identified by young readers as they talk and write about their transactions with the stories. This phase of the research has not yet begun but will build on a series of reader-response studies previously completed by this author[2] as well as on the analysis in the first three phases of this research design. A major factor to be considered in this phase, as in my earlier reader-response studies, is the role of the adult intermediary in such transactions between young people and literature. Of course, the adult intermediaries selected for these studies will be knowledgeable about feminism, literature, and young people and will approach this research from the standpoint of those concerned with the full development of all in a gender-fair, multicultural world.

WOMEN'S VOICES IN YOUTH LITERATURE

Feminist literary critics have, in the past three decades, worked diligently to identify women's texts that had almost been lost in the obscurity created by the domination of the male literary canon. As women's voices from the past have been rediscovered and heard by modern women, a new view of women's history and female achievements in literature and in other disciplines can be seen and appreciated. At the same time, modern women writers are finding and trusting their own authentic voices to tell their stories to others through fiction, biography, autobiography, poetry, and informational narratives. This generation of girls and young women is the first to have access to such a range of resources.

In spite of their efforts, feminist literary scholars are a long way from the establishment of an inclusive canon that affirms women's lives and represents female heroes independent of the male model. In order to make such changes, we must begin early; and an examination of the literatures shared with young people is an obvious starting point. There have been many bibliographies of children's and young adult stories with female protagonists labeled "feminist." The female protagonist, however, no matter how feisty or independent, is not enough. We must consider the richness and complexity of feminist texts and subtexts as they are present in youth literature. The model permits us to see some of the range of feminist themes explored in literature for young people. One may assume somewhat of a logical progression clustered around the center as fictional females developed from secondary characters to protagonists who were either universal, essentially genderless, characters or those presented as gender reversals to females who are truly strong and independent in their own right. Beyond that inner circle, the feminist themes represented are placed around the center with no attempt to demonstrate particular relationships because many texts include various themes located at disparate parts of the model. It is important to note, however, that, as works of literature, the texts discussed in relation to this model may be perceived from multiple perspectives and are certainly not limited to meanings made in this context. That multiplicity of meanings is, of course, characteristic of feminist thought as well as of literature and should encourage young people to construct and communicate their own meanings made in transactions with literary works.

Although male paradigms persist, contemporary books do provide many opportunities for young people to encounter strong female voices in a variety of times, places, roles, and literary styles. Books such as those listed in Appendix A go beyond just having female protagonists. They are not only gender-fair; they are multicultural, international, and represent a diversity of ages, classes, and personalities. Some assist in the process of researching women's history, others celebrate women's forms of expression, others tell of a young woman's relationship with parents or grandparents, and still others offer new perspectives on other women in the lives of young people. This literature is also beginning to present alternative, more inclusive, views of everyday human lives and of scholarly disciplines than ordinarily represented in traditional school curricula. As these materials are more widely read, both by young people and by those adult intermediaries whose own education was bound by eurocentric male canons; feminist historians, for example, may not forever have to recover and introduce to adults a new version of history inclusive of women and minorities. Through youth literature, probably more readily than through authorized textbooks, young adults can become familiar with aspects of human life absent in most school curricula.[3]

Unfortunately, as evidence indicates, the increased production of feminist texts does not necessarily mean these resources are readily available to young readers. With dwindling budgets for school and public library collections, fewer materials are purchased; and priority is often given to resources for young people that support school curricula. If these curricula emphasize a traditional male-dominated view of the world, as most still do, supporting that view is a denial of women's contributions and a silencing of women's voices. Of course, more enlightened curriculum developers are demanding histories of all disciplines that are more inclusive of women and minorities, but the textbook industry is so firmly entrenched in our schools and so much a part of the financial structure of public education that change is almost impossibly slow. In the meantime, publishers, facing their own downsizing and cost-cutting measures as they are bought up by huge international multimedia conglomerates, allow all but the best-selling works to go out of print almost before parents, teachers, librarians, or young people have the opportunity to learn about them and certainly before many libraries can muster the monies to purchase them. Even those who try to supplement authorized curricula by providing alternative views, especially those of women and minorities within our culture as well as the perspectives of other cultures and nationalities, face difficulties in doing so. Short print runs, limited in-print times, and tax laws that discourage the storage of backlists, along with bottom-line mentalities that encourage emphasis on established markets, work together to limit production of alternative texts by major publishers. Smaller presses with limited resources for both production and advertising may not have adequate access to reviewing media and may not even be handled by the largest distributors. Thus, their materials are not only more difficult to locate, they are more costly to access both in time and dollars.

COMING OF AGE IN AMERICA

Of all the feminist themes identified in this model, coming of age is the one most obviously related to the lives of young adults. One could speculate that the coming of age process is more difficult for those growing up in a young and diverse country like the United States that has few traditional rites of passage from one stage of life to another. Without formal ceremonies or rituals generally recognized as marking the move into adult society, both young people themselves and the adults to whom they look for guidance may be uncertain about when and how one is truly "grown up." Extended periods of economic dependence which accompany the increased demand for higher education only complicate this issue. The dilemma is compounded by the fact that young people today can no longer assume that, even with their extended educations, they will be more successful or more prosperous than their parents' generation. In fact, an alarming number of young people worry about whether they will even live long enough to become adults, which is not surprising given the juvenile mortality rate in this country. In a society that fosters such adolescent angst, it is understandable that young adults' self-determined rites of passage often take a dangerous turn. Teenage rebellion and risk-taking have traditionally represented both the breaking from childhood restrictions and an imagined sense of invincibility, even immortality. Today's young people are still marking the transition from child to adult, but they may also be tempting fate in different, less positive, fashions than earlier generations. Young adults who experience, at least intermittently, a sense of hopelessness, may feel that they have little to lose by demonstrating their independence from adult authority through drinking and driving, other forms of substance or self-abuse, or unsafe sex. A generation reared on images of violence, hate, death, destruction, and inhumanity, both in newscasts and in entertainment broadcasting, may suffer a kind of duality of consciousness. On the one hand, they want to cower in childhood for what little protection is available to them there while, on the other, they feel the need to rush into adult life before they lose that possibility altogether.

That duality and the contradictions of young people coming of age are often especially acute for females who are simultaneously expected to assume nurturing, caregiving roles and to remain dependent and subservient. Often one is called upon to be "Little Mother" to siblings, sometimes even to parents, while remaining "Daddy's Little Girl." Unfortunately, this kind of duality has historically been perpetuated in the adult lives of women who provide physical and emotional support for others but must accept a childlike dependence to acquire the resources necessary for such a role. When they try to gain the emotional and financial independence which would enable them to perform that role on their own, they are accused of abandoning those who need them or of being "unnatural." Of course, feminist research has greatly expanded our perceptions of what is "natural" for women, and these new views of women are present in fiction as well as in scholarly reports, and informational narratives.

YOUNG ADULT FEMALES AND THEIR LITERATURE

American literature is rich in both young adult novels and in our own versions of the *bildungsroman*, the novel of education or of initiation in which the central character learns about the world while growing up and into that world. In fact, as a young country, many of our classic stories are about rebellion, loss of innocence, and coming of age, the staples of young adult literature. One will note, however, that from *The Adventures of Huckleberry Finn* to *The Catcher in the Rye* to *A Separate Peace* to *Rule of the Bone*, most of the protagonists in these books are male. Even *The Outsiders*, considered one of the foundations of contemporary young adult literature, has a basically all-male cast of characters, although it was written by a young adult female. Of course, talented authors regularly write from the perspective of those unlike themselves; some might consider this an ironic reminder that young women have grown up identifying with male protagonists in required texts and have become so adept at it that only recently have feminists forced us to examine these responses to literature as another example of women living through and for others rather than creating their own self-identities as females. Judith Fetterley writes eloquently about this in *The Resisting Reader*, describing the process by which women must actively resist the male paradigms dominating literature and scholarship. Such paradigms demand that females identify against themselves, that is, they identify with male characters and situations, often those exhibiting stereotypical views of women.

The books discussed as exemplars in this chapter express the voices of young adult females whether they are published as young adult novels or as adult novels in which adult characters look back retrospectively at their earlier coming of age experiences. Several points must be made about this literature and those who read it. One, we live in a society in which young people are, in many ways, coming of age earlier than previous generations. That fact, combined with the knowledge that young people generally like to read about those at least slightly older than themselves so they can vicariously experience what lies ahead, means that novels labeled "young adult" are commonly read by ten- to twelve-year-olds. Two, although women in many societies have had to assume "adult" responsibilities at an early age, such responsibilities have been more likely to delay than to hasten a true sense of coming of age in which one establishes a personal identity in coming to know both oneself and the world. Thus, many of the female coming of age stories are set later in life than most such male stories and may take place in the character's twenties, thirties, or even beyond. Third, the primary literature of many in this media-saturated age is not print but aural and visual media in other formats. The Model of Female Voices might, therefore, be useful in an analysis of television show and other popular media, as well as of print literature.

Young adults who do read, however, are often avid readers who, although they may read primarily adult works, enjoy a variety of genre, including young adult literature, and are powerfully affected by what they read. Even those who seldom read may be greatly influenced by their transactions with a single book or set of books. Those who read genre fiction read the same mysteries, romances, and science fiction as adult genre readers. The same is probably true for those who gravitate toward informational narratives or more general categories of fiction. Young adults, however, have a special affinity for stories written for adults about young adults. In a way, such stories provide opportunities for them to eavesdrop on what adults are saying and thinking about them and their peers and perhaps to gain insight into their own lives. Also appealing are those adult stories about younger children that enable young adult readers, with adult authors and readers, to look back from a position of greater maturity on those without the benefit of their experience.

FEMALE COMING OF AGE STORIES

One of the most critical and most fascinating elements in the Model of Female Voices in Youth Literature for those who work with young adults is obviously that of coming of age. Readers look to stories for confirmation and illumination of their own life experiences and for vicarious experiences very different from their own reality but that, nonetheless, extend their perceptions of the world and their understandings of those who share that world. In Heilbrun's words, these are "stories to live by," stories that portray strong models for young women coming of age in difficult times and difficult circumstances.

One might posit that almost all young adult literature is coming of age literature; that is, it is a literature in which young protagonists are engaged in the process of separating from childhood, of making the transition from the security of family and then from peers to independence and maturity, and ultimately of integrating their lives into a community of adults. Of course, not all young adult books include the entire range of this process. Younger young adults, approximately ages ten to twelve, often read stories that focus on young characters rebelling against parental authority as they develop new interests in the opposite sex and in their own appearance and establish strong ties with peer groups. In real life this is a dangerous time for girls when they suffer a loss of confidence and too often begin a cycle of eating disorders in response to unrealistic concerns with body images. In the literature, however, the real physical and emotional changes facing young girls are seldom dealt with. While boys are breaking boundaries with rebellious adventures, girls are most often featured in stories in which an animal character has co-billing or those which perpetuate the paradigms of male power.

In the transition stage, both male and female characters usually go on a journey and face some sort of isolation, either physical or psychological. For girls, the journeys and isolation are frequently internal as they face the personal tragedy of being different, while the conflicts faced by young men are most often physical ones. As indicated earlier in this chapter, most of the novels young people read in schools are male coming of age stories and require the resistance of female readers to avoid that crisis of consciousness all too commonly experienced by young females. It is at the third stage, as young people take their places in the adult community, when we have traditionally seen the most dramatic differences between male and female characters. While young men are portrayed as establishing separate identities, beginning careers, and embarking on life's journeys, females are pictured as reconciling themselves to their circumstances, assuming new responsibilities, and settling in as if at the end of a journey. Thus, it is imperative that we identify powerful young adult novels with strong feminist themes that will increase the awareness of male dominance in literature and help young women to begin their own resistance as readers. In fact, it would be most effective to begin with a study of contemporary picture books with strong feminist themes because of the brevity of these works and the clarity of the themes. Young adult and adult stories are often too dense, too complex, and too layered with ideas to readily identify specific feminist themes. In a well-written story, such themes are so integrated into the totality of the composition that one would have to re-read the entire work several times to verify the existence and the importance of such themes in the story.

YOUNG ADULT NOVELS

One young adult novel with an adult protagonist from the realm of folklore that can serve as a transition between the books for young children and those for young adults and adults is *The Magic Circle* by Donna Jo Napoli. This book is a powerful rendering of an alternative version of the Hansel and Gretel story as told in the first person by the hunchbacked old woman who has become the witch. The "Ugly One" had been a midwife and a healer until, tempted by a golden ring, she steps from the magic circle of God's power to the powers of evil, making her a witch who craves the blood of children. Isolating herself in the woods away from all human life, she vows to resist the evil that has possessed her. When Hansel and Gretel arrive at her cottage, she takes them in and, drawing upon what remains of her inner beauty and purity, hides their presence from the demons and treats them as her children. But the demons are not to be denied and the witch/mother cannot forever resist their powers. In a hauntingly fascinating twist of the old tale, the witch plots her own death and, in death, frees herself from the powers of evil as she frees Hansel and Gretel from the demons who would use her to destroy them.

Young people familiar with traditional folk literature may also have read some of the many contemporary stories which present alternative versions of these tales; often switching the point of view from antagonist to protagonist. In this instance, the alternative perspective is that of the older female character portrayed as evil in the original story. This change of point of view encourages young people to look sympathetically at those who have been marginalized or portrayed negatively, an ability that, one hopes, may be transferred from literature to life. Young adults may even want to explore the more scholarly feminist literature on crone theory as a result of reading this and similar stories.[4]

A more realistic older female character is the eccentric and somewhat acidic grandmother in Lensey Namioka's *April and the Dragon Lady*. The dragon lady of the title is a seventy-year-old Chinese grandmother who sneaks around putting empty soap boxes in the neighbors' garbage cans on a rainy night, plays mahjongg with the ladies at the nursing home and wins their valuables, and escapes from her own birthday party to join, uninvited, another party at the restaurant. Grandma may appear confused at times, but she rules the family with the full power of Chinese tradition behind her. Fifteen-year-old April has to plan her life around Grandma's care in spite of the fact that "I didn't count with her because I was only a granddaughter, a girl." (9) Her older brother, Harry, on the other hand, enjoys the benefits of a tradition in which men are all-important and have only to marry and raise children to carry on the family name. Although this is a typical young adult coming of age novel, it is also the story of three generations of women trying to remain true to themselves while coming to grips with changes over time and across cultures. Between the two title characters, both in age and in coping strategies, is Ellen Wu, the thirty-something divorced university teacher who is involved with April's widowed father but reluctant to join a household ruled by the grandmother. Each of these women faces her own inner turmoils and finds her own ways to bend the walls of tradition without breaking them down completely. Symbolically, the gift of the jade bracelet which April loved, and which, along with the grandmother's other woman's things—fans, a locket, embroidered silks, and clothing, "are for Harry, of course" (12) shows the grandmother's reluctant willingness to change.

One of the most popular heroines of contemporary young adult literature is Dicey Tillerman, the protagonist of several of Cynthia Voigt's novels. In *Homecoming*, Dicey successfully completes her journey shepherding her three younger siblings, on foot, from Massachusetts to the Chesapeake Bay area and to the grandmother they had never met. It is in *Dicey's Song*, however, that we most clearly see her coming of age as she begins to learn who she is as a person, apart from the provider and guardian she has had to be. As she opens herself to new possibilities and to new relationships with others, so too does Gram who had kept her own feelings packed up with the remnants of the past hidden away in her attic. Throughout the novel, Dicey and Gram help each other learn about holding on, reaching out, and letting go. Until now, Dicey has concentrated so hard on holding on to what little she had that she was unable to reach out to others, even to those closest to her. In an effort to prevent Dicey from making the same kind of mistakes she made, Gram tells her how she allowed her husband to dominate her life and keep her from reaching out to her own children. She says:

> I let the children go away from him. And from me. I got to think-
> ing—when it was too late—you have to reach out to people. To
> your family too. You can't just let them sit there, you should put
> your hand out. If they slap it back, well you reach out again if
> you care enough. . . . You don't go reaching out with your hand
> closed up. (119–120)

Dicey does reach out—to Gram; to Mina, a classmate; and to Jeff whose music gains him entrance into the Tillermans' lives. Dicey also learns that one way of holding on is to let go. "But part of holding on was letting him [her brother James] do things his own way." (90) The most important "letting go" for Dicey, however, was her learning to let go of the past, to give up some of her adult responsibilities and perhaps even to learn to be the child she never was.

The metaphors that move this story so powerfully are those of music, the sea, and wood. Wood and water are pictured on the front of the dust jacket with Dicey leaning against an old wooden boat at the seashore, and the wood is picked up again in the image of the paper mulberry tree on the back of the jacket. The boat symbolizes being a part of the family who has owned the boat, and the family is represented by the branches of the tree. The boat also reminds readers of the ability to control the tiller and to set one's course on the sea of life. (Most readers see, rather quickly, the association with the family name; young feminists note the final syllable—Tiller*man*.) The most poignant image of wood is that of the wooden box in which Dicey and Gram carry Dicey's mother's ashes home to be buried by the mulberry tree, to bring her once again into the encompassing branches of the family tree. Dicey describes the boxes in the woodworker's shop:

> They were simple boxes with lids that fit down over the tops. But all of them had been constructed out of a variety of woods, and the woods seem to fit together as the pieces of a patchwork quilt do. The different woods talked together, Dicey thought, look at them; only it was more like singing in harmony than conversation. (173)

The rhythms and the syncopation of the sea pervade this story's plot and the lyrical sound of its language. Dicey herself is compared to a sailboat sitting at anchor, not anchored as a tree is planted but safely at rest in the quiet ebbing and flowing of a calm sea. It is Dicey's song, of course, that is noted in the title and is the central metaphor of this story. It is the movement of music that draws Dicey toward others and enables her to find and listen to her own voice so that she can enter into harmony with those whom she learns to care about and to trust. Ultimately Dicey moves out of a lonely silence into a song of celebration with friends and family.

ADULT NOVELS

Ellen Foster, the title character in Kaye Gibbons' first novel, is a tough, street-smart, eleven-year-old innocent who looks back from the security of her new life in a foster home to years of abuse at the hands of her severely dysfunctional family. It is that combination of childlike innocence and tough-minded survival skills that is so appealing. Young adults may smile with a kind of caring but bemused condescension as they read of Ellen's initial misinterpretation of *foster family*. When she could no longer tolerate living with relatives who didn't want her, Ellen determined to pick out a new mama for herself and decided that "the woman with all the girls lined up by her" (98) in church "fit my description perfect and I started thinking hard about how to be her new girl." (98) Thinking the foster family was a family named Foster, Ellen decided to take Foster as her surname. On the other hand, Ellen has the kind of savvy, good humor, common sense, and strength of character that enable her to endure severe emotional brutality, to outwit her drunken father, and to survive deprivation while maintaining a positive outlook on her future. Although Ellen is only eleven years old at the novel's end, she has, in many ways, already come of age and readers leave her story confident that, despite hardships yet to come, she will make a secure future for herself.

The emergence of sexuality is evident in a number of coming of age novels. For instance, a soft approach is used in Jamaica Kincaid's *Annie John,* in which Annie begins to be noticed by boys and hears her mother's sharply toned voice saying:

> . . . after all the years she had spent drumming into me the proper way to conduct myself when speaking to young men, it had pained her to see me behave in the manner of a slut (only she used the French-patois word for it) in the street and that just to see me had caused her to feel shame.

> The word "slut" (in patois) was repeated over and over, until suddenly I felt as if I were drowning in a well but instead of the

well being filled with water it was filled with the word "slut," and it was pouring in through my eyes, my ears, my nostrils, my mouth. As if to save myself, I turned to her and said, "Well, like father like son, like mother like daughter." (102)

From early childhood, Annie had loved her mother intensely. In fact, the essay she reads in school is a poignant expression of those feelings for her mother. (41–45) After reading her powerful and moving essay Annie writes:

Often I had been told by my mother not to feel proud of anything I had done and in the next breath that I couldn't feel enough pride about something I had done. Now I tossed from one to the other: my head bowed down to the ground, my head high up in the air. (45)

By the time Annie has decided to go to England and study nursing, although not truly committed to the field, the relationship with her mother is tense and painful. Typical of mother-daughter relationships at this age, Annie is backing away from her mother while recognizing the bond between them.

Another adult novel dominated by a mother-daughter relationship and emerging sexuality is Jeanette Winterson's *Oranges Are Not the Only Fruit*, set in an evangelical home in the industrial midlands of England. Jeanette is adopted to be raised as a young Christian woman, home-schooled until her mother is forced to send her to the local school. Jeanette is extraordinarily sheltered by a determined and religiously focused mother and is very much disliked by her classmates and her teachers. She embroiders religious samplers and shakes her tambourine with the other church people. Her mother sees herself as a missionary who will raise up her child to actually go to the missions. The chapters share their titles with chapters from the Bible, emphasizing the driving force of missionary zeal, but occasional glimpses of folktales and the Arthurian legend also enter the story. Eventually, Jeanette comes to recognize that her sexuality draws her to other females; and, when this is discovered by her mother, a great battle for her soul ensues. This mother-daughter relationship is severely strained, and their Pentecostal church offers potential correction to the situation but never actually changes Jeanette.

The House on Mango Street by Sandra Cisneros is a series of vignettes in the coming of age process of Esperanza Cordero, a young Mexican-American woman growing up in Chicago's Hispanic community. The short chapters capture the essence of her life and that of her friends and are very appealing to young readers. Esperanza hates her name, is quite conscious of her poverty, and yet believes winning the lottery may be a reality. She shares the pathos of a friend who is the victim of abuse, both physical and psychological, in her chapter "What Sally Said." Esperanza describes this schoolmate's pain-wracked life:

> But Sally doesn't tell about that time he hit her with his hands just like a dog, she said, "like if I was an animal. He thinks I am going to run away like his sisters who made the family ashamed. Just because I'm a daughter, and then she doesn't say." (92)

Esperanza has a strong community anchoring that enables her to write:

> One day I will pack my bags of books and paper. One day I will say goodbye to Mango. I am too strong for her to keep me here forever. One day I will go away.
>
> Friends and neighbors will say, What happened to that Esperanza? Where did she go with all those books and paper? Why did she march so far away?
>
> They will not know I have gone away to come back. For the ones I left behind. For the ones who cannot out. (110)

Her ability to share her cultural identity with flamboyant colors and keen observations all around her reveal Esperanza's coming of age with power and beauty.

How to Make an American Quilt by Whitney Otto is an innovative and compelling novel that uses the metaphor of the quilt to look at patterns of women's lives in twentieth century America. The stories of the eight members of a small town quilting circle are interspersed with instructions on quilting, so that both scraps of fabric and fragments of the life stories come together in wholes greater than the parts. The thread tying these pieces together is the visit of the granddaughter of one of the quilters prior to her impending marriage. This young woman, Finn, hears the stories of all the quilters and gains an appreciation for several generations of women. Sophia Darling's story, beginning at age seventeen, is one that may give young adults a great deal of insight into what coming of age meant for women of their mothers' and grandmothers' generations. Sophia is a water creature who loves diving for "the feeling of falling. Of the water rushing toward you and there is nothing to be done about it. You cannot alter your course once you jump from the board . . . I guess you could say it combines certainty and the unexpected" (56). This combination of certainty and the unexpected is played out when she meets a young geology student with whom she wants to travel the world, swimming in all its various bodies of water while he studies the earth. Both earth and water come together on their very first date, and a pregnant Sophia marries Preston and convinces him:

> that if I have to stay, so do you.
>
> . . .
>
> Sophia lives with the inheritance of her mother, who lived with the inheritance of her mother. She is not expected to attend to her own intrepid journeys or follow her own desires. Her time does not encourage it. (73)

Sophia has had to give up her dreams but so too has her husband, and his point of view is also presented. He wonders:

> "Who am I, what does being like me mean? . . . A romantic? A wanderer?" Surely he is neither of those, if he examines his life. He was once someone who moved without thought of the consequences, acted on nervy impulse. Like his marriage to Sophia, his fishgirl, who adapted herself to home and hearth with a vengeance, like someone who has something to prove or a debt to pay back. (78–79)

Sophia, Preston, and their three children are bound together by blood, love, convention, and the certainties of their small town lives. Yet when sixteen-year-old Edie, sent away to give birth to a child whose father she does not want for a husband, disappears in her ninth month, Preston goes to search for her and, at the end of Sophia's chapter, he has not come home or been heard from. One wonders if this too is part of the inheritance of her mother whose own husband, Sophia's father, had deserted them during the Great Depression.

At the end of Sophia's story, when Sophia is home alone with the son who gave up his dreams to stay with his mother, the author reflects upon the relationship of Sophia's quilting preferences and the patterns of her life.

> Sophia does not enjoy the freedom of color and pattern in the Crazy Quilt. . . . Sophia prefers the challenge of a traditional, established pattern. That is the true challenge, she thinks—to work within a narrow confine. To accept what you cannot have; that from which you cannot deviate. (79)

This novel, using the quilt as a frame, with the quilters telling their individual stories, may encourage young adults to investigate the role of quilting in women's lives in American society as a means of communication, of community-building, and of self-expression.[5]

The Scent of the Gods by Fiona Cheong is the story of Esha, called Su Yen by her grandmother. Su Yen is the eleven-year-old teller of the family story, detailing life in Singapore during the trying times of the 1960s. Clearly, the grandmother dominates the clan who all live in one household. Su Yen is a keen observer who describes her grandmother and her influence:

> She was sitting near a window that opened out from the kitchen, and in the light that fell onto the porch, I could see how she kept her hands folded in her lap, neatly, the way she had taught me, many times, to fold my hands so that people would know that I was a proper young lady. These things were important, she told me. Men were going to treat me according to how I behaved. One day when I was older, she said, I would understand what she meant, and I would be grateful that she had taught me the proper graces. (9)

The sharing of these times of upheaval and death reflects the cultural pattern of this Chinese family combined with typical events in a girl's coming of age. The girls in Su Yen's school are fascinated with the sexual behavior of the boys in the nearby school, although they only vaguely grasp what is really happening. Again Grandmother adds her viewpoint: "Do you think about boys yet, . . . You are too young. Boys are trouble for you, you understand? . . . Concentrate on your studies" (95). Nonetheless, young Su Yen, after watching an incident of the local boys taking pictures of Patricia climbing a tree they had rigged, writes: "I had wondered how much a Catholic schoolboy would pay for a photograph of Patricia's panties" (96). She goes on to say "Until then I had believed that the thing called sex was a thing only grown-ups understood, a thing only grown-ups could feel" (100). Later, Su Yen writes of the rape and subsequent pregnancy of Aunt Daisy; the killing of her dearly loved and protected cousin, Li Shin; and her own final departure from the household on the onset of her first menses. Fear of the government and its agents permeate this story, reflective of the time period in that country. Su Yen's family stories, told mostly by her grandmother, also reveal bits and pieces of the history of Malaysia, particularly the immigration of the Chinese to Singapore. Su Yen grows up in this book, and her narrative demonstrates a universality in the coming of age experience.

CONCLUSION

The brief discussions of the young adult and adult novels included here give some indication of the richness of these works. My research to date supports the premise that many texts from the body of literature read by young people do contain strong feminist themes. As one might expect, such themes are presented more strongly and more obviously in recent publications, although they can certainly be found in earlier works. It also seems clear that a concentration on a particular feminist theme or on a cluster of such themes is dependent, at least in part, on the anticipated audience for a text. Obviously, books for young adults are more likely to focus on emerging sexuality and mother-daughter relationship. On the other hand, these books seem to be less concerned with ecofeminist concepts of reverence for and an integration with the natural world. That kind of ethic of reciprocity and responsibility for nature is more evident both in stories for young children and in adult books. Specific themes are also treated differently, depending upon the anticipated audience. For instance, emerging sexuality is a common theme in young adult literature, but that theme is dealt with far more explicitly in adult novels about young adults. It is expected that, with further research, clearer patterns will emerge.

One thing that is absolutely clear from the work to date is that both adults and young adults find it enlightening and rewarding to discuss feminist themes in picture story books and/or young adult novels as a means of introduction to this topic. The simplicity and clarity with which the best authors and illustrators present such themes in these works is both a useful starting point for older readers and a hopeful sign that the next generation of readers may not need the kinds of remedial efforts that require young women to be resisting readers. Those of us now working with the Model of Female Voices in Youth Literature are eager to begin the final stage of the research study, that is, to study the ways young people respond to and make meanings from their transactions with these texts. Informal discussions with young people encourage me to believe that these books are indeed catalysts to focus attention on issues that will help young people, both male and female, to create a more integrated, gender-fair, multicultural world in which women's ways of knowing are truly valued.

NOTES

1. Beginning with the AAUW Report *How Schools Shortchange Girls*, there have been a number of studies and monographs that examine the female child-adolescent in our society. See, for example: *Meeting at the Crossroads* by Lyn Brown and Carol Gilligan; *The Difference* by Judy Mann; *Reviving Ophelia* by Mary Pipher; *School Girls* by Peggy Orenstein; *Failing at Fairness* by Myra and David Sadker; *Gender Play* by Barrie Thorne; and *Beyond Silenced Voices* edited by Lois Weis and Michelle Fine. The curriculum entitled *The Girl Child*, developed by UNICEF/Ontario, is an outstanding document for study of issues related to female children.
2. Among the author's most applicable studies are: "The Child's Meaning-Making in Response to a Literary Text," "Meaning-Making and the Dragons of Pern," and "Exploring the Concept of Contextual

Void." Discussion of this research is also found in her *Children's Literature: Theory, Research, and Teaching.*

3. Although the focus of this chapter is on female coming of age stories, it is equally important to present alternative views of the male coming of age story. Appendix B includes a sampling of such stories from different cultural perspectives.

4. One aspect of my current research focuses on the concept of the crone in stories for young people. Both visually and textually, the old woman, the healer, the midwife, the witch, the wise woman, the hag, the crone, and the Baba Yaga have been portrayed in a range of forms. Studies such as the following have provided a framework for my examination and should prove helpful in understanding the concept: *The Goddess Re-Awakening* compiled by Shirley Nicholson, Barbara Walker's *The Crone*, Mary Daly's *Gyn/Ecology*, Donna Wilshire's *Virgin Mother Crone*, and *Weaving the Visions* edited by Judith Plaskow and Carol P. Christ.

5. Quilting plays prominent roles in many stories from picture books to others listed in Appendix A to young adult novels such as Ann Rinaldi's *A Stitch in Time*. "Catching the Shape of Their Dreams: Quilts As a Medium," Tess Beck Stuhlmann's chapter in this book, further discusses the stories of quilting in women's lives.

WORKS CITED

American Association of University Women and Wellesley College Center for Research on Women. *How Schools Shortchange Girls.* Washington: AAUW Education Foundation, 1992.

Anderson, Bonnie S., and Judith P. Zinsser. *A History of Their Own: Women in Europe from Prehistory to the Present.* Vols. I & II. New York: Harper, 1988.

Apter, Terri. *Altered Loves: Mothers and Daughters During Adolescence.* New York: St. Martin's, 1990.

Banks, Russell. *Rule of the Bone.* New York: Harper, 1995.

Belenky, Mary Field, and Others. *Women's Ways of Knowing: The Development of Self, Voice, and the Mind.* New York: Basic, 1986.

Braxon, Joanne M. *Black Women Writing Autobiography: A Tradition within a Tradition.* Philadelphia: Temple UP, 1989.

Brown, Lyn Mikel and Carol Gilligan. *Meeting at the Crossroads: Women's Psychology and Girls' Development.* Cambridge: Harvard UP, 1992.

Cheong, Fiona. *The Scent of the Gods.* New York: Norton, 1991.

Christian-Smith, Linda K. *Becoming a Woman through Romance.* New

York: Routledge, 1990.

Cisneros, Sandra. *The House on Mango Street*. New York: Vintage, 1989.

Clemens, Samuel L. *The Adventures of Huckleberry Finn*. New York: Bantam, 1981.

Collins, Patricia Hill. *Black Feminist Thought: Knowledge, Consciousness, and the Politics of Empowerment*. New York: Routledge, 1991.

Conway, Jill Ker, ed. *Written by Herself: Autobiographies of American Women*. New York: Random House, 1992.

Cranny-Francis, Anne. *Feminist Fiction: Feminist Uses of Generic Fiction*. New York: St. Martin's P, 1990.

Dalsimer, Katherine. *Female Adolescence: Psychoanalytic Reflections on Literature*. New Haven: Yale UP, 1986.

Daly, Mary. *Gyn/Ecology: The Metaethics of Radical Feminism*. Boston: Beacon, 1978.

Davis, Flora. *Moving the Mountain: The Women's Movement in America since 1960*. New York: Simon & Schuster, 1991.

Eller, Cynthia. *Living in the Lap of the Goddess: The Feminist Spirituality Movement in America*. New York: Crossroad, 1993.

Evans, Sara M. *Born for Liberty: A History of Women in America*. New York: Free P, 1989.

Fetterley, Judith. *The Resisting Reader: A Feminist Approach to American Fiction*. Bloomington: Indiana UP, 1978.

Flynn, Elizabeth A., and Patrocinio P. Schweickart, eds. *Gender and Reading: Essays on Readers, Texts, and Contexts*. Baltimore: Johns Hopkins UP, 1986.

Gaard, Greta, ed. *Ecofeminism: Women, Animals, Nature*. Philadelphia: Temple UP, 1993.

Gibbons, Kaye. *Ellen Foster*. New York: Random House, 1988.

Gilligan, Carol. *In a Different Voice*. Cambridge: Harvard UP, 1982.

Gilmore, Leigh. *Autobiographics: A Feminist Theory of Women's Self-Representation*. Ithaca: Cornell UP, 1994.

The Girl Child: An Investment in the Future. A Project of the UNICEF Ontario Education for Development Committee. Ontario: UNICEF/ Ontario, 1994.

Hancock, Emily. *The Girl Within*. New York: Fawcett Columbine, 1989.

Heilbrun, Carolyn G. *Writing a Woman's Life*. New York: Ballantine, 1988.

Hinton, S. E. *The Outsiders*. New York: Viking, 1967.

Hite, Molly. *The Other Side of the Story: Structures and Strategies of Contemporary Feminist Narrative*. Ithaca: Cornell UP, 1989.

hooks, bell. *Ain't I A Woman: Black Women and Feminism*. Boston: South End P, 1981.

_____. *Feminist Theory: From Margin to Center*. Boston: South End P, 1984.

_____. *Talking Back: Thinking Feminist, Thinking Black*. Boston: South End P, 1989.

Jacobus, Mary. *Reading Woman: Essays in Feminist Criticism*. New York: Columbia UP, 1986.

Kerber, Linda K., Alice Kessler-Harris, and Kathryn Kish Sklar, eds. *U.S. History As Women's History: New Feminist Essays*. Chapel Hill: U of North Carolina P, 1995.

Kincaid, Jamaica. *Annie John*. New York: Plume/Penguin, 1986.

Knowles, John. *A Separate Peace*. New York: Macmillan, 1959.

Lerner, Gerda. *The Creation of Feminist Consciousness: From the Middle Ages to Eighteen-Seventy*. New York: Oxford UP, 1993.

_____. *The Creation of Patriarchy*. New York: Oxford UP, 1986.

Lorde, Audre. *Sister Outsider: Essays & Speeches*. Freedom, CA: Crossing P, 1984.

Mann, Judy. *The Difference: Growing Up Female in America*. New York: Time Warner, 1994.

Mills, Sara, ed. *Gendering the Reader*. New York: Harvester/Wheatsheaf, 1994.

Moraga, Cherríe and Gloria Anzaldúa, eds. *This Bridge Called My Back: Writings by Radical Women of Color*. New York: Kitchen Table/Women of Color P, 1981.

Morton, Patricia. *Disfigured Images: The Historical Assault on Black Women*. New York: Greenwood, 1991.

Namioka, Lensey. *April and the Dragon Lady*. San Diego: Browndeer P, 1994.

Napoli, Donna Jo. *The Magic Circle*. New York: Dutton, 1993.

Nicholson, Shirley, comp. *The Goddess Re-Awakening: The Feminine Principle Today*. Wheaton: Theosophical, 1989.

Noddings, Nel. *Caring: A Feminine Approach to Ethics and Moral Education*. Berkeley: U of California P, 1984.

_____. *Women and Evil*. Berkeley: U of California P, 1989.

Orenstein, Peggy. *School Girls: Young Women, Self-Esteem, and the Confidence Gap*. New York: Doubleday, 1994.

Otto, Whitney. *How to Make an American Quilt*. New York: Ballantine, 1991.

Palmer, Paulina. *Contemporary Women's Fiction: Narrative Practice and Feminist Theory*. Jackson: UP of Mississippi, 1989.

Pipher, Mary. *Reviving Ophelia: Saving the Selves of Adolescent Girls*. New York: Grosset/Putnam, 1994.

Plaskow, Judith, and Carol P. Christ, eds. *Weaving the Visions: New*

Patterns in Feminist Spirituality. San Francisco: Harper, 1989.

Rinaldi, Ann. *A Stitch in Time.* New York: Scholastic, 1994.

Ruiz, Vicki and Ellen Carol DuBois, eds. *Unequal Sisters: A Multicultural Reader in U.S. Women's History.* 2nd edition. New York: Routledge, 1994.

Sadker, Myra, and David Sadker. *Failing at Fairness: How America's Schools Cheat Girls.* New York: Scribner's, 1994.

Salinger, J. D. *The Catcher in the Rye.* Boston: Little Brown, 1951.

Shapiro, Ann-Louise, ed. *Feminists Revision History.* New Brunswick: Rutgers UP, 1994.

Showalter, Elaine, ed. *The New Feminist Criticism: Essays on Women, Literature and Theory.* New York: Pantheon, 1985.

Thorne, Barrie. *Gender Play: Girls and Boys in School.* New Brunswick: Rutgers UP, 1993.

Vandergrift, Kay E. *Children's Literature: Theory, Research, and Teaching.* Englewood: Libraries Unlimited, 1990.

_____. "Exploring the Concept of Contextual Void: A Preliminary Analysis," in *Library Education and Leadership: Essays in Honor of Jane Anne Hannigan.* Ed. by Sheila S. Intner, and Kay E. Vandergrift. Metuchen: Scarecrow, 1990, pp. 349–363.

_____. "A Feminist Perspective on Multicultural Children's Literature in the Middle Years of the Twentieth Century," *Library Trends.* Vol. 41 (Winter 1993): 354–377.

_____. "A Feminist Research Agenda in Youth Literature," *Wilson Library Bulletin.* Vol. 68 (October, 1993): 23–27.

_____. "The Child's Meaning-Making in Response to a Literary Text," *English Quarterly* 22 no. 3–4 (Winter 1990): 125–40.

_____. "Meaning-Making and the Dragons of Pern," *Children's Literature Association Quarterly.* 15 (Spring 1990): 27–34.

_____. "Peacocks, Dreams, Quilts, and Honey: Patricia Polacco, A Woman's Voice of Remembrance," in *Ways of Knowing: Literature and the Intellectual Life of Children.* Lanham: Scarecrow P, 1996, pp. 259–288.

Voigt, Cynthia. *Dicey's Song.* New York: Atheneum, 1982.

_____. *Homecoming.* New York: Atheneum, 1981.

Walker, Alice. *In Search of Our Mothers' Gardens.* San Diego: Harcourt, 1983.

Walker, Barbara G. *The Crone: Woman of Age, Wisdom and Power.* New York: Harper, 1985.

Warhol, Robyn R., and Dianne Price Herndl, eds. *Feminisms: An Anthology of Literary Theory and Criticism.* New Brunswick: Rutgers UP, 1991.

Weis, Lois and Michelle Fine, eds. *Beyond Silenced Voices: Class, Race, and Gender in United States Schools.* Albany: State U of New York P, 1993.

Wilshire, Donna. *Virgin Mother Crone: Myths & Mysteries of the Triple Goddess.* Rochester: Inner Traditions, 1994.

Winterson, Jeanette. *Oranges Are Not the Only Fruit.* New York: Atlantic Monthly, 1987.

Zinsser, Judith. *History and Feminism: A Glass Half Full.* New York: Twayne, 1993.

APPENDIX A

FEMALE COMING OF AGE STORIES IN ADULT LITERATURE

Allison, Dorothy. *Bastard Out of Carolina.* New York: Plume/Penguin, 1993.

Alvarez, Julia. *How the Garcia Girls Lost Their Accents.* New York: Plume/Penguin, 1992.

Angelou, Maya. *I Know Why the Caged Bird Sings.* New York: Random House, 1970.

Atwood, Margaret. *Lady Oracle.* New York: Fawcett Crest, 1976.

Bedford, Simi. *Yoruba Girl Dancing.* New York: Viking, 1992.

Bolton, Ruthie. *Gal: A True Life.* New York: Harcourt, 1994.

Brown, Rita Mae. *Rubyfruit Jungle.* New York: Bantam, 1977.

Cahill, Susan, ed. *Growing Up Female: Stories of Women Writers from the American Mosaic.* New York: Mentor, 1993.

Campbell, Bebe Moore. *Sweet Summer: Growing Up With & Without My Dad.* New York: Ballantine, 1989.

Cary, Lorene. *Black Ice.* New York: Knopf, 1991.

Chase, Joan. *During the Reign of the Queen of Persia.* New York: Ballantine, 1983.

Cheong, Fiona. *The Scent of the Gods.* New York: Norton, 1991.

Chernin, Kim. *In My Mother's House: A Daughter's Story.* New York: Harper, 1983.

Cisneros, Sandra. *The House on Mango Street.* New York: Vintage, 1989.

Cofer, Judith Ortiz. *Silent Dancing: A Partial Remembrance of a Puerto Rican Childhood.* Houston: Arte Publico P, 1990.

Corman, Avery. *Prized Possessions.* New York: Simon & Schuster, 1991.

Delany, Sarah Louise and A. Elizabeth Delaney. *Having Our Say: The Delaney Sisters' First 100 Years.* New York: Kodansha International, 1993.

Dillard, Anne. *An American Childhood.* New York: Harper, 1988.

Erdrich, Louise. *Love Medicine*. New York: Holt, 1984.

Esquivel, Laura. *Like Water for Chocolate: A Novel in Monthly Installments, With Recipes, Romances, and Home Remedies*. Trans. by Carol and Thomas Christenson. New York: Doubleday, 1992.

Eulo, Elana Yates. *A Southern Woman*. New York: St. Martin's P, 1993.

Fraser, Sylvia. *My Father's House: Memoir of Incest and of Healing*. New York: Harper, 1987.

Gibbons, Kaye. *Charms for an Easy Life*. New York: Putnam, 1993.

_____. *Ellen Foster*. New York: Random House, 1988.

Greenberg, Joanne. *No Reck'ning Made*. New York: Holt, 1993.

Hurston, Zora Neale. *Their Eyes Were Watching God*. New York: Harper, 1937.

Kaysen, Susanna, *Girl Interrupted*. New York: Turtle Bay, 1993.

Kincaid, Jamaica. *Annie John*. New York: Plume/Penguin, 1986.

_____. *Lucy*. New York: Plume/Penguin, 1991.

Kingston, Maxine Hong. *The Woman Warrior: Memoirs of a Girlhood among Ghosts*. New York: Random House, 1976.

Laurence, Margaret. *A Bird in the House*. New York: University of Chicago P, 1993.

Leffland, Ella. *Rumors of Peace*. New York: Harper, 1979.

Loeb, Karen. *Jump Rope Queen & Other Stories*. Minneapolis: New Rivers P, 1992.

Lorde, Audre. *Zami: A New Spelling of My Name*. Freedom: Crossing P, 1982.

McCullers, Carson. *The Member of the Wedding*. New York: Bantam, 1966. (c. 1946)

McKinley, Robin. *Deerskin*. New York: Ace, 1993.

Mairs, Nancy. *Remembering the Bone House: An Erotics of Place and Space*. New York: Harper, 1989.

Marshall, Paule. *Brown Girl, Brownstones*. New York: Feminist P, 1981.

Minatoya, Lydia. *Talking to High Monks in the Snow: An Asian American Odyssey*. New York: Harper, 1992.

Moody, Anne. *Coming of Age in Mississippi*. New York: Dell, 1982. (c. 1968)

Morrison, Toni. *The Bluest Eye*. New York: Pocket, 1970.

Oates, Joyce Carol. *I Lock My Door upon Myself*. New York: Plume/Penguin, 1991.

Otto, Whitney. *How to Make an American Quilt*. New York: Ballantine, 1991.

Palwick, Susan. *Flying in Place*. New York: TOR, 1992.

Piercy, Marge. *Braided Lives*. New York: Fawcett Crest, 1982.

Quindlen, Anna. *Object Lessons*. New York: Random House, 1991.

Riley, Patricia, ed. *Growing Up Native American*. New York: Avon, 1993.
Robinson, Marilynne. *Housekeeping*. New York: Bantam, 1982.
Sanders, Dori. *Her Own Place: A Novel*. Chapel Hill: Algonquin, 1993.
Santiago, Esmeralda. *When I Was Puerto Rican*. Reading: Addison-Wesley, 1993.
Sarton, May. *Mrs. Stevens Hears the Mermaids Singing*. New York: Norton, 1975.
Shange, Ntozake. *Betsey Brown*. New York: St. Martin's P, 1985.
_____. *Liliane: Resurrection of the Daughter*. New York: St. Martin's P, 1994.
Smith, Lee. *Fair and Tender Ladies*. New York: Putnam, 1988.
Sone, Monica. *Nisei Daughter*. Boston: Little, 1953.
Tan, Amy. *The Joy Luck Club*. New York: Putnam, 1989.
Thisman, Jean. *Molly Donnelly*. Boston: Houghton, 1993.
Walker, Alice. *The Color Purple*. New York: Washington Square P, 1983.
Winterson, Jeanette. *Oranges Are Not the Only Fruit*. New York: Atlantic Monthly P, 1987.

APPENDIX B

MALE COMING OF AGE STORIES IN ADULT LITERATURE

Banks, Russell. *Rule of the Bone*. New York: Harper, 1995.
DeMarinis, Rick. *The Mortician's Apprentice*. New York: Norton, 1994.
Doyle, Roddy. *Paddy Clarke Ha Ha Ha*. New York: Viking, 1993.
Forman, James. *My Enemy, My Brother*. New York: Scholastic, 1970.
Galarza, Ernesto. *Barrio Boy*. New York: Ballantine, 1972.
Grossman, David. *The Book of Intimate Grammar*. Trans. from the Hebrew by Betty Rosenberg. New York: Farrar, 1994.
Mathabane, Mark. *Kaffir Boy: The True Story of a Black Youth's Coming of Age in Apartheid South Africa*. New York: Macmillan, 1986.
Mattera, Don. *Sophiatown: Coming of Age in South Africa*. Boston: Beacon, 1989.
Mehta, Ved. *Daddyji*. New York: Norton, 1989.
Ramusi, Molaptene Collins. *Soweto, My Love*. New York: Holt, 1989.
Rodriguez, Richard. *Hunger of Memory: The Education of Richard Rodriguez*. New York: Bantam, 1983.
Santiago, Danny. *Famous All Over Town*. New York: New American, 1984.
Shusterman, Neal. *Dissidents*. Boston: Little, 1989.

Soto, Gary. *Living Up the Street: Narrative Reflections*. San Francisco: Strawberry Hill P, 1985.

Standing Bear, Luther. *My Indian Boyhood*. Boston: Houghton, 1931 [reprinted Lincoln, NE: U of Nebraska P, 1988].

Unger, Douglas. *El Yanqui*. New York: Ballantine, 1988.

Wain, John. *The Free Zone Starts Here*. New York: Delacorte, 1984.

Watkins, Paul. *Night Over Day Over Night*. New York: Knopf, 1988.

CHAPTER THREE

Coming-of-Rage: Young, Black and Female in America

Pamela E. Groves

I t could be said that coming-of-age black in the United States is, in part, a coming-of-rage—coming into an understanding of one's own devaluation that grows out of the pervasiveness of controlling images in society and the way those images catalog people. For young black women, the challenges are even greater. One way to explore this issue is through young African American female voices in young adult and adult literature. While young African American women share many of the general concerns which face all adolescents, their race and gender affords them unique and substantial obstacles. In discussing this topic I acknowledge a profound emotional engagement. I admit that my identification with the victims of sexism and racism is unambiguous since the oppressed are my sisters, my brothers, in other words, my loved ones.

All forms of literature have the potential to evoke a wide range of responses in readers. This reality must be taken into consideration as we, as professionals and caring adults, make recommendations to the youth we serve. I share the following experience as an example of the power of literature, as well as the context in which it is discussed.

Ann Rinaldi's young adult historical novel *Wolf by the Ears* describes the story of Harriet Hemings, a slave of Thomas Jefferson's, and, perhaps his daughter. Harriet's coming-of-age cannot be disengaged from her historical placement and at age nineteen she comes to understand, from Jefferson's son-in-law, that she is a slave. Albeit one who is tutored and dressed most properly, but, still a slave. Light-skinned Harriet decides to "pass" for white in order to escape slavery. Rinaldi writes a moving account of the pain of having to choose between freedom, on the one hand, and her family and race on the other. I was a student in an all-white class where we discussed the book. When the issue of "passing" came up, those who spoke dealt with it flippantly: "We all pass for something in life," one person piped up; "I can't imagine a white man coming to marry a black woman—then or now," expressed another, exposing her distaste at the concept of the mixing of the races. I sat dumbfounded and silent. I could only express my feelings through the following poem, which I wrote during that class:

I have so much to say
but sit here with frozen lips
and timid heart.
Who are you all and
what does passing mean to you?
Stars and clouds in a black sky?
Or masked faces at a costumed ball?

But tell me
have you wanted to pass for black?
To kink your hair
and scorn blue eyes
and shed the privilege
of the skin
you're living in?

And tell me
Do I have a responsibility to say
what I feel
when what I feel
shows too much of me to you
and what you say
makes my insides shake
like a yolk
fragile and raw?

How can I crack
my black shell
and let your too rough hands
pass
over me?

The above experience, while painful, was instructive as it brought to light the significance of both the impact of literature and the inadequacy of discussion in certain settings. Had I, or the professor, been able to confront the students on their insensitivity as well as their apparent ignorance, there may well have been some meaningful discussion. As it was, the issue of "passing for white" passed unexplored.

As a black woman from the African diaspora, my own coming-of-age was painful. Although I grew up in Jamaica, much of what I describe below was present in either my childhood or in those of my friends and loved ones. The struggle to understand one's history, relate it to one's present, and integrate the complex consequences inherent in these matters, is an important element of coming-of-age as a black woman in this hemisphere.

FRAMES OF REFERENCE

There is no doubt that Carol Gilligan has done important work at the Harvard Project on the Psychology of Women and the Development of Girls, as she forges new territory in the area of developmental theories. However, I wanted to use feminist theories which would include race as a defining factor. White feminists have generally avoided the race issue in their research; and, in fact, many of these theories are mired in the Eurocentric discipline of psychoanalysis, which has been linked to the success of Europe's history of conquest and violence. Hussein Bulhan in his book *The Psychology of Oppression* makes the point that "Eurocentric psychology revealed itself more as a part of the problem of domination than as a discipline readily amenable to the resolution of oppression" (5). This situation has contributed to the fact that studies on black girls' development are limited. This general disinterest demonstrates a lack of understanding of the interrelated nature of racist and sexist systems of domination. Black feminist scholars like Patricia Hill Collins and bell hooks have revealed the inadequacies inherent in this silence and evasion, and have insisted that the parameters of scholarship and criticism be broadened so that those who have occupied the shadows of the discourse may now be fostered and united at its core.

In order to expand the discussion, I will add the psychological and developmental theories of Frantz Fanon, a revolutionary black psychiatrist. Fanon's insights into the psychology of oppression revealed how Eurocentric psychology was as much a part of the problem of domination as the military force that existed to produce and preserve the colonialist empires in the 1940s and 1950s. Inasmuch as brilliant social thinkers such as Fanon confronted the relationship between race and oppression, they too demonstrated a lack of awareness in the connectedness of different forms of oppression. In his important work *Black Skins, White Masks*, Fanon refers primarily to the white male colonizer and the black oppressed male. There is little analysis of the plight of the black woman in the society or of the impact of oppression on the white men *and* women who perpetuate it. However, these criticisms do not diminish the important contribution made by Fanon and white feminist researchers. In this chapter I shall focus the discussion around Fanon's theories and black feminist thought.

Few human encounters are exempt from oppression of one kind or another. By virtue of our race, sex, or class, each of us happens to be a victim and/or perpetrator of oppression. However, the roots of black-white as well as male-female conflict run deep in our collective histories. The catastrophe of slavery and subsequent racial discrimination perpetuates a disease with many victims. To discuss the legacy of slavery as it pertains to African Americans today would take this paper beyond its scope. Suffice it to point out, however, that black women received the brunt of the mass brutalization and terrorization; and, therefore, it is important to incorporate the lessons learned from this period, when racism and sexism were skillfully combined to reduce the black woman to the lowest form of life. This initial status shaped all successive relationships that have existed between black women and others and formed a powerful conditioning force in the form of a group memory that lingers into the present. bell hooks takes a comprehensive look at sexism and the black female slave experience in her book *Ain't I a Woman* which provides the foundation for understanding the continued devaluation of black womanhood.

This historical devaluation is important to any critique of

literature which serves to explore black female consciousness and development. Black women are still the lowest paid group in the nation by sex and race, and they face a double dose of contempt as they are the victims of the white racist society as well as the black sexist community. Black feminists have spoken eloquently of this oppressive corner to which young black women, by virtue of their race and gender, are increasingly being confined. It is a corner strewn with emotional and psychological, as well as physical and sexual, violence. But it is also decorated with creative resistance, spirituality, integrity, and grace.

Gender, race, and culture certainly are important determinants of an individual's identity. Ethnicity, socioeconomic level, education, religion, sexual orientation, geographic location, and the degree of assimilation or acculturation also constitute some of the many factors that impact one's coming-of-age. It should come as no surprise, therefore, that there are numerous (but not sufficient) books published (both adult and young adult) which describe the realities and diversity of coming-of-age as a black woman in the United States. Writers in this sub-genre have undertaken the job of exploring these issues, and the variety of techniques help to inform this complex debate.

I have identified six challenges related to "becoming" or "coming-of-age" as a black woman today. These six elements are to be found in varying degrees in much of the coming-of-age literature written with black female protagonists. They are: invisibility/otherness, negative self-image, sexual and other violence, drug abuse and crime, lack of faith in black men, and a loss of voice.

In order to illustrate these elements, I have chosen the following six books: Alice Childress' *Rainbow Jordan*, the Delany sisters' *Having Our Say*, Rosa Guy's *The Music of Summer*, Audre Lorde's *Sister Outsider*, Toni Morrison's *The Bluest Eye* and Walter Dean Myers' *Motown and Didi*. Except for Myers who is a black male, the authors are black females.

A LOOK AT THE LITERATURE

INVISIBILITY/OTHERNESS

Morrison deals implicitly with racial self-loathing and invisibility throughout her book *The Bluest Eye*. Pecola desires the bluest eyes so that she will no longer be ugly to her mother and invisible to society. When she presents herself in the local candy store armed with three pennies safely tucked away in her shoe, this is the white storekeeper's response:

> Mr. Yacobowski looms up over the counter. He urges his eyes out of his thoughts to encounter her. At some fixed point in time and space he senses that he need not waste the effort of a glance. He does not see her, because for him there is nothing to see. . . . She looks up at him and sees the vacuum where curiosity ought to lodge. And something more. The total absence of human recognition—glazed separateness. (48)

Pecola believes that she would be better off invisible and prays desperately "Please, God, please make me disappear" (45). She often got her wish—everything but the eyes. They were always left. And so, she prayed for the bluest eyes.

Audre Lorde relates the pain of invisibility she felt as a child growing up and the anger which it fueled. She is seated next to a fur-lined white woman on a Harlem subway. The woman finding her repulsive, "plucks at the line where my new blue snowpants and her sleek fur coat meet" (147). Believing that there must have been a roach between them, Lorde pulls away also, before realizing that it is her that the woman does not want her coat to touch.

Pivotal to theories of oppression is the view that the psychology of Europe divided the world and its people into either/or compartments. In other words everything and everyone could be divided into good versus evil, beautiful versus ugly, intelligent versus stupid, white versus black. This intellectual construct is an integral part of all forms of oppression as it allows people, things, and ideas to gain meaning only in relation to their complements (Bulhan, 140). As we watch the characters in these books struggle with their sexual and racial identities, we are able to see the destructiveness of this world view. It is because the fur-coated woman sees Lorde as evil, ugly, black, and possibly stupid, that she is driven to repulsion.

Many black feminists and writers have described this phenomenon that seeks to render black women invisible. Lorde comments that "within this country where racial difference creates a constant, if unspoken, distortion of vision, black women have, on the one hand, always been highly visible, and so, on the other hand, have been rendered invisible through the depersonalization of racism" (42). Patricia Hill Collins asserts that the process of objectification is in accordance with either/or logic. "One element is objectified as the Other, and is viewed as an object to be manipulated and controlled" (69). Black women as the Other allows the dominant group to justify and maintain their oppression by defining our reality and identity and limiting our growth. In keeping with this notion, Collins goes on to describe the struggle facing many black women who embark on a process of self-definition amid a society that "denigrates African ideas and peoples" (27). Sarah in Rosa Guy's *The Music of Summer* exhibits the characteristics of an unarticulated consciousness. She seems to embark on a self-conscious struggle and begins to question and explore the Afrocentric worldview held by Jean Pierre, an articulate black nationalist who describes Africa as "the oldest civilization in the world . . . the richest continent in the world" (111).

NEGATIVE SELF-IMAGE

From as far back as the late thirties and early forties, American society was provided with convincing evidence of self-hatred in black children through the doll tests of Kenneth and Mamie Clark. These studies found that nearly all the black children tested, regardless of geographic region, chose to play with a white doll over a black doll. Claudia in *The Bluest Eye* understands intuitively the power behind white dolls' representation and exerts her own personal rebellion as she states precisely: "I destroyed white baby dolls" (22).

We see an extreme representation of self-hatred in the frail, festering character of Pecola in *The Bluest Eye*. Her world conspires to envelop her in a violent and dehumanizing cloak, which renders her as an absolute victim. While we may almost be willing to accept society's treatment of her, we are sickened when we realize that her home is not a haven: Cholly, her father, and Pauline, her mother, are crucial agents of her demise. When she accidentally spills a blueberry cobbler in the white family's kitchen, her mother hastens to punish and abuse her while comforting the "little girl in pink" (109).

The teenagers in Rosa Guy's *The Music of Summer* express openly their internal conflict over one's outward appearance. Although close during childhood, Cathy Johnson and Sarah Richardson are growing apart in their teenage years as their skin color and hair texture become an issue. Cathy and her light-skinned black friends identify completely with their European heritage while casting aspersions on anything associated with Africa and blackness. An outing to the beach brings out both issues as reference is made to "good (straight) and bad (kinky) hair" as well as the undesirability of a dark complexion. We see that Cathy's statement "Before I leave this summer I intend to be as black as Sarah" (67) is meant as a slur, and later Cathy turns the blade as she tells Sarah that due to their pale complexion they are admitted wherever they go "without having to beg or being insulted. We're accepted, Sarah Richardson—so long as you're not tagging along" (123). Associating blackness so deeply with oppression and unattractiveness, both Cathy and Pauline struggle with self-hatred for they can neither accept Sarah's and Pecola's blackness, nor their own.

This is an integral part of the psychology of oppression, which posits that the rejection of one's own and the total acceptance of the 'other' may successfully breed psychopathology. Bulhan explains that the oppressed "internalize the oppressor, assimilate his image and become agents of their own oppression" (126). Collins describes Pauline Breedlove as typifying the internalization of the mammy image. She neglects her own children while lavishing attention and concern on the white children. "It is only by accepting this subordinate role to white children could she, as a poor Black woman, see a positive place for herself" (83).

There are a number of questions that arise in biracial individuals. Does one identify exclusively with the European ancestry or with the African? Or does one attempt to meld these two parts into an integrated individual? And finally, what do either of these choices mean in terms of a healthy identity? These are some of the issues being dealt with in coming-of-age literature for both adults and young adults.

We can see the destructiveness of complete Eurocentric identification in *The Music of Summer*, both for Cathy and for those around her. She is threatened by Sarah's self-confidence and self-respect. This fear is only heightened when Jean Pierre, a handsome black nationalist originally from Martinique but living in Africa, comes to visit and is attracted to and interested in Sarah. They share a love of jazz and she speaks his native language, French. Cathy's insecurity is increased as Sarah, fascinated by Jean Pierre's knowledge of Africa and his social and political explanation for its poverty, begins to explore her African heritage in a surprising way.

Frequently there are buffers which protect individuals in their community, as seen in the strong extended family presence in Rosa Guy's novel. Mama Dear, Cathy's grandmother, is sympathetic to her granddaughter's 'confusion' and recalls that it started at a young age when Cathy would tell her friends that Mama Dear was the housekeeper. She attributes much of it to the fact that Cathy's father was protected from knowing the world outside of his Quaker schools and friends, and could neither assimilate nor acculturate into the larger society. However, Mama Dear takes the time to tell Cathy about her dead father and the history that forms the contour of their lives. It is this connection that serves to educate, challenge, and support Cathy in her turmoil.

The transition from childhood to adulthood is a stressful time in the best of families. However, for African American youth, there are some added stressors caused by profound social forces. Fanon asserts that there are close connections between the structure of the family and the structure of the nation. Therefore, a child who grows up in a 'normal' stable family then comes to the wider social world as a normal adult. However, even when African American families are intact, the attack on the self is merely postponed and "a normal Negro child . . . will become abnormal on the slightest contact with the white world" (143). Thus black children who grow up in a healthy family environment sooner or later come up against massive social forces that undermine and sometimes overwhelm their development. Fanon maintained that every society needs an outlet—a vent through which "the forces accumulated in the form of aggression can be released" (145). The black person acts as a stimulus to anxiety and, therefore, is the recipient of repressed aggression and frustration. I believe that it is this encounter with the larger society which contributes to the coming-of-rage of African American girls.

The voices of centenarians Bessie and Sadie Delany ring loud and strident as they talk about growing up black and female through decades of Southern social terror and the Jim Crow period. Perhaps it is Bessie's statement in the recent stage production of their bestselling book *Having Our Say* that captures a great deal of their life: "I never thought I'd see the day when people would be interested in what two old Negro women have to say."

The Delanys' elongated view of society through the post-Reconstruction South and into the present shows us the strength and determination necessary to succeed in the country when you are young, black, and female. Both sisters speak of the difficulties they experienced in all aspects of their lives, and their personal resistance. Sadie Delany describes her experience as a student at Pratt Institute as lonely and demoralizing. Since black schools had no money, their students' early training in certain courses was limited and by the time they got into a white college they had to struggle to keep up or be labeled "dumb." As a teacher she was sexually harassed and provoked.

Bessie's college experience was even more difficult than Sadie's. It might have been because she was darker and quieter, or perhaps "it was easier to accept a colored woman studying to be a teacher than learning to be a dentist" (151). Nevertheless, her experiences there compelled her to say of Columbia "they let me in but they beat me down for being there" (162).

Particularly relevant to this chapter is their reference to what Kevin Gaines describes as "the tragedy of parents reduced to uncharacteristic fury or helpless silence by their inability to protect their children not just from external dangers but also from being consumed by self-destructive anger" (5). Gaines states that rage, a principal theme of the book, is inevitable, as the Delanys were "privileged among blacks while at the same time members of a proscribed caste" (5).

SEXUAL AND OTHER VIOLENCE

The tyranny of the male within the home is apparent in a number of adult coming-of-age stories, both black and white. bell hooks in her book *Talking Back* underscores the fact that the home is the first place where girls (black and white) may experience the devastation of coercive and often violent male domination. Since there is an inability to resist domination by those closest, it follows that resisting more distant exploitation might be unimaginable. While racist oppression is present in the lives of these young protagonists, it is inextricably entwined with patriarchal domination.

Growing up female in a working-class, father-dominated household can mean tremendous hardship as we see in Toni Morrison's *The Bluest Eye*. Eleven-year-old Pecola Breedlove falls victim to her father's sexual betrayal as he "dropped his seeds in his own plot of black dirt" (5). Cholly's rape of his daughter is inexorably linked to his "rape" by white men earlier in the book. It occurs when Cholly and Darlene are having sex in the woods. Two white men come upon them and, under poised guns, they force Cholly to simulate the act so that they may watch with delight. This humiliating experience fills him with impotent rage for he cannot strike the perpetrators who stand close enough that he can even "smell" their whiteness. Unable to prevent Darlene from seeing him in this insulting position, Cholly, instead, projects his fury onto her, and wishes that he could do it [the act] to her, "hard, long, and painfully, he hated her so much" (148). In this vivid scene we see the making of Cholly, and begin to understand the relationship of his status in society to issues such as parenting and male-female relations.

In Alice Childress' book, Kathie at twenty-nine seems hardly much older than her fourteen-year-old daughter, Rainbow Jordan. Kathie regularly abandons Rainbow in search of adventure, money and male companionship. In the first chapter we learn that Rainbow's father, Leroy, left them soon after she was born. Subsequent relationships with men are sustained under the threat of violence. Burke turns up one night with suspicions that Kathie has "another man." After searching the apartment, he threatens, "If I catch you two-timin me somebody's gon die!"

Later on Kathie is disillusioned with Burke: "How can he *love* me and do nothin but make lotta damn-ass trouble? . . . So busy lovin me till he knocked me almost senseless. Talkin bout I was gettin too chummy 'with the damn desk clerk'" (74). In the same chapter, he holds her prisoner and forbids her to call first Leroy then Rainbow, even though she had abandoned her again. As she tries to go out, he grabs her arm and "almost pulls it out the socket. Sends me sprawlin cross the bed. 'Bitch, don't turn your back on me!'" he yells. Underlying sexual and physical violence as portrayed in Childress' novel is very much a part of inner city family life today.

DRUG ABUSE AND CRIME

Walter Dean Myers, in his book *Motown and Didi*, presents characters who are complex and multi-dimensional against a backdrop of harsh reality in Harlem. We meet Didi discussing her continuing education prospects with her mother. Although her mother wants Didi to go to a nearby college, Didi wants to go very far away from the caregiver role she has had to adopt with her mother since her father had left them when she and her brother, Tony, were young. She also wants to get away from the neighborhood with "the junkies and the dope and the stealing and the cheap wine smells that filled the halls and dulls the crispness of the morning" (17). When she returns one day to find Tony shot up on dope she is blind with rage. She turns to the police for help but her plea is greeted with disdain and ridicule by the two policemen who address her. Myers does not let us know the racial identity of the officers, for in fact, it does not matter. When the officer refers to her as the "cutie", Myers introduces the second fate of the black woman, namely, sexism. There is no empathy and her complaint is not taken seriously by the law enforcement agency.

As discussed earlier, internalization of oppression often manifests itself as the oppressed group become their own worst enemy. Bulhan states that "because of this internalization and its attendant but repressed rage, the oppressed may act out, on each other, the very violence imposed on them" (126). After her brother dies from a drug overdose, Didi, enraged, decides that pusher Touchy must be killed. This is a pivotal moment in the novel, as Didi's pain from losing her brother mixes with her rage at the quality of life in Harlem. These two realities are highlighted in the scene in which she tells Motown of Tony's death.

> "Tony's dead," she had said. Fierce-eyed, a nightmare she-wolf, a stranger, a banshee come screaming from the streets to stand in the hallway of the first apartment he had ever had in his entire life . . .
>
> "What happened?" he had asked, his heart breaking to feel her pain.
>
> "He died from the dope." She looked up at him, searched his eyes. Searched his thoughts. Searched back to the mama he didn't remember and the father he had tried so hard to forget.
>
> "Didi," her name came out slowly. Motown sensed that she would explode. Sensed it and wanted to grab her before it was too late.
>
> "I want you to kill him," she said. Her nose was running. She was crying. "You got to kill him. He killed my brother!"
>
> "Touchy?"
>
> "I hate him!" she screamed. She picked up a magazine and threw it across the room. "I hate him!" (160)

It is this intersection of the oppressed community and the individual's impotence which significantly affects the individual's growth and development.

The use of drugs and alcohol in the black community is well documented. However, less well known is the disgraceful role of alcohol in the slave trade as well as the imperialism of Europe. There continues to be a presence of mind-altering substances in the black community, which brings with it tremendous personal and economic costs. Didi's coming-of-age is filled with anger and helplessness as she comes to terms with the loss of another male family member to the ravages of inner city turmoil.

LACK OF FAITH IN BLACK MEN

Oppressive relations between black men and women as well as whites and blacks have conspired to either physically remove the black male or to make him impotent when he does remain. Michael Tonry, in his book *Malign Neglect*, describes the impact that the current crime control policies have had on black communities. With more than a quarter of young black males in jail or on probation or parole, these communities "cannot prosper when so many of their young men are prevented from settling into long-term personal relationships, getting or keeping jobs, and living conventional lives" (vii). Young adult writers who write for and about African Americans no doubt reflect this reality.

Didi speaks clearly of her anger and disdain for men as we learn of her father's abandonment of the family and her brother's good-for-nothing lifestyle. One male is absent while the other is ineffective. This is why she finds herself taking care of both her single mother as well as her feckless brother. Billy "Touchy" Jenkins, the area pusher with whom Tony is involved, becomes the conscious object of Didi's simmering rage.

At the same time, Motown, young, black and unemployed, enters Didi's life. She sees Motown as another black loser, and does not want to be distracted by him. Robinson and Ward argue that in this current hostile sociopolitical climate African American girls develop survival strategies, but they fear that some of these strategies of resistance are adopted for survival and are often destructive. "Resistance strategies most frequently adopted by African American girls have been crisis-oriented, short-term strategies, and resistance strategies toward liberation are, regrettably, the exception" (97). We see Motown as caring, responsible and loving, and worry that Didi, given her negative experiences with black men, will remain blind to Motown's sincerity until it is too late.

Bessie Delany makes a point of stating that although she and her sister are unmarried, that was not to be taken as indication of lack of popularity: "We were popular, good-looking gals, but I think we were too smart, too independent for most men" (121). Reading between the lines, we sense the dilemma that black women have experienced for decades: a limited number of marriageable men. In the early 1900s, when Bessie and Sadie Delany would have been ready for marriage, most black men occupied an undesirable position in society, and few white men crossed the color line to marry a black woman. While they have clearly enjoyed their single lifestyle, it seems obvious that this position was attained only after years of bitterness and heartbreak. Bessie's rage is apparent throughout the book and climaxes when we realize that she is willing to be lynched rather than back down from a confrontation with an insulting white man.

Kathie in *Rainbow Jordan* begins to see her poor judgment in the men she chooses, and states "No matter how hard I try to do the right thing . . . I always mess up. . . . Not a man in this world is takin care-a me . . . except this clown, Burke" (80). But it is not a problem of her own making, and we understand the impact of society on the lives of black men such as Burke, Motown, Touchy, Tony and Cholly.

LOSS OF VOICE

Research shows that preadolescent girls, roughly between age seven and puberty, are outgoing, energetic, interested in widely variant topics, talkative, and adaptive. Mary Pipher's *Reviving Ophelia* describes this stage as a time when girls "are free to act without worrying if their behavior is feminine or masculine" (21). However, girls experience a marked transformation as they enter adolescence. The adolescent self is often described as conflicted and confused, mired in self-doubt, and marked by fluctuating poles of low and high self-esteem, self-worth, and self-confidence. The hunched shoulders, timid glances and faded optimism may indicate a shrinking of the self through this unstable period.

African American adolescent girls, too, are engaged in the process of identity formation and self-awareness, and experience similar changes. However, we cannot understand this process without an appreciation of the concept of racial identity. Adolescents need to identify with a group. And for black teenagers, being black begins to take on new significance. Black adolescence may be able to articulate some of these realities, but far more likely, is a complex set of internal negotiations which Collins describes as necessary "to reconcile the contradictions separating our own internally defined images of self as African American women with our objectification as the Other" (94). While researchers such as Gilligan indicate that a loss of voice occurs in girls as they enter puberty, much of the coming-of-age literature this writer investigated suggests that African American girls begin to lose their voice earlier than whites. Where there should be anger, instead there is shame; where there should be resistance, instead there is denial and where there should be integration, instead there is dislocation. Eleven-year-old Pecola in *The Bluest Eye* is perhaps an extreme manifestation of what it means to lose one's voice. Pecola remembers Mr. Yacobowski's eyes and is angry, but only briefly for "the anger will not hold; the puppy is too easily surfeited. Its thirst too quickly quenched, it sleeps. The shame wells up again, its muddy rivulets seeping into her eyes" (50).

By age 10 or 11 black girls and boys have already endured up to five years of systematic negative sexual and racial conditioning in schools. By the time black girls become teenagers their voices have either been buried or have taken on a timbre adopted for survival rather than for strength and enrichment.

This occurs not only in school, however, for many black households engage in strict punishment of misbehaving children. bell hooks explores the effect of this in her book *Sisters of the Yam*, noting that this punishment was enacted when parents felt that the children "might assert themselves in ways outside that might lead white people to abuse and punish them" (37). Therefore instead of developing strategies that would uplift and enrich them, they worked at developing strategies to avoid punishment. It is no wonder that we see black mothers speaking harshly to their children in apparently unprovoked situations, and it is similarly not surprising that coming-of-age stories such as Alice Childress' *Rainbow Jordan* depict an underlying diet of micro-violence. When Rainbow's mother Kathie realizes that the three dresses she has spent hours sewing will not fit Rainbow, she is furious.

> She got mad and slap me so hard, with the dress still halfway over my head. I couldn't get my arms out. She hittin and hittin hard and screamin. "Nothing fits you! What the hell is the matter? I do and I do and for what? Things always goin wrong with you . . . I'm sick-a you!" (31)

The fixation on control is a prominent feature of white domination over people of color and is a legacy of slavery. bell hooks states this clearly and she says "We need to better understand how black folks who feel relatively powerless to control their destiny exercise negative power over one another in hierarchical settings" (36).

TOWARD LIBERATION—STRATEGIES OF RESISTANCE IN AFRICAN AMERICAN ADOLESCENT FEMALES

I want to stress that the concerns listed above are not the only themes in this literature. Personal integrity and the importance of community is at the heart of all the books included in this chapter. Motown and Didi convey a great deal of personal integrity as they struggle with coming-of-age in their vibrant yet challenging community. The decisions they make reflect both a moral and spiritual core which keeps them centered. There is a deep sense of family and community conveyed in *The Music of Summer* as well as *Having Our Say* and we are left with the sickening feeling that it is the lack of integrity and community which contributes to Pecola's disintegration.

Gilligan and others have spoken about the importance of attachment and relationship as critical issues in female identity formation. I would suggest that for African American girls these relationships often involve a sharing of history as well as a sharing of the rage with the outraged mother or grandmother, who is affronted at the abuse of her people and her personhood. We observe this in the way Mama Dear engages Sarah Richardson, and affords Sarah the opportunity to identify with her past. She uses this growing relationship with Mama Dear to resist the negative pressure of her peers. Although she desperately wants to restore her childhood friendship with Cathy, she realizes she must first be true to herself. Similar to this phenomenon is the relationship between the Professor and Motown, which has an indirect but important impact on Didi in her relationship with Motown. When the Professor tells Motown "we're all in the tribe from the moment that we're named," and that "the tribe has got to have numbers and the strength of each person" (54), he is educating Motown and helping him to form a healthy identity which encompasses personal principles as well as community consciousness. The Professor is the father who Motown,

Cholly, and Leroy never had.

The Delany sisters emphasize the significance of education and parental support to their physical and spiritual survival, and for Didi, like many African Americans today, education, family and community continue to be the most certain way out of a life of hardship and despair. However, while education has been accepted by many as a way out of oppressive family and environmental conditions, black adolescent girls fall victim to the accusation that they are acting "white" if they are conscientious students. Black girls, therefore, are often having to choose between their identity and success.

CONCLUSIONS

Coming-of-age stories offer their readers an opportunity to see and understand their own experiences and allow them to get a vicarious insight into the lives of others. One of the goals of young adult novels written with African American female protagonists is to resolve the rage and restore the selves of these girls by offering strategies of resistance as they work toward liberation.

As a black female adolescent, race and gender begin to take on new meaning for her social and political identity. It is often a time when racial pride is strong, and, familiar with the demeaning stereotypes held about her and her racial group, Ward states that she must insist that "I am not what you believe black people to be, and I am black" (219). Readers identify with individual characters as well as the larger group in these stories, and are offered new ways of defining themselves. They can view themselves and their lives in a safe, nurturing place, before having to confront an oppressive world. We sense Sarah's struggle to define herself in a world that rejects her history and ethnicity, and we admire her ability to listen and incorporate those things which help her create an independent identity. Readers can also identify with the complex characters of Motown and Didi, and can take inspiration from their resistance to negative representation, violence, drugs and hopelessness.

These books are important to the adolescent during a time when their perceptions and view of life are fluid and perhaps

more easily influenced than later years. Books with female protagonists validate female voices and female ways of knowing. In
this literature, girls talk to their mothers, sisters, grandmothers,
and friends, inviting readers to explore issues vital to their own
growth and well-being.

The tentacles of racism and sexism reach far and wide and
make the necessity for change all the more urgent. Books such as
these can be used as a window into understanding the emotional and psychological challenges faced by our young people
today. In particular, the inquiry into the role of anger in African
American adolescent girls is a worthwhile study, for while we
can do nothing to alter the past, we can perhaps channel this
rage towards healthy forms of resistance so that we may forge
new truths for future generations.

WORKS CITED

Bulhan, Hussein Abdilahi. *Frantz Fanon and the Psychology of Oppression.*
New York: Plenum, 1985.

Childress, Alice. *Rainbow Jordan.* New York: Coward, 1981.

Collins, Patricia Hill. *Black Feminist Thought: Knowledge, Consciousness,
and the Politics of Empowerment,* Boston: Hyman, 1990.

Delany, A. Elizabeth, and Sarah L. with Amy Hill Hearth. *Having Our
Say: The Delany Sisters' First 100 Years.* New York: Dell, 1993.

Fanon, Frantz. *Black Skin, White Masks.* New York: Grove, 1967.

Gaines, Kevin. Living History Bears Witness. *New York Times,* April 2,
1995, Sec. 2, p. 5.

Gilligan, Carol, Annie G. Rogers, and Deborah L. Tolman, eds. *Women,
Girls & Psychotherapy: Reframing Resistance.* New York: Harrington
Park, 1991.

Guy, Rosa. *The Music of Summer.* New York: Delacorte, 1992.

hooks, bell. *Ain't I a Woman: Black Women and Feminism.* Boston: South
End Press, 1981.

_____. *Sisters of the Yam: Black Women and Self-recovery.* Boston: South
End, 1993.

Lorde, Audre. *Sister Outsider.* Freedom: Crossing, 1984.

Morrison, Toni. *The Bluest Eye.* New York: Pocket, 1970.

_____. *Playing in the Dark: Whiteness and the Literary Imagination.* Cam-
bridge: Harvard UP, 1992.

Myers, Walter Dean. *Motown and Didi.* New York: Viking/Penguin,
1984.

Pipher, Mary. *Reviving Ophelia: Saving the Selves of Adolescent Girls*. New York: Grosset/Putnam, 1994.

Rinaldi, Ann. *Wolf by the Ears*. New York: Scholastic, 1991.

Smith, Karen Patricia, ed. *African-American Voices in Young Adult Literature: Tradition, Transition, Transformation*. Metuchen: Scarecrow, 1994.

Tonry, Michael. *Malign Neglect: Race, Crime, and Punishment in America*. New York: Oxford UP, 1995.

Ward, Janie Victoria. "Racial Identity Formation and Transformation" in *Making Connections: The Relational Worlds of Adolescent Girls at Emma Willard School*, edited by Gilligan, Carol. Nona P. Lyons, Trudy J. Hanmer. Cambridge: Harvard UP, 1990.

CHAPTER FOUR

Loss of Voice in Women's Coming of Age Stories

Mary K. Lewis

L oss of voice, or loss of self has recently been recognized as a problem facing most girls coming of age in a male dominated culture. Dana Crowley Jack, Lyn Mikel Brown and Carol Gilligan, and Mary Pipher have documented this struggle to maintain a positive identity in girls and women in the United States, and Terri Apter has noted the same phenomenon in her studies of adolescents and young women in the United Kingdom.

While the literature of psychology has only recently dealt with this subject, women's fiction indicates that the problem of loss of voice is not new, and that on some level, women themselves have been aware of the struggle for a long time. Five female coming of age stories reflecting a variety of cultures, spanning a publication period of over fifty years, illustrate that the struggle to retain a sense of identity is not limited to modern white Anglo/American women. *Their Eyes Were Watching God*, by Zora Neale Hurston, was first published in 1937. It tells the coming of age story of Janie, a young Black woman in a Black community in Florida. Maxine Hong Kingston takes a retrospective look at her coming of age as a first generation Chinese American in the 1950s in *The Woman Warrior*, first published in 1975. *Shabanu: Daughter of the Wind*, although written by an American, Suzanne Staples, is the story of an 11–13-year-old Pakistani girl who grows up in a nomadic desert family. *A Thousand Acres*, by Jane Smiley, originally published in 1991, is the narrator's reflection on growing up in the fifties on an Iowa farm, but coming of age as an adult in the seventies. *Like Water for Chocolate*, by Laura Esquivel, written in 1989, is a Mexican coming of age tale set at the turn of the century. Each of these novels explores the protagonist's struggle to resist loss of voice or to regain a voice or self that has been lost.

There seem to be some universal psychological factors that make adolescents and young women especially susceptible to crises of identity, but the agents of suppression, the degree and methods of resistance, and the effects that are experienced are as diverse as the personalities and the cultures in which the young women grow up.

Loss of voice is a hesitancy or refusal to express true feelings. It is a suppression of emotions and desires for fear of a variety of social, economic, emotional, and physical consequences.

Brown and Gilligan, Jack, Pipher, and Apter, as well as other relational theorists agree that a central aspect of women's personality and development is their ability to feel a sense of connection with others. Jack suggests that attachments form a foundation for the self, mind, and behavior of all humans, but especially women. She believes that women's self-esteem is closely tied to the quality of these attachments. Brown and Gilligan note that women generally speak of themselves in connection with others, whereas men often speak as if they are autonomous, and are free to do and say as they please, seemingly unburdened by a need to be in relation with others. When this basic emotional need for connectedness collides with women's cultural surroundings, they give up their voices and abandon themselves to stay in relationship. They deny their needs and desires to avoid rejection.

Ironically, the most basic need, to achieve and maintain relationship, is often one women must deny. Jack points out that society, and, therefore, women themselves, often see the need for relationship as negative because traditionally maturity has been characterized by self-sufficiency and autonomy. Women are, therefore, forced to see themselves as immature or dependent, both of which are words with negative connotations—things to be outgrown.

Yet, while emotional dependence is seen as bad, in male dominated culture it is extremely difficult, and until recently was virtually impossible, for women to escape social and economic dependence. Because women are traditionally excluded from social and economic power, they have often been dependent on males—their fathers and husbands—for economic support, and to write the codes by which they live in society.

Therefore, their own emotional needs and the cultural norms imposed upon them cause women to modify their behavior, their words, and sometimes even their thoughts in an attempt to be desirable daughters, companions, or wives to others. They need to be "good" according to the cultural models that have been set for them.

CULTURAL, SOCIAL, AND FAMILIAR CAUSES OF LOSS OF VOICE

Some of the forces that bring about self censoring and cause the struggles to maintain identity that are described in these novels include cultural and social expectations, family traditions and loyalty, and parental fears for the future of their daughters. Many of the heroines are subject to a combination of these pressures.

Like Water for Chocolate is the only one of these five books in which male domination of the culture is not described. Mama Elena, Tita, and her sisters Gertrudis and Rosaura, along with female servants Nacha and Chencha, are the significant characters in the story. It is their decisions that move the plot. There is no father at all. Pedro, Tita's lover and Rosaura's husband, is cowardly and ineffective. He is as much dominated by Mama Elena as her own family is. John, Tita's friend and fiance, is kind, knowledgeable and sensitive, but still relatively unimportant, except in providing a haven for Tita to wait to recover her voice. He is unable to get Tita to speak. Rather, it is Chencha who finds the way to cure Tita with her ox-tail soup. The smell of onion, and memories of cooking with Nacha bring the tears that allow Tita to release her grief and to use her voice.

While this story is fantastic, it makes a believable case for loss of voice occurring whenever one grows up dominated by another male or female. The De la Garzas are a strongly matriarchal family.

Mama Elena is a tyrant who demands unquestioning obedience. "In the De la Garza family, one obeyed—immediately" (Esquivel 10). Her orders not only must be carried out, but they must be done in the way she specifies. Her daughters, especially Tita, have no opportunity to think for themselves or to make their own decisions. Thus, even when Tita has sewn a perfect seam, she is made to rip it out and resew it because she hadn't basted it first.

Punishment for failure to meet Mama Elena's expectations is often physical. For Tita, failure to speak her mother's name with the proper respect has often caused her to be slapped (11). And, when she expresses unhappiness at Roberto's death, suggesting that her mother is responsible, Mama Elena beats Tita's face and breaks her nose with a wooden spoon.

Mama Elena uses family tradition to maintain control of Tita. This tradition says that the youngest daughter of the family may not marry, but must care for the mother until the mother's death. Tita is not only prevented from marrying Pedro, but she is virtually enslaved to her mother as a cook and personal maid. When Tita tries to express an opinion, her mother tells her:

> "You don't have an opinion, and that's all I want to hear about it. For generations, not a single person in my family has ever questioned this tradition, and no daughter of mine is going to be the one to start.". . . From then on they knew, [Tita] and the table, that they could never have the slightest voice in the unknown forces that fated Tita to bow before her mother's absurd decision. . . (9).

Her mother's domination and family tradition are the main forces that work to silence Tita, but they are not the only ones. She is also concerned with social ideas of decency and good manners. She repeatedly curses the etiquette manual she's learned to follow, for making her act in ways that are contrary to her feelings. "Damn Carreno's etiquette manual," she says, at one point suggesting that he should be punished and made to disappear a little at a time (54).

Tita censors herself, using moral language just like the girls and women Brown, Gilligan, and Jack have interviewed. Although Tita knows that she will always love Pedro, she feels that she must deny this even to herself. "It wasn't decent to desire your sister's future husband. She had to try to put him out of her mind . . ." (17).

The language of the book is explicit about the silencing that occurs. As Pedro is leaving, Tita would like to be able to tell him she wants to go with him, but she cannot. Social expectations, and fear of her mother keep her silent: "Tita, for her part, was trying to shout to Pedro . . . but not a single sound came out of her mouth. The words formed a lump in her throat and were choked one after another as they tried to escape" (54).

The Chinese culture of Kingston's mother's era, passed on to her Chinese American children, and described in *The Woman Warrior* is clearly male dominated. It is a culture in which female children are not wanted, are seen as a burden, and are sold as slaves, while the birth of boys is feted with month-long celebrations. Women's feet are bound to limit their freedom, and education is denied to most of them. Kingston notes that Chinese would execute women who were caught disguising themselves as students or soldiers, regardless of their skill, bravery, or intelligence (39). She tells us that the descent line in Chinese families is passed on only through sons, so a woman without father or husband is literally no one. Even the language reflects and reinforces the subservience of women. "There is a Chinese word for the female *I*—which is 'slave.' Break the women with their own tongues!" (47).

Most of Kingston's cultural indoctrination comes from her mother, and as in *Like Water for Chocolate*, there are no significant male characters in this book. But, Kingston makes it clear that her father is a force in teaching her about women's place in society. He tells her stories of Chinese who smeared honey on their "bad" daughters-in-law and tied them naked on ant hills; and he warns her that on Confucius's authority husbands can kill disobedient wives (193).

Cultural expectations for women's behavior are very much tied to the importance of family, and so Kingston's dream of the warrior is a dream of "perfect filiality" (45). The stories she is told by her mother, and warnings she receives tell her that if she fails to be the good daughter, she will cease to exist in the minds of her family. She is told about a table for outcasts, where people who brought shame upon their family were fed separately from everyone else, and ignored. The threat of loss of relationship is imposing in this culture.

Brave Orchid silences her daughter with a cautionary coming of age tale about Kingston's paternal aunt's betrayal of her family. Her words, the very first words of the book impose silence and secrecy: "You must not tell anyone . . ." (3). When the aunt became pregnant she humiliated her family, was disowned and even allowed to be stoned by the villagers. So great was the punishment of being ignored by her family that the aunt drowned herself and her newborn baby in the well. Kingston's mother tells her not to speak of this to her father, who denies that he ever had a sister; and warns her: "Now that you have started to menstruate, what happened to her could happen to you. Don't humiliate us. You wouldn't like to be forgotten as if you had never been born" (5).

Kingston is silenced by her belief in the unacceptability of saying some things. She feels she can not ask about her aunt because she has no known name, and the only way to refer to her seems inappropriate. " 'Remember Father's drowned-in-the-well sister?' I cannot ask that" (6). Additionally, she is afraid of the power of her words to hurt. She says that she believes that words are so strong that the word " 'aunt' would do my father mysterious harm" (15).

Ginny's father, Larry, and the culture of the farming community where they live create an insurmountable silencing force in *A Thousand Acres*. Ginny is terrified of her father, who has always seemed to her to be larger than life. She tells of how, as a young child, she could not believe other children who said their fathers were farmers. She believed her father to be the epitome of both fathers and farmers: "To believe that others even existed in either category was to break the First Commandment" (Smiley 19).

Ginny's earliest memories of her father are associated with fear. She remembers being afraid to speak to him and even to look at him (19). What Ginny doesn't remember until the summer during which the events of this story take place, when she is in her mid-thirties, is that one of the ways her father instilled this fear was by beating her when she was a child.

Ginny tells us that appearances are very important in the farming community. Neighbors judge each other by the appearance of the farms, and the cleanliness of the homes, and they pay attention to the way families interact. She says that "a good appearance was the source and the sign of all other good things" (199). She expresses concern about how the community would view the fighting among her family members, suggesting that the "paramount value" of maintaining appearances made it "imperative that the growing discord in our family be made to appear minor" (199).

Things that are considered aberrant are not spoken of, and one pretends that they are forgotten. When Jess Clark leaves the country to avoid serving his military time, it is an embarrassment, and no one, including his family, speaks of or to him for years until he returns. Jess, himself, says that the wisdom of the plains is to "pretend nothing happened" (22).

Ginny's mother, while she is alive, plays a part in passing these principles on to her daughters by serving as a model and by teaching them to be good. "We were told, when we had been 'naughty'—disobedient, careless, destructive, disorderly, hurtful to others, defiant—that we had to learn" (278). Ginny remembers that her mother "fit in" and did what was expected. She raised her children to behave, and didn't argue with her husband, keeping him in his position of authority. She recalls her mother standing by while Larry beat Ginny for losing a shoe at a school dance. Ginny suggests that much of her self-consciousness may have come from being taught to behave.

The silencing is so effective, that when Ginny is 15 and her mother dies, she has no real choice but to assume the responsibility for raising her youngest sister, taking care of the house, and all of her father's needs. She submits to sex with him, because there is no one she can tell. The horror and pain are so great that in pretending nothing happened, Ginny can only survive by denying and forgetting how she feels.

In *Their Eyes Were Watching God*, Janie's grandmother's fear for her granddaughter's future makes her try to force Janie to deny her feelings and dreams and forget her need for relationship. While Janie, unlike the other four protagonists, has no mother that she ever knew, her mother's existence is a force with which she has to contend. Nanny doesn't want Janie's life to turn out as unhappily as her mother's or her own. She wants

Janie to be settled, cared for, protected, and proud. She says she wants to see Janie "safe" before she dies (Hurston 15). Nanny's fears are related to the fact that this, too, is a male dominated culture, and the only way to see Janie safely cared for is to have her married to someone with land or wealth.

Wife beating is so common and accepted that, when Janie comes home to see Nanny after three months of marriage, Nanny asks if Logan has "already" started beating her. When she learns that he is good to Janie and doesn't beat her, she tells Janie that because of what Logan owns and all he does for her, Janie should want him.

In Janie's second marriage to Joe Starks, she is required to behave in ways that are considered appropriate to Joe's status as mayor of the town. Generally this means she must remain silent and, like Ginny, must maintain expected appearances. Janie herself has little fear of poverty or of being socially excluded and remains with Joe for 20 years, trying to make the marriage work because she still has little idea that real love might be anything other than what she has experienced.

The Pakistani culture in which Shabanu is raised, as it is described in *Shabanu: Daughter of the Wind*, like the Chinese culture of Maxine Hong Kingston, is one where men and boys are clearly more important than women. This is often explicitly stated. Because she has two sons, Shabanu's aunt feels superior to Shabanu's mother, who only has daughters. The prayers said for Phulan's marriage are that she should have sons, and even strangers think nothing of commenting to Shabanu's family on their misfortune of having only daughters.

Sharma is considered a great oddity because she left a husband who beat her for having a daughter instead of a son. One of the reasons Shabanu is forced to marry Rahim is because women require a husband to protect them and care for them economically.

Both of Shabanu's parents try to teach her to obey. Her mother tells her: "You must learn to obey. Otherwise . . . I am afraid for you. . . . You aren't a child anymore. You must learn to obey, even when you disagree" (Staples 28).

Mama also sets an example of goodness which Shabanu finds difficult to live up to. Her mother helps Dadi with the work, repairs the mud walls of the house, cleans, cooks, sews, and nurtures; and Shabanu is somewhat in awe of this, saying that she doesn't know how Mama finds the time (21).

Although the culture and her parents work to make Shabanu "good" and to deny her feelings and desires, ironically, it is her independent cousin Sharma, whom she greatly admires, who is most effective in finally silencing her. Sharma is the one who gives Shabanu the advice to keep her soul to herself and to maintain a relationship with her future husband by refusing to make a real emotional connection with him.

RESISTING LOSS OF VOICE

Girls and women have different ways in which they resist or merely attempt to cope with the cultural censoring that can bring about loss of voice. Brown and Gilligan have found four methods: some resist openly, making their struggle political; some find a creative means of expressing themselves; for some, resistance is moved underground, where they feel more free to share thoughts and feelings secretly with others; and some attempt to protect themselves by keeping their feelings private, allowing no one to see.

Like the real girls interviewed by Brown and Gilligan, the heroines of these five novels use these same coping and resisting mechanisms. Often, they do not resort to a single type of behavior, but rather use them in combination, trying them out at different times, in different situations.

Many of them attempt to resist openly, at least early on, when they first become aware that choices are being made for them without consideration of their feelings and desires.

Janie, at 16, tries to refuse to marry Logan Killicks, a man she finds repulsive. Twice she tells her grandmother that she will not marry him (Hurston 12, 13).

Tita, at 15, first learning that Mama Elena will not allow her to marry Pedro because of the family tradition, does not want to accept this decision, and tries to argue: "Discussion was not one of the forms of communication permitted in Mama Elena's household, but . . . she intended to protest" (Esquivel 9). In fact, Tita does try to express her opinion before being cut off by her mother; and, although Esquivel makes the claim that Tita is protesting for the first time in her life, this is not really accurate.

For Tita, Shabanu, and Kingston, their early rebellion is a carry over from childhood and a result of their incomplete understanding of the strength of the forces against which they struggle. Tita is reported to have been a rebellious child, who often did not show her mother the proper respect. For example, Mama Elena prefers to be called "Mami" and has ordered her daughters to use this term from their early childhood, because she believes that "Mama" sounds disrespectful. Apparently Tita has refused to do this as her mother wishes. "The only one who resisted, the only one who said the word without the proper deference was Tita . . ." (Esquivel 11).

Shabanu also reports that she has not learned to obey: "Dadi is a wise man, and I've never truly learned to obey him" (Staples 30). One gets the impression that throughout her childhood her spiritedness and her disobedience have been indulged and her feelings have been considered. After selling her favorite camel Guluband, her father gets her a puppy to try to make her feel better, even though she has screamed, kicked, and fought against him in anger and despair.

Kingston writes of having had tantrums as a child in rebellion against injustices to girls in general: "When one of my parents or the emigrant villagers said, 'feeding girls is feeding cowbirds,' I would thrash on the floor and scream so hard I couldn't talk" (Kingston 46). She also strongly resisted the personal injustice of being called a "bad" girl because she knew that she wasn't bad, and she seemed to understand that merely being a girl was enough to make people believe she was inherently and inescapably bad. " 'I'm not a bad girl,' I would scream . . . I might as well have said, 'I'm not a girl' " (46).

Regardless of how their childhood resistance is dealt with by their parents or societies, open rebellion and disagreement with authority and cultural expectations at the point when these heroines are perceived to have become physically mature or sexually aware is no longer indulged or tolerated. It is often met with physical punishment or emotional withdrawal, and put down quickly and decisively.

Tita, who has been punished for resistance since childhood,

dares to attempt to express an opinion on the subject of the family tradition that won't allow her to marry. Her mother silences her immediately, telling her she doesn't have an opinion even before Tita can say what her opinion is. Then she refuses to speak to Tita for an entire week (Esquivel 9).

Nanny sees Janie kissing Johnny Taylor and believes this marks the end of Janie's childhood. She feels that she must get Janie safely married right away. Janie is slapped by her grandmother for pouting at the thought of marrying Logan Killicks. Nanny wants not only Janie's compliance, but her appreciation as well. She scolds Janie: "'Don't you set dere poutin' wid me after all Ah done went through for you.' She slapped the girl's face violently, and forced her head back so that their eyes met in struggle" (Hurston 13).

Shabanu, who appears never to have suffered more than a scolding or a shaking for disobedience, also is slapped for suggesting that she will disobey her family and go to live with her aunt rather than to marry Rahim: " 'I'll go to live with Sharma,' I say, and Mama's slap sends my head flying and my eyes reeling. 'Shabanu,' she says, her face harder than I've ever seen it before, 'you are to say nothing more. It is done'" (Staples 193). Her mother not only hits her but, in hardening her face, she withdraws emotional support and sympathy.

Shabanu knows when her parents discover that she's begun menstruating that she will be forced to marry Rahim immediately, and she tries to make one last refusal by running away. Although she has been mostly gently treated as a child, she is aware that the consequences if she is caught will be more severe. Her father has told her that some Bugti tribal men they met on a trip would kill the daughter of one of their members who eloped with a Marri tribesman instead of obeying. She knows that the least she can expect if she's caught is a beating, but she attempts this last rebellion anyway. When her father catches up to her he beats her just as she expected, using a stick, until she bleeds.

Janie continues to try to stay true to her feelings and tries to express them openly from time to time. In her marriage to Joe Starks, she repeatedly tries to tell him what she thinks. His responses escalate from disagreeing with her and telling her how she should feel; to assaulting her self-esteem by insulting her intelligence, her appearance, and her actions; to beating her. "Time came when she fought back with her tongue as best she could, but it didn't do any good. It just made Joe do more. He wanted her submission and he'd keep on fighting until he felt he had it" (Hurston 67).

Kingston relates several attempts to speak out about her truth as a young adult. Speaking up for what she believes is so difficult that, in trying, her actual, physical voice is unreliable. The consequences are predictably negative. At best she is ignored. When one boss tells her to order more "nigger yellow" paint, she rebels: " 'I don't like that word,' I had to say in my bad, small-person's voice that makes no impact" (Kingston 48). In this instance, her voice truly does not have an impact because she gets no response at all. On another occasion she disagrees with a boss's choice of a banquet site because the restaurant is being picketed by CORE and the NAACP. " 'I refuse to type these invitations,' I whispered, voice unreliable" (49). Without further discussion she is fired.

MOVING UNDERGROUND

Usually, the severe reprisals against expressing their thoughts or acting on their feelings lead these characters to abandon this as a primary form of resistance. Their thoughts and feelings are to a large extent driven underground. In their novels, Kingston and Esquivel describe several creative outlets young women have for expressing what cannot be directly stated.

When Tita realizes that she has no voice in the decisions that shape her life, she puts her feelings into her cooking. Her desires and disappointments find their way into her recipes magically, through her bitterness, tears, and blood. They make themselves felt anonymously by all who eat what she cooks.

Kingston, whose silence was imposed from early childhood, describes two attempts at creatively expressing what has been repressed. As a child, she seemed aware that silence concealed important thoughts and feelings—possibilities of self. She expressed this through her art, by covering up the representations of her personality that were her drawings.

My silence was thickest—total—during the three years that I covered my school paintings with black paint. I painted layers of black over houses and flowers and suns, and when I drew on the blackboard, I put a layer of chalk on top. (165)

Much later, after years of struggling with silence, trying to understand who she is and to speak of the wrongs she has been unable to talk about, Kingston writes her story. Her art, her words, represent not just resistance, but a form of revenge. They are her attempt to exorcise the ghosts, like her dead aunt, that have haunted and silenced her. "My aunt haunts me—her ghost drawn to me because now, after fifty years of neglect, I alone devote pages of paper to her . . ." (16).

She compares herself to the folk tale swordswoman, Fa Mu Lan, suggesting that her own writing, like the words carved on Fa Mu Lan's skin, are an important and heroic resistance. She says that what they have in common are "the words. . . . The reporting is the vengeance—not the beheading, not the gutting, but the words" (Kingston 53).

Her writing as a creative form of expression is more direct and less anonymous than her drawing or Tita's cooking, but still is done from a safer distance than speaking or acting.

Ginny, like Kingston, seems to have been silenced from earliest childhood, and her coming of age is a struggle to gain an awareness of herself and bring her resistance to silencing forces out in the open. For most of her life, almost everything she does and says is with careful consideration of avoiding open conflict. To this end, she alters both what she says and how she says it. When she would speak to her father, she says she would make her voice "as inoffensive as possible" (Smiley 81). Later she notes that something she does often to avoid giving offense is "phrasing and rephrasing of sentences in my mind, scaling back assertions and direct questions" (115).

Ginny seems, at least initially, most comfortable keeping her resistance underground, sharing her opinions and feelings secretly with her sister Rose. She and Rose privately discuss the irrationality of their father's behavior, and resentment over their sister Caroline's failure to understand their point of view. Ginny tells about how, after their mother died, she and Rose plotted secretly to be sure Caroline had social opportunities that they felt were important, but they knew their father would never have permitted.

It is to Rose, and not to her own husband, that she confides her fourth pregnancy and miscarriage, because she doesn't agree with Ty's decision to give up trying to have children, but she doesn't want to argue about it with him.

Ginny reflects on the importance of having another woman with whom to share her feelings, and to help her gain perspective to her suffering. She describes some of the ways women use secret communication without saying directly what they mean. They maintain an ongoing commentary through "rolled eyes . . . sighs and jokes and irritated remarks" (113). Ginny feels that this indirect communication helps to prepare women for their misfortunes, and provides a source of support for women that is unavailable to men.

Shabanu's resistance also takes the form of sharing her feelings secretly sometimes. One night she sneaks out to Sharma and Fatima's house to discuss her feelings about the marriage that her father has arranged, and to plot a course of action. Sharma and Fatima sympathize with her in a way she knows no one else will, and offer her the choice of going to live with them.

All of the heroines of these novels sometimes resort to protecting themselves or others by keeping their feelings entirely private, and sharing with no one. Janie speaks of learning not to speak as a part of growing up. "No matter what Jody did, [Janie] said nothing. She had learned how to talk some and leave some" (Hurston 72).

After Joe beats Janie the first time, she realizes that there are many thoughts and feelings she hasn't shared with him. She talks about having inside and outside selves that are different, and that represent what she feels and what she shows.

> She found that she had a host of thoughts she had never expressed to him, and numerous emotions she had never let Jody know about. Things packed up and put away in parts of her heart where he could never find them. . . . She had an inside and an outside now and suddenly she knew how not to mix them (68).

Later at Joe's funeral, she uses her inside–outside awareness.

She talks about "setting" her face to show what people expect to see, but she knows that inside she feels freed.

Tita also has thoughts she will not voice, even to God. Although she wishes her mother dead, Tita prays that nothing bad will happen to Mama Elena. Esquivel says that these hopes are unconscious, but it seems that Tita is actually aware of them, because we are told that she is ashamed of them (Esquivel 89).

Shabanu, like Janie has learned how not to speak. She tells us, "I have learned to keep my mouth shut . . ."(Staples 196). She is willing to tell her sister, Phulan, only a limited amount of what she thinks about her future husband because she is afraid of punishment. "I clamp my mouth shut, but I am not ashamed of what I think. I decide not to say more for fear Phulan will tell Dadi" (213).

In the end, when her father has caught her and she has no escape from marrying Rahim, she remembers Sharma's advice to keep to herself and let no one see her feelings. As Dadi beats her, she tells us:

> I am silent . . . I refuse to cry out . . . I take Sharma's advice. I recall the beautiful things in my world and, like a bride admiring her dowry, I take them out, one by one, then fold them away again, deep into my heart. . . .
>
> 'The secret is keeping your innermost beauty, the secrets of your soul, locked in your heart,' Sharma's voice whispers in my ear, 'so that he must always reach out to you for it' (240).

Not only does she withdraw herself from her father; but, in the last sentence of the book, she vows that she will do the same with her future husband. "Rahim-sahib will reach out to me for the rest of his life and never unlock the secrets of my heart" (240).

When girls or women like Janie, Ginny, Tita, Shabanu and Kingston keep their feelings private in these ways, they are not merely trying to avoid physical punishment. They are enacting the relational paradox that Gilligan and Brown describe. They withdraw themselves from relationships for the sake of maintaining relationships. They cease to speak their true feelings, saying or doing what others expect—or saying nothing at all. They abandon themselves to become "good" women according to their cultural norms, and look for acceptance, which they may measure through their ability to maintain successful (i.e. lasting) relationships. The paradox is that while they may manage to maintain the appearance of a relationship, the relationship is false.

A true relationship is of paramount importance to Janie. She values it more than material goods or prestige, and her life purpose seems to be to find it. Therefore, she tries to convince herself that, however Joe behaves, she needs to maintain a relationship with him. She needs him to be important to her. She thinks:

> "Maybe he ain't nothin', but he is something in my mouth. He's got tuh be else Ah ain't got nothin' tuh live for. Ah'll lie and say he is. If Ah don't, life won't be nothin' but uh store and uh house" (Hurston 72).

Janie stays married to Joe for twenty years, until he dies, but there is no emotional sharing in their marriage.

Ginny clearly expresses the importance of staying in relationship in talking about her relationship with Rose. She describes setting aside herself and her jealousy to do this. She says:

> I was so jealous . . . every time I saw [Rose's babies], that I could hardly speak. . . . We've always known families . . . for whom a historic dispute over land or money burns so hot it engulfs every other subject, every other point of relationship or affection. I didn't want that, I wanted that least of all, so I got over my jealousy and made my relationship with Rose better than ever . . . (Smiley 88–89).

Ginny represses her jealous feelings and acts selflessly in taking care of her ill sister, attending to Rose's personal needs as well as her household chores. Without doing these things, she fears she would lose her closeness with Rose. Yet, their relationship is not as strong as Ginny would like to believe. There are many more secrets between them; and later, when Ginny learns of them, she is so angry she attempts to poison Rose.

LOSING THE SELF

A danger in denying one's feelings or hiding them from others is that they may soon become lost to women themselves. Brown and Gilligan found that by removing themselves from relationships, adolescents and women lose the ability to articulate their true feelings, then they become confused, and they may ultimately forget what these feelings are—or what relational truths they used to know. Jack also believes that by presenting an unauthentic version of herself to the person with whom she lives most intimately, a woman may begin to experience a loss of her own self.

All of these psychologists agree that many girls or young women are aware of the games they play and the things they leave unsaid in the interest of maintaining relationship. Ginny, for example, displays an awareness of pretending to have certain feelings in order to keep her father from being angry, when she says that once offended, her father could be easily mollified if she spoke a "prescribed part with a proper appearance of deference" (Smiley 33).

Janie also seems aware of saying and doing things that are not true to her feelings. Early in her marriage to Joe, when he refuses to allow her to make a speech, silencing her for the first time, Hurston tells us, "Janie made her face laugh after a short pause, but it wasn't easy" (Hurston 40–41).

In telling the story of her dream of becoming a warrior, Kingston relates an exchange between her seven-year-old dream self and the old mentors. The parenthetical explanation of what she really felt and would like to have said echoes the voices of the girls and women in *Meeting at the Crossroads* and *Silencing the Self* when they describe what they say in contrast with what they think. When the old man and woman ask if she has eaten, the dream child replies:

> "'Yes, I have,' I said out of politeness. 'Thank you.'
>
> ('No, I haven't,' I would have said in real life, mad at the Chinese for lying so much. 'I'm starved')" (Kingston 21).

If they are lucky, women who become silent at least maintain an awareness of how they feel. In many respects, Janie doesn't lose touch with herself altogether, though she does become confused. "The years took all the fight out of Janie's face. For a while she thought it was gone from her soul" (Hurston 72). But even after twenty years of marriage to Joe, when he is dying she knows enough about how she feels and about what their relationship has been like for her that she is able to pull it up out of her soul and tell it to him.

On the other hand, Joe's death also frees her to realize in a new way, how much she resents her grandmother for not allowing her the chance to experience life or love. These feelings seem to have been entirely lost to her. When she thinks of returning to where she came from, she decides she can't because that place is full of thoughts of her grandmother—now dead. "She hated her grandmother and had hidden it from herself all these years under a cloak of pity. . . . She hated the old woman who had twisted her so in the name of love" (85).

Kingston, like Janie, manages fairly well to hold on to her self, even while she is silenced. She is, at all points in the telling of her story, able to describe how she felt at those times. However, even though it doesn't happen to her, she is still afraid that her silence will cause her to lose her awareness of self or to lose her mind. She says, "I thought talking and not talking made the difference between sanity and insanity. Insane people were the ones who couldn't explain themselves. There were many crazy girls and women" (Kingston 186).

Tita becomes one of these crazy women Kingston describes, at least temporarily. Years of oppression and mistreatment by her mother cause her to lose her ability to make choices or to think about how she feels. When Roberto dies and Mama Elena will not allow Tita to mourn, the accumulated suppressed pain seems to become suddenly and violently more than Tita can bear, causing her to lose control and refuse to obey while screaming that she is sick of her mother's orders (Esquivel 95–96).

After her outburst, Tita goes to the dovecote over the barn, where she is later found acting crazy, staring vacantly, trying to feed a dead pigeon, and finally curled in a fetal position (97). Tita becomes completely silent for weeks and is like an insane person because she has no ability to express, even to herself, how she feels, or to make choices based on what she wants. For years she has practiced not knowing how she feels. It seems easier for her to escape from herself than to cope with all of the

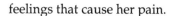

feelings that cause her pain.

> She preferred silence. There were many things she needed to work out in her mind, and she could not find the words to express the feelings seething inside her . . . she would stare at her hands for hours on end. At her mother's, what she had to do with her hands was strictly determined, no questions asked. . . . Now seeing her hands no longer at her mother's command, she didn't know what to ask them to do, she had never decided for herself before. . . . She raised her hands to heaven; she wanted to escape from herself, didn't want to think about making a choice, didn't want to talk again. She didn't want her words to shriek her pain (104–105).

Although she doesn't become crazy, Ginny has lost contact with herself even more completely than Tita. Through years of learning to be good, acting selflessly, submitting to her father's authority, beatings, and sexual assaults, and trying to keep up appearances in the community, she no longer even knows how she really feels. Just as she has misjudged her relationship with Rose, Ginny believes her marriage to Ty is good and thinks he makes her happy, only to realize later that this isn't true.

When she tries to express an opinion, and her father, like Tita's mother, tells her she's not entitled to have an opinion, she acquiesces easily, saying, "It was silly to talk about 'my point of view.' When my father asserted his point of view mine vanished. Not even I could remember it" (Smiley 176). So when her father proposes forming a corporation and selling the farm to Ginny and her sisters, Ginny's reaction comes only after checking for others' responses (Harold and Ty) and then what she says is not what she feels. "In spite of that inner clang, I tried to sound agreeable" (Smiley 19). She is not even able to define for herself what her opinion is, beyond a general unease—an "inner clang."

Ginny has lost more than her feelings. She has lost events as well. For about twenty years she has no memory of the incest. Later on, in reflecting on her life, she describes her old life before the memories as one where many things went unsaid and were forgotten: "What was never given utterance eventually becomes too nebulous to recall" (305).

The reason Tita and Ginny lose their minds is that the

amount of suffering they are required to deny exceeds even the considerable strength they possess. Brown and Gilligan have observed that resisting loss of voice requires of young women a courage and strength that is heroic because, beginning at adolescence, for girls to say what they feel and think means that they risk losing their relationships and may find themselves powerless and alone.

It is important, however, not to regard loss of voice or loss of self as weakness or as a flaw of character. It is generally a state of being that is culturally imposed. Jack notes that while a woman's behavior may appear passive or dependent or helpless, playing a compliant role actually requires tremendous cognitive and emotional activity to silence the self. Silencing negative feelings, therefore, is active and requires at least as much strength as speaking them.

Shabanu and Ginny both speak of their weariness and exhaustion when they are obedient or act as expected, when they are actually feeling differently. Told to come to her father to accept a gift from Rahim that Shabanu does not want because she resents being bought, she nevertheless obeys her father: "wearily, as if my body is making a great effort to overcome the laws of nature I get down from Xhush Dil and stand before my father" (Staples 197).

Ginny refers to her "molasses feeling of fatigue" in a tense relational situation with her sister Caroline, when she is trying to think of what Caroline wants her to say rather than saying what she is feeling (Smiley 98). Another time, trying to maintain an appearance of harmony at dinner with Rose's family and her father, Ginny comments that it is "exhausting" simply to stay at the table (101).

Later, when Ginny has begun to recover her voice, she finds that, even though she risks changing their relationship completely, she is able to tell Ty what she really feels. While it requires tremendous courage to do this, she does not describe the effort as exhausting:

> We had spent our life together practicing courtesy, putting the best face on things, harboring secrets, the thought of giving that up, right now, with my next remark, was terrifying. Finally, I summoned a firm voice, in which I said . . . (260)

COMING OF AGE: FINDING THE LOST VOICE

For all of these heroines, coming of age has different complications, different meanings, and happens at different times in different places. Their ages at the time of the telling of their stories ranges from 11 years old to about 40 years old. What their individual stories have in common is that for all of them the process of coming of age involves the struggle to maintain or to find a voice or an identity of their own.

For Janie, coming of age is ultimately finding a real relationship with Tea Cake. This relationship allows her to experience what love and sharing really are. Tea Cake not only allows Janie to express herself, he encourages her to do this, admonishing her to have the nerve to say what she means (Hurston 104).

The end of Janie's childhood is kissing Johnny Taylor, but coming of age is a 21 year struggle with loss of voice until she meets Tea Cake and becomes convinced of their connectedness. Finally, Janie's life depends on her ability to find the words to tell the truth about her relationship with Tea Cake, and she manages to do this at her trial.

For Kingston, the beginning of coming of age is clearly marked by physical maturity, but involves years of sorting out conflicting stories, desires and responsibilities. As it does for the woman warrior of her dream, coming of age means assuming the expectations of her family bit by bit until finally they are all but carved upon her back. These expectations are conflicting and confusing: she must be a hero as a daughter, wife, and mother in a culture where she cannot be a hero because she is female. For Kingston, coming of age and figuring out what is true and what is false requires that she leave home. She tells us that this is the only way she can come to see the world "logically" (Kingston 204). Having left, and continuing to look for explanations even into her forties, she still finds telling difficult but says that regardless of the possible consequences, she needs to express her real thoughts, because to fail to do so is too painful (205).

Coming of age for Ginny doesn't even begin until she is in her mid thirties. In this sense she is like many of Mary Pipher's adult clients who struggle with adolescent issues twenty years behind schedule. Ginny, like the women Pipher describes, has spent her adolescence and young adulthood occupied with the thoughts and feelings of other family members rather than her own. In the summer of the story, when Jess returns, the farm is sold, her nieces are home from school, and her father loses his mind, Ginny begins to struggle with her unresolved adolescent questions about friendships, honesty, her physical appearance, her own values and needs.

The beginning of her new adult life comes dramatically when her memories and feelings return and she finds her self and her voice in screams. "I screamed in a way that I had never screamed before, full out, throat-wrenching, unafraid-of-making-a-fuss-and-drawing-attention-to-myself sorts of screams. . . . My new life, yet another new life, had begun" (Smiley 229).

From this moment on, Ginny stops censoring her thoughts and says what she really feels. Ginny, like Kingston, needs to leave her home and family to find herself completely.

Tita's coming of age begins when she is 16 and falls in love with Pedro, and it continues as she loses her voice and struggles to regain it, until her mother and her sister die allowing her finally to be with Pedro. Like Janie, she desires a truly fulfilling relationship. She cannot be satisfied until she finds someone to "light her inner fire" (Esquivel 239), and only Pedro can do this. For Tita, her coming of age struggle ends only with her death and Pedro's.

Shabanu's story is unfinished in this book.[1] Coming of age for her is tied closely to physical maturity, and begins with puberty. In this story, it ends with her decision to silence herself, to keep her soul hidden from Rahim. This novel, of all of the five discussed here, ends the most disturbingly for this reason. Thinking of the emotional costs to women of silencing their voices, her ultimate decision makes the ending pessimistic and leaves one wondering how Shabanu will cope with silence and whether she, like the other protagonists, will ever regain her voice.

NOTES

1. Shabanu's story, and her struggle with loss of voice remain unresolved in the sequel, *Haveli*. This story begins six years after *Shabanu: Daughter of the Wind* ends.

WORKS CITED

Apter, Terri. *Altered Loves: Mothers and Daughters during Adolescence.* New York: St. Martin's (1990).

Brown, Lyn M., and Carol Gilligan. *Meeting at the Crossroads: Women's Psychology and Girls' Development.* Cambridge: Harvard UP (1992).

Esquivel, Laura. *Like Water for Chocolate: A Novel in Monthly Installments with Recipes, Romances and Home Remedies.* (C. Christensen & T. Christensen, Trans.). New York: Anchor (1992) (Original work published 1989).

Hurston, Zora N. *Their Eyes Were Watching God.* New York: Harper (1990).

Jack, Dana C. *Silencing the Self: Women and Depression.* Cambridge: Harvard UP (1991).

Kingston, Maxine H. *The Woman Warrior: Memoirs of a Girlhood among Ghosts.* New York: Vintage/Random House (1989).

Pipher, Mary. *Reviving Ophelia: Saving the Selves of Adolescent Girls.* New York: Putnam's (1994).

Smiley, Jane. *A Thousand Acres.* New York: Fawcett Columbine (1992).

Staples, Suzanne F. *Haveli.* New York: Knopf (1993).

_____. *Shabanu: Daughter of the Wind.* New York: Borzoi Sprinter/Knopf (1991).

CHAPTER FIVE

Oh Mom,
What Am I Made Of?

A Daughter/Woman

O h mom, what am I made of ?
I am made of you, my silent mother.[1] You in the kitchen taking workshirts out of the dryer, while daddy and I fight in the livingroom. A fight I can never win (because I am a child, because I am a young girl, because I am a teenager, because I am an insecure college student, because I am a broken thirty—just divorced—who daddy "sure as hell wouldn't want to be married to," because I've been told for years and years by the father and the brother that I am "ugly," "stupid," "a flake," and best, "crazy").

Look, mom! Look at that. Look above at the gap between college and divorce, the time when I was safe from the father and the brother. The time when I was legitimate. Legitimate because I was married, "belonged" to the man. Do you see? Did the same thing happen to you? Were you safe from grandpa, were you made legitimate, when you married daddy on your college graduation day?

Listen, mommy. Listen to me. Because I'm reading books now. The ones you don't want to read. In the books I meet girls and women who you need to meet. And from them learn things you need to know. Try to hear me, now. Please.

I have learned:

We live in a patriarchal society. Do you know what that means? I didn't. It means that since the time of the Bible and the Talmud, since the Greeks, women and children have been considered property. We were bought and sold and traded. Our bodies belonged to the men to whom we belonged. If we were raped, we belonged to the men who raped us. So. Your father didn't touch you when you were married, because you belonged to another man, mom. Daddy and Jimmy didn't attack me when I belonged to another man. And we are so much a part of this patriarchy, mom, that we knew (unconsciously) to marry another man to make ourselves safe. But it didn't work. Why? Because the safety we found, the legitimacy, wasn't respect for us; it was respect by men for other men's property. Because in the end, the men we married didn't respect us anymore than the men from whom we ran. *This is the truth.*

(Or shouldn't I speak for you? It is not for me to say that your marriage was awful. That daddy treated you as a workhorse. That he treats you like . . . like shit, mom. That our world revolved around him, then around him and Jimmy, then around him and Jimmy and Chad. No, it's not for me. But mom, you're not speaking for yourself. So I, who was your protection, diverting daddy's anger, who for years cried your tears, confused because I didn't know why I cried all the time, now here am I still: doing your reading, so I can be your voice, and trying to hear your voice in the voices in the books.)

Mom. Becky. We are transferable, usable, rapeable, disposable. And to them, none of this has much to do with us.

What I mean is, the men come first.

So when my husband gave me back to my father, and I understand now that that is how they saw it, my father's first response was disappointment that he wasn't going to get free flying lessons and then understanding for my husband—my father sure as hell wouldn't want to be married to me either. And my brother's priority is his relationship to my husband. He needs to stay best-friends with the-man-who-gave-me-back because they are such good buddies, car buddies, flying buddies. For my brother is also understanding—he grew up with *stupidcrazyuglyflake*, helped name her, in fact.

What I mean is, the men come first.
They have the power.
So you didn't protect me.

So your mother didn't protect you.
And somehow you accepted that.

So you never cried all these years.
Maybe two or three times I remember you crying.
Then you told me about your father.
And now you cry every time we speak.

You admitted my father's cruelty,
my brother's meanness,
that you didn't protect me.
And I don't need to cry all the time anymore.

And suddenly I am not "crazy."
Because you have heard me, and believed me, and told me
that my truth was real.
So I can question *UglyStupidFlake.*

Because I understand now why you let them name me *Ugly* and *Stupid* and *Flake* (though I hurt and cried without anyone to contradict the names, though I acquired the other name, *Crazy,* because I "let" the words upset me, and though eventually I learned to call myself those names and will now spend the rest of my life learning how not to do that). I understand now that to you it must have seemed that I was safer as an ugly stupid crazy flake of a girl than as a beautiful, bright, together young woman. The type of young woman to whom fathers and brothers are attracted. (Girls like my friends. Like Marian, named Marian-the-Beautiful by Daddy and Jimmy—and who Jimmy dated. And voluptuous Thea, who felt uncomfortable when Daddy praised her looks—and who Jimmy slept with that summer you sent him, not me, to Europe.) I was safer despised than "loved."

I am suddenly so angry, mom. I am angry that I have to understand your life in order to understand my own. I am angry that I can't stop writing to you. I am angry that I am angry. I am angry that I find my life and yours in these horrible, wonderful books, but that I have to tell you about them (and about me and about you) in an essay you will never be willing to read.[2]

Would you read books looking for me?
To find my life and yours?

To find Tish whose stepfather named her too. He named her "Shit". He said that shit had the same letters as Tish, and so he'd say "Tish," but he'd say it in a certain way, so that they both knew he was really calling her "Shit." And she was supposed to think he was witty, and so she learned to laugh along. That's my life mom. The learned ability to turn Shit and Ugly into love, until I couldn't do it anymore. Until in a big confusing painful mess, I finally saw shit for shit, because if I didn't I would either truly go crazy or die. Like some of the girls in the books—not everyone makes it, you know. I almost didn't.

And now, I am weary.

So let me tell you what I learned about incest. Let me tell you what I learned from Tish and Abby and Celie and Pecola, from Maya and Sylvia, Laurel and Jen, and from the nameless sister of Benjamin. Let me ask the questions that led to questions:

> *What kept you silent?*
> Or is the real question how could you have spoken?
> Could you, a young girl, break silence in a world that might punish your voice by punishing you and the only people you loved?
> Could you choose yourself in a world that taught you that you, the girl child, are the sacrifice, the one of least value?
> Could you, alone, make decisions about your own fate and the fate of others, with no one to protect you or to help you to think?
>
> *What kept you silent?*
> Was it shame and confusion about your feelings?
> Had you accepted incest as your lot in life?
> Were you afraid you would not be heard?
> Did your father threaten you?
> Did you protect others?
> Or did you learn to forget what happened to you?
>
> And how could this happen, that **you** felt the shame?
> Like Maya, did you like the attention from your father, did you feel "precious,"at first?
> Or like Benjamin's sister, were you told that you were

somehow asking for his abuse, and were you confused by your body's response?
Like Tish, did you learn to read your father's bad thoughts and to then believe they were your own?

And how did you decide that you should not tell?
Did you understand that, like Jen and Celie's fathers, your father considered you a possession, and that the world considered you his possession too?
Did you believe that it was your job to take care of your father, like Benjamin's sister, Jen, and Celie?
Like Benjamin's sister, did you think that your family was all that you had.
Or did you fear the courts and foster homes for you and your three younger brothers?
Fear that, as for Jen, "the system" wouldn't protect you—that you would end up back at home, or someplace worse.

And how did you know that you would not be heard?
Did you try, as Tish and Benjamin's sister tried, to speak to a teacher, only to have her tell you in actions or in words that she was not going to hear you?
Like Tish, did you try to tell your mother, only to have her call you a liar and walk away?
Or beat you, like Pecola's mother?
Or tell you to keep the secret, like Abby's mother?
Or simply not hear your words, like Jen's mother?
Or did your mother have a habit of telling you that you imagined things, as Laurel's mother did, ignoring the message behind the dishes that you smashed.

Did your father use your love to keep you silent?
Did you know he was a violent man?
And loving others more than yourself, did you stay silent to protect them?
Celie protected her sister.
Jen and Abby protected theirs.
Maya protected her brother.

> Little Sylvia, the life of her teddybear.
> She and Jen, the lives of their pets.
> Benjamin's sister protected what was left of her family.
> And all the girls who had mothers protected their mothers.
> (We girls are taught early that we come last.)

We girls are taught early that our lives are for others.

In Jen's story, written by a man, Jen decides to prosecute her father in order to protect the girls in her father's new family. She does not need to protect herself. The existence of a video makes her safe. (And this video is worth thinking about. Without Jen's permission (!), her friend, Dillon, used a hidden camera to film Jen's father raping her, and in order to develop the film, he must view its contents. To prosecute her father, she must allow the video to be viewed by strangers. By now I am sufficiently cynical to find this necessity of plot distasteful and suspect. Voyeuristic. Pornographic.) In the story, written by a man, Jen does not prosecute her father because he repeatedly molested her, but rather, to help somebody else.

And you, mom, your story still written by men, told about your father not to help yourself but to help me.

You still don't help yourself.

Or do you? Is not getting help for your self still somehow the way you keep your world safe? Is it the best help you are able to give your self at this time? Are you helping your self in ways I don't know about or can't see?

And what did you do to help your self then, when you were living through the incest? What did you do to cope, to function?

> Did you create another self, a facade, who went out into the world for you?
> Like Sylvia's femme fatale?
> Like Tish's cool girl?
> Like Abby's Millicent Fillmore?
> Like Benjamin's sister's regular girl?
> Like Jen's super-achieving athlete?
> Like Pecola's bluest eyed self?

Like Laurel's Rose-White?
Who is the girl I've seen in pictures? The girl who got her-
self a scholarship for college, who worked in Macy's, who
wore a jaunty scarf tied around her neck?

Or did you have another self inside?
Who told you to tell or not to tell.
Who told you he loved you or didn't.
Who kept your scream inside you, kept you calm.
Who helped you believe things were OK.
Like Sylvia, like Pecola, like Tish, like Ben's Sister?

Did you write your truth, like Celie and Ben's sister and Tish,
in a journal or letter that you hid away? Like Laurel, did you
imagine painting your truth? Did you mail your truth to someone who never answered?

Did you learn to disappear, to dissociate, to float
away from your body?
Like Celie and Jen and Sylvia and Tish and Laurel,
did your mind go away and your body become numb
when you were touched?
Like Tish and Jen and Abby, did you drift off in the
middle of a conversation?
You do that now, you know. I do too.
Did you, as Sylvia and Laurel did, completely forget
a part of your self? Is there more to your story than
you remember?
Like Laurel, did you seem to have done things that
you didn't remember doing?

Did you wrestle with insanity?
Fear that you would scream like Tish and Laurel,
unable to stop?
Do things that made no sense to you, like Sylvia?
Did you begin to realize, as Laurel did, that you were
the someone who moved things, smashed things, left
doors open?
Fear losing the boundaries between real and unreal
as Pecola did?

(Reading, our omniscient eyes see that what looks like crazy makes sense.)

Did you fear pregnancy?
Were there pills then? Like Tish, did you steal them?
Like Benjamin's sister, did you live in wait for your period?
Like Laurel and Pecola were you pregnant by your father?
Like Laurel (like me), did you have an abortion?

Did you consider ways to escape?
Consider the perils of running away, as Abby and Maya considered them?
Consider the release of suicide, as Abby and Jen and Tish considered it. As Tish's classmate chose it?

How did you survive?
And what if?

What if you had been able to break your silence? If you had hollered like Tish? Or like Benjamin's sister, handed your journal to a grownup, squeaking "read it." What if you had been discovered, as Maya was? Or become pregnant as Pecola did? Or had told a friend, who told safe adults, who had gotten you help as Jen and Abby did? What if you had completely forgotten as Sylvia did? Or if your father had died, and you told your mother, as Laurel did?

If life were a story written for teenage girls, girls the age you were when you were abused, then if you didn't choose suicide, and kept on telling, or had remembered and told, you would eventually have found the person who could hear you and help you. And your life would have improved. You would have found, perhaps, some peace, or at the least, some safety. As Laurel did, as Jen did, as Abby did, as Benjamin's sister did, and as Tish, we believe, will.

Like Tish, you might have still needed a knife to feel safe, but you'd have had a lawyer on your side, to hold your written story, to call you twice a day, to defend you if you needed him, to speak for you when you were ready. Or, like Benjamin's sister, you might have been taken by courts and put into a foster home with your brother(s), a home that was a better place. Or, like Jen and Abby, your father might have gone away, and you and your mother and siblings might have begun to work to heal yourselves with a therapist's help. Or, like Laurel, with your father dead, you would have been able to scream, to tell your mother who would hear you, to let go, and to go on with your life. You would have had hope for the future. And your story would end there.

But eventually, incest is a story told for grownups. There are life-long consequences. So Pecola and Sylvia and Celie's stories show the fallout from disaster, and sometimes, the healing. As Tish's lawyer says: you can't expect to go through something like this and not have scars.

Pecola isn't strong, mom; she didn't make it. There wasn't enough in her world to sustain her. And disbelieved when she tried to tell, her pregnancy screamed too loudly to be ignored. But by the time she had her child, she was gone, believed her eyes were blue and wandered around in search of something no one could help her to find.

But you survived, mom; recognize that. You are a casualty but not a loss.

Celie recognizes early that she is just surviving. Her young adult life offers no escape. It takes her years and years to learn that she has value, to get angry at men, to find her own life, and to find some peace. It takes Sylvia years and years too. It takes her until her 40's to be able to remember what happened to her. And many more years after that to reconstruct her life, mourn her losses, and find some peace.

Though it takes a lifetime these two women find some peace, and they learn to love themselves. Their stories, made of pain and loss, are in the end triumphant. The cliches here are true.

So can you heal at fifty-six years old? At thirty-two can I? You have started, mom. You have spoken some truths. And though you are running from them now, you can't take them back, and you don't really want to. You've started to cry. Your eyes leak, almost without you. Sometimes you sob. You are angry. Interesting that the anger is directed at me now and at your mother. Still not at your father, still not at your husband, still you protect them. Your emotions haven't yet caught up with your words. But that's alright, you have started.

And me? Well, I'm writing this. I don't cry every day anymore. I don't want to die all the time. And I surprise myself again and again by choosing to protect myself, to take my time, to act as if I count. I am reading. I am speaking. And have begun letting all of you go. I thought the pain unbearable (chest axed in two, ribs split open, raw heart a bleeding bunny, wildly alive in my hands). But to my complete amazement, I too have survived.

I carry all of you with me everyday. Mommy, Daddy, Jimmy, Chad. And I know that I will never love again as I loved all of you. As I love you still. But neither will I return.

NOTES

1. Two years ago, my mother told me about what she called "a wrong relationship" with her father. When she was fourteen until the time she left for college at seventeen, she was sexually abused by her father. I was the first person she had ever told. What kept my mother silent for forty years? Why did she keep his secret?

   I am alone in my life, and she is alone in hers. Yet for the first time, for a little while, she was my mother and I her daughter. And if her words say the opposite now, because she is still and again faithful to the man, I know that really, somewhere inside, she is rooting for me. She wants me to live and be safe and to have the strength she did not have. The strength to say no. The strength to get away. The strength to make my self safe.

2. To help understand the characters referred to in the text the following list is provided: Maya in *I Know Why the Caged Bird Sings*, Laurel in *The Hanged Man*, Jen in *Chinese Handcuffs*, Sylvia in *My Father's House*, Benjamin's sister in *A Solitary Secret*, Abby in *Abby, My Love*, Pecola in *The Bluest Eye*, Tish in *When She Hollers*, and Celie in *The Color Purple*.

WORKS CITED

Angelou, Maya. *I Know Why the Caged Bird Sings*. New York: Random House, 1970.

Block, Francesca Lia. *The Hanged Man*. New York: Harper, 1994.

Butler, Sandra. *Conspiracy of Silence: The Trauma of Incest*. San Francisco:

New Glide, 1978.

Crutcher, Chris. *Chinese Handcuffs*. New York: Greenwillow, 1990.

Fraser, Sylvia. *My Father's House: Memoir of Incest and of Healing*. New York: Harper, 1987.

Hermes, Patricia. *A Solitary Secret*. San Diego: Harcourt, 1985.

Irwin, Hadley. *Abby, My Love*. New York: Atheneum, 1985.

Morrison, Toni. *The Bluest Eye*. New York: Holt, 1970.

Rush, Florence. *The Best Kept Secret: Sexual Abuse of Children*. New York: McGraw-Hill, 1980.

Voigt, Cynthia. *When She Hollers*. New York: Scholastic, 1994.

Walker, Alice. *The Color Purple*. San Diego: Harcourt, 1982.

The Making of a Heroine: A Feminist Approach to the Representation of Heroines in Selected Historical Novels

Hilary S. Crew

> *Women's heroism has been equally brave and equally original as that of men. But because in some of its forms it differs from the traditional pattern of heroism, it has often gone unrecognized . . .*
> (Polster 19).

Our knowledge and understanding of history is gleaned from certain stories told from particular perspectives. Through the way traditional historical narratives have organized and represented historical events, young people have had access to certain ways of knowing about the past. The absence of women and their contributions to history from these narratives, and thus from the school curriculum, has been an issue for those concerned with the intellectual life of young people. It has been noted that the "role of American women in history has been consistently overlooked and undervalued, in the literature, teaching and study of American history" (National Women's History Project 26).[1] "Students" are said to "sit in classes that, day in and day out, deliver the message that women's lives count for less than men's" (American Association of University

Women 67).

For young people to know how the lives of women have counted, and continue to count, towards the enrichment of intellectual, aesthetic, and everyday life, other stories of history need to be told from different perspectives. They need to see beyond the limited and biased constructions of history that have placed most value on progress that evolves through the domination of those in political and economic power. Young people are said to look often to the past for inspirational models of heroism, but these models should be inclusive of men and women's contributions to history from all cultures, races, and ethnic backgrounds.

Literary experiences with historical novels offer young people alternative ways of knowing that go beyond linear narratives of history, new ways of creating their own mosaics of meaning. Historical novels can be used as catalysts for critical approaches to history, questioning how and why only certain stories are told, and who has been included and excluded from the written records. In particular, the representations of strong female characters in historical novels have the potential to engage young people in thinking about the centrality of women's experiences and lives in history and to place value on their different contributions and heroism in shaping the past. Historical novels for children, writes Suzanne Rahn, have featured strong girl protagonists, particularly since the 1920s. Rahn suggests that feminism influenced American women writers who "established a claim through fiction to a place in history which textbooks were not to recognize for another forty or fifty years" (11).

Feminist critical theories make women's contributions central to their inquiries and question the way in which male models of experience and male narratives have been used to construct universal ways of knowing for all. In the discipline of history, this has involved re-examining history from a "woman-centered" perspective (Lewis 57). Bringing a feminist critical approach to historical novels for youth can raise questions about how conceptions of gender and femininity in different historical contexts work to constrain girls to certain expectations of behavior and asks how, in view of this, they are represented and valued as heroines in the texts of these novels.[2] The question can be raised whether a feminist consciousness informs these texts.

Neither women's nor men's heroism has to be interpreted and represented through narrow, stereotypical male models of the heroic. Miriam F. Polster argues that the heroic journey can follow different paths and be represented through alternative heroic qualities other than the "male-skewed images" of aggressiveness and physical strength. Rather than the journey of the hero who is summoned away from family to the unknown, women's heroism, often unrecognized, is "rooted in the particular circumstances and values of women's lives, where connection and relationship may not be quickly stated in adversarial terms" (18).[3]

Polster's feminist revision of heroism is inclusive of different forms of heroism that bind neither men nor women to gender constrained interpretations of what it means to be heroic. Her five characteristics of heroism include: respect for human life and dignity; a "strong sense of personal choice and effectiveness"; a "perspective on the world" that is "original" in going "beyond" what others "think is possible"—which involves questioning assumptions and the status quo while risking ostracism to self; "physical and mental courage"; and impact on others, whether in a public or a more private setting (22–31). When the concept of heroism is so defined, an alternative knowing can value the contributions of men and women in helping others as well as valuing their different kinds of work. Collective action and leadership in the context of reform movements can also be perceived as heroic.

This feminist perspective of heroism is particularly useful in providing alternative ways of thinking about the representation of heroines in historical novels. Discussion of the novels selected for this chapter focus on how much the making of a heroine is contingent on male patterns of the heroic and on the different forms and patterns of girls' heroism that are made evident and valued. The novels were chosen because they represent heroines with strong voices in texts that raise questions about gender and other constraints in relation to how girls and their achievements are represented in different historical contexts.

MARGUERITE LEDOUX: A BOUND-OUT GIRL

Set in 1743 on the rugged coastline of Maine, Rachel Field's
Calico Bush tells the story of Marguerite Ledoux, a twelve-year-
old French girl who has lost her family and is now a "Bound-out
Girl" to Joel and Sally Sargent—pioneers in the New World. She
is bound to the Sargents until her eighteen birthday and "would
be answerable to these people for her every act and word,
bound to serve them for six long years in return for shelter,
food, and such garments as should be deemed necessary" (9).
Marguerite's task is to help care for the Sargents' five young
children and undertake general household tasks as the Sargent
family voyage to Penobscot and settle on their claimed land.

The motif of the bound girl is a useful concept that can be
used to think about the different gender, social, and cultural
constraints which are shown generally to bind heroines in different social and historical contexts and to define girls' actual
bondage as servants or slaves in specific contexts.[4] Social and
economic constraints, and racial prejudice are represented as
forming the binding of a young girl in this novel in which Marguerite is also represented as a servant. A bound girl, or indentured servant, is shown to have endured a life of hard servitude
in colonial times when they "were forbidden to leave or marry"
until their service was over (Rappaport 9). Not only is she
bound in servitude, Marguerite is represented as an outsider—a
"Frenchee" whose loyalty and up-bringing is liable to be suspect
in the context of the war between the English and the French.
Her identity as a young French girl is stripped from her as she is
made to answer to the name of "Maggie."

Marguerite is represented in this text as a strong heroine who
earns her freedom from bondage through her demonstrations of
bravery. The making of a heroine in this text is a strong example
of how a girl's heroism is often defined and represented as emulating the traditional universal traits of heroism associated with
boys. There is an emphasis on Marguerite's physical endurance.
Helping Caleb prevent the sheep from being swept off the boat
during a storm, heading out in a skiff to head a cow and calf
back to shore, and crossing the frozen channel of ice to obtain
help from the Sargents' neighbors, Marguerite demonstrates that

her courage and strength are equal to those of thirteen-year-old Caleb—son of Joel Sargent. As she rows the skiff, the analogy to a male feat is made clear:

> Then the oars were clumsy affairs, made to fit a man's hands rather than her own thin brown ones. Nevertheless she gripped valiantly, bracing her feet against a wooden cleat till her toes ached with the pressure. Drops of sweat rose on her forehead and trickled down over her face. She felt them on her cheeks and lips as she tugged tirelessly at the oars (45).

Her deeds are described and praised in terms of "grit," "spunk," and bravery by the males in the text: "The Captain had praised her, and Joel Sargent had admitted that she had grit. Perhaps even Caleb would be less scornful of her now" (20). It is made clear that her bravery transcends that which is considered normal for her sex. A male voice narrates that he "guessed Caleb would stick fast . . . but why *she* ain't gone to the bottom traipsin' out there in all that blow is past me. She's got grit, wherever she was raised—I'll say that for her" (20).

The narrative plot continues to be built around incidents, such as a foraging bear and a potentially dangerous encounter with American Indians, in which Marguerite's heroic attributes are demonstrated.[5] She is represented as capable of acting alone, a trait which reproduces the valued tenets of independence and individualism of the American pioneer. "She saved us, all by herself," Dolly Sargent comments in praise (191). In her original approach of erecting a maypole to distract the American Indians from attacking, Marguerite uses skills of communication and persuasion. These are skills, as Polster points out, that are often used by women in lieu of force and which have not always been perceived as heroic, since they are used to influence rather than overpower (39). In the context of Marguerite's action, they are represented and acknowledged as heroic.

Demonstrated through her character are the stamina and fortitude that are necessary for survival in the rugged setting of the wild and untamed frontier. She will "weather" the settlers' life, she is told. She is a heroine capable of sharing the traditional heroic terrain of men, but this ability goes beyond the settlers' objective of taming the land. One of the strongest and most beautiful components of this text is the illustration of Marguerite's close affinity with the land as what she sees and feels about her environment is described in detail. Looking at the scenery around her, "it was as if she knew herself for a part of all this miracle of land and sea and sky" (54). At the closure of the novel, "her bare feet" knew "the hollow and rooty places so that she had no need to look down as she went" (200). These expressions of being in relationship with the land, learning to love and know it, is a way of knowing about the land that women have demonstrated in opposition to the more heroic attribute of subjugating virgin territory (Polster 104–06). Marguerite is represented as being metaphorically linked in legend to the "island-scattered coast of Maine" as "a flowering sprig in the wilderness" (xi).

It is her possession of the heroic traits which emulate those associated with men, however, that is given as the reason for Marguerite's freedom from servitude. Joel Sargent wishes to do the "right thing" by Marguerite. She had "been a good girl," he tells her, "an' a brave one. I ain't said much, but I know grit when I see it, an' you've got more'n your share." She has "earned" her "freedom" and the right to join her "own folks" (197). She has proved her equality and capabilities. Her identity and freedom restored, Marguerite chooses of her own free will to remain with the Sargent family. Marguerite Ledoux's heroism can thus be interpreted as an exemplar of the male traditional model. However, Marguerite's demonstrated relationship with the land, her caring and devotion to the Sargents' young children, and her ability to deal with a dangerous situation by her quick-thinking and inventiveness are attributes that broaden the archetypal model of bravery.

Gender is not foregrounded consciously in this text as a constraint that binds Marguerite Ledoux. For Marguerite to become a heroine is to transcend rather than transgress gender boundaries; since her emulations of men's courage is praised. As the courage and fortitude of the frontier woman has so often been celebrated in romantic form, so is Marguerite Ledoux remembered as legendary heroine and pioneer woman in the ballad, "Maypole Point." Reproduced in the text through Marguerite's character are the attributes deemed necessary for the survival of the pioneer woman. It is useful from this perspective to discuss the representation of Dolly Sargent, who is shown to lose her small daughter through lacking the toughness to "burn" the child's fingers "on purpose" to show her the danger of fire (88). In contrast, represented through the elderly, resilient Aunt Hepsa, are the attributes needed for a quintessential model of the pioneer woman who must civilize the land.

Although women in colonial America were still subordinated to patriarchal family structures, they are documented as receiving respect and independence for their sharing of essential work in an "agricultural economy." Although "work proceeded along gender lines," these "distinctions were easily blurred" (Lerner xxvi–xxvii). Frontier women shared with men the hardship of everyday life in stringent conditions. Perceived from this perspective, one way to approach a discussion of this novel might be in the context of the Equal Rights Amendment (introduced in Congress in 1923) whose supporters "believed that women were similar to men in capabilities and merely needed to be afforded equal opportunities and accorded natural rights" to achieve equality (Donovan 60).

DACIE TYBBOT: A REVOLUTIONARY HEROINE

The settings of many historical novels follow the linear, chronological great events sequence of history which is familiar from traditional history textbooks. The Revolutionary War has been the background for several historical novels written for youth. Mary Stetson Clarke's *Petticoat Rebel* can be discussed in the context of another rebellion—a girl's rebellion against the gender restrictions under which women were bound in a specific historical context. Dacie may not be bound as a servant girl, but the title of the novel alone draws attention to sixteen-year-old Dacie Tybbot's resistance to her subordination as a female. In American colonial society, females were "generally assigned to subordinate positions" with "universal insistence upon sex-appropriate language, clothes, work, and recreation" (Kiefer 2–3).

"To want to become a heroine, to have a sense of the possibility of being one," writes Rachel M. Brownstein, "is to develop the beginnings of what feminists call a 'raised' consciousness: it liberates a woman from feeling (and therefore perhaps from being) a victim or a dependent or a drudge, someone of no account" (xix). Set in Gloucester, Massachusetts, 1774, in the context of the Revolutionary War, Clarke's novel foregrounds issues of gender constrictions which are centered on the right for equal education for girls. Dacie is represented as a young woman conscious of and frustrated by the restrictions imposed on her because of her sex.

Dacie is aware that she is excluded from the "exciting business of life"—that the only way to be part of the real action is to be disguised as a boy in a men's and boys' world. Her statement that she wished she had "been born a boy!" so that "there'd be something" she "could do" in the war reinforces the division made between her world and that of her father and older boys (157). Either the desire to dress, or actually dressing in male attire, is a motif that is frequently reproduced in historical novels (and other genres) as a way of girls accessing those places of power and action from which they are barred.[6] It is thus reproduced as a wish to transgress gender boundaries in a patriarchal society.

Throughout the novel, the rigid divisions between the private sphere of women and the public sphere of men in colonial New England are made clear. Dacie is expected to take her place bound within the traditional role of women and girls who would be spinning and weaving coats for the soldiers (157). The role of women who were dependent and confined to the "domestic scene" in supportive or ancillary roles to men at war were often awarded "low status," argues Polster. When heroism is defined as that achieved on the battlefield, women have limited possibilities to be heroic (12). When the fringes of war do touch the boundaries of Dacie's life, she is represented in ancillary and supportive roles through the re-loading of a musket for her grandfather and by helping the doctor with the wounded. Dacie's heroism is not, as in *Calico Bush*, reproduced through the emulation of men's heroism; this she is denied. The making of a heroine in Clarke's novel can be interpreted through alternative values and definitions of heroism.

Clarke has chosen to represent a protagonist with a raised consciousness about what is at stake in relation to girls' education and their future status in society. With a "sound" educational "background," Dacie thinks, girls would be "able to understand government and politics, and could discuss them ably with men. Perchance men would even listen to such educated women and let them have a part in the business of the world" (213). The emphasis on Dacie's interest and love for education provides the context for her courage in advocating education for girls. Her vocation for teaching is represented through the lessons she gives to freed slaves. Dacie's voice is presented as gathering strength as she continues to speak up for the education of girls at a time when education for girls was little valued over and above the elementary skills of reading and writing, and for girls of Dacie's class, extra education in the form of elocution and needlework.

She faces ridicule and disapproval as she first quietly voices her opinion "that parish schools ought by rights to be open to girls" (118). Later, she is represented as strong enough to defy prominent citizens when they offer her the official post of school teacher in lieu of the school master who has enlisted. "Unless girls can come to school on an equal footing with boys," she informs them, "I don't care to teach" (242). Despite the disparity in power relationships between herself and the male citizens of Gloucester, she recognizes a responsibility to the girls she teaches. However, her position is clearly represented as subordinate in the context of patriarchal colonial society; she cannot make decisions, only suggest. Her advocacy for teaching is at the grassroots level. It is in the classroom that she "faced a challenge" when the girls she teaches must "demonstrate how well they have been taught" to prove "that they should be granted equal educational opportunities with their brothers" (242–43).

Dacie is eventually granted the position of teaching boys and girls so that the official school master may go to war. Her contribution is valued, her young man, Rafe, tells her for the grander purpose of freeing the school master so that he "can follow his larger sense of duty to our whole country" (254). However, Dacie's new position is represented in the text as important in its own right. "It's almost as if I were fighting, then!" she tells Rafe. "Exactly," he tells her. "You're doing something no woman before you has ever done—at least, no woman in this town.

You're freeing a man to go to war." As she "matched her pace to Rafe's," she feels

> herself a part of the vast army of patriots working for America's freedom. Now she was one with Zeke and her father and Rafe and all the others who were fighting for liberty. There were more ways than one of helping to win a war, and in the schoolroom she could be working for the cause of liberty as surely as if she were on the battlefield (255).

It is through the representation of a raised consciousness—one that "liberates" Dacie from feeling that she is "someone of no account"—that a heroine is made in this text. Dacie is represented as neither transcending nor transgressing gender or societal boundaries but achieves her goal through pushing at the boundaries from within. Dacie does not go "beyond the confines of 'proper behavior'" that Polster argues is characteristic of a heroine in her actions (32), but her ideas about education are represented as revolutionary in the context of the setting. In terms of Polster's feminist revision of heroism, the novel is a recognition of women's work that has often gone unrecognized, particularly in the historical narrative. This novel can also be discussed in relation to knowing how women have contributed to the intellectual life of young people in the field of education.

It is not known if Clarke consciously uses the colonial era—a time when women's status was changing and under debate—in which to explore issues that were being raised in relation to women's status and education during the 1960's when the novel was published, but it is an interesting supposition. In a "Foreword" to the novel, Clarke makes the link between slavery and illiteracy, pointing out that "changes in public opinion" were brought about to both issues in Gloucester, Massachusetts because of the Revolutionary War (9). Certainly equality through equal education has long been a tenet of the feminist movement. The analogy of uneducated women to slaves had been made by Mary Wollstonecraft in the eighteenth century (Donovan 9). In the following novel, published thirty years earlier, the issue raised in the text is the socialization of boys and girls into appropriate and different gender roles and is framed around a very different kind of heroine. Although this "different" heroine is younger than other protagonists included here, she is well-known and serves as an exemplar of a particular form of heroism in historical fiction.

CADDIE WOODLAWN: HEROINE AS TOMBOY

The crossing of gender boundaries is a motif that is frequently used in specific historical contexts as a way of drawing attention to the kind of constraints that bind girls and young women in particular periods, and which also demonstrates the way gender is socially constructed. A clear example of how a heroic action by a young girl is able to be carried out, in part, because she has been encouraged to step out of the bounds of appropriate gendered behavior is reproduced in Carol Ryrie Brink's *Caddie Woodlawn*. Based on the stories of Brink's grandmother growing up in Wisconsin in the nineteenth century, Caddie is eleven years old in 1864 at the beginning of the story and "as wild a little tomboy as ever ran in the woods of western Wisconsin" (1).

Throughout the text is a strong questioning of appropriate gender behavior as Caddie is first allowed to "run wild" with the boys. "Don't keep her in the house learning to be a lady," her father had asked his wife, having lost one daughter to frailty. "I would rather see her learn to plow than make samplers, if she can get her health by doing so" (13). Caddie is reined in by her mother when Caddie's behavior has gone too far away from what is appropriate and she behaves like a "hoyden" towards a young lady guest (129–30). It is time for Caddie to grow up into a woman, her father tells her (240).

Caddie's action as a heroine is to ride through melting snow and to cross an iced-over river to warn her American Indian friends of the settlers' threatened attack. Her action is based on her own decision that the action planned by her father's neighbors, in his absence, is wrong. Caddie's heroic action, brave, resourceful, individualistic—based on familiar heroic attributes—is performed, therefore, while she is still represented as having the same freedom as her brothers. Writing in the 1930's, Brink foregrounds the issue of gender dichotomy and how young girls and boys were inculcated with a particular value system in the context of a specific period. Caddie's father tells her: "A woman's task is to teach [men and boys] gentleness and courtesy and love and kindness" (240). Caddie's future work is not undervalued in the text. "It's a big task," Caddie's father tells her:

> harder than cutting trees or building mills or damming rivers. It takes nerve and courage and patience, but good women have those things. They have them just as much as the men who build bridges and carve roads through the wilderness. A woman's work is something fine and noble to grow up to, and it is just as important as a man's (240).

A woman's responsibilities are thus described in heroic terms by her father to reconcile and persuade the adventuresome Caddie to her future womanhood. Brink's novel has been singled out for its feminist approach and for its representation of an adventurous heroine. Hancock uses the representation of Caddie to illustrate the freedom that is given to young girls before they reach the gender constraints they encounter at puberty. She is described by Hancock as a "noble heroine" whose action depends on physical strength and an "outreaching spirit" (11). Zilboorg argues that Caddie is an "important example of a genre of works by American women for a young female audience that present admirable girl heroes as feminist role models" (116).

In relation to Polster's shared characteristics of heroism, Caddie is represented as demonstrating physical and mental courage as she questions the actions of the settlers, risks disapproval for her action, and shows respect for human life by valuing the lives of her American Indian friends which is motivated by Caddie's sense of connection and responsibility to them. The fact that the American Indians were indeed represented as "other" to the settlers lends even more credence to her heroic act. Her heroism can thus be discussed in wider terms than emulating a male pattern of heroism.

However, Caddie's actual heroic *deed*, with which young readers are most likely to identify, is possible only because she has been able to live without the constraints of behaving as a young woman as an "experiment." As in several other historical novels, girls have adventures because they cross gender boundaries; Caddie had ventured from the private sphere of home to the public sphere in visiting the Indian reservation and had built up her physical stamina through her play with her brothers. How much, then, is her specific act of heroism attributable to freedom from the constraints of womanhood and to exposure to male territory in this particular historical context? Brink's text is useful for discussion since it remains popular with young people and certainly is open to critical interpretation and debate on issues of gender socialization in relation to how Caddie is represented as a heroine. It can lead to ways of thinking about how cultural differences are constructed between gender resulting in the dichotomy of the private, feminine and public, masculine spheres, respectively.[7]

GRACE DARLING: THE MAKING OF A HEROINE

> . . . Darling is one of the two individuals who have so honourably distinguished themselves, the other being Grace Darling, his daughter, a young woman of twenty-two years of age! The latter prompted by an impulse of heroism which in a female transcends all praise, seeing that it would have done honour to the stoutest-hearted of the male sex, urged her father to go off in the boat at all risks, offering her self to take one oar if he would take the other! (*Grace* 89).

Walsh's novel does not just tell a story of an actual young woman's courageous rescue of nine survivors from the wrecked passenger ship, *Forfarshire* off the coast of North Sunderland, England on September 7, 1838. Far more than this, it reconstructs from a feminist perspective, how Grace was expected to fit into a certain idea of a heroine. She was to possess the kinds of attributes acceptable in a young woman for public adulation in the Victorian era. The focus in the novel is on the process of the molding of a heroine in a particular social and historical context in that it shows how Grace's bravery was perceived and interpreted in different ways, according to the perceiver's gender, class, and religion in Victorian patriarchal society.

Grace is represented as risking her life to save the survivors of the wreck. Despite the warning given by her father that although they may get to the wreck, they may not get back unless one of the rescued would be "strong enough to help" them, she chooses to take action out of respect for human life. The alternative, she asks her father, is to "otherwise . . . stand and watch" the stranded passengers "die?" She "would try it alone, if [she] had to," she tells him (12). The newspaper clipping quoted above describes Grace's bravery as transcending that of men. Her father speaks of the "mettle" needed to save lives at sea and states: "A man couldn't have a pluckier daughter, even if she was a son" (123). The clergy, among others, however, were anxious to prove that Grace did not act from avarice for the premiums paid to those who rescued survivors from the high seas, but acted rather, from the "compassionate emotions [that] womanhood" had "so much to teach, mankind so much to learn" as an Archdeacon puts it to Grace (217).

It is through Grace's subjective voice as she narrates her thoughts and feelings, that Walsh chooses to reconstruct a heroine who was publicly heralded in the nineteenth century, much as a celebrity is constructed through the media today, as she was thronged by crowds, asked for personal mementoes, and had her portrait painted. Rather than gaining in confidence and self-esteem from her brave action, however, Grace is historically documented by Walsh as being castigated by the local community for encroaching on the Sunderland's lifeboat crew's domain. She is represented as finally living in a state of torment —beset by doubts that her act was indeed selfless; perhaps she had, after all, saved lives for the wrong reasons. "In that case," Grace narrates, "if I had indeed done my deed for money, then all the presents, all the praise and love I had been given had been given in error, taken on false pretences. I would cough, and toss and turn, and wrestle with thoughts like these" (219).

Dying at the age of twenty-four from consumption, Grace is represented by Walsh as enduring personal suffering rather than gaining pride and confidence from her very real heroic act —despite her national popularity. Strong and full of confidence at the beginning of the novel, Grace is represented as gradually losing voice and self as she is burdened with the identity of being "a beautiful example of lowly virtue!" (245). In the context of her own time, Grace was brought up against a patriarchal culture which denied her a sense of joy in her heroic deed without feelings of guilt. She is only accepted as a role model and heroine by her own sex when they are reassured that Grace's looks and dress conform to their ideal of femininity. The Lukas sisters had expected "some kind of Amazon . . ." (86). Grace can, however, comments one sister, "prove one may be pretty as well as brave!" (88). She had given them:

> A testimonial that the noblest feelings may inhere in a womanly bosom! That our sex is not for ever cut off from the possibility of heroic acts; that to be female is not always to be weak and helpless! You have reconciled us to our gender, Miss Darling, and we must thank you for it, however deeply you blush! (87–88).

It is only at the closure of the novel, when one of the rescued passengers tells her that it did not matter *why* she did it, asking that if she had done it "for rage and spite and greed," was he "the less living for that?" that Grace is able to believe in herself again. "What coin was ever minted, Miss Darling, that made a brave man of a coward, or could buy what you did for me?" (251). Despite her impending death, Grace is represented as feeling restored to a sense of self with his words—no longer burdened by those who attempted to bind her heroic act within the definitions of a "pure and perfect compassion for suffering humanity" (217). "Heroes," writes Polster, "are not measured by publicity. Whether a heroic act receives worldwide attention or occurs in an obscure setting with only a single witness, a heroic act is still heroic" (22–23). Interesting to consider are questions of how publicity affected a young heroine in Victorian society as she is lauded for risking her life (like a man), yet whose act had also to be perceived as fitting Victorian definitions of femininity.

Feminist scholarship has focused both on the discipline of history and the field of literary criticism in writing women into history. Scholars have rescued and reinstituted in the records of history and literature those women, their deeds, and their works who have been absented by a male hierarchy which has controlled the way knowledge is constructed and studied. Women, it is noted, with those "others" who are not of the dominant ruling groups, have been marginalized; they remain on the outer boundaries of what it is important to know and record. The inclusion of women's contributions and experiences to the historical record involves viewing "the past from an entirely new perspective" (Lerner xxii).[8]

Walsh's text, published in 1992, would seem to be informed by a feminist consciousness of this absence of women in the patriarchal record through the choice of language and foregrounding of the written record. Emphasized is Grace's discovery that her name is absent from her father's journal in his written record of their joint rescue. Her name and heroic deed are hidden under the patriarchal name, "The Darlings." She narrates that this caused her "grief"; she felt that she was a "person missing, a person lost from view" (213). She further discovers that her brothers' names are entered for their part in a rescue at sea and that not even her birth is recorded in her father's journal. She is, she notes, "off the margins of his page" and that her "thoughts if I cannot remember them are lost . . ." (213).

This feminist approach of writing women into history would seem to inform the following four novels discussed in this chapter. Avi's novel reproduces this feminist perspective through the representation of a strong, romantic heroine whose recorded heroic deeds are threatened to be erased from her journal by a patriarchal father. Unlike the actual historical figure of Grace, Charlotte Doyle is represented as a fictional heroine who is able to break away from the constraints of Victorian definitions of femininity.

CHARLOTTE DOYLE: AN UNNATURAL GIRL

When the transgression of boundaries is made most visible, heroines are represented as "unnatural." In *The True Confession of Charlotte Doyle*, Avi's representation of Charlotte Doyle is a clear example of how a young girl becomes a heroine through transgressing boundaries of gender, class, race, and the Victorian ethic of femininity, and who is thus branded as "unnatural." The unnaturalness of Charlotte is represented through the opening sentence of the text: "Not every thirteen-year-old girl is accused of murder, brought to trial, and found guilty" (1). Set in 1832, as she is ready to begin the voyage to America, where she is to rejoin her parents, Charlotte describes her dress, education, and background as befitting a young woman whose "destiny" was "to be a *lady*" (1). She crosses gender boundaries as soon as she is instructed to embark upon the voyage without female companionship—an impropriety of which she is well aware: "But . . . but that would be all *men*," Charlotte protests. "And . . . I am a girl. It would be *wrong!*" (14). She was, she realizes, "where no proper young lady should be," and it is her *father's* voice that she hears saying those words (25).

The social and class barriers of Victorian society are made clear throughout the text as Charlotte is represented, at first, as naturally aligning herself with the Captain—reinforcing the boundaries of social class and race—as she finds prospects of being friends with the "forward" black cook, Zachariah, "unpleasant." She will be a civilizing and moral influence on the disorderly crew, the Captain tells her. As the voyage proceeds, the order and hierarchical structures of Victorian society are shown to collapse, and Charlotte is represented as fighting against the disorder and wildness that threatens her identity as a young Victorian lady as she begins to cross over the boundaries to join the mutinous crew.

After donning the clothing made for her by Zachariah, which is not "proper" for a lady and finding it "surprisingly comfortable," she spends "two hours composing an essay" in her "blank book on the subject of proper behavior for young women" (66–67). As the voyage proceeds, however, it is, rather, the unnaturalness of Victorian definitions of femininity that are uncovered. The natural order of things masked by constraints of Victorian femininity is symbolized through Charlotte brushing her hair "wanting it smoothly drawn—anything to keep it from its natural and . . . obnoxious wildness" (62–63).

The text is structured throughout by the oppositions of natural/unnatural and order/disorder. Charlotte's transgression of boundaries is represented by Jaggery as creating chaos out of his orderly world. She has upset the "rightful balance between commander and commanded," Jaggery tells her (188). "It doesn't matter that" *she* is "different," he continues. "The difficulty is that your difference encourages *them* to question their places. And mine. The order of things" (188). Reproduced in the text are the shifting re-alignments of the seemingly fixed differences between hierarchies of gender, race, and social class caused by Charlotte's "difference." Perceived by Jaggery as unimportant as a girl in her own right, she is threatening because she symbolizes a marker of instability through her transgressive behavior. The realization by Jaggery that the surface order of things is an illusion is symbolized by his attempts to restore order to the disorder of his cabin—damaged in a storm. By candlelight, the cracks and splinters are visible; but by blowing out the candle, he demonstrates to Charlotte that "it's hard to notice the difference. Everything appears in order" (190). When Charlotte finally becomes a member of the crew through the male initiation right of climbing "to the top of the royal yard," she is represented through the language of the Captain as "unnatural." Refusing her own definition as being "unusual," Jaggery identifies her as "an unnatural girl, dressing in unnatural ways, doing unnatural things . . ." (169). "Who shall be blamed for this disastrous voyage?" Jaggery asked. "It cannot be me, can it? No, it must be someone from the outside. The unnatural one" (189). Represented is the girl, without bounds, who can naturally be sacrificed and hung by Jaggery for the murder of the ship's first mate.

The perception of Charlotte's behavior as unnatural can be understood in the context of the Victorian definition of femininity which was believed to be "natural." Women and especially daughters were conceptualized as innately "innocent, pure, gentle and self-sacrificing" (Gorham 4–5). Charlotte is represented as a heroine through transgressing boundaries. Crossing over to a male-ordered setting, she emulates the traditional heroic pattern of courage through her physical courage as a member of the ship's crew. Charlotte, however, is also represented as intellectually and emotionally engaged in an alternative way of knowing. In the context of Polster's model, she demonstrates mental courage and responsibility in re-aligning her values with a different moral order. She acts upon her own sense of fairness and responsibility in response to the whipping of Zachariah in contrast to the Captain's "justice" dictated by "admiralty codes" (93). Her heroism might, then, also be usefully discussed in terms of women's "heroism in the service of connection and responsibility to others" as distinct from "heroism in the service of abstract principle" (Polster 33).

No longer restrained by rigid divisions of gender, class, and race, or by Captain Jaggery's and her father's definitions of order and morality, Charlotte returns to sea with Zachariah, where "winds have a mind of their own" (210). In relation to Polster's model, she is represented as an "original" heroine with "a strong sense of personal choice" as she displays physical and mental courage in "going beyond what other people think is possible" (Polster 22).[9]

The absencing of women from the patriarchal record is fore-grounded in Avi's text. The journal, in which Charlotte records her heroic deeds on her fateful voyage on a ship with a muti-nous crew from England to America is burned by her father. It consists of "the most outlandish, not to say *unnatural* tales," her father tells her. She is "forbidden—*forbidden* to talk about" the voyage to her siblings (207). Charlotte is confined to her room with a "vast quantity" of her father's books "deemed suitable for [her] reclamation." She does not read them. "Instead," she narrates, "I used the books, the blank pages, the margins, even the mostly empty title pages, to set down secretly what had hap-pened during the voyage. It was my way of fixing all the details in my mind forever" (208). Unlike Grace, Charlotte is repre-sented as writing her own memories into the patriarchal record so they might not be forgotten. It is this revision and alteration of the patriarchal annals of history that is represented in Kathryn Lasky's novel through her heroine, Meribah.

MERIBAH SIMON: A HEROINE BEYOND THE DIVIDE

Beyond the Divide is the story of an Amish girl, Meribah Simon, who in 1849, accompanies her father on the pioneer trail. In writing about her work, Lasky makes the distinction between historical fiction and the fiction of history and thus between the different ways of knowing about history. In the fiction of his-tory, facts are covered up, erased, abused and distorted.[10] Her novel, *Beyond the Divide*, she writes, is historical fiction of the pioneers emigration to the West rather than fiction of history which she had grown up watching on television and film, which had erased the history of violence against women in the West

(Lasky "The Fiction" 159). In this novel, Lasky writes into history this violence against women on the Overland trail through the raping of the young woman, Serena Billings, who is subsequently criticized and ostracized by the company. Through the representation of how the rape of a girl is covered and concealed—the "nameless" fear "within" the community—Lasky doubles the violence done to a young woman with the violence done to the historical record through its omission. Through Meribah, the record is set straight as she climbs alone to Independence Rock and inserts there, the lost women's initials with the other names of their company.

It is men who have officially recorded the historical narratives.[11] In Lasky's novel it is a young woman who is represented as actively shaping history and the land as Meribah creatively maps the pioneer trek across the West. Her mapping is described as "totally original and not reliant on the usual cartographic symbols" (205). She tells the official Government cartographer, Goodnough (based on J. Goldsborough Bruff) that she makes "new symbols to show the shape and feel of things out" there. "Dost thou know that sometimes, no matter how real I know this land is and however long it has been here," she asks him, that "I sometimes I feel as if I am reinventing it as I move through it?" (209–10). She is a recorder of history—a scribe—a function historically allotted to men; but more than this, she shapes and molds the land to her own view of it. Goodnough compares his skills at cartographer to Meribah's and finds for all his knowledge of "trigonometry, calculus" and his scientific tools of measurement, it is Meribah who has the deeper knowledge. "As a cartographer he knew the land, but she knew nature. He drew boundaries. She didn't. He measured. She invented" (251).

In terms of the representation of Meribah as a heroine, she is an active shaper of her own history. With her strong voice she represents attributes from Polster's five shared characteristics of heroism. She is represented as showing dignity and respect for life in caring for her father when he is fatally injured and in her love and friendship for the raped Serena; she is one of the most original heroines represented in these novels as she maps her own perspective physically and metaphorically as she travels the Overland trail; she possesses mental and physical courage in her ingenuity in mending her father's broken wagon and in surviving the hardship of winter on her own in the wilderness; and she represents the strength of a woman who can make her own way in community and in solitude in what was predominantly represented as a male setting. Meribah's model for selfhood is thus composed of many attributes from patterns of both traditional and female heroism.

Going beyond the historical narrative, *Beyond the Divide* represents another way of knowing about history for young people. There is an emphasis in the text itself on the different ways of knowing as Meribah considers the difference between the Amish ways of understanding justice, family, work, and religion and the different "ways" of her father—the reason why her father must leave the Amish community. Meribah's own selfhood is represented as being constructed through the difference between what she had known before and what she subsequently learns.

The "divide"—that "ridge that separates the waters flowing to the Atlantic from the waters flowing to the Pacific"—is represented as a symbolic divide of knowing for Meribah as she notes the triviality and hypocrisy of the travellers who speak of the "crowning glory of our achievement" on reaching the ridge. "If she felt anything at all; it was a dividing within—self out of self" (146). Meribah's map of the divide represents the uncertainty and future of ways of knowing (although not directionless) rather than fixed and unalterable systems of knowledge:

> Meribah marked the divide on her map in a way that she herself only half understood. She did not print the words. She did not stipple the ridge or crosshatch a mountain range. She made a few, very faint lines for the dividing rivers. But what she did mark on her map were the two oceans. In the wide margins of her paper she printed PACIFIC on the left and ATLANTIC on the right. In printing the names on her map, she reversed her usual mapmaking procedure, for she had never seen either ocean. But this did not bother her. She had marked what she had never seen, but could only believe to be (147–48).

LYDDIE WORTHEN: MILL GIRL

Feminist scholarship has involved "asking new questions of new topics" (Lewis 57). This includes researching women's place in the home and the work place as well as their work as leaders in reform and emancipation movements. Factories and mills, for example, are some of the new contexts in which women's heroism is recognized. Katherine Paterson has also written women into history in her story of *Lyddie*, which is based on research of the New England mill girls in Lowell, Massachusetts.[12] In contrast to Meribah's story set in the pioneering West, Lyddie's story, beginning in 1843, is narrated in the context of working girls in the industrial East, recreating the history of farm girl to factory girl.

The attributes of heroism, represented through Lyddie, are those of grit, hard work, and a fierce determination to be independent—the Protestant work ethic—in a text that eschews the romantic treatment of a heroine. From the time she and her brother struggle to keep the small farm going after her mother's breakdown and departure, Lyddie determines to be "beholden" to nobody. After being hired out on her mother's instructions as a servant in a tavern, Lyddie decides on a journey of "freedom" to Lowell, where she will work as a "factory girl." She will be "free," she narrates. "I can do anything I want. I can go to Lowell and make real money to pay off the debt [on the farm] so I can go home" (45).

The concept of the bound girl is reproduced in a different social and historical context in this novel. The differences and contradictions between freedom and slavery in relationship to working girls is made throughout the text. At the tavern, Lyddie defines herself as "no more than a slave. She worked from before dawn until well after dark, and what did she have to show for it?" (43). Working and earning more money in the mill, Lyddie refuses to be identified as a "wage slave" by those girls working for better working conditions. "I ain't a slave!" she tells them "fiercely" (92). Lyddie opposes signing the "petition" because she has "got to have the money" (92). She does not wish to help the new Irish girls manage the looms. "She could not fall behind in her production, else her pay would drop and before she knew it one of these cussed papists would have her job" (100).

Through the representation of Lyddie, the alternative values of working in relationship and caring for others are also represented when her life is turned upside down by the arrival of Rachel, her young sister, for whom she is now responsible. The care of Rachel is shown to demand a different set of values than those of the Protestant ethic of individuality and success (Polster 20). Lyddie's journey, as heroine, is represented as taking a different path as she develops compassion and a larger sense of responsibility towards others culminating in her rescue of Brigid, an Irish girl, from the sexual molestation of an overseer. Lyddie risks and loses her job through her action. The reason given for her dismissal—"moral turpitude" not only belies the moral integrity that is represented by Lyddie as a heroine but makes visible the sexual harassment that lies under the respectable veneer of the mill's regulations supervising the moral behavior of the factory girls.

Free from the constraint of being a "wage slave," Lyddie chooses to attend a college for women in Ohio rather than stay to marry Luke Stevens (181). Represented once again in these novels, through the choice of a heroine, is the equation between education and equal opportunity. A different form and pattern of heroism is reproduced in the novel through the valuing of collective action and "raised consciousness" of women as they engage in labor reform and compassion for each other. "A distinctive quality of women's heroism," Polster points out, "is the form of aggregate action" (36). There is, in this novel, a different conception of the "freeing" of a bound girl. The making of a heroine in this text is through the demonstration of tenacity, physical, and moral courage in obtaining independence while retaining a sense of responsibility towards others.

RIFKA NEBROT: A VOICE FROM OUTSIDE

The writing in of women into history and literature includes those women from other races, cultures, and ethnic groups. *Letters from Rifka*, by Karen Hesse, is the story of twelve-year-old

Rifka's flight, with her Jewish family, from Russian persecution in Berdichev in 1919 and their journey to America. Rifka is separated from her family when she contracts ringworm and must stay alone in Antwerp until her ringworm is cured. On her eventual arrival in the States, she is confronted with discriminatory immigration laws because of her lack of hair. Without hair, she is told, she may not "find a husband to take care of" her and thus be "a social responsibility" (95). Detained on Ellis Island, helping the nurses and doctors care for the other detainees, Rifka demonstrates her linguistic skills and also the "skill and talent," and compassion that would enable her to study medicine. Through her strong voice, Rifka argues her own case to be allowed into the States, irrespective of her bald head, thus freeing herself from the constraints of gender biased immigration laws.

Rifka's journey, like that of the hero's, is represented as one of courage in the face of fear. On account of her physical looks and linguistic ability, she poses as a "Russian peasant" girl distracting the Russian guards with bayonets searching the train where her parents and brother are hidden (8). "Inside," she narrates, "I twisted like a wrung rag" as she is pawed over by one of the guards (7). Rifka also represents, however, the attributes of care and relationship in the compassion she shows towards a small Russian boy on Ellis Island, who refuses to speak or eat, despite the fact that he represents the Russian soldiers who would have killed her and her family. "Compassion is a part of medicine you can't teach," a doctor tells an immigration official. "Compassion is a quality I have often seen in Rifka" (138). Rifka is represented as gaining entry to the States from the "outside" through her courage and compassion, her respect for human dignity, and her originality—an inclusive pattern of heroism which is reproduced in these novels.

Hesse bases her novel on "the memories" of Lucy Avrutin, her great-aunt (x). The form of the text emphasizes the personal histories of women that are being written into historical narratives from their formerly unpublished letters, diaries, and journals.[13] Rifka writes letters to her cousin back in Berdichev throughout the vicissitudes of her long journey on the margins and blank pages of the new volume of Pushkin's poetry that her cousin had given her before leaving. Rifka, like Meribah, is represented as a creative and inventive heroine as she creates her own poetry (also written on the blank pages of the Pushkin volume) that contributes towards her acceptance as an immigrant into the United States. Reproduced in the text is an intertwining of a Jewish girl's written record of her courageous journey and her poetry with one of Russia's foremost writers. Pushkin's verses, in turn, are reproduced in the margins of the text of Rifka's story. Again a feminist consciousness would seem to inform the text as a young female "outsider"—persecuted as part of the Jewish community in the Ukraine—writes in her history and verses on the margins of a dominant culture, and whose story in this text is now told in its own right.[14]

ANNIE METCALF: FACING A DIFFERENT KIND OF FEAR

Women's heroism, Polster reminds us, has often gone unnoticed because it has been undertaken in the everyday "ordinariness" of women's lives away from the traditional arenas of heroism, such as the battlefield. Heroism can take place in "commonplace settings and in response to everyday challenges" by family members, neighbors and those with whom we work (21). This form of heroism often is undertaken in the caring of others; it can involve the overcoming of fear and prejudice in helping others. This quiet form of heroism is represented through the character of thirteen-year-old Annie Metcalf in Margaret I. Rostkowski's historical novel, *After the Dancing Days*, set in the context of home and hospital in a small town near Kansas City in 1919.

As Annie and her mother meet her father, a doctor, just returned from the Great War at the train station, Annie experiences the fear and repulsion at the sight of the badly wounded soldiers who disembark from the train with him. Her initial reaction is typical of the feeling of the community of the town. "Now the war is over. We can forget all those horrible things now," Annie's friend comments. "Besides, it's true, those men *are* scary to look at . . ." (55). Annie's personal courage is demonstrated as she overcomes her fear and prejudice as she learns "to look" into the "faces" of the young men whom the community wished to ignore and forget. When she meets the young man, Andrew, who has returned from the Great War with severe burns caused by mustard gas, she literally has to face Andrew's burns and the pain that he feels. "I wanted to turn and run away," she narrates, "not in space, but in time, to the moment before I had seen him" (47). Annie, however, faces her own fear and is able to see Andrew as a person.

In her determination to continue visiting Andrew, Annie risks the disapproval of her mother. She questions her mother's attitudes and behavior towards the wounded soldiers, who cannot "face" them and wishes to protect her daughter from the "ugliness" of war that is personified in their burned and wounded presence. Despite her love and respect for her mother, Annie goes against her wishes. She has the courage to tell her mother that she was "wrong." Andrew, she tells her mother, "needed" her:

> And because they aren't terrible or awful the way you and everyone else seems to think. They fought, just like Uncle Paul! They were brave like he was. They can't help what happened to them! Andrew can't help it that he was hurt. Why can't you see that? His own father won't come to see him! But I will. He's my friend and I'm going back out there again (152–53).

Represented is a heroine whose voice is strong as she uses her own judgment and initiative to free herself from the unjustified fears and prejudices of her mother and others. She stands up for what she believes in and influences her mother's opinion and behavior. Through the representation and viewpoint of Annie, the perception of fear and bravery takes on different forms and meanings than that of the traditional model of heroism. Her heroism may be made in very different circumstances and take a very different heroic pattern from that of Grace Darling's, but the principal motivation on which she acts is the same—"a profound respect for human life." The "risk" she takes is one made in the context of risking disapprobation with her mother, rather than the risk of her losing her life, but her actions and choices are represented as strong and effective in helping others.

Annie's personal courage is reproduced in relation to larger questions about what are considered as acts of courage and who are remembered as heroic. Throughout the text, the heroism of those who died sacrificing their lives in battle is raised in relationship to those soldiers who returned but were not remembered as heroes. Raised is the issue of respecting and valuing those soldiers who lived but still bore the scars of war. The text opens up new ways of thinking about the concept of the heroic as Annie pursues the reason for her uncle Paul's death and discovers that he died of measles rather than fighting at the front as his family had been led to believe. "And then Uncle Paul didn't die the way we thought, not helping someone. Not brave and splendid. He got sick and died because nobody could take care of him" (167). Andrew had been burned, he tells Annie, because he had lost his gas mask (167).

Literally and metaphorically, the novel opens up questions about facing death and pain through Annie's persistence in discussing and dealing with these issues. "And it doesn't seem right to me that you and everybody else just want to forget" the men who did not die but shall live, Annie tells her mother (168). Annie's bravery is represented as that of the everyday—experiencing and facing up to the human experiences of fear and loss while retaining the courage to go on loving and caring.

SUMMARY

These historical novels can construct different ways of knowing about history to enrich the intellectual lives of young people. They can show that history indeed can be constructed through stories from different viewpoints; and that knowledge is not fixed and unalterable. Through these *different* stories, women's experiences and lives are represented as central to the past so that young people do not discount the contribution of young women in a society that has often valorized and defined the past through narratives based on men's contributions. From bound girls to mill girls, from pioneer women to teachers, to those who have gone beyond the divide, these heroines are reminders of women's history. Many of their names are forefronted on the title-pages: Caddie Woodlawn, Lyddie, Rifka, Charlotte Doyle, Grace Darling. Often represented as behind the lines of the historical narrative, they are represented in the front lines in these novels. Their voices are represented as strong in self-affirmation.

A feminist approach to history and literature provides a way of asking different questions about how women are perceived and recorded in the fictions of history and historical novels. The novels reproduce an awareness of how gender has constrained and constructed heroines, and therefore, heroes, in different social and historical contexts. This awareness can open ways of thinking about current constructions of gender and how they may relate to young people's perceptions of the achievements they might make. Carolyn Heilbrun points to the contradiction in her own thinking about heroism that often seems to be reproduced in these novels:

> On the one hand I deplore the fact that women of achievement, outside the brief periods of high feminism, have become honorary men, have consented to be token women rather then women bonded with other women and supporting them. On the other hand, I find that those women who *did* have the courage, self-confidence, and the autonomy to make their way into the male-dominated world did so by identifying with male ideals and role models (31).

Heilbrun's position is that women need not eschew attributes associated with a male model of achievement if they "recognize the importance of taking these examples as women, supporting other women, identifying with them, and imagining the achievement of women generally" (32). Polster's definition of heroism, inclusive of both male and female models provides yet another model of ways of knowing that can be brought to bear on discussion and reading about the heroic, and provides different models of self-hood for young people.

Through the representation of heroines in historical novels, young people have access to various and differing constructions of heroism with which they can identify. They open up ways of thinking about the heroic. The journey of the hero has provided one rich model. Polster's model can be used to enrich young people's ways of thinking about ways the heroic may be interpreted in history, literature, and in mosaics of their own everyday lives.

NOTES

1. For multicultural resource materials on women's history for the school curriculum, see National Women's History Project.
2. For ways in which feminist criticism can be brought to bear on research on literature for youth, see Vandergrift.
3. Polster bases the relational aspects of her conception of women's heroism on the work of Carol Gilligan in *A Different Voice*. See Gilligan.
4. For an example of a historical novel set in New Jersey and Philadelphia, 1837, in which the heroine is represented as a bound girl—a "taken girl"—in the sense that she is a servant, see Vining. For examples of historical novels in which heroines are bonded through slavery see Hurmence and Lyons.
5. It should be noted that, written in 1931, the text is not sensitive to the stereotypical representations of American Indians.
6. Women have historically disguised themselves as soldiers. For an example of a fictional account of Deborah Sampson who actually served in the Revolutionary War as a soldier see Clapp. For an example of a novel set in the same historical context as Clarke's novel, see Cavanna.
7. For discussion and historical documents relating to "childhood experiences of nineteenth-century women, focusing particularly on sex role indoctrination" in which boys were encouraged to explore the world while, "for girls the home was to be the world," see Lerner 3–41.
8. For a feminist history using documentary sources to record the experiences of women in American history from a "female point of view," see Lerner.
9. Women are historically documented as serving at sea as captains or crew members in the nineteenth century; see De Pauw. For an example of a children's picturebook documenting the true story of a wife's captaincy of a ship during her husband's illness, see Lasker.
10. For a historical novel which also writes into story a different perspective on the lives of pioneer women, see Conrad.
11. For alternative sources on the West which document women's history on the frontier, see Blenz-Clucas.
12. For women's narratives of their personal experiences as mill girls, see Eisler.
13. For examples of letters and diaries used as documentary sources of women's history, see Lerner and Rappaport.
14. For the story of the young Jewish heroine, Sashie, and her family's

flight from Russia in 1900, told by Sashie to her great granddaughter, see Lasky, *The Night Journey*.

WORKS CITED

American Association of University Women. *AAUW Report: How Schools Shortchange Girls*. Washington: AAUW Educational Foundation, 1992.

Avi. *The True Confessions of Charlotte Doyle*. New York: Orchard, 1990.

Blenz-Clucas, Beth. "History's Forgotten Heroes: Women on the Frontier." *School Library Journal*. 39 (1993):118–123.

Brink, Carol Ryrie. *Caddie Woodlawn*. 1935. New ed. New York: Macmillan, 1973.

Brownstein, Rachel M. *Becoming a Heroine: Reading about Women in Novels*. New York: Viking, 1982.

Cavanna, Betty. *Ruffles and Drums*. New York: Morrow, 1975.

Clapp, Patricia. *I'm Deborah Sampson: A Soldier in the War of the Revolution*. New York: Lothrop, 1977.

Clarke, Mary Stetson. *Petticoat Rebel*. New York: Viking, 1964.

Conrad, Pam. *Prairie Song*. New York: Harper, 1985.

De Pauw, Linda Grant. *Seafaring Women*. Boston: Houghton, 1982.

Donovan, Josephine. *Feminist Theory: The Intellectual Traditions of American Feminism*. Rev. ed. New York: Continuum, 1992.

Eisler, Benita, ed. *The Lowell Offering: Writings by New England Mill Women (1840–1845)*. New York: Harper, 1977.

Field, Rachel. *Calico Bush*. 1931. New York: Macmillan, 1966.

Gilligan, Carol. *A Different Voice*. Cambridge: Harvard UP, 1982.

Gorham, Deborah. *The Victorian Girl and the Feminine Ideal*. Bloomington: Indiana UP, 1982.

Hancock, Emily. *The Girl Within*. New York: Fawcett, 1989.

Heilbrun, Carolyn G. *Reinventing Womanhood*. New York: Norton, 1979.

Hesse, Karen. *Letters from Rifka*. 1992. New York: Puffin, 1993.

Hurmence, Belinda. *Tancy*. New York: Clarion, 1984.

Kiefer, Monica. *American Children through Their Books, 1700–1835*. Philadelphia: U of Pennsylvania P, 1948.

Lasker, Joe. *The Strange Voyage of Neptune's Car*. New York: Viking, 1977.

Lasky, Kathryn. *Beyond the Divide*. New York: Macmillan, 1983.

Lasky, Kathryn. "The Fiction of History: Or, What Did Miss Kitty Really Do." *The New Advocate*. 3.3 (1990): 157–166.

Lasky, Kathryn. *The Night Journey*. New York: Warne, 1981.

Lerner, Gerda. *The Female Experience: An American Documentary*. 1977.

New York: Oxford UP, 1992.

Lewis, Jane. "Women, Lost and Found: The Impact of Feminism on History." *Men's Studies Modified: The Impact of Feminism on the Academic Disciplines*. Ed. Dale Spender. The Athene Ser. New York: Pergamon, 1981. 55–72.

Lyons, Mary E. *Letters from a Slave Girl: The Story of Harriet Jacobs*. New York: Scribner's, 1992.

National Women's History Project. *Women's History Catalog*. Windsor: National Women's History Project, 1994.

Paterson, Katherine. *Lyddie*. 1991. New York: Puffin, 1992.

Polster, Miriam E. *Eve's Daughter: The Forbidden Heroism of Women*. San Francisco: Jossey, 1992.

Rahn, Suzanne. "An Evolving Past: The Story of Historical Fiction and Nonfiction for Children." *The Lion and the Unicorn*. 15.1 (1991): 1–26.

Rappaport, Doreen, ed. *American Women: Their Lives in their Words*. Harper, 1990.

Rostkowski, Margaret I. *After the Dancing Days*. New York: Harper, 1986.

Vandergrift, Kay E. "A Feminist Research Agenda in Youth Literature." *Wilson Library Bulletin*. 68.2 (1993): 23–26.

Vining, Elizabeth Gray. *The Taken Girl*. New York: Viking, 1972.

Walsh, Jill Paton. *Grace*. New York: Farrar, 1992.

Zilboorg, Caroline. "Caddie Woodlawn: A Feminist Case Study." *Children's Literature in Education* 21 (1990): 109–117.

CHAPTER SEVEN

A Lesson in Activism for Young Adults: Danish Resistance during World War II

Karen Toron Cooper

I
n her 1994 Newbery acceptance speech, Lois Lowry relates a series of stories which illuminate episodes in her life that forced her to journey consciously from everyday, essentially safe, and not particularly dimensional points of view to moments of clarity and questioning which had profound impact on her intellectual development and on her subsequent writings. She implies that, like Jonas in her Newbery winner, *The Giver*, she understands the appeal of "the familiar, comfortable, and safe" in life, but that, in order to find dimensions, one needs to journey, like Jonas, on "other rivers" to "Elsewhere" (Speech 365, 367). "Elsewhere" contains variety; it contains both pleasure and pain. Yet, as a writer, Lowry relates that "each time a child opens a book," he or she enters a world of the imagination which allows "choices" and which grants "freedom." In the world of literature, young people find that their intellectual life expands, for in this world there are "magnificent, wonderfully unsafe things" (Speech 367).

In her speech, Lowry also relates that she still receives questions regarding her earlier Newbery winner, *Number the Stars*. She has been asked whether or not it is necessary to tell the stories of the Holocaust "over and over" (364). Lowry replies with a response from her German daughter-in-law, who insists that events of the Holocaust must be told "again and again" (364).

Yet, perhaps no other world is so difficult to capture in literature, for its Elsewhere involves a perilous journey with unexplainable boundaries.

For young people, an alternate approach to that journey can involve entry through an examination of four young adult historical fiction novels, all of which are set in Denmark during the war years, and all of which involve young people choosing activism as a response to evil. These four books—Lois Lowry's *Number the Stars*; Carol Matas's *Lisa's War* and its sequel, *Code Name Kris*; and Bjarne Reuter's *The Boys From St. Petri*—have been selected after both online Dialog searches and extensive reviews of bibliographies in print on the Holocaust and on Denmark's role during World War II.

In the section on Denmark in *The World Must Know: The History of the Holocaust as Told in the United States Holocaust Memorial Museum*, Michael Berenbaum points out that "of all the countries of Nazi-occupied Europe, only Denmark rescued virtually all of its Jews" (157). Characters in these four books frequently raise such questions as how the Danes could resist despite the German occupation of their country, and several become directly involved in the Jewish rescue effort. The intellectual development of these young characters stems from their increasingly conscious choice to care and to act. They move, as Denmark itself actually did, from passive resistance to active involvement.

These books were also selected because each of their authors has based them on historical facts, because each received positive reviews in the press, and because Matas and Lowry are well established young adult authors. Reuter joins them, for I wanted to see if a Danish author offers the same themes and perspective. His concept of the social and aesthetic viewpoints in Denmark turns out to be very much like the others'. Finally, while these books appeal to a young adult audience, they range from Lowry's work, geared toward younger teens and preteens, to Matas's and Reuter's, which could interest a wide audience from approximately age twelve to adult. Along with Lois Lowry, each of these authors has the skill to relate stories of "Elsewhere" after carefully lulling the reader into a sense of how cozy and safe regular life could be.

These authors add dimension to their portrayals of Denmark by having characters recognize what Denmark was like before the war. Danes speak of "hygge" as something which defines them. It is a difficult word to translate, but essentially a world of hygge is a world of comfort, a world in which all one's senses are satisfied. One book on Denmark, *Of Danish Ways*—with its chapters on Kings, Queens, Vikings, and Danish customs and holidays—gives an effective hint as to how Danes define themselves, for chapters on "world consciousness" and "social consciousness" are included along with a chapter on "courtesy and humor" (MacHaffie contents page). This somewhat quaint book, written by two Danish sisters, nonetheless, pinpoints something all three authors capture in their historical fiction. Over and over again, the occupiers are seen as rude and bullying. Over and over again, the Danish characters lament the loss of innocence— of Denmark as the home of Tivoli amusement park, which is "lit up with thousands of lights and looks like every child's dream of fairyland." This type of description from Matas's *Code Name Kris* (16) appears in both Matas's and Lowry's works. Both authors use descriptions of fairy tales and Denmark as a sort of fairy tale kingdom not only to define it, but also to emphasize how its children are robbed of their idyllic dreams.

This description and others exemplify the loss of innocence as a theme that runs through all four works. In keeping with this theme, each of the books strongly stress peer and sibling relationships that frequently involve characters in the switch from passive to active resistance. As they move away from parental control and toward peer or sibling relationships, their intellectual development reflects an inner questioning that is marked by their increasingly outward participation in active, more dangerous sabotage actions. In her review of *The Boys from St. Petri*, Hazel Rochman aptly describes this book as "exciting adventure in the ever-popular World War II genre of ordinary kids fighting the Nazi occupation" (1003). She also explains that "what will hold readers is the action, the story of the boys' secret sabotage, and their loss of innocence" (1003).

Although historical fiction remains a popular genre for young adults, as Elizabeth Howard points out in *America As Story: Historical Fiction for Secondary Schools*,

> there is a growing awareness being voiced both in the literature of education and in the general press that today's graduates of American high schools have little knowledge and less understanding of their country's past (xi).

In fact, this complaint extends to a lack of knowledge of history in general. Howard advocates incorporating historical fiction along with classroom texts so that students can begin "to see that history is alive. This will happen when they are able to think of history first of all as story" (xi). She suggests "that teachers consider assigning an appropriate novel (or novels) at the beginning of each new unit" as a means of "revitalizing history" (xii). This takes us back to Lois Lowry's definition of literature as appealing to the minds and hearts of young people because the stories move them deeply. It also corresponds to Michael Berenbaum's suggestion in *The World Must Know* regarding study of the Holocaust. He emphasizes that

> the material is vast and can be overwhelming. A word of advice may help. Interweaving history with biography and reading primary material in conjunction with secondary sources are good ways to strike a balance between the bleak depersonalization of Holocaust history and the vivid power of individual stories. Diaries and memoirs, oral histories and novels should be read alongside the standard works in the field (224).

As a companion work to the four suggested historical fiction novels, I strongly recommend that any teacher or librarian include *The Rescue of the Danish Jews: Moral Courage under Stress*, which contains not only historical background on Denmark during the war years but also personal narratives of Danes who participated in resistance efforts or who, as Jews, were helped in their escape to neutral Sweden. Students will relish these actual narratives, both for comparison with the events and characters in the novels and for the very real adventure stories the individuals tell with grace, humor, knowledge, and courage. This text also has contributions by academics who review the social, historical, and aesthetic character of Denmark in relationship to questions regarding the sense of collective responsibility the nation exhibited in its resistance efforts.

Thus, librarians and teachers could effectively use any one or all of these suggested historical fiction books along with *The Rescue of the Danish Jews*. At the very least, these works could be included in suggested reading lists or in bibliographies on the Holocaust years. However, these books could be used more effectively either in an introductory unit to the Holocaust or in library book discussion groups. In my own work as a Youth Services/Reference librarian, I have been able to keep a young adult bookclub alive and well by allowing its members choices in their selection of books and subjects. Dealing with a subject like the Holocaust for young adults ranging from sixth grade through high school was made possible by affording them the variety represented in these works.

Before more closely examining the four novels and such themes as the movement from passive to active resistance, I would like to add some personal and general background information. The subsequent analysis of the historical fiction selections which follows this background could then easily serve to stimulate questions on which teachers or librarians could base their discussions.

As Lois Lowry related, every family has its stories, and among those stories each member finds special relevance in the narratives that best help to define and shape his or her lifelong interests. For me, tales of World War II, of the German occupation of my native Denmark, and of my family's history during those years served to fortify my belief that individual acts of moral courage can spread beyond the individual to produce countrywide activism and empowerment. I have spent most of my life in America, but my interest in Denmark as a positive example during the dark years of the Holocaust has grown.

Nineteen ninety-three marked the opening of the U.S. Memorial Museum in Washington, D.C., and it also marked the 50th anniversary of the rescue of the Danish Jews. Groups like Thanks to Scandinavia have encouraged the "memorializing ... [of the] incredible stories" which documented that rescue (*Thanks to Scandinavia* 2). Much more massive in scale, the U.S. Memorial Museum, which was "established by an Act of Congress ... is this country's official witness to the atrocities committed by the Nazis. ... but the museum provides hope as well as remembrance" in its displays on various resistance movements against the Nazis. These displays underscore the truth that there "is tremendous evil in the world, but tremendous good as well—and inside each of us is the power to choose" (Ryan).

Among these resistance displays is a small wooden boat that a Danish fisherman used to carry refugees to safety. My father and most of his family were among the 7,500 Jews rescued by a massive Danish resistance to the German roundup attempts of September 1943. They landed safely in neutral Sweden. Unfortunately, my teenage aunts, Aunt Eva and Aunt Ruth, were among the 481 Jews whom the Germans captured and sent to Theresienstadt, a concentration camp in Czechoslovakia. Yet, even there, continued support "from the Danish civil service and church organizations" meant monthly "packages of clothing, food, and vitamins" as well as "Danish Red Cross" inspections of the camp. Eventually all but a few of the Danish Jews were able to return after the war to Denmark. "Protected for over five years by the heroic and persistent Danish people, the Danish Jews were spared from near certain death in Birkenau-Auschwitz and from being victims in the Final Solution" (Thanks to Scandinavia, *Resistance* 4–5).

Central to my personal response to the above facts has been the knowledge that my Aunt Ruth was able to save Aunt Eva's life in Theresienstadt. Like many others, they almost starved, for many of their food parcels were in fact appropriated by camp personnel. However, Aunt Ruth generously shared her food with Aunt Eva, enabling her to survive. As this story was retold during the years that followed, my family was empowered by the knowledge of how the sisters had been able to support and sustain one another. Although both teenage girls had been turned over to the Nazis by a Danish traitor, during their capture my red-headed Aunt Ruth was at first not believed to be Jewish. She could actually have escaped, but she chose to stay with her older sister, insisting that they were in fact sisters and refusing to be separated. Both my emotional and intellectual response to their story has extended to a professional interest in displaying and collecting Holocaust material. Material such as the recently expanded second edition of Volavková's *I Never Saw Another Butterfly: Children's Drawings and Poems from Terezin*

Concentration Camp, 1942–1944, testifies that unlike the Danish Jews, so many others were sent to killing camps.

Sidra DeKoven Ezrahi writes on the Holocaust in literature, trying to see how and if words can ever capture the reality of that period. She finds that even

> the most vivid presentation of concrete detail and specificity, the most palpable reconstruction of Holocaust reality, is blunted by the fact that there is no analogue in human experience. The imagination loses credibility and resources where reality exceeds even the darkest fantasies of the human mind; even realism flounders before such reality. (3)

Young adults frequently study the Holocaust in middle school and again in high school as part of curricula that focus on "the history of the murder of the European Jews" in lessons centered on "Global Studies" and "World Cultures" (Dawidowicz 67). Curricula attempt to "do two things, first, to give students basic information, and, second, to provide appropriate moral education. They are better at the first task than at the second, and better at describing what happened than explaining why it happened (Dawidowicz 69). In order to provide lessons in both the "what" and the "why," it is possible to use Danish resistance as a symbol of moral courage by tracing the obstacles that the characters in the young adult novels above must face. Empowerment in these novels is possible, for characters live in a society in which ultimately all facets—from the King, to the Church, to the Jewish population, to individual students—accepted the moral challenge of staying positively active despite individual fear.

Still, these books can provide only an entry into any larger discussion of the Holocaust. As stated, Danish Jews were not sent to killing camps. These narratives, like many other works of fiction, stay outside the camps. "In the history of Holocaust literature there are relatively few stories which are actually located in the camps; most of them ... reach the periphery of the concentrationary universe ... [for the] concentration camp is a world without exit" (Ezrahi 52). For students looking for works inside that concentrationary universe, Art Spiegelman's *Maus* and Jane

Yolen's *The Devil's Arithmetic* provide vivid entry. Abraham J. and Hershel Edelheit's *Bibliography on Holocaust Literature* is one of many excellent bibliographies that lead to additional sources.

In the *Supplement* volume to this collection, the Edelheits define different categories of resistance: there are the "spiritual, moral, individual, collective, spontaneous, and organized" forms, as well as different activities from "sabotage" to "anti-German propaganda and espionage" to "armed resistance" (7). Certainly in Denmark early resistance efforts lacked organization, as early "resistance meant action first—policy later" (Hæstrup *Secret Alliance* 203). Anger and dissatisfaction over an unwanted German occupation consistently propelled the Danish resistance members, many of whom, like the characters in historical fiction, were teenagers—teenagers who like Stefan in Matas's two books lacked patience with Denmark's occupation from the beginning: "Surrendered! We never even tried! We hardly fired a shot! Should we all go out there and lick the German's boots now, too" (*Lisa's War* 3)? Teenagers like Stefan entered the resistance early, aflame with passion and indignation, while much of Denmark, like their beloved King Christian X, favored displays of quiet dignity, aware of Germany's power and of the long history of hostility between the two countries.

Denmark was central to the "Nazi ideology which saw Scandinavians as Aryan brothers and aimed at making them German satellites" (Seymour 49–50). In addition, "the Germans wanted Denmark to be neutral because of her importance as a supplier of food to Germany and her strategic position at the entrance to the Baltic" (Seymour 50). In contrast, many Danes felt that the Germans had no understanding of them—of their humor, tolerance, and essential lack of racial or religious stereotyping. This difference appears over and over again both in informational narratives on the war years and in fiction. Central to the increasing activism shown in all sources is the Danish conviction expressed from the King on down that "there was no Jewish problem in Denmark." Ironically, this

> attitude was so widespread that [even] German publications took note of it. In the spring of 1941, the official German journal *Die Judenfrage* carried an article under the headline DENMARK—A COUNTRY WITHOUT A JEWISH PROBLEM? The author went

on to complain that preoccupation with racial problems was considered "un-Danish." (Petrow 197)

From a historical perspective, this opposition to anti-Semitism was part of a tradition dating back to 1690, when

> a Danish police chief was relieved of his duties for daring to suggest that Denmark should follow the example of other European countries and establish a ghetto in Copenhagen. The Danish Parliament had immediately followed the dismissal of the police chief by passing a resolution condemning the very idea of a ghetto as "an inhuman way of life." (Flender 30)

Thus, Danes have historically been unwilling to isolate any one group. In Danish society this attitude strengthened during World War II. The Danish historian, Jørgen Hæstrup, has written extensively on Denmark during World War II. In the second chapter of *The Rescue of the Danish Jews*, he clearly outlines events of this period. The German occupation began on April 9th, 1940. Initially, passive resistance was the dominant response, but as time passed "scattered incidents of active sabotage and the beginning of an extremely significant underground press (growing steadily to more than five-hundred separate papers and three-hundred books and pamphlets)" helped prompt a more and more active resistance (Hæstrup 19). Among the Jewish population in Denmark, not only Danish citizens but "almost 2,200 individuals who did not hold Danish citizenship" (20) were fully integrated into Danish society. At no time did Danes allow ordinances against the Jews to go into effect.

While this paper cannot possibly cover all the fascinating details of how Denmark managed to maintain this situation until 1943, young people will appreciate individual episodes outlined in Hæstrup's chapter. So, for instance, the Danish Supreme Court actually "sentenced ... [a] would be arsonist of the synagogue ... on the ground of anti-Semitic activities" to jail time "despite the fact that Denmark was occupied by the Germans" (32). By 1943, this and other types of spirited behavior resulted in severe crackdowns, which in turn prompted nationwide protests and strikes. The Germans ended their "so-called moderate" approach: they "declared a state of emergency" and eventually placed the Danish King under "house arrest" (38, 45). By early October of 1943, the attempted roundup of the Jews in Denmark began. The events surrounding that attempt actually served to unite the Danish resistance effort. Each of the four historical fiction novels also stresses this point of view.

For one thing, Danes prided themselves collectively on not succumbing to propaganda efforts. Currently, Bjarne Reuter, an extremely popular author of many Danish books, follows this tradition. In *The Boys from St. Petri*, Mrs. Balstrup does not know that her two sons, Gunnar and Lars, are members of the resistance. Their father is the local minister, and the young men join their friends in a secret organization that meets in the church loft. Their family has strong ties to the town's organist, Filip Rosen, who as a Jew typifies Danish Jews of the time. Since religion was typically considered a private matter, Danish Jews were integrated into all aspects of society. Thus Rosen, famous for his exquisite playing, lives in the rectory. Throughout this novel, Reuter contrasts Rosen's individual musical style with the brass band music that the Germans love to play. When Rosen is forced to flee the rectory, the Balstrups find the sound of that band almost unbearable: they sit in their living room, listening to this music now "swelling, crescendoing, filtering in through every crevice." To them, it oppressively mingles with the sounds of "German boots marching down Østergade as if that were the most natural thing in the world" (Reuter 155).

Before Rosen is forced to flee, Mrs. Balstrup briefly wonders whether the town's increasing sabotage activity is somehow to blame. Her son Lars turns their discussion into an ethical debate. He quickly convinces her not to fall for German propaganda. Lars reminds his mother that he agrees with the position of his father, who had in an earlier scene defiantly told the Nazis searching Rosen's room that Rosen had not engaged in any resistance or broken any Danish laws (Reuter 148). Lars warns his mother against blaming the saboteurs for the gestapo actions. The gestapo seeks "excuses" for their actions "so as to turn ordinary people against both the Jews and the saboteurs" (150). Ultimately he pleads, "I can't bear to see you falling for their propaganda too" (150), to which she poignantly replies: "All I know is we're losing Rosen" (150). Lars rationalizes to himself that "of course there was nothing really the matter with her powers of judgement—if these methods worked in the huge county of Germany, then why wouldn't they work in Denmark too" (150)? Ultimately, Reuter concludes this passage by having Lars's mother take her son's side. Lars confides that he hates the Germans, and Mrs. Balstrup responds, "Yes. ... To hell with them all" (150).

Mrs Balstrup, much like the other mothers in the four historical fiction novels, functions as representative of "hygge." Not only do mothers frequently recall home life before the occupation, but their children also remember instances before the war when their mothers could protect and nourish them. Both children and their mothers must recognize the new reality that the war imposes upon them. It takes them from the comfort of home to the obstacles of Elsewhere. So, for example, Jesper in *Code Name Kris* can only allow himself a brief visit home after he has gone underground in the resistance movement. His mother sees him after a long absence, and she speaks in a choked, whispering voice of how he has changed (Matas 63). She notes his growth, wonders how he eats and whom he lives with; he in turn longs to stay at home with her. He does return to his resistance work, but only after an internal struggle, for at heart he still wants the comfort of childhood—he still longs for normality. He finally leaves, but only after inwardly admitting that

> I wanted to go to sleep in my own bed, and to go to school in the morning and to start studying English literature again. I wanted my mother to take care of me and baby me; regret poured over me as I understood that would never happen again (63).

This longing for childhood will be readily understandable to adolescent readers, for theirs is an age of increasing peer relationships, and they frequently struggle to gain independence from parental control. So too, Lars in *The Boys from St. Petri* discovers that it is one thing to choose that independence as a natural part of growing up, but another thing to have it thrust upon one in response to a national crisis. Once Rosen flees their home, Lars, like Jesper, recognizes that the old order has passed. He finds no comfort in his mother's afternoon coffee rituals; he sits with his family in their dining room, looks around, and listens to "the grandfather clock routinely slicing the hours into little bits" (155). Lars senses that now Rosen is no longer among them, their inability to protect him has left them with hollow rituals. Rosen "had left a gaping black hole, a dreadful sense of loss, behind him" (155).

Nonetheless, for the Danes in these fictional accounts, as with the Danes in historical accounts, the attempted roundup of the Danish Jews ultimately unites the nation. In *The Rescue of the Danish Jews*, one of the most moving personal narratives is by Dr. Jørgen Kieler, who recalls his activist student days. He feels that the Germans made a giant "blunder" in attempting to "persecute Danish Jews" (146)—that the attempt propelled many in Denmark from passive to active resistance and granted them "the opportunity to 'protect one's younger brother with one's own body.' The opportunity was seized by numerous people who had been living in an ethical conflict for months" (146). Dr. Kieler's narrative retains the intensity of his student days; like the leading characters in the fictional accounts, Dr. Kieler indicates that for his group of friends no compromises were possible. For them "an occupied country has a choice between two alternatives, i.e., collaboration with the enemy or active resistance" (142).

In the historical fiction, such ethical conflicts result in several symbolic extensions like Dr. Kieler's, extensions in which central characters enlarge their family structures. So in *The Boys from St. Petri*, Rosen is accepted as a family member with the approval of the whole family. So too in *Number the Stars*, the parents of Annemarie Johansen, the central character, value her friendship with her Jewish friend, Ellen Rosen. When the October 1943 roundup begins, Annemarie's parents agree to hide Ellen with them. Their family has lost a beloved daughter, Lise, to the resistance, but Lise's death is not talked about, and young Annemarie nurtures her memory in private. Mr. Johansen speaks of Lise out loud for the first time in years when he suggests that Annemarie and Ellen pretend to be sisters. He counsels them not to be afraid, and he inspires them to be brave by relating that "once I had three daughters. Tonight I am proud to have three daughters again" (38). Annemarie, Ellen, and

Annemarie's little sister all benefit by such adult examples of courage. Annemarie is in turn able to help Ellen once the soldiers arrive to brutally question them. She quickly hides Ellen's Star of David necklace, and she finds that after the soldiers leave she has its "imprint" firmly edged in her palm (49). By extension, she and Ellen become not just close peers or intense friends; they unite as symbolic sisters.

Several such relationships exist in Carol Matas's accounts, too. In *Lisa's War*, Lisa's family "adopts" two new members as the war worsens. Lisa and her friend Susanne both carry out resistance efforts. Matas knows the types of details guaranteed to grab young adults' attention. Susanne's beautiful long blond hair is completely burned off in a German bombing. Susanne arrives at Lisa's apartment in a state of shock. Lisa opens the door to find that "Susanne is looking at me. She has no hair—only charred frizz is left. Her clothes are simply tatters. She is covered in blisters. I look at her. I think I'm screaming. I must be" (41). Soon Matas has Lisa's family take in Susanne, whose parents were killed; and they take care of a little girl, Sarah, whose parents are also killed in a vivid scene in the hospital where Lisa's father is a doctor.

That adoption adds another ethical dimension, for the baby—unlike Lisa's family—is not Jewish. Soon Lisa faces a most painful dilemma when her family has to escape to neutral Sweden. She holds Sarah, but she finds herself sitting or lying awake all night, for she cannot stop thinking of the impossible position they place her in. She wonders "if these will be my last memories. ... Sarah is my only comfort, but also my greatest burden. Could they kill a little baby like her?" she questions. Finally she must conclude that she knows "they could. And they want to. They want to. They want us all dead" (81).

Thus these authors, while they do not enter the world of concentration camps, do, nevertheless, have their characters face one of the most terrifying aspects of the Holocaust. During this period, parents lost the ability to protect the lives of their children; during this period, children had no special protection. Nothing, not even the great resistance stories, can ease the intellectual leap that young adults must make in facing that fact. Books such as these, in which characters unite to save each other and each other's children, soften the larger picture as well as provide alternative examples, but ultimately, as *The World Must Know* relates,

> in the end, children were deported along with their parents to concentration camps. Mothers and fathers could no longer protect their young. Parents who refused to be separated from their children were sent at once to the gas chambers. ... The young children, and the parents who insisted on staying with them, went to their death (Berenbaum 194).

Similarly, Jeshajahu Weinberg, the Director of the United States Holocaust Memorial Museum, asserts powerfully that the "understanding of the passive bystander's inadvertent guilt is probably the most relevant moral lesson the museum can teach its visitors" (Berenbaum xv). Berenbaum himself emphasizes that the Danish response, in contrast, may stem from the fact that Danes "simply treated Jews as the neighbors they were, and one does not allow the enemy who occupies one's country to deport neighbors. The explanation for their behavior may well be as simple as that" (159).

Clearly in the four historical fiction novels and in historical narratives, the portrayal of neighbors as heroic helpers is repeated in many exciting examples. In all four works of historical fiction, as in actuality, Jews could turn to their neighbors for help once the attempted Nazi roundup of the Danish Jews began. So too, characters are peers and friends who have established close ties based on proximity and daily exchanges. In *Number the Stars*, Annemarie and her best friend, Ellen, live in the same apartment house, attend school together, and at times exchange visits during their respective Christian and Jewish holidays. Likewise in *Lisa's War* and its sequel, *Code Name Kris*, Stefan and his sister Lisa, who are Jewish, grow increasingly close to Jesper, who is not. At one point Lisa passionately questions, "What does it matter that we are Jewish? I don't feel any different from anyone else, and I'm not treated differently" (*Lisa's War* 57). If anything, war and the Nazi's increasing anti-Semitism function to heighten the brotherly tie between Stefan and Jesper, as well as the growing romance between Lisa and Jesper. Before the war, their families exchanged visits during Easter and Passover, while during the war their relationship takes on new dimensions. In *Code Name Kris*, Jesper relates an example of their new roles. He explains that their activism grows alongside their romance, that in reality the excitement of each spills over to the other: "Lisa and I would go to a movie in the afternoon and a sabotage action after dinner. By that time there were six or seven sabotage acts every day" (13).

Effective dramatic tension builds throughout both books as Carol Matas has the three become involved in increasingly dangerous acts; they go from distributing underground newspapers to eventually participating in sabotage and armed resistance during the attempted roundup of Denmark's Jews. Danger to all of them increases as their activities intensify, but Matas especially underscores Lisa and Stefan's unique position as Jews. Neither is welcomed at first in underground activities. Stefan must initially fight to be allowed to participate

> because the resistance doesn't want Jewish people in dangerous situations, situations where they can be caught. The Germans will only use that as an excuse. "See, here we have Jewish saboteurs. Now you see why we have to round up the Jews and send them away. They threaten the very peace of Denmark." (*Lisa's War* 15)

Here too, young activists like Stefan refuse to let a power from without segregate them from activities within Denmark. In the personal narrative of *The Rescue of the Danish Jews*, the same type of struggle Stefan faced in order to be included in resistance efforts is chronicled. As Jørgen Hæstrup points out, Jewish participation in the resistance seemed "contrary to the Jewish leadership's strategy, which called for trustful loyalty to the government" (39). He indicates that "even minor indications of Jewish resistance activity could have … carried severe consequences for the whole Jewish community" (39).

In *Code Name Kris*, Stefan, who at the end of *Lisa's War* has sailed to safety in neutral Sweden, returns to risk his life to further the resistance because he cannot in all conscience let Jesper or Denmark fight on alone. Increasingly throughout *Code Name Kris*, Matas shows her characters making moral choices that reflect their evolving perceptions of what constitutes right and wrong. Realistically, she has them enter a grey area of not easily chosen options once their lives are actually threatened. Lisa especially fears that their actions change them beyond control: "My God, I think, these Germans are dragging us all down to their level. How will we keep ourselves better than them" (*Lisa's War* 46)? By the end of this novel Matas has Lisa and Jesper share in the killing of a young German soldier who is trying to prevent the escape of several Jewish families to Sweden. Matas has just shown how absolutely terrified the escaping families were; in fact, she has the father of one family slit the throats of his wife and two young children just before they think they are to be captured. Obviously, this is difficult for both the young reader and the characters to witness. In this section Lisa's internal debate consists of grotesque questions. Matas has taken her characters one step further into the war. They enter the realm in which children die, and Lisa struggles with her thoughts. She keeps remembering what the children looked like, and she compulsively wonders if their mother held them while the father carries out his actions (88).

Immediately afterwards, Lisa and Jesper kill the soldier, with Lisa narrating how really frightful the act was: he "shrieks, then falls over. ... He's screaming horribly" (94) until Jesper finishes the killing. Early on we learn that Lisa has a weak stomach, as she constantly fears vomiting during times of stress. Now she "retches" in the bushes, feeling worse afterwards, with no possible relief. In contrast, the aware reader remembers the younger Lisa, who in her first resistance effort threw up all over a soldier on a streetcar as she tried to distribute underground papers. She and the others had roared with laughter, but now she can only keep working to save others until she too is finally on a boat to Sweden. At the conclusion even Stefan and Jesper have tired. They also long for liberation from the reality of fighting.

Still, their friendship unites them, both in *Lisa's War* and in *Code Name Kris*. Their bond is based on a shared history. So too does Bjarne Reuter focus on the friendships of the young characters in *The Boys from St. Petri*. But while he begins this book by showing characters like Gunnar and his brother Lars entering resistance work with a group of lifelong friends, Reuter soon builds dramatic tension by having an outsider, Otto, join them. Suddenly Lars and his friends, with their elaborate rituals and joining ceremonies, seem like naive schoolboys in contrast to Otto, who unlike the others is private, untalkative, and from a working class background.

Otto's home life is also different. He functions like a parent to his younger siblings, and his mother is in his own words an "army mattress," a prostitute for German soldiers (Reuter 161). Otto's anger at that leaves him frequently silent, certainly not a joiner in the others' club, yet in the end he is the one to lead the group into action. He brings them their first gun, and he has no problems with dangerous sabotage missions; in fact, he longs for them. At the end of this work Reuter has the others taken prisoner, yet Otto escapes. Reuter seems to say that Otto, who works best alone and follows "his own strategy, carrying out his own plan," represents the new order of survival (85). He is the foil for the other characters.

In her Master's thesis on *War and Peace in Adolescent Literature,* Faye Lander comments that an

> important aspect in most books for students is character development and growth. Many of these stories deal with adolescent struggles. Most works continuously emphasize that even in wartime or in concentrations camps, life continues as before with familiar patterns and social institutions. ... Adolescents, particularly those who remained with their parents, exhibited rebellion or resentment against their parents. (19)

With the exception of Otto, however, teenage and youthful rebellion in all four novels is directed not against parents but against the larger Nazi authorities. Family and resistance members learn to keep secrets from one another as their activities increase, but this was a typical precaution. The family remains important.

In Lowry's book, with Annemarie as its young protagonist, there is a pull or a wish for normality, parallel to the "normality" Denmark hoped for during the earlier occupation period. Both Annemarie and Ellen look to adults in their family for guidance. Likewise, Lars and Gunnar find much to respect in their father's actions. The minister seldom misses a chance to let his opinions show in his sermons, and he "listened avidly to the radio—the broadcasts from London were positively sacred"

(Reuter 49). Similarly, Lisa's father, a doctor, is able to help in his own right, much like actual Danish doctors. Once the roundup began, hospitals served as hiding centers, and many physicians helped in the rescue operation.

But just as the attempted roundup of the Jews involved all segments of Danish society, so Denmark, as it rebelled and entered into a nationwide strike against its oppressors, found that there was no turning back. Martial law and increasing activism prevailed. All of this is depicted, especially in Matas's books. She does have her characters work independently from their parents, but with the implication that those parents fear yet understand the activities they assume their children engage in. Ultimately, and this would appeal to adolescent readers, young characters make their own decisions. In a very real sense, group activity within the resistance legitimizes the natural inclination young people have to favor and relish peer relationships. Thus, Lisa poignantly thinks of her parents on the way to Sweden while she hunts the shore for Germans. She pictures "Mother and Father looking back through the dark, wishing Stefan and I were with them," yet she can act on the choice to stay behind. She stays behind with her sibling, and with their peer, Jesper. Together they move out of the realm of parental control (*Lisa's War* 96).

Lois Lowry also has ten-year-old Annemarie Johansen make brave and moral choices, yet ironically it is her mother who has to push her into the adult world of responsibility. All along in *Number the Stars*, adults set moral examples. Annemarie's uncle questions her carefully to see if she intellectually understands concepts of bravery. He finds her responsive, and she gradually is told more and more about their attempts to have Ellen's family and others escape. Having proved herself brave beyond her years, Annemarie eventually risks her life to spirit the Rosen family to freedom once her mother is injured, and she has to journey alone through the woods in her mother's place in order to deliver a specially scented handkerchief to her Uncle, the fisherman. The handkerchief is soaked in a special formula designed to throw Nazi guard dogs off the scent. While the adults shield Annemarie from the details of what she carries and how it might help, she cannot be spared the long journey through the woods.

Interestingly, in that journey Lowry has Annemarie comfort herself by reciting parts of *Little Red Riding Hood*. However, as Annemarie carries out her journey through the woods, armed soldiers pursue her with "two large dogs, their eyes glittering, their lips curled," combining into a horrible image of the menacing wolf (112). Surely, Denmark as the fairy tale kingdom—as the place where "all Danish children grew up familiar with fairy tales"—has changed, but Annemarie's ability to act out those tales in fact saves her (Lowry 11). Earlier she had told them to lull her younger sister to sleep, now she uses this one to calm herself as she walks, and she uses a version of it in acting out the part of "a silly little girl" who keeps "chattering away" until the soldiers leave her alone (114).

Earlier it is also Annemarie who symbolically hides Ellen's Star of David necklace among her own dead sister's belongings, and it is Annemarie who, at the end of the novel when newly freed Denmark awaits the return of its Jews, decides to wear the necklace until Ellen comes back. Denmark alone, with its protests against discrimination, manages to survive without Jews' being forced to wear the Star of David as a badge to segregate and identify them. By extension, it is Annemarie who voices one of the moral lessons of the novel. Previously, her father had commented on how brave King Christian X was. His daily horseback rides through Copenhagen rallied the whole country behind him. Annemarie's father relates that all of Denmark serves as the king's bodyguard, and that "any Danish citizen would die for King Christian, to protect him" (14). Once the Danish Jews are threatened, it is Annemarie who expands on this symbolic concept. Young as she is, she intellectualizes this image one step further by realizing that "now I think that all of Denmark must be bodyguard for the Jews, as well" (25). Both in action and in thought, Annemarie carries out her convictions. She emerges as a young heroine easily identifiable to young people. *Booklist's* review rightly stresses that while "the novel has an absorbing plot, its real strength lies in its evocation of deep friendship between two girls and of a caring family who make a profoundly moral choice to protect others during wartime" (Olderr and Smith, 86).

In wartime, death and loss—or the possibilities of death and loss—hover together. Otto breaks up the friendship of Gunnar and his lifelong friend, Søren, who quits their group once Otto shows himself willing to kill Nazi soldiers. In Otto's view such things happen; after all it is wartime, but in Søren's view there are no fine lines to ponder. He denounces his friends and their group; he quits after calling Otto a "murderer". In the end, he wants out from under the burden of Gunnar's intellectualizing. Gunnar had quietly asked him "where do we draw the line between what you call murderers and what the rest of Denmark calls patriots" (Reuter 145)?

That type of question ultimately haunts many of the characters in these books. At the close of *Code Name Kris*, Jesper hopes to find release through his skills as a journalist. He learns them writing for underground papers, but at the end he hopes to tell his story and somehow purge himself of its horrors. His first person narrative is penetrating throughout. Carol Matas respects her audience; she does include explicit passages, but she carefully and clearly leads her characters through the types of ethical debates young people can identify with.

Finally, both Lowry's and Matas's versions of the occupation also underscore the danger of the war years by having important characters die; each author is willing to show her audience that resistance efforts could lead to profound loss, especially in *Code Name Kris*. Matas's haunting description of the death of Janicke, a young resistance fighter, comes as a shocking climax to a long period in which the relationship between Janicke, Jesper, and Stefan has been carefully detailed.

Likewise, as we have seen in *Number the Stars*, Annemarie's intense sister-like bond with her best friend Ellen is strengthened by the earlier death of Lise, Annemarie's older sister. Yet, as is appropriate for a younger audience, we do not "witness" death. Instead, Annemarie frequently recollects previous times when Lise had celebrated her engagement to fun-loving Peter. Annemarie lovingly looks through the blue trunk in their bedroom in which "were folded Lise's pillowcases with their crocheted edges, her wedding dress with its hand-embroidered neckline, unworn, and the yellow dress that she had worn and danced in, with its full skirt flying, at the party celebrating her engagement to Peter" (16).

As we have seen, in all four books Denmark becomes increasingly tense under German rule; but in Lowry's version, the most hopeful of the four, we, along with Annemarie, do not learn until near the end that Lise and Peter were both in the resistance and that Lise's death occurred during a Nazi raid. Young Peter's letter, written the night before he is executed by the Nazis, asks his loved ones to remember that "he was proud to have done what he could for his country and for the sake of all free people" (129). His thoughts echo the words of an actual Danish resistance fighter who on the night before his own death wrote:

> I want you all to remember—that you must not dream yourselves back to the times before the war, but the dream for you all, young and old, must be to create an ideal of human decency, and not a narrow-minded and prejudiced one. This is the great gift our country hungers for. … (Thomas 107)

WORKS CITED

Berenbaum, Michael. *The World Must Know: The History of the Holocaust as Told in the United States Holocaust Memorial Museum.* Boston: Little, 1993.

Colarusso, Kathleen Dale. "World War II and Its Relevance to Today's Adolescents." *The Alan Review* 13.2 (Winter 1986): 12–14.

Dawidowicz, Lucy S. *What Is the Use of Jewish History?* New York: Schocken, 1992.

Edelheit, Abraham J., and Hershel Edelheit. *Bibliography on Holocaust Literature: Supplement.* Boulder: Westview, 1990.

Ezrahi, Sidra DeKoven. *By Words Alone: The Holocaust in Literature.* Chicago: U of Chicago P, 1980.

Flender, Harold. *Rescue in Denmark.* New York: Simon, 1963.

Hæstrup, Jørgen. "The Danish Jews and the German Occupation." *The Rescue of the Danish Jews: Moral Courage under Stress.* Ed. Leo Goldberger. New York: New York UP, 1987. 13–53.

———. *Secret Alliance: A Study of the Danish Resistance Movement 1940–45.* Trans. Alison Borch-Johansen. Vol. 2. Odense: Odense UP, 1976. 3 vols.

Howard, Elizabeth F. *America as Story: Historical Fiction for Secondary Schools.* Chicago: ALA, 1988.

Kessler, Kate. "Teaching Holocaust Literature." *English Journal* 80.7 (November 1991): 29–32.

Kieler, Jørgen. Personal Narrative. *The Rescue of the Danish Jews: Moral Courage under Stress*. Ed. Leo Goldberger. New York: New York UP, 1987. 141–155.

Lander, Faye. "War and Peace in Adolescent Literature." Master's Thesis. U of Akron, 1981.

Langer, Lawrence L. *The Holocaust and the Literary Imagination*. New Haven: Yale UP, 1975.

Lowry, Lois. *Number the Stars*. Boston: Houghton, 1989.

_____. "1994 Newbery Acceptance Speech." *Journal of Youth Services in Libraries* 7 (1994): 361-367.

MacHaffie, Ingeborg S., and Margaret A. Nielsen. *Of Danish Ways*. New York: Harper, 1976.

Matas, Carol. *Code Name Kris*. New York: Scribner's, 1990.

_____. *Lisa's War*. New York: Scribner's, 1987.

Olderr, Steven, and Candace P. Smith, eds. *Olderr's Young Adult Fiction Index 1989*. Chicago: St. James, 1990. 86.

Petrow, Richard. *The Bitter Years: The Invasion and Occupation of Denmark and Norway April 1940–May 1945*. New York: Morrow, 1974.

Reuter, Bjarne. *The Boys from St. Petri*. Trans. Anthea Bell. New York: Dutton, 1994.

Rochman, Hazel. Rev. of *The Boys from St. Petri*. *Booklist* 1 February 1994: 1001, 1003.

Ryan, Michael. "It Should Shake People Up." *Parade* 18 April 1993: 18.

Seymour, Susan. *Anglo-Danish Relations and Germany 1933–1945*. Odense: Odense UP, 1982.

Thanks to Scandinavia, Inc. *Resistance and Rescue: Denmark's Response to the Holocaust*. New York: A Scholarship Fund, 1992–1993. A photographic exhibition by Judy Ellis Glickman.

_____. *Thanks to Scandinavia: Fiftieth Anniversary Report*. New York: A Scholarship Fund, 1992–1993.

Thomas, John Oram. *The Giant-Killers: The Danish Resistance Movement 1940/5*. New York: Taplinger, 1975.

Volavková, Hana, ed. *I Never Saw Another Butterfly: Children's Drawings and Poems from Terezin Concentration Camp, 1942–1944*. 2nd ed. New York: Schocken, 1993.

CHAPTER EIGHT

Finding The Way: Morality and Young Adult Literature

Carol Jones Collins

T he question of what makes a moral life has resonated in philosophical thought from the time of the ancient Greeks and Romans to the present. Some who spend their time thinking about such things have devoted their entire lives to unraveling this question. Homer, Socrates, Plato, Kant, and Nietzche, to name but a few, have all explored the question of morality or knowledge of what is right and what is wrong (Frankena 3). And although philosophers have not always agreed, their pursuit of the issue has been persistent and often passionate. In our present American society, the question of morality has become the subject of much debate, especially as it concerns those in or seeking public office. Around the office of the President of the United States have swirled questions of propriety, honesty, and integrity. And while these questions are not new to the presidency, they now seem much more urgent, more strident. The same can be said of other elected or appointed positions in this country, including those in the Supreme Court and Congress. With the rise of violent criminal acts among teenagers, these questions have deepened and broadened.

Morality is a hot topic. But what do we really know about morality? How do the young, particularly young adults, learn the moral life, since, as with most things, early exposure is critical? Are children taught in their homes or in schools? Are they exposed in their churches, synagogues, temples, or mosques? Although these questions cannot be fully answered because of the diversity of peoples and lifestyles in this country, some thought has to be given to how the young develop a sense of morality.

Indeed, the history of ethics, that branch of philosophy that studies morality, reveals a multiplicity of voices (Bourke). Some of these voices have viewed the acquiring of morality as a purely intellectual act. To become a moral being is to think one's self to morality, to use judgment, and to consciously make the decision to be moral. Others have described coming to morality as intuitive, as a natural act, which somehow is embedded in the very fiber of each person. Still others have seen the doing of moral acts as simply actions that allow the agent to avoid punishment; that is, the individual only follows the rules set down by society and nothing more. Alasdair MacIntyre, in *After Virtue: A Study in Moral Theory*, contends that no consensus exists among philosophical thinkers as to what constitutes the moral life, how it is achieved, and the extent of its rationality (1–5).

Whether one accepts the notion that an individual becomes moral through an act of the intellect, through the emotions, or intuitively, it is clear that acquiring a moral sense and becoming moral involves a kind of knowing. Acquiring a moral sense, then, is yet another way of knowing. The mechanics of that knowing, however, are still very much under investigation. But because an upright and moral citizenry is so crucial to any society, this way of knowing, this moral awareness, is critical. Creating in children and young people an awareness of right and wrong as defined by the society in which they live and empowering these young people to do what is right is one of the most important things a society can do to protect and preserve itself.

Scholars concerned with moral education, with the genesis of moral judgment in children, and the place of morality in the lives of young children have approached these issues from a number of often very differing perspectives. Few, however, have examined the role that literature can play in imparting to young people, and especially to young adults, moral values. This chapter examines young adult literature in this light, as a conduit through which moral values can be communicated to the young.

Certainly, books have been written for young people that contain moral lessons. The past century is famous for producing a juvenile literature that depicts morally upright characters, created to be moral exemplars for the young reader. The McGuffey readers, the Horatio Alger stories, Jacob Abbott's Rollo series, the works of Juliana Horatia Ewing and Mrs. Molesworth are most representative of a moralizing nineteenth century juvenile literature. That is to say, this is a literature that deals with moral issues in a rather heavy-handed manner, doing its preaching, moreover, to the children of the privileged. It is a literature that talks at and not to young people. Still, for all their "preachy" set pieces, these books did provide the young reader of that day with a vast store of morally behavioral do's and don'ts.

The literature produced in the last half of the twentieth century, aimed at young adults, differs markedly from the juvenile literature of the last century. This contemporary literature treats contemporary problems in ways that reflect the concerns of young adults, as they struggle to become adults in a complex, technological society. It is a rich and growing body of literature whose moral power has been too long neglected by literary critics and ethical theorists alike. For this chapter, a small number of young adult books have been chosen for discussion. These are books that have the potential to foster in young adults a sense of responsibility for their moral acts and feelings.

This way of thinking about books as moral conduits has support from several sources. Rita Manning singles out fiction as having an impact on the moral lives of young people (28). She argues that fiction can help the young reader determine and understand his or her own ideas about morality and can help that reader work through moral confusions. In short, Manning contends that fiction, along with other human interactions, can help young readers find their moral voice (28).

Wayne Booth speaks to the ethical role literature can play when he describes it as having the possibility of "building a richer character out of adopted roles, roles critically chosen from those stories our society offers us" (251). John Gardner concurs with this position:

. . . wherever possible moral art holds up models of decent behavior; for example, characters in fiction, drama, and film whose basic goodness and struggle against confusion, error, and evil—in themselves and in others—give firm intellectual and emotional support to our own struggle. (106)

William Kilpatrick writes in *Why Johnny Can't Tell Right from Wrong* that along with the family, books can serve to anchor children to moral values (88). MacIntyre argues that to deprive children of stories is to "leave them unscripted, anxious stutterers in their actions as in their words" (216). To this he adds that the moral tradition from the heroic age through medieval times has depended principally on stories for moral education.

Mark Tappan in another work contends that gradually, over the course of years, moral authority emerges from one person listening to the narratives or stories of others (5–25). But here, this description of the narrative interaction focuses on the oral narrative. James Day, in discussing the power of narrative, builds on and extends Tappan's analyses by including the written text, or what he calls the "fixed" narrative (40). Day argues that the structure of the moral life is so complex that only a recognition of the tremendous interrelatedness of a number of factors which include fixed narratives, dialogues, personal narratives, and other persons, among others, can explain how the moral life develops (40).

Reader response theory provides another support for the importance of literature in the moral development of the young. Wolfgang Iser explains that through reading, the reader's experience is transformed, because reading has the same structure as experience (107). The reader's interaction with the text stimulates change in the reader and enables that person to go beyond his or her experience. This is exactly what is required when young readers encounter a narrative text that allows them to gain what Manning calls their "moral voice." Louise Rosenblatt, among the first to contribute to the field of reader response theory, calls this encounter, this kind of merging or meeting of the minds, a transaction between the reader and the text (28).

Reader response theorists view the act of reading as achieving a myriad of things. Reading allows the reader to explore who he or she is or can be, exposes the reader's untapped emotions and feelings, and enables the reader to acquire a perspective on life once unavailable. Most reader response critics would agree that reading is a powerful tool for a number of reasons, not least of which is its power to convey to the reader a sense of morality.

Social construction theory provides yet another support, primarily in its treatment of the concept of the self. Kenneth Gergen argues that the concept of the self as an autonomous, single individual, with the capacity for self-direction and self-reliance is an outmoded concept (8). He contends that the notion of selves "as possessors of real and identifiable characteristics, such as rationality, emotion, and will are dismantled" (7). For Gergen, the old ideas about the self have been replaced by the view that "persons exist in a state of continuous construction and reconstruction" (7). The self is created, then, through a series of social relationships. Peter Berger and Thomas Luckmann add that the face-to-face encounter is by far the most important social encounter, that the self is really a reflection of the attitudes, behaviors, and emotions of significant others (27).

Social construction theory suggests that morality is created through social interaction, that it is, in fact, a product of that interaction. Gergen takes this idea one step further and adds other forces at work on the self's construction. These include memory of other selves, imagined selves, and interaction with the selves in poetry, drama, novels, movies, speech, dreams, and fantasy. All of these forces can easily act as substitutes for face-to-face encounters (68–71).

Reader response theory and social construction theory converge in their implications for how morality is learned. Both speak to moral development by placing interaction in the foreground. That the interaction is of a face-to-face nature or takes some other form is less important than the interaction itself. Both reader response theorists and social construction theorists see this interaction as a means by which change can take place in the individual. Interaction and change, then, are the critical elements in both theories. As such, they provide a framework for assessing literature as one more source for moral development in the young. Moreover, agreement with this position comes from other theorists as well. William Damon, for example, in *The Moral Child: Nurturing Children's Moral Growth*, agrees that "morality arises naturally out of social relationships, and children's morality is no exception" (2).

Yet, what exactly is this moral life we speak of? MacIntyre argues that our concept of morality is fragmented, disjointed because we have, over the centuries, lost our sense of what morality actually is. We have picked up bits and pieces of concepts and terminology, but have no real theoretical or practical framework upon which to view morality (2). There is no moral consensus within our society. Because of this discontinuity, he contends, we are unable to resolve any argument about the nature of morality or the moral life:

> . . . modern moral utterance and practice can only be understood as a series of fragmented survivals from an older past and that the insoluble problems which they have generated for modern moral theorists will remain unsoluble until this is well understood. (110–111)

MacIntyre points out that ethicians still view philosophers from the past as essentially contributing to one single debate, with one single subject matter. This is a mistake, which, he argues, serves to remove these men from their social and cultural contexts (11). It is only when men such as Plato or Aristotle and the others who came after them are placed in their own cultural milieu, can we make some sense of their concepts of morality and its implications for us.

By MacIntyre's account, at least three different concepts of morality, what he calls virtue, emerge when the history of ethics is investigated (185). The first concept of virtue comes from Homer's Heroic Age. Here, it is a quality that centers on a man's or woman's social role. To be virtuous in the world of the *Iliad* and the *Odyssey* is to know and be able to discharge one's duty according to the social role he or she inhabits. The hallmark virtues here would be physical courage, fidelity, loyalty, friendship, and cunning (123). It should be noted that the roles spoken of are those of the privileged classes, since little is said in the Homeric poems about the lower classes, or women, for that matter. For Aristotle, the New Testament prophets, and Thomas

Aquinas, virtue is what enables a person to set about achieving a particular human end. Virtue here is a means to an end, defined by these men as those qualities that enable a person to achieve happiness or blessedness. Agreeableness, obedience, and friendship are three of the virtues prized by them, but in the context of a unique political state. For Benjamin Franklin, virtue is what enables the individual to achieve worldly success (185). Thrift and perseverance would constitute two quite Franklinesque virtues.

Obviously, these are widely differing conceptions of what constitutes the moral virtues. Other, later philosophic thinkers were to build on these various themes. Bourke begins his discussion of the history of ethics with Aristotle and Plato, observing that for them the ideal moral person was the male Athenian aristocrat. Their approach to the moral life was intellectual. Aristotle's *Nicomachean Ethics* and *Eudemian Ethics* both discuss what Aristotle considered the major virtues. It is these virtues that have come to be the foundation for our modern list of virtues. These include, but are not limited to, the virtues of courage, temperance, truthfulness, modesty, wittiness, and friendliness (23–31).

Augustine was to argue that those who truly love God would always act in accord with God's will and moral law (57). Thomas Aquinas, perhaps the most outstanding moralist of the Middle Ages, took a different approach. He saw moral actions as being altogether voluntary acts, completely under human control. Aquinas reasoned that the forces that swayed moral activity in humans were sensual desire, feelings in response to threats, intellectual appetite, and intellectual acts having to do with reasoning, judgment, and understanding (97). For each of these forces, according to Aquinas, there was an appropriate moral response, such as temperance in response to sensual desire or courage in response to feelings of threat.

During the eighteenth century, Immanuel Kant worked on some major ethical questions. Considered by many to be the greatest modern moral philosopher, he began a revolution in ethics which is still being felt in the twentieth century (167). Kant's most important propositions, and the ones now widely studied, include the following: to be morally worthy, an action must be done from duty; acts are considered worthy not because of their results but because of what produced them; duty is necessary when an act is done out of respect for law (169). Auguste Comte emerged in the nineteenth century as not only the father of sociology, but as an ethician. His concern was for the "collective being," for humanity. His is an humanitarian ethics, which has "love for principle, order for basic, and progress for end" (223). In the early twentieth century, John Dewey, America's best known ethician, wrote a series of books on ethics. His is a naturalistic, pragmatic ethic. For him, every moral situation is unique and cannot be resolved by appealing to some abstract moral law (268).

Clearly, these various approaches to morality are conflicting and confusing in their variation. Moreover, these represent only some of the major thinkers in the field. In more recent years, the debate has turned from the question of what morality is to that of whose morality. Carol Gilligan began the discussion by disputing the findings of Lawrence Kohlberg, her former teacher. Kohlberg built his theories on those of Piaget, but also on those of Dewey and Kant. His studies of boys between the ages of ten and sixteen confirmed for him that the level of a child's moral development is dependent on age. Developing in six stages, children acquire their moral sense independently and not simply through learning standards set by adults. Identifying the first and most important moral virtue as justice, Kohlberg places moral development within a "stages" framework, each stage bringing with it better and more effective ways to resolve issues of justice (xii–xiv). His is a universal and nonrelative conception of morality, with moral virtue always in the same form no matter what the time or place (xxix).

In *The Education Feminism Reader*, Gilligan is critical of Kohlberg on several counts. Her primary criticism, however, centers on his perception of women as lacking in moral development, since they are locked at his third stage, that of relationships (36). She finds major fault in the way Kohlberg structures his studies, using only boys from the United States and then universalizing their experiences. In essence, she finds fault with Kohlberg's equating male development with child development and male moral development with moral development.

Gilligan's investigation of the moral development of women led her to findings that were quite different from those of Kohlberg. Her essay in *Mapping the Moral Domain* discusses these findings (Prologue). Conducting studies with both male and female participants, questions were asked of them that elicited responses based on their own experiences. Analyses of those responses led Gilligan to conclude that women, on the whole, are interested in relationships, not in rules. Because of this, according to Gilligan, women and girls base their moral decisions on the relationships they have with others, not on abstract principles of right and wrong. She, along with Jane Attanucci, argue that there is a relationship between "moral orientation and gender such that both men and women use both orientations, but Care Focus dilemmas are more likely to be presented by women and Justice Focus dilemmas by men" (82).

In subsequent studies, Gilligan concluded that the people who participated in the various studies were concerned with issues of both justice and relationships of care. But when decisions were made in resolving moral conflict, the person made that decision based on one or the other, justice or care, not both (xviii). She describes two voices that emerge in resolving moral issues: "one speaks of connection, not hurting, care, and response; and one speaks of equality, reciprocity, justice, and rights" (8). Gilligan finds that there are basically two moral principles. The first involves not treating others unfairly and the second involves helping others in need (73).

Other feminist voices have contributed to this debate on gender and moral development. Nel Noddings maintains that the language of ethics has traditionally and historically been discussed through the voice of the father and that the voice of the mother has been silent (1). While the father has spoken in terms of justice and fairness, the mother has said nothing. She argues that any moral virtue must now be viewed within the context of caring, the mother's voice (96). In fact, Noddings sees this feminine voice as far superior to that of the masculine voice.

In presenting these arguments, there was no intention to enter the debate, only to provide a framework for discussion of the moral dilemmas faced by the young adult characters in the books selected for this chapter. This framework, however, does reject abstract ethics and emphasizes an ethic that allows young people to behave "well" in the day-to-day problems they face. In assessing this "behaving well" behavior, morality is seen as vastly complex, with race, class, culture, and gender influencing how one morally acts. Thus, this framework incorporates an ethic of justice with that of care, recognizing that no situation is ever clear cut, but almost always ambiguous, and using care as the foundation ethic. Characters are judged against criteria created by Rita Manning (89–114), who looks at how well people function in seven care situations: caring for the helpless, caring for the relatively helpless, caring for peers, caring for family, caring for friends, caring for enemies, and caring in conflict. Using MacIntyre's contention that the classical philosophers and philosophies functioned within their own cultures, moral values no less so, a morality based on care and justice are values well suited to this society. However, in no way is this position a bow to relativism, for these ethics, those of care and justice, exist in some form in all societies. They should form the foundation for any society, and, as such, they should be valued and nurtured in those young people who live in this particular society.

The following young adult books demonstrate these care and justice values in a number of ways. These books were chosen, for the most part, because they make the reader wonder what he or she might do in situations such as the ones described in the books. They force readers to think about how they should treat other people and about what it really means to be both fair and caring. These books, through the exploration of friendship and self-esteem, examine what it means to be a friend, to be honest, to be fair, to be a community.

In *Staying Fat for Sarah Byrnes*, the author, Chris Crutcher, explores the nature of friendship. What is a healthy friendship? How does one show friendship? How far does one person go to befriend another? He examines the very complex nature of friendship by placing it within the context of caring. Eric Calhoune cares very deeply for his best friend, Sarah Byrnes. Yet, Sarah Byrnes is a very unlovable and, quite frequently, unfriendly person. She is often mean tempered, angry, and hostile to everyone around her, including Eric. She is psychologically and emotionally closed off from other people; yet, Eric is the only person she has allowed into her life, but just barely. Sarah Byrnes is psychologically scarred, but she is also horribly physically scarred. Her face is a mass of scars, incurred as a toddler, when her father deliberately burned her.

Eric is the only person in school who shows Sarah kindness, but he too has problems. He is fat and, as a result, has few friends. Sarah and Eric cling to each other for comfort and for protection. Where Eric is shy and reticent, Sarah is forceful and vocal. Where Eric hangs back and follows, Sarah comes forward and leads. They complement each other, this odd couple. But through swimming, Eric begins to meet other people, to gain other friends, and, most importantly, to lose weight. When this happens, Sarah begins to turn away from Eric and to turn into herself. In a desperate effort to preserve their friendship, Eric eats not to become thin, but to remain fat. He believes he owes her something and acknowledges his debt to her when he remembers their times together:

> . . . thinking of those days long ago when I held onto Sarah Byrnes like the only life raft in truly tempestuous, treacherous seas. She pushed her scars directly into our tormentors' faces, while I disappeared into my cottage cheese carcass like a scared turtle in a soft shell, watching her wage our war of the outcasts alone. (31)

Because Eric is not burdened with the kind of physical disadvantages that Sarah faces, he has more opportunities available to him. But he is determined to maintain his relationship with her by attempting to include her in the things that he does:

> I made it my life's resolution to refuse any invitation that excluded Sarah Byrnes. Even though she rarely agreed to go anywhere with me, when I brought her name up, if one nose crinkled, I uninvited myself on the spot. (68)

Eric realizes that Sarah needs his friendship and that she needs his help in breaking free from her abusive father. To do this, he goes to see her regularly in the hospital when she has a kind of emotional breakdown. He pries and probes and discovers the secret that Sarah has been keeping for so long, that her father burned her. He enlists other responsible people to help

Sarah. He even puts himself at physical risk by confronting her enraged father. All this Eric does because he cares for Sarah. At no time does he turn his back on her, and there were times when he could easily have done so.

But Eric's relationship with Sarah is unusual. In their school environment, no one else has gone out of his or her way to befriend her. Most looked away when she came near. Others no longer noticed her or even wondered about her and her life. Except for Eric, she was truly alone. Only Eric's friend, Ellerby, an iconoclast and a minister's son, seems to acknowledge this as a moral issue, and he does it in a classroom discussion:

> My subject will be shame. . . . I was embarrassed that I didn't know her [Sarah] better, that I ever laughed at one joke about her. I was embarrassed that I let some kid go to school with me for twelve years and turned my back on pain that must be unbearable. I was embarrassed that I hadn't found a way to include her somehow the way that Mobe [Eric] has. (62)

As a result of Eric's caring, Sarah is saved from the miserable life she led, and she is essentially saved by Eric. In the end, Sarah recognizes what Eric has done for her:

> And then there's you. When we were younger I kept you around because you were an easy friend. And it's only been since I got here, since that girl hugged me, that I figured out if I have a chance it'll be because I let somebody like me. You saved me, Eric. (130)

Certainly, most young adult readers will never encounter so dramatic a situation. What they will encounter are people, fellow students, who are different from them, who are handicapped in some way. What is the reaction when a young person is white in a predominately white school and community and encounters a black or Asian student in his or her midst? What happens when a young person is physically sound and encounters a student who is deformed physically, emotionally, or intellectually? These are situations that most young people experience daily. What is their response? Do they turn a deaf ear to suffering in those immediately around them or do they attempt to bring comfort to those who need it? These are all moral issues involving care for other people. Eric was faced with the moral dilemma of how and when to care for another human being, and he acquitted himself well. But what if Eric had not been fat and himself socially disadvantaged? Ellerby faced that question and was ashamed of what he learned about himself and his fellow students. No one had cared enough about Sarah Byrnes to get to know her or to even speak to her, despite years of seeing her in the halls and in classes. Somehow the ethic of care, an ethic central to this book, had broken down in Sarah's school and in her community.

Stephen Hoffius in *Winners and Losers* looks at the ethic of care within the context of friendship, just as Crutcher did, but explores what happens when no one is willing or able to act on that ethic. Daryl Wagner is a wonderful athlete, the top half-miler in his school and possibly in his division. His best friend is Curtis, also an athlete, but seen always in Daryl's shadow. Daryl Wagner has it all, popularity, a beautiful girlfriend, and an excellent academic record. His future is exceptionally bright. His father, however, is demanding and critical, often pushing Daryl beyond his physical and mental endurance. This is no more evident than when Daryl collapses during a track meet from a rare heart ailment. His athletic future now in doubt, his father turns his attentions to Daryl's friend, Curtis. Now Curtis has it all—a new girlfriend, new friends—he is big man on campus. And although he often resents the treatment he receives from Daryl's father, he relishes his newfound life:

> You're number one now . . . Just like you've always wanted. . . . Now it's your turn to shine. . . . Daryl could have won the conference before this happened. Now you can. (19)

No one seems to give Daryl much thought. True, he seems at first to be adjusting to life without athletics, but he desperately wants and needs his father's approval and attention. Curtis has that, and the only way Daryl feels he can regain that approval is to once again run track, even if it means risking his life.

Curtis never talks to Daryl about how he feels about himself, about his illness, or about his father. Much is left unsaid between them. Where Curtis could have spoken out, where he could have made a difference, he remains silent and takes no action. In place of care and concern, there is rivalry and competition. When Curtis's father enlists the aid of both Curtis and Daryl in shingling a house being built for the poor, Curtis, reluctant to go in the first place, sees the activity they both engage in as a kind of race:

> He [Daryl] had always been a better everything than me. Once Mr. Wagner had said to me, 'Somebody's got to win every race, and somebody's got to lose . . .' I was the loser at shingling. But at least, I realized, I was now better at *something* than he was. I was a better half-miler . . . (71)

Unlike Sarah Byrnes, Daryl does not get a second chance at life. He is neither enabled or empowered to find out a truth about himself, a truth that can stop his fall. He practices for the big meet, begins to gradually run well, and finally is back to his old form. But in the final race, leading in that race, he collapses and dies. As his friend, Curtis had some responsibility to Daryl, yet he abdicated that responsibility and the results were deadly. Daryl was left to wrestle with his demons alone.

Eric Calhoune had little to lose by maintaining his friendship with Sarah. He was already an outcast. But what about Curtis? He had always secretly coveted what Daryl had. When all that Daryl had was given to Curtis by none other than Daryl's own father, this was hard to resist. Few could have withstood the external and internal pressures that were at work on Curtis. Blind to the danger, he allowed Daryl's father to coach him and all of his time to be consumed by track. He seems to have given the matter little thought. Most of all, he did not think about the effect of his actions on Daryl.

It is only when Daryl dies in his arms, does Curtis seem to realize what has happened. Yet, it is not clear that even then he sees his role in the drama. Curtis is guilty of not being a good friend, of allowing envy to get in the way of friendship, of seeing his best friend as a competitor, and of not practicing an ethic of care. Daryl might have been helped by his friend, might have wanted that help, despite an aloof and disinterested facade. In turning a deaf ear and blind eye to Daryl, Curtis contributed to his death.

How many friendships are built on competition and on

rivalry? Far too many. Hoffius shows the underside of friend-ship, the side lacking an ethic of care. Certainly this is a dra-matic situation, and few young adults will have to face this kind of situation. Yet, it is not a highly unusual situation—an excel-lent athlete, at the top of his or her form, must decide to compete or not to compete because of a life-threatening illness. We've seen the headlines announcing the shocking death of an athlete in his or her prime, dead because they chose to gamble with their lives.

In *Heart of a Champion*, Carl Deuker uses baseball as a meta-phor for life. This is another story centering around a friendship, that of Seth Barham and Jimmy Winter, both talented baseball players. Jimmy Winter, however, is a baseball fanatic, willing to do almost anything to play. Seth is more introspective, more willing to see life beyond the playing field. Jimmy takes his tal-ent for granted, thinks he should be given special privileges because of that talent. He is reckless, staying out late at night drinking, and frequently driving far too fast for his own good. He is also a selfish player, seeing himself as the center of his high school team. Seth, on the other hand, sees effort and dedi-cation as important in his life. He is willing to work for what he has:

> I was afraid that if I backed off on the schoolwork, I might start backing off on hard ground balls. I might start stepping in the bucket on inside fastballs. I was afraid if I didn't go all out in everything, I wouldn't go all out in anything. (62)

Seth does not lie, and he abhors cheating. He is kind and car-ing, even comforting a cocker spaniel that has been hit by a car. Yet, recognizing that his friend Jimmy is making some serious mistakes, he does nothing to help him. He knows that Jimmy drinks heavily, but he never confronts him on this, even joining him at least once in his drunkenness. Seth is hard on himself, holding himself to very high standards, but he never sees the need to hold his friend to the same high standards. When Jimmy takes two champagne bottles from his father's wedding to drink, Seth says nothing, does not even think to say anything. In fact, he and Jimmy both get drunk that night. When Jimmy asks Seth to write a paper for him so that he will not fail a course, Seth does it, choosing not to see any harm in this act.

In effect, Seth abdicates any and all responsibility for Jimmy and Jimmy's acts. He calls himself Jimmy's friend, but he does not act as a friend should. He is tolerant of everything Jimmy does, hoping things will work out. Of course, they do not. Jimmy is killed one night in a one-car accident, having run into a tree at a high rate of speed while drunk. Here again is the underbelly of friendship. But this book does pose two very critical ethical questions for its young readers: What is the nature of friendship? What are the responsibilities of one friend toward another?

In an ethic of care, a friend would not stand idly by and watch a friend make life-threatening mistakes. A friend would not allow another friend to draw him or her into cheating. A friend would reach out to a friend, attempting to learn what problems the friend has. A friend would not be put off by a friend's weakness and vulnerability. None of these things happened in *Heart of a Champion*. Friendship, the right kind, can make a difference. Sarah Byrnes might have been destroyed emotionally and psychologically had she not enjoyed Eric's friendship.

Out of Control by Norma Fox Mazer explores both the ethic of care and the ethic of justice. Valerie Michon, an outspoken, artistically talented young woman, is assaulted by three football heroes. She is not raped, but she is terrorized and physically groped by the three young men in their high school hallway. For her, this is a terrible experience; yet, the young men, with the exception of Roland Wingate, feel they have done nothing wrong.

For the most part, the school administration agrees with the boys and wants to sweep the incident under the rug, but Valerie is supported by some of the other young women in the school who have had similar experiences. Together they form a mutual support system. Julian Briggers and Kevin Candrella act as if nothing major has happened. Only Roland experiences confusion, shame, and remorse.

Roland has done something he deeply regrets because of his concept of friendship. Because he does not know who he is or what he wants, he accepts anything. He goes along with the flow. Whatever his friends decide is all right with him:

> I love that word. You can just . . . say it. Drawl it out. And the moment you do, you can relax. You don't have to choose: Candy or Brig. You don't have to decide if you want cheese pizza or pizza with sausage, if you want to go swimming or play racquet-ball, if you want to see a movie or rent a video. You don't have to think about anything. You don't have to think about . . . her. You don't have to figure out if what you did was right or wrong. You can just sort of blank your mind and go . . . *whatever*. (6–7)

This is the attitude that gets Roland Wingate into moral trouble, the one that does not question his friends or their friendship, the one that allows him to infringe on the rights of another person, and the one that absolves him of any sense of responsibility for any of his actions. For him, doing what his friends do is friendship, not thinking for himself is friendship, and having fun is friendship:

> The thing is, you're not thinking, even if on one level you know what you're doing isn't right. The thing is, there's something in you that's saying don't think about it . . . so you don't, and that's easy, because you don't want to think about it, anyway, you don't want to say something and be a jerk, you just want to do what your friends are doing. So you do it. (146)

Being with those you like and who like you is one level of friendship, but it is not the cornerstone of friendship. Friendship that excludes an ethic of care and an ethic of justice, as Roland's friendship with Candy and Brig does, is not true friendship. Their friendship allowed them to terrorize Valerie Michon and to lie about the incident. Their friendship allowed them to delude themselves into thinking that Valerie was overreacting and exaggerating what really happened. Their friendship allowed them to believe that because they were who they were, they could do anything they wanted.

Only Roland Wingate sees what they have done as wrong. He is both surprised and shocked by his own actions, and seeks to make amends to Valerie by calling her to apologize. He wants desperately to make everything as it once was, but that can never be. Roland Wingate is the moral battleground in *Out of*

Control. His struggle is with what is right and wrong, good and evil, and he comes up short. The principal of the school has a struggle also, but his is not much of one, since his is the way of political expediency. Where his struggle should have been with justice, what is fair and unfair, he takes the easy way out. Among those in the wider school community, feelings and reactions are mixed. A few young women, some of whom did not really know Valerie Michon before the incident, come to her support. They do this because they empathize with her plight or they have had a similar experience. They create a small, but powerful community of care, but one that is also quick to point up both the injustice of the attack and its unjust resolution by the school administration.

Twelve Days in August by Liza Ketchum Murrow is another book for young adults that treats the ethics of both care and justice. Alex Beekman and his twin sister Rita are new kids in town from California. Alex is a phenomenal soccer player, whose skill and talent is a threat to Randy Tovitch, the school's soccer star. Because Randy cannot hope to compete with Alex on the field, he conspires with the other players to keep Alex out of key plays, and in the process taunts and picks fights with him. Finally, he spreads the rumor that Alex is gay.

The other players on the team have no problem with treating Alex unfairly, and they stand idly by while Alex is verbally and physically attacked by Randy. But it is Todd O'Connor who has the power to change things for Alex. Because he is respected by the others, he can do this by becoming Alex's friend and treating him as he would treat any other of his friends. He does not do this, despite his attraction to Alex's sister. Because Todd does not want to be labeled gay by his teammates, he attempts to avoid Alex when he can and remains silent about the treatment Alex is receiving from Randy and the rest of the team.

Todd takes a morally neutral stance in the book, and it is only through the urgings of Craig, the only black player on the team, that he begins to feel some sense of responsibility for what is going on. Murrow implies that there is no neutral ground, that to be neutral is in reality to side with evil and injustice. But Todd feels that he is fine morally because he never called Alex a "fag," that he never treated him unkindly, and that all he wants to do is play soccer. Craig, however, sees the situation a little differently:

> Craig pointed to the chain-link fence behind the bleachers, separating the field from the parking lot. 'See that fence there? You think you can sit on it, not taking sides, hoping if you don't take a stand, everything will work out fine.' He clenched his fists. 'But it doesn't work that way. There's no place in the middle.' (103)

Sometimes caring means that you have to take a stand, as Craig has done. Perhaps being black has made him more sensitive to the issue of being different and the price one pays for it:

> Todd asks, 'What *about* Alex. Do you think he is a fag?' Craig stared at me, then scrambled to his feet. 'What if he is? I don't give a damn, and you shouldn't either. . . . Calling Alex a fag might be like calling me nigger.' (103)

Todd's problem is that he fears what he does not know. He does not know or care about anyone who is gay, or so he thinks, so he is indifferent, even callous, toward Alex. It is only when he learns that his own uncle is gay that he begins to change. Even his younger sister is more aware than he:

> 'You're not very nice to Alex, you know' . . . 'Alex is all right,' I mumbled. . . . 'So how come you make fun of him—along with everyone else?' 'I don't . . . I'm just—' (171)

A care ethic dictates that one cannot be neutral, cannot sit on the fence when another human being is being unfairly treated. An ethic of justice dictates that one must not stand by while the rights of others are being abrogated. Yet, in this instance Alex has no one to support him except his sister and Craig. But they do not have the same standing in the community as does Todd. It is Todd who has standing by right of respect, and as such, he has power. He chooses not to use that power because he doesn't recognize it for what it is. He remains silent when he should speak out. He feels himself to be merely "one of the boys," but sometimes being one of the boys is not enough. Todd is guilty of not taking a stand and of being morally irresponsible.

Just as Murrow relates issues of care and justice to bigotry against gays, Marsha Qualey relates these same issues to bigotry against Native Americans. *Revolutions of the Heart* takes place in Summer, Wisconsin, predominately white, but with a sizable Cree population. It is Cory Knutson who sets the moral tone in this story of young love, family ties, community, and racism.

Seventeen-year-old Cory meets and falls in love with a young Cree Indian at a powwow. Until that moment, although literally surrounded by Native American students in her high school, she has never really thought much about them, in fact, has never really seen them:

> She realized that not long ago it was as if they were invisible to her, people who were there but not seen. Now she couldn't help but look surreptitiously, fascinated with the faces, body types, and, especially the varied palette of skin colors. (53)

Cory's mother sounds the initial alarm when she points out bigotry in a town Cory thought was free of it: "The bigotry. Where does it come from? Is it possible people are born with hate?" These are interesting questions which neither Cory nor her mother can answer. But Cory's mother, unlike Cory, has Cree friends and is more open to interacting with them than many of the other residents in Summer.

When Cory's mother becomes seriously ill, and money is needed for a heart transplant, the town comes together to raise the much needed funds. Cory views the group as basically good, concerned people, who cannot be criticized for anything. But a friend takes a different tack, saying, "Maybe so, but they all live separately. Look around. This is the first integrated event I've seen since I moved here" (50). So the town is separated, divided, not a true community at all, at least not in the sense of its residents living together in close, friendly association, or in fellowship. And it becomes even more divided when the Crees and whites in the town clash over fishing rights. With the introduction of the traditional rights of Native Americans versus the rights of the larger white society, the moral questions asked in this book are stretched to encompass not only those of care, but also those of justice.

In time, Cory comes to know and care about one Cree Indian. Through that one, she comes to see other Native Americans in a different light. In fact, she is now quite literally able to see them, where once they were all but invisible. Before Mrs. Knutson's death, she talked to Cory about what a change of heart can accomplish, explaining, "Change a heart, you change the world. But doing it one heart at a time is the best you can hope for" (64). Cory changed her heart, embraced an ethic of care, and began to see the unfair ways Native Americans were treated. Through her change of heart, she began to care about what happens to one Cree Indian, then to care about what happens to the many Cree Indians in her community. They, through her change of heart, became a part of her community, a community, we can only hope, governed by both care and justice.

Thus far, the discussion has gradually moved from young adult books involving individual acts of care and justice to a discussion of those young adult books with community as a locus of these ethics. *Toning the Sweep*, by Angela Johnson, looks at an ethic of care within an individual, fourteen-year-old Emily, but also within the context of a community. And what a community it is. Ola, Emily's grandmother, lives in California on the edge of a desert. She loves the desert and the ragtag group of people who have shared this place with her for thirty years. Ola herself is black, but there are Native Americans, whites, the young, and the old. They are all different, some even strange, but they share two things, a love of the desert and a love and concern for each other. *Toning the Sweep* is two stories in one. It is the story, movingly told, of the efforts of Emily and her mother, Diane, to accept the imminent death of Ola from cancer. The second deals with Diane's efforts to work through the pain of the tragic and violent death of her father many years ago. Both resolutions take place in this one desert community over the course of a few weeks.

Emily and her mother are in the desert to take Ola home with them to Ohio. This task is painful for all of them, but there is joy here too and reconciliation. Yet, it is the community, this community in the desert, that provides the care and support that Ola and her family so desperately need. In the time it takes Ola to pack her belongings and dispose of the things she has accumulated, the community has wrapped her and her daughter and granddaughter in a blanket of love, reminiscences, and warm memories. They have showered each with a special kind of love, a love that makes what is happening and will happen much more bearable.

This desert community is full of characters who know when and how to laugh and to enjoy life, no matter what the situation:

> In the living room now they are finishing each other's sentences and slapping their legs when the talk gets too funny. . . . Ruth leans against Ola and they about fall over laughing. Everything explodes into laughter. Ola lies down on the floor. Mama and Martha lean against each other and snort. But the aunts . . . the aunts lose every bit of control they have and roll across the floor. (42)

They are close-knit, this group of people, taking in orphans, and caring for the sick and dispossessed. No one has very much money, but each is rich in other ways. They have learned to share themselves and to support one another. True, they may all be eccentrics, but they are all good-hearted and kind. There is, first of all, Martha Jackson, Ola's best friend, who takes in home-less children. There is David Two Starr, Emily's friend. There is Roland, an artist, who has carved a beautiful house, full of lush green plants, out of the desert sand. There is Miss Sally Hirt, who runs the local general store. And there are Margaret Title and the aunts. All are Ola's friends. All have formed one, solid community on the outskirts of a harsh desert.

Years ago, Ola escaped to this California desert from Ala-bama, when her husband was gunned down in his car for being an "uppidy nigger." Neither she nor her daughter have ever quite gotten over the loss. Diane is still tortured by the murder of her father, and, on some deep level, resents her mother for having left Alabama for such a desolate place. Yet, all three women are engulfed and cleansed by this desert community, a community that seems to have unlocked the secret of caring for one another through laughter, empathy, and love.

Two books by Jacqueline Woodson, *Between Madison and Pal-metto* and *Maizon at Blue Hill* look at what can happen when a young person moves from a community that exemplifies an ethic of care to one where that ethic is missing. The main charac-ter in both books is Maizon Singh, a black seventh grader, who lives in Brooklyn, New York, in a tight-knit, caring community.

In *Maizon at Blue Hill*, Maizon moves from that community to an elite, boarding school for girls, where an ethic of care is not so evident. In one community, Maizon is surrounded by friends and family, people who love her and wish her well, with no strings attached. These are people who accept Maizon for what she is and for what she will become. Maizon knows that she belongs here and that this is her home, even telling her best friend Margaret that "none of them—Ms. Dell, your mom, my grandma, Li'l Jay, even Cooper and Hattie—none of them would ever let anything happen to us."

Nevertheless, Maizon's grandmother makes the decision to send Maizon to Blue Hill. She must leave the only place she's ever known and go to another state, to a school other than Baldwin Prep. The results are disastrous, not because the people at Blue Hill are particularly malicious or bigoted, but because Maizon is not prepared to enter so alien an environment, where care, the kind she's always known is so obviously lacking. There is a distance between Maizon and the people she encounters at Blue Hill, a distance created by race, culture, and class:

> 'Maizon?' Sandy nearly whispered. 'Why do you have to think about it [racism] all the time?' I shook my head and brushed her hand away. 'You don't understand, Sandy. And I can't explain it to you.'
>
> Sandy sighed and walked back to her bed. It felt like there were a million miles between us. But the miles weren't about distance, they were about knowledge and experience and pain. (103)

Taken from her home and familiar surroundings, Maizon isolates herself, rejecting those who offer her friendship or counsel. She is confused and lonely, seeing everyone as a racist. Maizon spends one very miserable semester at Blue Hill, wrestling with her own internal demons, finally getting relief only when she decides to leave Blue Hill and return to Brooklyn.

Blue Hill is not able to provide Maizon with the emotional supports she needs. It tries, but its ethic of care is hollow and forced, and by its very nature, artificial, compared with what Maizon has experienced in her own community. Sometimes the best intentions will not suffice when the only things needed are the warmth and care of home. Sometimes, there really is no place like home. This too is an ethical issue, and care is central to this ethic.

In *Others See Us*, William Sleator poses an ethical question similar to the one posed by Glaucon in Plato's *Republic* (359–360). Both want to know how a person would act if that person knew he or she could do wrong with impunity. Glaucon, in a challenge to Socrates, describes what happens when a lowly shepherd discovers the secret of invisibility and uses that power, not for good, but to murder, plunder, and seize power from the king. Glaucon used that story to prove his contention that people will do evil if they know they will not be discovered and punished. Several characters in *Others See Us* fall into a toxic waste swamp and acquire the power to read minds. Annelise, the relative who is clearly a sociopath, uses the power for evil. But in the cases of Grandma, Jared, and Lindie, the situation is not so clear. Sleator leaves the reader wondering what kind of woman Grandma really is and what Jared and Lindie will do with this terrible "gift."

The overarching ethical question, however, is the issue of care. Where was that ethic in this summer community of relatives and friends? Unfortunately, it did not exist, thereby allowing an atmosphere of envy and rancor to fester, grow, and tear that community apart. That small community was ripe for the havoc those mind-reading, toxic dump mutants created. When care is weak in any community, terrible things can, and usually do, happen.

Lois Lowry's *The Giver* represents the ultimate end of any community that does not value a care or justice ethic, that places lack of strife above all else. This future society has no need for care or justice because its residents no longer feel normal human emotions. Their emotions have been dulled by drugs and deadened by an inhuman regimentation, which the people gladly accept. This is a society where the word "love" is obsolete, where babies are murdered at birth and the old when they become useless. This is a society where the concepts of love, warmth, and care are vague memories, held in the head of the man called the Giver, the one person assigned the task of remembering for the entire society. The society is, as a result, a cold and sterile community, what a place without care ultimately becomes.

The books chosen for this chapter are few in number and are meant to be merely representative of books for young adults that present some type of moral dilemma. Many more books could have been selected. For that matter, a completely different kind of book could easily have been chosen. The results would have been the same, however, for so frequently overlooked is the undeniable fact that all fiction, whatever the genre, has an ethical core and takes an ethical position. This is not to say that this ethical position is explicit; often it is not. Nevertheless, each reader, on some level, is able to determine what is morally wrong and what is morally right, even morally reprehensible in a book.

Frequently, writers take a morally neutral position. This is true of Peter Dickinson in *Eva*. Here, the situation described by Dickinson is heavy with moral overtones; yet, he merely describes them. The reader is left to take his or her own position. The same is true of Thomas Baird's *Smart Rats*. The protagonist in this story commits murder twice, one victim being his younger sister, and compounds this by piling up other misdeeds. Again, readers are left to draw their own conclusions. But in the drawing of these conclusions, an intellectual and emotional struggle has to take place within the reader. The evoking of this struggle is the strength of these books. In *The Drowning of Stephan Jones*, Bette Greene takes a clear and explicit moral position. She is an advocate of fairness and care and a denouncer of hate and intolerance. The same can be said of all the works of Mildred Taylor. Because the author does not take a clear moral position does not in any way mean that the book does not have a moral point. All books do.

What this all means is that books, all books, that young adults read have power. Their power rests in their ability to sway and to change the reader in so many ways, not the least of these is morally. These books can create a moral sense in the young by demonstrating what is morally right and what is morally wrong. They can raise and resolve ethical issues. The reader may not agree with each resolution, but is certainly forced to think about issues he or she may never have thought about before.

To use an ethical framework of care and justice is yet another critical approach to young adult novels. The ways of knowing available to young people must not exclude the ways of knowing that ethics provides. Our youth are too valuable a national commodity to miss any opportunity to expose them to a morality that will help guide them in an ever changing society and world.

WORKS CITED

Baird, Thomas. *Smart Rats*. New York: Harper, 1990.

Berger, Peter, and Thomas Luckmann. *The Social Construction of Reality*. New York: Doubleday, 1966.

Booth, Wayne C. *The Company We Keep: An Ethics of Fiction*. Berkeley: U of California P, 1988.

Bourke, Vernon J. *History of Ethics*. Garden City: Doubleday, 1968.

Crutcher, Chris. *Staying Fat for Sarah Byrnes*. New York: Greenwillow, 1993.

Damon, William. *The Moral Child: Nurturing Children's Moral Growth*. New York: Free P, 1988.

Day, James. "The Moral Audience: On the Narrative Mediation of Moral 'Judgment' and Moral 'Action.'" *Narrative and Storytelling: Implications for Understanding Moral Development*. Ed. Mark Tappan and Martin Packer. New York: Jossey, 1991. 27–42.

Deuker, Carl. *Heart of a Champion*. Boston: Little, 1993.

Dickinson, Peter. *Eva*. New York: Dell, 1988.

Frankena, William K. *Ethics*. Englewood Cliffs: Prentice, 1963.

Gardner, John. *On Moral Fiction*. New York: Basic, 1978.

Gergen, Kenneth. *The Saturated Self: Dilemmas of Identity in Contemporary Life*. New York: Basic, 1991.

Gilligan, Carol. Prologue. *Mapping the Moral Domain*. Ed. Carol Gilligan, et al. Cambridge: Center for the Study of Gender, Education and Human Development, 1988.

_____, and Jane Attanucci. "Two Moral Orientations." *Mapping the Moral Domain*. Ed. Carol Gilligan, et al. Cambridge: Center for the Study of Gender, Education and Human Development, 1988. 73–86.

_____. "Women's Place in Man's Life Cycle." *The Education Feminism Reader*. Ed. Lynda Stone. New York: Routledge, 1994. 26–41.

Greene, Bette. *The Drowning of Stephan Jones*. New York: Bantam, 1991.

Hoffius, Stephen. *Winners and Losers*. New York: Simon, 1993.

Iser, Wolfgang. *The Act of Reading: A Theory of Aesthetic Response*. Baltimore: Johns Hopkins U P, 1978.

Johnson, Angela. *Toning the Sweep*. New York: Scholastic, 1993.

Kilpatrick, William. *Why Johnny Can't Tell Right from Wrong*. New York: Simon, 1992.

Kohlberg, Lawrence. *The Philosophy of Moral Development: Moral Stages and the Idea of Justice.* New York: Harper, 1981.

Lowry, Lois. *The Giver.* Boston: Houghton, 1993.

MacIntyre, Alasdair. *After Virtue: A Study in Moral Theory.* West Bend: U of Notre Dame P, 1984.

Manning, Rita. *Speaking from the Heart: A Feminist Perspective on Ethics.* Lanham: Rowman, 1992.

Mazer, Norma Fox. *Out of Control.* New York: Morrow, 1993.

Murrow, Liza Ketchum. *Twelve Days in August.* New York: Holiday, 1993.

Noddings, Nel. *Caring: A Feminist Approach to Ethics and Moral Education.* Berkeley: U of California P, 1984.

Piaget, Jean. *The Moral Judgment of the Child.* Trans. Marjorie Gabain. New York: Free P, 1965.

Plato, *The Republic of Plato in Ten Books.* Trans. H. Spears. New York: Dent, 1908.

Qualey, Marsha. *Revolutions of the Heart.* Boston: Houghton, 1993.

Rosenblatt, Louise. *Literature as Exploration.* New York: The Modern Language Association of America, 1983.

Sleator, William. *Others See Us.* New York: Dutton, 1993.

Tappan, Mark. "Narrative, Authorship and the Development of Moral Authority." *Narrative and Storytelling: Implications for Understanding Moral Development.* Ed. Mark Tappan and Martin Packer. New York: Jossey, 1991. 5–25.

Woodson, Jacqueline. *Between Madison and Palmetto.* New York: Delacorte, 1993.

_____. *Maizon at Blue Hill.* New York: Delacorte, 1992.

CHAPTER NINE

Greybeards and Grannies: Pariahs of Young Adult Fiction

B. Elizabeth Mina

Despite the fact that nearly 11% of all Americans are now considered elderly, modern authors of young adult fiction have had real trouble in presenting representative numbers of older characters in their books for ten- to eighteen-year-old readers. And when these writers do introduce the elderly on their pages, they often demonstrate a real dilemma in deciding how to portray this rapidly increasing group of greybeards and grannies. Perhaps one of the reasons for this bewildering situation is that adolescents tend, at least on the surface level, to be absorbed primarily in themselves, their peers and the unique and rich cultures they together keep creating and recreating around their lives. Young adult authors respond readily to this focus. But the overriding cause of the often wacky and bizarre ways in which older people are treated in this genre can probably be attributed to the fact that American society itself, and the writers who mirror it, are themselves perplexed about their feelings towards the elderly and their place in society.

The pervasively negative thoughts we have about the elderly are readily reflected in every-day advertisements, television shows, and newspaper cartoons. But society's thoughts here are probably best seen in a thesaurus, which gives us the words that we Americans characteristically use for all aspects of our society. Although some of these terms for older people, such as "venerable," are positive, the derogatory ones permeate the listings. Commonly listed are adjectives about older people such as decrepit, feeble, senile, withered, fossilized, doddering, time-worn, and stricken in years. Nouns are even more graphic; aged men are called geezers, codgers, old duffers, while elderly women are frumps, old hens, hags, old battle-axes. Together they are referred to as old fogies, fuddy-duddies, or even old stodges. The words evoke images of crabby, infirm, and inca-pacitated people stuck in old-fashioned and ineffective ways of life. American writers featuring elderly characters within any genre of literature can easily be influenced by this choice of words for older people as they echo society's thinking about them.

THE DILEMMA OF THE ADOLESCENT PSYCHE

If modern adult fiction produces a sharp-focused snapshot of today's culture within its volumes, then modern young adult fiction gives us a zoom lens with which to take intricately detailed close-up pictures of the psyche of adolescents. Honing in on an introspective and confusing time of transition from childhood to adulthood, these pieces of literature show up as relatively short, quick-read books written in the first person about problem-oriented situations. Sometimes grim and almost maudlin in content, plots have increasingly centered on adoles-cents involved in the worst possible experiences life has to offer: physical abuse, death, mental illness, drug dependency, disabili-ties, divorce of their parents, and incest. The pattern in these books is for the storyline to ignore most adults, or present them as incompetent, unhelpful, hypocritical, or even harmful, echo-ing the disdain teenagers often express for their elders. Genera-tional conflict is alive and well, as it has been through the ages. So the question is: Why should older people, as adults, and as adults two generations apart, be treated any differently in fiction for adolescents?

Part of the reasoning behind this enigma lies in the efforts that young adult writers make to present books of a crisis-intervention nature that are both believable to the adolescents who read them and emotionally stimulating at the same time. Considering that essential components of the enjoyability factor of any fiction work are the offering of escapism along with a disregard for what the readers consider to be unimportant issues, authors for teenagers quite successfully meet these goals. Escapism in fiction for adolescents comes through in carefully crafted blends of plots and characters that position the young protagonists—who in real life often have great feelings of impotency in regard to running their own lives—as autonomous in working out viable solutions to problems. And by leaving out references to concerns that most teenagers find trivial or boring, these books usually do not discuss the problems of young children or the intricacies of marital relationships, for example. Nor do macro-problems such as political upheavals or state economic crises figure into the formula either, unless, of course, these circumstances have a direct effect on the adolescent character's story.

Another topic dismissed as irrelevant by young adults is nearly any issue involving old people and their problems. Sociocultural changes in the United States, such as the isolation of the growing number of the elderly in retirement communities or nursing homes, have reduced the amount of daily contact youngsters of all ages have with older people, even though, paradoxically, there are more of them than ever before. A natural consequence is for adolescents to not even think of these elders as a recognizable group with its own unique problems. After all, if most teenagers fit the pattern of only seeing their grandparents once or twice a year for Thanksgiving and/or another holiday, it follows that their limited contact will spur a disregard for the aged. Adding to what seems to be a selective ignoring of older people is a common feeling amongst ten- to eighteen-year-olds that they themselves are immortal—and will never get old either. This distortion of reality is understandable when one thinks of it as a protective mechanism of the adolescent growing-up process, a process that requires inordinate amounts of energy to accomplish, even poorly. These youngsters frequently feel so incredibly overwhelmed with their own concerns that they have nothing left for investment in trying situations that they do not need to confront. In fact, often if teenagers actually do have to worry about extraordinary (and, to them, unnecessary) items in the midst of managing their own existences, their lives become that much more fragile and personally threatened.

This psychological self-absorbed predisposition of teenagers turns up in the pages of young adult fiction as one of the two main biases the genre exhibits toward older people: the almost complete absence of the elderly from many books in the genre. In her 1978 Master's Thesis "The Role of the Elderly Adult in Recent Young Adult Fiction," Janette Rutherford blamed their nonexistence in this genre on the then current emphasis on the nuclear family, which she said did not allow for teenagers to come in contact with many elderly individuals (1). Whether this notion is or was ever true is immaterial; what is important to note is that the phenomenon of absence has been maintained into the 1990s, with maybe only a quarter of young adult fiction books having even one minor elderly character in them. But perhaps the explanation as to why there are so few novels for any age reader about older people may simply have to do with the nature of the beast: Sven Birkerts in a 1994 *The New York Times Book Review* about an adult book featuring an elderly person explained it by saying, "Fiction has always been more about becoming than about being or ceasing to be" (12).

Related to this absence of older people in young adult fiction is the fleeting presentation of the elderly in insignificant character roles almost extraneous to the plot. One of the first studies to quantify this bias was a 1976 analysis by D.A. Peterson and E. L. Karnes, who examined older characters that appeared in all Newbery Medal books from the award's inception in 1922 through 1975. Representing the finest American books written for children of all ages each year, the 53 volumes were found to include a total of 159 older persons, but mostly as peripheral characters with no effect on the action (1). Although the researchers concluded that more positive than negative descriptions were made of the elderly in these particular books with virtually no age stereotypes promoted, there was also no attempt to deal with these characters on a real-life basis.

STEREOTYPING OF ELDERLY CHARACTERS

As distorting and damaging as the absence of older people in young adult literature may be, it is nothing compared to the second, and definitely more harmful portrayal of these characters in adolescent literature in a stereotypical fashion that pegs them as either eccentrics or incompetents. These older eccentrics are usually superheroes or villains capable of physically, emotionally, and economically ignoring the conventions of society and the realities of life. Although many of these portraits can be positive and even uplifting, eccentric characters presented so ludicrously as to be silly or entirely unbelievable are not beneficial to the story or to the image of older adults. Meanwhile, incompetent characters are nearly always very negative, painted as infirm, mentally incapacitated, or otherwise pathetic skeletons of human beings. Presentations of this latter type can be easily associated with and identified as ageism, or the discrimination against older people in the form of prejudicial stereotyping.

In the early days of young adult fiction at the turn of the century, just about every character that appeared in books created specifically for older children was a stereotyped portrayal of a human being. Part of the reason for this practice was the Victorian philosophy that these books existed primarily to provide moralistic lessons to guide readers through their tender growing-up years. Bad characters were totally evil, and their losses in life were always directly attributed to their devious ways. Likewise, good and honest people were rewarded for the fruits of their labors with respect, honor, happiness, and love. There were no shades of gray. The few authors who persisted in bucking tradition by creating fully-developed young characters and down-to-earth plots (Mark Twain with *The Adventures of Tom Sawyer* and *The Adventures of Huckleberry Finn* are notable exceptions) wrote the books that many today revere as true classics in the field. These non-preachy stories even featured prominent elderly characters in fairly representative numbers for their times, although their portraits were inarguably not always entirely flattering. The more traditional books of the times consistent with the old philosophy have largely been forgotten.

Reality and complexity did not hit the ranks of young adult books in a revolutionary way until the still controversial *Catcher in the Rye* by J. D. Salinger stormed onto the American scene in mid-century. Covering two days in the life of a sixteen-year-old boy who was severely depressed by the death of a younger brother, this novel chronicled the confusing experiences Holden Caulfield got himself into after he was expelled from his fourth prep school. The shock of exposing to possibly unsuspecting readers then that, yes, teenagers can become depressed and self-destructive and, in the process, act out in ways that flaunt societal conventions, started breaking down all manner of stereotypes about the coming-of-age process. Soon it became clear that books for adolescents with goody-goody one-sided protagonists in socially-acceptable plots with obvious moralistic lessons were a dying breed. Stories about girls preparing for high school proms as their defining life experiences and boys solving intricate mysteries and winning acclaim for their fantastic ventures began vanishing. Authors slowly began writing more about what was really happening in the lives of teenagers.

The breaking down of other stereotyped characters in this genre was only possible because of a corresponding opening up of American societal values in the 1960s and 1970s that culminated in unprecedented freedoms for many peoples. In banning discrimination based on a person's color, race, national origin, or religion, the Civil Rights Act of 1964 facilitated the path for young adult authors to begin producing books featuring individualistic characters of different racial, ethnic, and religious backgrounds. These types of books today constitute a substantial and popular chunk of the young adult fiction market, celebrating differences and pride in all aspects of multi-culturalism. At the same time, the fields of psychology and law were expanding the culture's understanding of the nature of deviance and crime, opening acceptance for the 1967 teen offering *The Outsiders* by S. E. Hinton, about a fourteen-year-old urban Texan boy, who witnessed several fatal shootings as part of gang activities. The feminist movement that gained strength around this same time led to the highlighting of stronger and more capable girl and women characters in young adult literature. More recently, the 1990 Americans with Disability Act prohibited discrimination against those with physical and mental handicaps, spurring another topic in adolescent fiction that is just starting to take off. (One book in this genre presaging the law is the 1988 *Probably Still Nick Swansen* by Virginia Euwer Wolff about a learning disabled boy in a special education class who yearned to be able to drive and be friends with non-disabled students in his high school.) Now it is nearly impossible to pick up a book at random when browsing in the young adult section of the public library that does not have at least a mention of some of these differences.

Meanwhile, civil rights for the elderly were achieved in the 1965 Older Americans Act after the birth and massive growth of a wide variety of lobbying groups ranging from the American Association of Retired People (AARP) and the then radical Gray Panthers. Equal opportunities for the elderly were ensured in the areas of employment, housing, and medical care; and personal dignity and social acceptance for them were widely promoted. It was at this time that age 65 was established as the age of retirement with conferral of full Social Security and medical benefits, officially creating the group of senior citizens in existence today. Soon thereafter, 50 became the lowest possible age that entitled one to most of the benefits of advancing years, such as membership in AARP or eligibility for housing in many retirement complexes.

One might think that this watershed legislation would have paved the way for a more even exploration of older characters in young adult fiction, as had the laws that expanded freedoms for other groups of peoples. However, not only did negativism persist in the portrayal of the elderly in television and print media, but also societal attitudes, in general, did not change as much as could be expected. In fact, more than ten years later older adults were still identified as one of the three "hidden minorities" neglected by educators and authors by Joan F. Jaffe in a paper she presented at the 1977 Annual Meeting of the National Council of Teachers of English (1), with the others being the handicapped and families with nontraditional lifestyles. Unfortunately, until very recently, research by both critics of literature and gerontology experts—those who specifically study the problems of the elderly—has revealed that trends in this area have been relatively static, with progress made in only a few isolated works for adults or teens. In other words, bias toward older people largely remains in the pages of books for young adults as well as in the minds of the American people as a whole.

One might question why any stereotypes still exist after they have been debunked, as have many in Western society. But in exploring the nature of stereotypes, one realizes that all of them carry at least an element of truth. For example, one cannot dispute the fact that in the early- to mid-1990s America's very vocal Christian Coalition was a group with an anti-abortion platform and strong anti-homosexual attitudes. Does this mean that all Christians are anti-abortionists and homophobic? Of course not; such a conclusion is a classic example of faulty logic. But a small minority of Christians are associated with these positions, and the resulting publicity about them can lead to the acknowledgment that there are small grains of truth in these assumptions.

ATTITUDES ABOUT THE REALITY OF AGING

By the same token, it is a known and accepted fact that as people age, this natural process will cause them to slowly lose some of their physical capabilities, which may lead to illness or disability, and, of course, ultimately death. Hair thins; movement may need the assistance of a walker; ears may require hearing aids; memories may have to be prompted. These are normal and expected parts of life. Does that mean that all older people have serious age-related physical and mental disabilities? Of course not. In fact, most of them are healthy, vibrant people who continue contributing their concerns, intellects, and talents to their families, jobs, and communities in inestimable ways. But, admittedly, when elderly people reach certain points in their lives, they cannot avoid the inevitable physical and/or mental declines of the aging process. This relatively new phenomenon, brought about by tremendous medical advances in the twentieth century, has been both a blessing and a curse. When life expectancy at the turn of the century was only around 47 years of age, fewer people (only 4% of the population) had to cope with the problems of old age: the profusion of arthritis, cancers, heart disease, Alzheimer's, and hypertension that often go hand-in-hand with today's life spans close to 80. An elderly person's death now is more often the result of a long and disabling illness rather than a swift blow from an infectious agent or an industrial or farm accident that could have easily occurred during the second or third decade of life in the early years of the 20th century. Most of us concur that it is indeed wonderful that many people can now live healthily through the primes of their lives, but we also admit that we do not know how to properly deal with the increasing number of elderly people (32 million of whom were on Medicare in 1994) whose bodies are failing them simultaneously in multiple ways. The psychological, socio-logical, medical, and financial costs of this situation are a drain on the citizens of our entire nation, both individually and collectively.

The question is: How should authors convey the reality of these cultural changes in literature, especially for adolescents? Naturally, they tend to emphasize the most disastrous compo-nents of the aging process, the ones with the grains of truth, the ones that bring about crises that teens have to confront and solve. But we cannot forget that the formula for young adult lit-erature tells writers to do exactly that, highlighting the extraor-dinary problems in teens' lives. So maybe the bias against the elderly in adolescent fiction is no more prejudicial than its bias toward any other group of people. Is this reality? Certainly not, if one is evaluating the entire collection of young adult litera-ture; however, just about any realistic fiction offering in the genre, if taken separately, could be deemed plausible.

Ironically, though, a 1981 review of literature highlighted a historical study conducted ten years earlier that showed a steadily *increasing* rate of negativism towards older adults in children's fiction published in magazines and books between 1870 and 1960 (Hannelore Wass, Dorothy Fillmer and Leola Ward, 357). This was an alarming development that could be at least partially attributed to America's extreme glamorization of the youth culture thirty years ago. The authors of this *Educa-tional Gerontology* article summed up the situation by saying there was "a strong counterforce of negative or ambivalent atti-tudes toward aging and the aged . . . [that are] deeply ingrained . . . reinforced by stereotypic notions and the persistence of mis-conceptions about aging and older persons even in the face of much new knowledge" (355). As specialists in the process and problems of aging, the authors represent a group much con-cerned about these unflattering and unrealistic presentations of the elderly in the various forms of media, and particularly those that affect children, who are forming attitudes that tend to color their outlooks on life. Obviously, older adults personally care a lot about the images presented of their age group, not wanting to be unfairly and negatively stereotyped, a situation that can lead to prejudice against them in areas of housing, health care, employment, and the like. In addition, though, seniors are deeply troubled over the perceptions that children and adolescents are creating in their minds about the aging process because they feel that the attitudes that result will make it difficult for these future generations to adjust to problems they themselves will have to face as they get older.

Indeed, a 1985 study of 790 Iowa students from 35 junior and senior high schools who completed a questionnaire called "My Views about Older People" exposed a multitude of misconceptions and stereotypes that adolescents commonly hold about the elderly. Even though most of the youngsters in the study had generally positive attitudes towards older people, their contacts with them tended to be limited in frequency and duration, and most often restricted to one person, a grandmother. Probably because of the scanty experience the teens had with the elderly, they held wrong ideas about both medical and psycho-social aspects of the aging process, making misjudgments about personality traits, interests, and, ultimately, the competence of this group of people (Ralston, 1). Certainly the attitudes held by these young adults are vital not only in paving the way for the adjustment and position of today's elderly in society, but also for the future adaptations these adolescents will make in their own eventual aging.

To this end, gerontologists and the senior citizens they represent have become active in exploring and attempting to correct negative portrayals of the aged, whether on television, in movies, or in print material. Some studies on the subject, particularly in regards to children's and adolescent literature, have, therefore, appeared over the last thirty years in the gerontology journals, and a limited number of books from the gerontological viewpoint have also touched on the topic. For example, the eighteenth book in the series "Bibliographies and Indexes in Gerontology" is Frank H. Nuessel's 1992 *Image of Older Adults in the*

Media: An Annotated Bibliography, which lists journal articles containing research about the portrayal of the elderly in the field of literature for children and young adults. Many of these studies are available through information furnished by the American Association for Retired Persons, such as its online data file "Ageline."

THE GERONTOLOGIST VERSUS THE LITERATURE CRITIC

However, gerontology experts do not necessarily agree with authorities in the field of adolescent literature about what types of portrayals of older people are best, and this disagreement is readily evident when examining the sources gerontologists recommend about the topic. For example, the gerontologist-compiled annotated bibliography mentioned in the previous paragraph highlights studies about older adults as portrayed in adolescent literature that had appeared primarily in gerontology journals, while not mentioning any of the landmark studies on the topic that had been published in traditional education or library journals. Many of these latter studies, by acknowledged experts in the young adult literature field, are instead abstracted in ERIC, the U.S. Department of Education's Resources Information Center, and come exclusively from education and library science journals. Although all researchers on the topic, whether gerontologists or educationalists/librarians, concur that the elderly are often presented in a stereotypical fashion as insignificant, incompetent, and uninteresting with a wide variety of infirmities, the two groups have very different ideas on how to correct the situation. In general, literature experts tend to feel that the goal is to strive toward realism with all of its warts, while gerontologists would rather see a more utopian picture of older people that emphasizes individuality and vitality while keeping the problems of aging to a minimum.

Some of the biggest clashes in these conflicting philosophies between literature authorities and gerontologists came to a head in the 1970s and 1980s as they independently critiqued the literature with wildly different interpretations. One of these works that could be regarded as a true breakthrough book in that the entire plot revolved around an older adult and the problems of aging was *A Figure of Speech* by recognized young adult fiction author Norma Fox Mazer. In this 197-page book, 13-year-old Jenny fought for keeping her beloved, but increasingly infirm, 83-year-old grandfather from being put into a nursing home, an action the rest of her family fully favored. Typical of most seminal works, the events and attitudes within the story were overemphasized to the point of being beyond credibility. For example, when Grandpa stormed into older granddaughter Gail's party to tell her teenage friends to quiet down, they taunted and physically handled the man, something that just would not have happened in a normal, middle-class family home. In addition, Gail's complaints about Grandpa having "ruined" her party were seemingly accepted by her parents without absolutely any word of retribution to their daughter for her obvious complicity in the verbal and physical abuse!

Another questionable tactic was the narrative of *A Figure of Speech*, which occasionally jumped from Jenny's point of view to that of Grandpa's, giving the reader a double dose of stereotypes coming from two sides. Once the reader heard multiple times how Grandpa awoke with "stiff swollen joints" (6), told the same stories over and over (26), wouldn't change his underwear for a week at a time (33), acted "narrowminded" and in "a rut" (89), mumbled to himself (112), etc., etc., nothing that Jenny could say to her family, such as ". . . you should think more about Grandpa's feelings" (33) could be capable of overcoming the negatives. He ate poorly, collected old newspapers in piles, was forced to pay for a burial plot out of his social security checks, missed the bowl when he went to the bathroom, and thought of himself as a "useless creature" (133) with the disgusting habit of sucking in his mouth and drooling. These stereotypes—even though they were openly criticized in the main—were so overwhelming in number that it was impossible for the author to defuse them, no matter how she might have tried. Even the story's end, which found Grandpa with the strength to rebel against his family's devaluation of him by running away to an abandoned old farmhouse, was muted by the implication of senility. By this time, the only resolution to the problem, as Grandpa saw it, was to die a benign suicide and get out of the way. Although *A Figure of Speech* was plainly written with attempts to expose this ageism for what it was, the fact that the author overaccentuated all of the problems associated with growing older resulted in exactly the opposite, reinforcing the negative stereotype of an infirm, incapacitated old man out of touch with reality.

However, when discussing this book, Carolyn Baggett, Assistant Professor of the University of Mississippi School of Library and Information Science, maintained that it featured a "compelling plot which deals with aging in a painful but forthright manner" (61–62). In her article called "Positive Portraits of the Elderly in Realistic Fiction for Young Adults," the author went on to champion the book as promoting the message that older people are "self-reliant" and should be able to maintain their independence (62). These views were supported by Richard R. Abrahamson, of the University of Iowa, whose opinion was quoted in the 1976 special issue of *Arizona English Bulletin* devoted fully to adolescent literature. He described the camaraderie between Jenny and Grandpa as one of the most "realistically portrayed teenage-senior citizen relationships" in young adult fiction, with Grandpa the "significant adult" in the life of Jenny, who spent virtually all of her time with him while neglecting other familial relationships (Donelson, 183).

These positive book discussions of *A Figure of Speech* differ markedly from the critique published in *Educational Gerontology* by Jeanne Gerlach, who found Jenny's mothering role of Grandpa, like others in the genre, to be "contrived" and "unrealistic" and "in complete contrast" to the kinds of relationships that actually exist between teens and older people (187). Her contention was that this book represented just one more example of an adolescent novel that presented an older person in a fashion atypical of real people in the age bracket, and she urged young adult fiction authors to write about the elderly in a more representative way. Meanwhile, Notre Dame College of Ohio Education Professor Regina Alfonso took a middle ground on the book in her practical guide "Modules for Teaching about Young People's Literature" published in *The Journal of Reading*. Recommending the book with reservations, along with others about the elderly on her 1986 reading list, she noted that *A Figure of*

Speech and others like it would be best read in a teaching situation so that adolescents could be made aware that the elderly characters in these books did not necessarily typify people of the age bracket (201–203). In this article, Alfonso did quantify in a unique way what she felt were the four main myths concerning the elderly that were frequently surfacing in young adult literature: that older people were senile (Myth #1), dependent on their families (Myth #2), stereotyped as passive, sedentary, and non-individualistic (Myth #3) and looked toward children to rescue and protect them (Myth #4) (202–203). All misconceptions, of course, promote ageism, which is why she advised the reading of these books only within a classroom setting that could ameliorate their possibly negative effects with a presentation of the facts.

During these two decades of debate, authorities on all sides also disputed the quality of presentation of older people in a number of other young adult books, especially in *The Dream Watcher* by Barbara Wersba, *Remove Protective Coating a Little at a Time* by Donovan, and *The Pigman* by Paul Zindel. In *The Dream Watcher*, 83-year-old Orpha Woodfin became an important adult in the life of teenage misfit Albert, who thought he was a complete failure in life. The sherry-sipping Mrs. Woodfin conveyed a romanticized view of herself as an animated, former grande dame of the theatre, a picture that was exposed as fraudulent upon her death. Yet, all the same, she had been the first adult to treat Albert as a real person, which changed his initial view of her from a lady "a thousand years old" (26) to one who was "a complete friend . . . the kind of person you could be with when you had a terrible cold" (100). Her walking with a cane, having white hair, and living in an unkempt house were irrelevant. Both Abrahamson (Donelson, 185–187) and Baggett (62) in their literature reviews said that the moral of the story—that even though Mrs. Woodfin was a liar, she gave Albert the support with which to face his problems and grow up—made the book positive. This verdict appears to agree with the protagonist himself, who at the very end of the book said that it had not ultimately mattered that Mrs. Woodfin had lied about herself, because she had made him "Albert Scully . . . [possibly] the biggest freak in the universe . . . but [someone] who would still be somebody" (Wersba 170). But gerontologist Gerlach blasted the book by asking why Wersba felt she had to "twist the plot" at the end, portraying Mrs. Woodfin as a "cheat" in life when the story could have remained as a "simple, believable tale" in which the older woman had simply died as a famous actress (189). She has a point, but not much of one here. Anyone of any age can be a liar, or an alcoholic, or on welfare, after all, but most importantly, we cannot forget that we are talking about literature, that unpredictable treasure, with all of its bolts out of the blue.

In the quirky *Remove Protective Coating a Little at a Time*, Harry, a 14-year-old well-off New York City boy who was a loner was befriended by 72-year-old Amelia, a homeless squatter he met in Central Park. When she, in her pink dress and sneakers, was not throwing a football to him or talking about the illegitimate children she had given away, Amelia was visiting with the teenager in questionable circumstances in her shabby room in an abandoned building. Again, Baggett found this book to be a realistic story in which Harry was "touched and nourished" by the worldly-wise woman, who was perhaps not a lovable character, but "courageous and gutsy and admirable" (62). Presumably one could call a destitute woman "gutsy" as she lured pigeons to her window sill with seed, killed them and then proceeded to cook them for dinner over her sterno burner, but it is certainly obvious that others could disagree. In typical, yet relatively muted fashion here, considering the book's many other provocations (such as Amelia asking Harry if he was circumcised and saying she was afraid she would be mistaken on the street for a "hooker"), Gerlach said this story was an illustration of an author presenting yet another unbelievable relationship between an older and younger person (184). But at least this strange book broke three of the four myths of the aged that often appear in young adult fiction, with Amelia in sharp mind, while remaining independent and individualistic —even though young Harry, did try to protect and save her (Myth #4).

Meanwhile, Pulitzer Prize winning author Zindel (for *The Effect of Gamma Rays on Man-in-the-Moon Marigolds*) was roundly criticized for his characterization of Angelo Pignati as a lonely, isolated elderly man whose only friend was a baboon at the city zoo in his book, *The Pigman*. Befriended by two troubled teenagers, who at first saw him through a society fearful of old age, Mr. Pignati reveled in the relationship, willingly believing that high schoolers Lorraine and John were charity workers. The portrait of the Pigman was universally panned by nearly all experts as a poor example of older individuals, who realistically would not invite strange people of any age into their urban homes, or give them checks addressed to "cash" (DeSalvo, 23, 26; Gerlach, 187). Yet, on the other hand, the neglected teens looked to simplistic Mr. Pignati, who sometimes acted as if he were regressing into a second childhood (having a heart attack while trying to go upstairs on roller skates, for example), as a source of unconditional love, which they had never had from their own dysfunctional families. The book may not have been evaluated so negatively had Zindel not put highly critical words about older people in the mouths of his teenage protagonists after the Pigman died at the end of the story. Frequently quoted was John's thought that ". . . you can grow old and be alone and have to get down on your hands and knees and beg for friends . . . [forgotten] because you get a little old and your mind's a bit senile or silly" (Zindel, 175). Lorraine, too, criticized the Pigman after his death for going backward, for "trespassing" in the grand scheme of life, something she said the aged were not supposed to do (180). However, it may just occur to some literature experts that perhaps *The Pigman* was written as a modern fairy tale rather than a realistic work, meant to pass judgment on some of the same aspects of modern society that gerontologists themselves criticize, such as the isolation of America's older citizens. The story was written from the point of view of two immature and admitted adolescent loners, after all. Are readers supposed to interpret the circumstances of the book merely from the protagonists' point of view?

OLDER CHARACTERS: ECCENTRICS OR GRANDMOTHERS?

This early focus of young adult fiction on eccentric, rather than realistic, elderly characters was found to be disturbing in some critics' reviews, yet delightful in others, who championed the individuality of the elderly that was exhibited. In any case, the trend spurred Mary W. Vraney and Carol J. Barrett to formulate a new study in 1981 that attempted, for the first time, to bring together all the prior research of both literature experts and gerontologists on the subject. Integrating research from all disciplines, the authors constructed a literature review with citations from seven articles and books from the field of gerontology, four from psychology or psychiatry, three from education and two from sociology (in addition to consulting Betty Friedan's *The Feminine Mystique*) for their 17 total sources. This *Journal of Reading* article, "Marital Status: Its Effects on the Portrayal of Older Characters in Children's Literature" set a new course in the evaluation of the treatment of older people in young adult literature, as the authors, with their counseling and psychology backgrounds, were better able to frame a comprehensive study that did not rely on the opinions of solely gerontologists or literature experts.

Although Vraney and Barrett had hoped to concentrate mainly on the different way characters were portrayed according to marital status, they came up with several surprises in their results that could be more universally applied. Examining 138 (or 5%) of children's and adolescent books picked at random from a comprehensive university library collection, the researchers found that although marital status had some effect on whether the elderly characters were presented negatively or positively, there were more curious results to be found when analyzing older characters categorized as eccentrics: those living as hermits or engaged in unusual and atypical activities for their ages. Eccentric older characters as a group were much more likely to be negatively portrayed (72%), with 100% of the widowed eccentrics in this category, as opposed to only 44% of those who had never married (490). In addition, 69% of all eccentric older adults were male, and of the positively-portrayed eccentric seniors, 80% were never-married females with men who were bachelors representing the smallest positive rating at 20% (491). Do these findings tell young readers that it is all right to be eccentric when one ages as long as one is a spinster, or that maybe spinstership leads to eccentricity? Does widowhood condemn an older person to a dull, uneventful life? Are aged bachelors a group to be feared or disliked? And how does this all square with reality?

Another shock came as Vraney and Barrett looked at children's and adolescent literature according to the decade in which it had been published, from the 1940s to 1980. Older widowed and never-married characters in these books were treated more positively (76%) in the 1950s, followed by the 1940s with a 67% favorable rating; this declined to 51% positive in the 1960s with a precipitous drop to 31% in the 1970s (491). We would do well to question why negativity is increasing rather than decreasing, a confirmation of the Wass, Fillmer and Ward study that analyzed a century's worth of children's and adolescent literature discussed earlier. Is this, too, a reflection of the direction of societal attitudes?

Also, Vraney and Barrett found that older people are likely to show up in the young adult genre most frequently as relatives, and specifically grandmothers (older females), who are depicted as having no lives except those in relation to family activities, such as preparing meals, bringing presents or offering nurturing (488). These elderly were often portrayed as ill, lonely, tired, bored, dull, and inactive, and certainly not complex individuals with complicated motivations (Wass, Fillmer and Ward, 357), unless, that is, they were cast as eccentrics or characters in fantasy tales. Gerlach says that these negative presentations of elderly characters foster attitudes like those expressed in an essay session she conducted with forty eleventh graders who were asked to write about their involvement with older people (Gerlach, 183). Representative comments that came out of the experiment were quotes such as, "When thinking of old people, I see gray hair, canes, shawls and wrinkles," and "I think of the aged as people who are sickly and want to sleep the rest of their lives away" and "They just sit alone wishing they were dead" (184).

A later Ph.D. dissertation came to similar conclusions upon examination of 37 favorite novels of teenagers combined with 37 of the American Library Association's "Best Books for Young Adults" when pinpointing the quality of roles older characters had in adolescent literature. The statistics extrapolated from Gail

Sylvia Rittenbach's analysis showed that grandparents in the more recent books of this genre are portrayed either very positively or very negatively, with nearly nothing representing the middle ground (1). Yet are not most people firmly in this middle area, whether they are children, teens, adults, or the elderly? Where is reality here?

Fortunately, a 1993 literature review of the topic presents us with a new perspective by pooling twenty-eight empirical studies that tie the portrayal of the elderly in young adult fiction to related studies, such as the analysis of aging themes as found on birthday cards or in magazine advertisements. Latika Vasil of Victoria University in New Zealand and Hannelore Wass of the University of Florida add to the knowledge by not only linking these and various historical studies in new ways, but also by discussing the resulting implications within the current context. In nearly all categories, including adolescent literature, they found that elderly women were underrepresented, not matching the three-fifths of the aged population in the United States that is female (79). Meanwhile, although young adult fiction was criticized for its relegation of elderly characters to minor roles, it received much higher marks than younger children's literature (picture books, magazines, and basal readers) for its fewer incidences of stereotyping (79). In fact, among the most offensive categories on the list showing bias toward the elderly were magazine cartoons and birthday cards, which were overwhelmingly negative, and newspapers, which were found to allot only 1% of their space for issues specifically important to the elderly (79). All in all, the treatment of older people in adolescent literature was much more positive as compared with the portrayals they were afforded in nearly every other category.

However, Vasil and Wass did not intend to let writers of adolescent fiction off the hook with their study, proposing seven detailed plans of action that they felt could help combat the abuse and neglect that the elderly receive from all sources of media. These included programs to foster an awareness of elderly concerns among parents, educational staffs, clergy and other community leaders, in addition to encouraging senior citizens themselves to become more in tune with children's and adolescents' issues so that their interactions with the younger generation could be more positive (81–83). The authors promoted these directives as efforts to aid in the prevention of negative stereotyping of the elderly becoming a self-fulfilling prophesy, not only for today's oldsters, but also for tomorrow's.

CONFLICTING PORTRAYALS OF OLDER CHARACTERS FROM MIDDLE AMERICA

Ironically, one of the ground-breaking books in the field of young adult literature, Salinger's *Catcher in the Rye*, presents perhaps one of the most negative portraits of older people still found. The scene towards the beginning of the novel in which Holden Caulfield visited his aged and at least temporarily infirm history teacher to tell him he has flunked out of prep school drags on for thirteen full pages with one unflattering description of old people after another. Speaking derisively—as he admittedly did about nearly every character in the entire book—the boy said "old Spencer" was so stooped over that he was incapable of picking up chalk if he dropped it on the floor in the classroom, an embarrassing and "awful" occurrence. He continued with a physical description of old men in general, particularly recoiling at the thought of their "bumpy old chests" and "white and unhairy" legs that showed when they were in bathrobes or at the beach. Having to speak up to be heard by Mrs. Spencer, the boy knocked the aged's hearing difficulties and mused later about ". . . what the heck [her husband] was still living for" (10). As derogatory as Holden's depiction here of the Spencers was, though, it must be noted that the aged Mr. Spencer was the only teacher to whom the boy wanted to say goodbye before leaving the school.

Further on in the story, an even worse picture of the elderly emerges in the mind of Holden when he encountered the old bellboy at the Edmont Hotel in New York City, where he hid out before getting the courage to go home and face his troubles. "Terrible" was the way the boy described how the bellboy combed his hair from one side over his head to vainly try to cover up his baldness, and the fact that this man, at his age, had to carry other people's suitcases and then wait around for tips was considered ". . . even more depressing than the room was"

(79). Salinger succeeded in covering nearly all the bases in degrading the elderly for their appearances, infirmities, poor economic straits and lack of intelligence, but one must remember that Holden saw the entire world in a stereotyped condition through his depression. Nearly no group of people mentioned in the book, from girlfriends to middle-aged adults, escaped criticism.

A more recent Newbery award winning book that contained an extremely disparaging account of an elderly person is Katherine Paterson's *Jacob Have I Loved*, set in a fishing village on an island in Chesapeake Bay during World War II. In this tale of jealousy of one non-identical 14-year-old twin girl toward her beautiful and talented sister, the grandmother served as an antagonizing wedge between them. As the 63-year-old woman became even more senile, some of her comments were so repulsive that the girls' father had to send the teens out of the room with the excuse that his mother's age made her "not responsible" (133). Towards the end of this book, the elderly woman worsened so much that every living minute was "poisoned by Grandma's hatred," according to her plain granddaughter (197).

As venomous as this atmosphere was, however, Sara Louise could not hate old people, for another character in the book, the Captain, was the most influential adult in her life, believing so strongly in her abilities that she was spurred to achieve her goals in life. At the same time, the girl became infatuated with the 70-year-old Captain, titillating the reader by the idea that elderly people can be sexually attractive. Captain, however, chose to marry his childhood sweetheart after the eccentric "old maid" with numerous cats in her smelly house came home from the hospital in a wheelchair with the crooked smile of a stroke victim. Perhaps making amends for the negative images of the elderly in this story, the author has Captain expound on the advantages of aging towards the very end of the book, as he opined that it was good being old because "youth [with all of its trials and tribulations] is a mortal wound" (191).

Many are the young adult fiction works with older people mentioned almost only in passing, as inconspicuous or insignificant characters who do not figure in much of the action of the plot. In Dorothy Allison's *Bastard Out of Carolina*, for example,

12-year-old Ruth Ann encountered two grandmothers, her maternal one and that of her half-sister Reese, but neither helped her in her struggle to escape the bad influence of her poor white trash family. Concerning the first, Ruth Ann described Granny as the kind of person who could call herself "ugly" and not even care about it, with her thin, gray hair and "strong" smell. Meanwhile, the teenager was jealous of Reese's grandmother as one you might "read about or see in a movie," with her blue gingham apron and thick braids (55). But as flattering as the portrait of the second grandmother was, it is the type that would be lambasted as stereotypical by gerontologists, showing a nurturing grandmother in the kitchen preparing a meal. However, these presentations are not nearly as negative as the one paragraph in Robert Cormier's *The Chocolate War* which acknowledged the existence of the elderly only as a few anonymous old women with "blue hair and big handbags" who conspicuously tried to ignore the teenage protagonist who got on a bus smelling of vomit after having been beaten up. The kinds of brief mentions of older people as illustrated by the Cormier book might actually be some of the most insidiously harmful since, being so short, they barely seem worthy of notice. But to adolescents, who are constantly forming and reforming their images of older people as they accumulate the wisdom of the world, these messages may serve as continuous, yet unrecognized, reinforcements of negative stereotypes, and ones that are perhaps not even necessary to the plot line.

MULTICULTURAL PORTRAITS OF ELDERLY CHARACTERS

The problem of ageism is not restricted to books for young Caucasian Americans either, but shows up in multicultural works as well. Although the reader does not find out until the very end of Jamaica Kincaid's *Annie John* that the Antiguan adolescent girl's father was thirty-five years older than her mother, and was, in fact, elderly during her entire life, we are not spared negative thoughts about his age. Upon leaving for nursing school in England at 18, Annie John reflected on her mother's having had to run "up and down stairs" catering to her husband's infirmities, which made her determined "never to marry an old man" (132). Again, though, this statement must be tempered with the understanding that the context of the young woman's thoughts were part of a typical full-blown teenage rejection of society.

Author Alice Childress featured a delightful elderly character in her young adult book *Rainbow Jordan* about a 14-year-old urban African American girl whose mother was neglectful, leaving her needs to be provided from time to time by a foster mother. Ironically it was not Miss Josie, the African-American foster mother, who was the model here, but her 78-year-old friend Miss Rachel, who exuded peace and truly lived her Quaker philosophy of helping people less fortunate than herself. The way 57-year-old Miss Josie was portrayed, depressed upon having been left by her husband, thrust it upon Rainbow to buoy her up (Myth #4, the saving of the elderly by the young). ". . . Plenty old people findin [sic] happiness," Rainbow had to tell her, with the obvious dictum, "Lotta elderly have dignity" (132). Here it was the teenager trying to break the stereotypical way in which the older Miss Josie thought of herself.

In Jane Leslie Conly's *Crazy Lady!* about an African American inner-city neighborhood rallying around the needs of Ronald, a teenage Down's syndrome boy, the crazy lady of the title was ironically not an elderly person, but Ronald's alcoholic mother. The older character featured in this story was instead Miss Annie, a wise and sympathetic former teacher who volunteered to tutor Vernon, the adolescent protagonist, who had recently lost his mother and was on an angry road to flunking English and getting into trouble with the wrong friends. One of the main lessons Vernon learned in this book was that all people— whether disabled, chronically diseased, or just old—need to be judged individually, like Miss Annie herself, whom Vernon used to call "the Lady from La-La Land" for the "great big dumb grin" she always had on her face when he and his pals had made fun of her before he got to know her (30). Although Miss Annie had trouble walking due to arthritis, she was given credit for her "sharp" mind, neat appearance, business-like demeanor, and her ability to get people to do what she wanted them to do. And she certainly changed Vernon's mind about another elderly neighbor woman, whom he had called "bitchy" and "gross," when Miss Annie told him something about her uniqueness (such as speaking five languages) emphasizing just how important it was to make the effort to get to know people different than himself before making judgments (155). This book presented itself as sensitive to all kinds of people, including those older.

Another healthy portrayal of an elderly African American woman is found within the pages of Angela Johnson's *Toning the Sweep*, in which 14-year-old Emmie and her mother flew to the California desert to help grandmama Ola close up her house and move back to Ohio with them to be treated for cancer. Although Ola was afflicted with a fatal disease, had arthritis and bottles of pills to take, she was still presented as a vibrant and strong woman who laughed frequently when visiting her individualistic older friends, who were active people, functioning as artists and foster parents. Always with fresh flowers in her bedroom, Ola had a daily ritual that included sweeping her sandy yard with a broom every morning, while winsomely brushing designs into it. Although Emmie herself said that Grandmama was "strange," she also knew that her friends secretly thought that the interesting woman was "cool" (46).

Three other multicultural books for young adults featuring elderly Asian characters provided some of the strongest portraits of people in the advanced age bracket; one was highly praiseworthy, the second realistically laudable, while the last leaned more negatively. Of the two that took place outside America (*Shizuko's Daughter* by Kyoko Mori was based in Japan, and *Year of Impossible Goodbyes* by Sook Nyul Choi was from Korea), grandparents played a great and positive influence in the lives of their families, certainly reflective of the cultures from which they came. It is only when multicultural values clashed in America, the theme of *April and the Dragon Lady* by Lensey Namioka, that the elderly grandmother became a manipulative busybody who tried to force Chinese ways on her 15-year-old Asian-American granddaughter and the rest of the family.

The grandfather in Choi's uplifting semi-autobiographical recounting of experiences that occurred during World War II under the Japanese occupation of Korea and the ensuing takeover by Soviet Communists, was the central inspirational character who helped 10-year-old Sookan grow and form her philosophy of life. As the family patriarch, he directed the children's activities by instructing them in the forbidden languages of Korean and Chinese while passing on the crafts of wood carving, knot-making, and the brush strokes of art. He also taught ways of living that embraced peace, harmony, forgiveness, and the path of the spirit with an optimism that sustained the family through the many atrocities afflicted upon them. Sookan described his physical appearance in old age lovingly, especially admiring his deep grooved wrinkles she longed to run her fingers in. The grandfather's wisdom and physical evidence of aging in this book were thus refreshingly considered assets, not liabilities.

In Mori's book, Yuki's grandparents are the most significant adults in her life even though they are not permitted to see the 12-year-old for several years after her mother committed her shameful suicide. The attention given to her grandparents' aging process was depicted as normal, but sad, with them having "slowed down," with weak legs necessitating the use of canes, and fingers "too stiff" to do many kinds of work they had formerly done. But both of these elderly people adapted their activities according to their capabilities, and were able to continue contributing to the important concerns of their extended family while maintaining their positions of high respect. Only after her husband died did the grandmother feel she was entitled to insist upon wearing the gray and brown kimonos of older, less modern women, rejecting brighter Western styles and colors.

However, in Namioka's book, grandmother was the Dragon Lady of the title, who disapproved of April's association with "white devils" at school, and especially her ambitions to further her education in college, hiding and tearing up her acceptance letter to Colorado School of Mines. As an Asian-American with mixed Chinese and American values, the girl had to question them all, particularly in regards to her overbearing grandmother. Presented as eccentric, first putting piles of empty soapboxes in neighbors' garbage cans and later, wandering off at her 70th birthday party at the banquet hall into someone else's celebration, the grandmother was found to be diabetic, requiring medication. The doctor told them the medical help would not change the woman's unconventional ways; but, at 70, she had the right to act crazily if she wanted. Although at the story's end, April and her grandmother did come to an understanding of each other, with both showing the ability to make changes, the overwhelming portrait of the Dragon Lady was very negative, at least from the viewpoint of adolescent readers who tend to dislike bossy authority figures. Meanwhile, one of the few other elderly characters discussed in the book was the grandmother of April's friend Steve, a "sweet old lady" who visited his family every Thanksgiving and Christmas, functioning in the key role of bringing presents. Even though this character was only mentioned briefly, it was almost worse in presenting the grandmother as so insignificant to Steve's family life. In any event, it is fascinating to contrast the Asian spin on the elderly in young adult fiction to those representing Middle America. We might ask if it is perhaps inherent within the United States' rapidly-changing society that the words of our elders are no longer considered wise or relevant. Or is it just within our way to debase the elderly and their importance?

THE EVOLUTION OF PORTRAYALS OF
ELDERLY CHARACTERS

In all of their critiques of the portrayal of the elderly in young adult fiction, gerontologists nearly never identify books that they think exemplify the types of treatments that they find ideal. However, one can infer that they might actually like the presentation of at least some older characters in many books that have been published for this age group in the last thirty years, and especially more recently. In the 1991 young adult historical fiction offering, *Wolf by the Ears*, author Ann Rinaldi featured the elderly Thomas Jefferson as a vital, intelligent, and active individual, still serving as a hero to the country, state, and town that he lived in. Never described as old in the sense of being incapable or infirm, he is always written about with great respect and admiration as he rode his horse around Monticello or worked on his famous gardens. The only attention that his age is given, in fact, is in parts of the book in which his slaves expressed worry that his impending age might soon bring about a death that could mean the breaking up of their families as they are dispersed to other plantations. Of course, since Rinaldi's book is a historical treatment, it may tend to reflect more of a 17th century attitude of how the elderly had been regarded in American society.

Similarly, there was only one mention of aging in Robert Newton Peck's *A Day No Pigs Would Die,* the best selling story about 13-year-old Rob growing up in backwoods Vermont under the shadow of his father's impending death. Upon giving instructions to Rob as to how to carry on the work of the farm, his father told him that his mother was "not young" and her sister who lived with them was "near seventy." This statement surprised Rob because he had never considered either of them as growing older, being totally unaware of their advancing ages. According to gerontologist Gerlach, relegating age to the back burner like this while developing characters as individual people is the best way to portray older adults.

Meeting these objectives in the main are at least five more books published in the last fifteen years that featured elderly characters who played major influential roles in the lives of adolescents in literature written specifically for them. In Norma Fox Mazer's *After the Rain,* 15-year-old Rachel was stunned by the news that her 83-year-old grandfather Izzy, whom she hardly knew, even though her family visited with him weekly, was going to die. At first Rachel was led to question just what it was like being old, especially in a life like that of her bullying and inflexible grandfather's, who had strong hands, but yet was frequently "popping his bridge" in his mouth (47). Even later the girl was surprised to discover ageism herself as she observed the doctor treating her grandfather like an irresponsible child, not even telling him how sick he was. Making a strenuous effort to discover what this elderly man was all about as a person, Rachel became enriched after becoming the only person in the family to understand Izzy within the context of his cantankerous existence. All this, though, did not stop the anger that welled up in the girl after her grandfather died, as she regretted the many years of love they had missed (a "goddam waste," according to Rachel) because Izzy had not bothered to reach out to her (279), a responsibility she put on him, as the adult.

However, at the same time in this book, it must be acknowledged that Rachel complained bitterly about her own aged parents, in their sixties, especially after comparing them to the younger and more vibrant parents of her friends. "If only they weren't so old . . ." Rachel wrote in a letter to her 35-year-old brother, who had grown up under them in a quite different way as part of their first generation of children (12). The teenage girl felt that she had to take care of her parents and guard their feelings, going with her mother to hear the doctor's diagnosis of Izzy, and taking over for them by supervising Izzy's walks after he had started falling (Myth #4 again). It is only on the last few pages when Rachel finds her grandfather's hand print in a masonry project he had worked on many decades earlier that the girl came to appreciate the immortality of his life. It is amazing the difference in Mazer's much more sensitive and realistic portrait of an elderly/teenage relationship in this book fourteen years after her problematic breakthrough book *A Figure of Speech* discussed on previous pages.

Malcolm J. Bosse's *The 79 Squares* dealt with a similar significant elderly/youth relationship in its story of the dying 82-year-old Mr. Beck and eighth grader Eric, who is on the edge of becoming a full-fledged member of a gang that had already gotten him into trouble with the police once. The elderly man's physical condition is described in mortifying detail, such as the picture of him in his "terribly bent" and frail body held up on "shaky legs" (54). Yet despite Mr. Beck equating age with taking pills, the old man had a pride that summoned a terrific strength of character, a strength that he was able to pass on to the youngster to enable Eric to contemplate changing the direction of his life. The fact that the older man was also presented as just out of prison, where he had been for most of his adult life for the murder of his wife, introduced a wrinkle into the story for which one might question the necessity. (Just how eccentric must these characters be, after all?) But as the old man and his young companion studied the 79 foot-square blocks of Mr. Beck's garden, they both learned something about their inner spirits, leading the boy to pull away from his gang and the elderly man to die in some possible state of peace.

Pappy's problem in Ron Koertge's *Tiger, Tiger Burning Bright* was that he had, in his own words, "lost" his mind (106), forgetting where he was going, what he was doing, and who he was with at inopportune times. An 82-year-old cowboy, he had been his grandson Jesse's male role model throughout the eighth grader's fatherless life, teaching the boy how to track animals, ride horses, and camp in the mountains of drought-besieged California. Yet at his age, Pappy began burning his food, starting fires with smoldering cigarettes, and insisting he had seen tiger tracks in the desert. It was Jesse who felt that he had to hide Pappy's infirmities from his mother, fearing she would put him in a nursing home where the proud old man would die of shame and loneliness. "It just killed me to see him standing there like somebody with a loose rope in his hands who knows there was something important at the other end but can't remember what," the boy said, agonizing over the situation (85). Pappy, too, was unhappy about his growing senility, and commented, when seeing an old friend who had had a stroke, "Some choice . . . you either have a stroke or forget which end of your horse to feed," (107). These humorous touches about the problems of aging added immensely to the charm of this sensitively-written, down-to-earth book.

Pappy's daughter took a more pragmatic view of the situation, admitting to Jesse that, although his grandfather's going to a nursing home would be unfair, it might be the best thing to protect him from his own careless actions. But she, too, was not thrilled at the prospect of placing her father in one of these settings, and expressed pride in Jesse's caring for Pappy when she knew that most boys his age would "want nothing to do with old people" (174). So when his grandfather found out for himself that a real tiger had, in fact, been in the mountains as part of an illegal private game hunt, Jesse and his mother felt that Pappy had been exonerated for his lapses, and vowed to keep him at home with them, as difficult as it might be.

The last two of these books, Ouida Sebestyen's *Out of Nowhere* and Cynthia Voigt's *Dicey's Song*, feature elderly characters with virtually no mention of any age-related infirmities or personality traits. In Sebestyen's book, 13-year-old Harley, the neglected son of an unwed mother, was abandoned in the Arizona desert, where he joined 69-year-old May journeying to California to live in her childhood home. Once there, he also got to know and appreciate the previous renter of the house, sixty-ish Bill, a junk collector, who had at least some of the answers to the problems of living in the kind of confusing, upside-down world Harley had been in. Both older people worked hard and were in control of what they were doing, but they saw they had to make changes, just as the teenage boy had to do, in order to adjust to new ways of living. The relationships that Harley, Bill and May were later beginning to develop led each of them to realize how important it was to open themselves up to the loving responsibility that comes with being part of a caring, albeit unconventional, family.

Gram, in the Voigt book, also is a strong, capable and wise individual who adopts the four children of her mentally ill daughter, including 13-year-old Dicey, when it appeared as if their mother would not ever get well. The reader sees the older woman as a wonderful mothering influence for the needy children, whose circumstances cry out for the shelter, sustenance and guidance of a secure and loving home. Her unique parenting methods turned out to be sound, such as the unusual tactic of challenging the second grade to a marbles tournament in order to solve young Sammy's problem with a bully, for example. The major theme of this story, the notion that people can learn lessons and change no matter what their age, is just the right philosophy for Gram and Dicey both, each of whom had hurt themselves over the years by not "reaching out" to people (119–120).

One of the most tender and sensitive treatments of older people in young adult fiction is found in Judy Blume's *Forever*, a book that has been panned and banned in American libraries for its explicit discussions about the first sexual experience of Katherine, a senior in high school. The attitude of Katherine's stylish and smart grandmother, nearly 70 years old, was much more nonjudgmental than that of the girl's parents as she became the significant adult to see that her granddaughter got proper birth control advice at Planned Parenthood. Although her husband had had a stroke with an inability to speak clearly and walk without a cane, both he and Katherine's grandmother were described as dynamic and involved in life, living in New York City and still going to their law offices and favorite restaurant for lunch daily.

Katherine discussed her grandfather's infirmity by saying it was "sad" to see him struggle to get his words out, but she admired how her grandmother was able to treat him the same "... like there's nothing wrong at all" (30–31). In other words, illness in old age (or at any time, for that matter), is a part of life. Even more enlightening is the picture the girl has of her grandfather after he died: the memory of the recent toast "To love!" he had made to her grandmother (118). Thus the desexualization stereotype of older adults was debunked.

But Katherine's feelings about the elderly were not always so positive, as she remembered visiting her father's infirm mother in a nursing home when she was young, seeing a scary nonperson "with crooked fingers and wrinkled skin" (32). But as a result of later making a better effort to know her maternal grandparents, the teen came to love them dearly and exercised her change in thinking by volunteering to work as a Candy Striper in the local hospital on the gerontology floor. Although she credited herself only with bringing them flowers or helping adjust the patients' beds, it is obvious that Katherine had come to appreciate the importance that older people had played in her life and in the lives of others, a feeling she wanted to pass on even to aged people unknown to her.

CONCLUSION

This examination of the content of some of the more recent young adult books with elderly characters brings one to the conclusion that more and more authors are beginning to portray older people as individuals in their own right, maybe with infirmities or other age-related problems, but also with dignity and admiration. Some of the relationships that the teenage protagonists have established with elderly grandparents or neighbors, too, have a real ring of truth to them. This is encouraging. Of course, gerontologists can still say that 11% of the characters in every adolescent book are not elderly, or that three-fifths of these elders are not women, the numbers that would constitute a representative match to American society. They could also criticize the books that discuss the physical and mental declines of older people, and urge authors to restrict their presentations of relationships between adolescents and the aged in a context whereby they are in complete empathy with each other's lives, growing together only in a meaningful manner. If following these rules, we can question next whether the proper idea is that all elderly people in young adult fiction should be portrayed as wonderful, interesting, healthy individuals with no problems, as the gerontologists might like to encourage.

Maybe if we turn the tables, we will find the answer to this question, for herein lies the crux of the matter. Should all of the books that elderly people write have a sample of teenagers in them that are representative of their numbers in American demographics? Ought those adolescents who are featured in these books to have only major roles in the storyline? Should ten- to eighteen-year-olds press for these standards, based on the reasoning that old people make so many negative prejudicial assumptions about teenagers? This begins to sound a bit nutty. More legitimately, perhaps, let us speculate about what an elderly person today would choose to focus on if writing a book about a relationship with an adolescent. Certainly, for the book to have any kind of engrossing nature, it would have to high-light some special problem or situation, such as a teenager's being in trouble and coming to live with an elderly grandparent, or a beloved adolescent having an illness that might be fatal. Does this mean that all teenagers are in trouble or have a poten-tially fatal illness? Of course not. But no fiction writer can spin an intriguing tale about characters who are idealistic, perfect models of their age groups with absolutely no problems in life.

Turning the tables back, we must remember that the world is fraught with misunderstandings, wrong conclusions, and mis-judgments about nearly every subject, not only the plight of the elderly. If young adult fiction writers present some of these problems of the aged in their literature for teens without making right or wrong judgment calls, are they necessarily promoting harmful ideas? Can we not give adolescents the credit to make at least some distinctions between good and evil, realism versus fantasy, quality versus fluff? The answer here is not a censorship of ideas, but a sensitivity of presentation. Of the increasing numbers of young adult authors who are choosing to structure stories that include elderly characters, more and more of them are highlighting the notions that our older citizens can live important and productive lives, with unique personalities and a wisdom that comes with cumulated years of experience. And they are doing it at the same time as sympathetically and passionately discussing the physical and emotional problems that naturally arise within this advanced age bracket. However, let us also not discount the fact that not all of our senior citizens are laudable people, so we will continue to see some realistically-based portraits of the elderly that are not always positive in literature for adolescents. It is ludicrous to press for inauthentic and hypocritical portrayals of the elderly from these authors, for there is nothing like a teenage reader to pick up on phoniness or hypocrisy within the pages of a book, and immediately toss it aside.

So let us continue to monitor the progress of more honest portrayals of greybeards and grannies, the pariahs of young adult fiction, and make certain that we witness realistic, fair and full presentations of their characters, with the elderly assuming the various statuses they require according to plot and character. This is the most we can demand of our writers of adolescent literature, who cannot be unjustly constrained by politically correct artifices within their pages.

WORKS CITED

Alfonso, Regina. "Modules for Teaching about Young People's Literature—Module 2: How Do the Elderly Fare in Children's Books?" *Journal of Reading* 30 (1986): 201–203.

Allison, Dorothy. *Bastard Out of Carolina*. New York: Penguin, 1992.

Baggett, Carolyn. "Positive Portraits of the Elderly in Realistic Fiction for Young Adults." *Catholic Library World* 54.2 (1982): 60–63.

Birkerts, Sven. "It Is Time to Be Old." *The New York Times Book Review*. May 22, 1994: 12.

Blume, Judy. *Forever*. New York: Bradbury, 1975.

Bosse, Malcolm J. *The 79 Squares*. New York: Crowell, 1979.

Childress, Alice. *Rainbow Jordan*. New York: Coward, 1981.

Choi, Sook Nyul. *Year of Impossible Goodbyes*. Boston: Houghton, 1991.

Conly, Jane Leslie. *Crazy Lady!* New York: Geringer/Harper, 1993.

Cormier, Robert. *The Chocolate War.* New York: Dell, 1974.

DeSalvo, Louise A. "Literature and the Process of Aging." *Media & Methods* 16.6 (1980): 22–23.

Donovan, John. *Remove Protective Coating a Little at a Time.* New York: Harper, 1973.

Donelson, Ken, ed. "The Elderly Person as a Significant Adult in Adolescent Literature." *Arizona English Bulletin* 18.3 (1976): 183–189. Adolescent Literature Revisited after Four Years (Special Issue).

Gerlach, Jeanne. "Adolescent Literature: A Misrepresentation of Youth-Aged Relationships." *Educational Gerontology* 14 (1988): 183–191.

Hinton, S. E. *The Outsiders.* New York: Viking, 1967.

Jaffe, Joan F. *The Hidden Minorities: Sex and Race Are Not Enough.* ERIC, 1977. ED149379 CS203910.

Johnson, Angela. *Toning the Sweep.* New York: Orchard, 1993.

Kincaid, Jamaica. *Annie John.* New York: Farrar, 1983.

Koertge, Ron. *Tiger, Tiger Burning Bright.* New York: Orchard, 1994.

Mazer, Norma Fox. *A Figure of Speech.* New York: Delacorte, 1973.

_____. *After the Rain.* New York: Morrow, 1987.

Mori, Kyoko. *Shizuko's Daughter.* New York: Holt, 1993.

Namioka, Lensey. *April and the Dragon Lady.* San Diego: Browndeer/Harcourt, 1994.

Nuessel, Frank H. *Image of Older Adults in the Media: An Annotated Bibliography.* Bibliographies and Indexes in Gerontology 18. Westport: Greenwood, 1992.

Paterson, Katherine. *Jacob Have I Loved.* New York: Crowell, 1980.

Peck, Robert Newton. *A Day No Pigs Would Die.* New York: Dell, 1972.

Peterson, D. A., and E. L. Karnes. "Older People in Adolescent Literature." *The Age of Aging: A Reader in Social Gerontology.* Prometheus, 1979. Dialog file 163, item 00011983.

Ralston, Penny A. *Secondary Students' Knowledge of, Attitudes toward, and Experiences with Older Adults.* ERIC, 1985. ED 271711 CG019250.

Rinaldi, Ann. *Wolf by the Ears.* New York: Scholastic, 1991.

Rittenbach, Sylvia Gail. "Authority Portrayal in Young Adult Fiction from 1974 to 1983." *DAI* 47 (1986): 12A. U of Washington, Seattle.

Rutherford, Janette. *The Role of the Elderly Adult in Recent Young Adult Fiction.* Denton: Texas Woman's U, 1978. ERIC ED 157498 IR005820.

Salinger, J. D. *The Catcher in the Rye.* Boston: Little, 1951.

Sebestyen, Ouida. *Out of Nowhere.* New York: Orchard, 1994.

Vasil, Latika, and Hannelore Wass. "Portrayal of the Elderly in the Media: A Literature Review and Implications for Educational Gerontologists." *Educational Gerontology* 19, (1993): 71–85.

Voigt, Cynthia. *Dicey's Song*. New York: Atheneum, 1983.

Vraney, Mary W., and Carol J. Barrett. "Marital Status: Its Effects on the Portrayal of Older Characters in Children's Literature." *Journal of Reading* 24 (1981): 487–493.

Wass, Hannelore, Dorothy Fillmer, and Leola Ward. "Education about Aging: A Rationale." *Educational Gerontology* 7 (1981): 355–361.

Wersba, Barbara. *The Dream Watcher*. New York: Atheneum, 1969.

Wolff, Virginia Euwer. *Probably Still Nick Swansen*. New York: Holt, 1988.

Zindel, Paul. *The Pigman*. New York: Harper, 1968.

CHAPTER TEN

Catching the Shape of Their Dreams, Quilts as a Medium

Tess Beck Stuhlmann

The colors sing out across the space between us, and I am lifted up in hope, dancing with stars, sliding down triangles, tumbled with feather-light forms in space. A quilt speaks directly to the unconscious with its rhythms of color, shape, texture and form. It is pared down language, rather like poetry, with its brevity and clarity. This essential quality of visual story appeals to the intuitive powers, where the word is bypassed and an experience is transferred in a direct way via color, shape and texture, crossing over in space to communicate an aspect of the emotional or spiritual state of the creator directly to the viewer's emotions or spirit. There is a pure uncomplicated pleasure in this type of transfer of knowledge, which is very satisfying. It augments communication by language, whether written or oral. Many years ago one might have said the reverse about written language, before it was common for "everyone" to read and write. In fact, in our society, not everyone does read and write, and of those who do, it remains true that reading is not the only way to absorb knowledge or gifts of value. Story precedes and outdates the written word; humans have woven and painted, carved, spoken, and sung their stories for far longer than they have read them. The many ways of communicating one's stories need to be seen as equally valid. The use of cloth stories in quilts has been traditionally part of American communicative arts. Most of the early quilters probably did not read or write, but they spoke with the tools and materials they had at hand, cloth, needle and thread. Their visual stories can call forth a unique response and can inspire young people to create their own story offerings, whether quilted, written, spoken or in some new way yet to be invented by some ingenious young person. For those who struggle with words, those for whom reading and writing is difficult, this old way of communicating becomes new and satisfying; for those who love words and reading, it can only add new dimensions of meaning and experience.

INTRODUCTION

There are so many ways that quilts can be used to enhance the lives of young adults and to extend their literary experiences. The making of quilts, intertwined with the history of the United States, from the Colonial period through the abolition movement to the times of pioneer experience and up through the suffrage movement. So looking at quilts can help bring the story of North America's growth to life. They can be linked to feminist studies, or seen as visual poetry or music; they can provide opportunities for creativity and fun, used for multicultural studies, seen as a treasury of memories, or a way of reconnecting with one's roots. The act of making a quilt can be an opportunity for emotional or spiritual integration. They can provide a source of inspiration for writing, acting, storytelling, and for living boldly. Quilts lend themselves to cooperative venture; many small squares join together, each one a small project which becomes part of a greater whole. Rich nuances and potential for learning exist in these textural arts pieces, and a study of them yields much that can be used to encourage and extend the learning process.

Young adults still have the child's ability to think in symbols and live in story, combined with the stirring of analytical and critical faculties. While this can lead to self-involvement, they do feel a hunger for social and personal justice, which sometimes turns to disillusionment in the face of our society's hypocrisy. They also possess a sensitivity which is best channeled into creative endeavor. Much of this sensitivity frequently produces extreme introspection, or preoccupation with sexuality and relationships. These are all important issues for a growing person to learn about and come to terms with, and they need ways to integrate all these new feelings and urges, information, and longings. While I would not suggest that quilting is a panacea, there is a redemptive, healing quality to the creation of a harmonious whole out of disconnected fragments which can be very valuable. The painter turned quilter, Joyce Parr, speaks of the remembering aspect of quilting, where by "integrating textiles, a woman integrates herself and her world" (Ferrero, *Hearts and Hands, the Influence of Women and Quilts on American Society*, 64). Since young adults have the child's ability to live story coupled with an awakening sense of social responsibility and an emerging emotional awareness, they respond well to stories dealing with situations of human struggle, and valor against great odds. So many quilts, quilters, or the situations surrounding their creations contain these qualities and can call them forth. I think of a poem by Patricia MacNeal Miner in her *Quilts from Appalachia*. It begins by telling of a woman trapped by her poverty and ends:

> Her faith she packs so carefully away within a bureau drawer.
> Her faith she sings.
> Her faith she spreads as covering to the bed.
> There lies displayed her claim to stars and roses, to fruits and birds of paradise singing within the tree of life. (67)

Bringing examples such as this to young people's attention can be very unifying for them. It can help them focus attention outside themselves and make sense of the incongruities of the world, which they are beginning to discover as confusing. Young adults are capable of dealing with reality if they are allowed a creative outlet and taught some tools of integration.

INFORMATION AND SOME DEFINITIONS

Quilting is an ancient craft. The oldest known functional quilt in the world was found on the floor of a Scythian chieftain's tomb at Noin-Ula near the Mongolian/Siberian border. It is thought to date from between 100 BC and 200 AD. The central portion shows a stylized spiral design in quilting, while exotic, possibly mythological animals appear to dance around this large central square. Pictures of it can be seen in Liddell's *Japanese Quilts* (3).

Ornamental quilts are known to exist from even earlier, in the Eastern Zhou dynasty of China, around 770–221 BC. (Orlofsky, *Quilts in America*.) A quilt is a simple thing really, a covering made up of three layers; the top layer is frequently pieces of fabric stitched together to create a design. This is called patchwork. Or it can be one piece onto which a design has been applied by using cut out shapes of colored fabric. This is called appliqué. Or it can be simply the three solid layers, the two outer being fabric, usually wool or cotton, and the central layer being batting of some sort. Usually this is cotton, wool or in modern times may be a polyester or Dacron fleece. All three layers are then stitched together to create one warm covering. At times the stitches are in the form of tufting, so that the central layer is held loosely in place. But the classic quilt is held together by a series of tiny running stitches which go through all three layers of fabric and create a pattern as they do so. I know a little girl who calls them "running mice feet," and there is that miniature, dainty quality to many of them. It is this process which gives quilts their name and adds depth to the finished product, although many African-American quilters add dimension to their quilts in other ways with color, texture, and embroidery and do very little of the actual quilting stitches.

When European women first came to America they had only the fabric they brought with them. There was nowhere to buy more, so they needed to be very frugal with the material they had. It was cold here, and the women pieced together scraps of fabric, laid them on to whatever warm material they could find and stitched the layers together to provide warmth for their families. The beginnings of the American patchwork quilt was just this humble and simple. Later, when African women were forced to come to North America to work as slaves, they had even less fabric. They too needed to keep themselves and their families warm. They took the scraps of material left over from the sewing room at the "big" house, and again fashioned warm quilts for their beds. They brought with them from African countries a rich lore and set of symbols, and just as the colonists had done, and as future immigrants would do, they incorporated their traditions and symbols into their quilts. The original use for quilts was practical—people needed them to keep warm.

But the artist in the human has prevailed and quilts became things of beauty, some very complex, others exquisitely simple. The scraps of cloth became the medium for the artists, as they were for Lucy Larcom, the well-known poet and writer, who as a child liked to play with colored scraps of cloth, arranging them into little visual poems.

Quilts are pictures in cloth, whether abstract or realistic, and as such they tell stories, as all pictures do. Because of the infinite possibilities inherent in the medium, it is possible to develop patterns and pictures of multiple dimensions, and many people have done so throughout history. Quilting is the art form of simple everyday people with great, colorful, intricate dreams.

INVITATION; RHYME AND REASON

My hope is that I can convince you to use quilts or some other form of symbol-packed textural art to help young adults discover the power of story in their lives, and in those of others. While I am aware that you could identify any craft in a culture and study it carefully with the young people for evidence of story, I hope to offer some compelling arguments for the use of quilts especially when working with this group, in order to awaken or extend a love of story in them.

There are quilts of compassion, those that attempt to raise peoples' consciousness on social issues. There are the quilts of oppression, giving voice to people who were denied other outlets for their stories and opinions. There are quilts of celebration, those that take joy in families, life's passages, community. There are quilts of integration where the quilter makes sense of an issue or heals herself by putting it all together in the quilts. There are quilts intended to teach and pass on information or traditions, and there are those that do all these things on some level. They are an art form and as such share the rich nuances and possibilities of all art.

I chanced on the value of quilts as a means of extending the literary meaning for young adults while pursuing another train of thought. My question was then: "What are the stories behind the symbols used by textile artists?" I was especially interested in the symbols used by women in their crafts. I wanted to know what the symbols meant, to discover the stories behind them, those signs woven into everyday life by the textural story tellers. I saw all the patterns woven into all the household articles by women of every culture, the rugs, sweaters, shawls, quilts, and laces, each one a rich treasure trove of stories waiting to be told. It was the triumph of the artist in the human spirit that made the work of women especially appealing. Limited in time to create, by their domestic duties, they made those very duties acts of creation, celebrations of who they were and are.

With this quest for the stories behind the symbols, there are many paths, and more groves, all connected more or less to the main pathway, and as many more questions emerge, so that it becomes a matter of deciding which aspect to explore, which influences to delve into, which path to follow.

I realized that one could choose to study the protective charm aspect in the patterns, such as those knit into the Irish/Aran sweaters. They are believed to protect the fishermen and children who live on and about the sea, the sea which gives them their living and can claim lives as though in payment. There are the protective devices embroidered on the jackets of small children in China, or a host of other charm devices used by mothers the world over, such as the charms appliquéd onto African cloth to keep the evil eye away from those resting beneath or wearing them. Young people have a particular fascination with this type of symbolism, as evidenced by the surge of interest in wearing clothing made of Guatemalan or other ethnic-type fabrics, and those with designs such as batik, tie-dye, appliqué, and patchwork. It seemed to me then, and also now, that these textural story arts are beautiful and valuable. Yet untranslated into words again, they are stories half-told, hinted at, sadly forgotten in fact, while the symbols alone are handed down. Mozell Benson, an African-American quilter, speaks of this experience when she says "Black families inherited this tradition. We forget where it came from because nobody continues to teach us. I think we hold to that even though we're not aware of it." (Wahlmann, 2). In a sense we are all librarians in a world full of stories written in languages no one can read. The bittersweet quality of these uninterpreted stories calls to us for translation. Each of us can translate one story in our own way, and the interpretation is valid if it works for the translator. Perhaps this is why quilts lend themselves so well to this type of study. They express the individual personalities and different heritages of those who made them so well. There are quilts like visual jazz, hot, spicy, asymmetrical, that grow out of the Southern slave tradition. Then there are the cool, restrained, clean lines of the Amish quilts, like Emily Dickinson's poems. For these reasons and for others, I finally settled on quilts, for my original studies, more especially African-American quilts. In some ways the drawing of the map became its own story and along the way I realized what a wonderful source of stories these quilts offered.

Young adults are intrigued by superstitions. Some playful pieces of "quilt trivia" superstitions are rather fun: if you sleep under a new quilt, all your dreams will come true! If a boy slept under a Turkey Track quilt, which was popular in the mid 1800's, and originally called Wandering Foot, then he would leave home and never return! They are also intrigued by the different beliefs of other cultures. One thing I learned from studying quilts and textiles that might interest them is the information that it is believed by more than one culture that evil travels in a straight line. Chinese prayer gardens have deliberately crooked paths and bridges at sharp angles to trick the evil spirits into falling off the edge and either drowning in the water or being eaten by the carp swimming below. The West Central African textiles use asymmetry and complex designs that do not line up easily in order to confuse, slow down or turn away the evil spirits from those wearing or using those textiles. Compare these to the Japanese textiles and quilts which show a marked preference for asymmetrical designs and which may have similar roots. This type of information lends richness to the learning process for young adults, and if they are further involved in the process of creating their own textiles to display and/or clothing to wear which thus wards off the "evil eye", one can see their imaginations being kindled and their interest engaged. The more one can involve young people in activities such as this, which enlarge and enrich what they can say with words, which call on the powers of the right side of the brain, the better. There is so much accent on the activities which call on the powers of the left side of the brain, that adults in authority need to tip the scales consciously in order to maintain a wholesome balance. Being involved with creating textiles, whether quilting or weaving, patching or beading, can be a way of involving the whole person in the process of learning. What a wonderful way to incorporate knowledge this can become.

QUILTS AS STORIES

In relationship to superstitions, many quilts do represent the religious beliefs of the maker using the symbols and tell of a spiritual journey or story. We can point out to young adults that often this is the same as identifying the essential story of the people, for their religious beliefs stem from the very heart of their being and both form and inform who they are. The Yoruba people of Nigeria, for example, believe that the Yoruba goddess, Yemoja, teaches women her symbols, which are found on Adire cloths, made with starch resist techniques and indigo-blue dye. Examples can be seen in Maude Southwell Wahlman's *Signs and Symbols*. Patchwork in Japan also seems to have religious origins. The indigenous religion is Shinto, which teaches that all things, animate or inanimate, have a spirit. Clothing is no exception; in fact it commands a very special reverence and love among the Japanese. So to incorporate scraps of old cloth into new creations becomes an act of reverence and respect, a continuation of the story; the spirit of the cloth continues in its new place in the universe. This type of information could enrich the study of books such as Kyoko Mori's young adult novel, *Shizuko's Daughter*, a luminous, tender story of a young woman who loses her mother. She is able to regain the spirit of her mother's gifts to her through a patchwork of fragile bright colors in spite of the rigid society which demands unrealistic behavior from all its participants and made it necessary for that very mother to commit suicide rather than live without her daughter. Examples of the distinctive and exquisite Japanese quilts and more information on their special place in the world of quilting can be found in *Japanese Quilts* by Jill Liddell and Yuko Watanabe. In a similar vein it was believed by Korean people that organizing scraps of fabric into a thing of beauty brought happiness not only to the maker but also to the recipient. Patchwork has an auspicious symbolism in the East. Since by patching fabric together one prolongs its life, it is believed that wearing clothes made of patchwork implies the hope of long life for the wearer. The number of patches in a special garment may equal the number of years of the recipient, especially for the honored birthdays of 77, 88, and 99. What better way to involve young people in developing and displaying a reverence for another culture and for the aged than to involve them in creating such an article of clothing for an elderly member of the community? Erica Wilson in *Quilts of America* also notes how the Chinese reverence old clothing. She says they rarely discarded old clothing because they felt that through use the fabrics became part of the wearer. So old fabrics were recycled onto new ones. Like the Chinese, early Americans also preserved memories of those gone by, handing down fragments of clothing, incorporating them into quilts filled with memories. Ann Rinaldi uses this as the theme for her young adult novel, *A Stitch in Time*, in which the heroine creates a family quilt composed of fabric given to her by each member and every special friend of the family.

POSSIBILITIES; THEMES, MOTIFS AND SYMBOLS

One could focus on a particular heritage and identify the way one story or significant stories are represented in different ways by that people, in all the art forms such as woven, embroidered, paint, pottery, sculpture, etc. One could focus on a common theme spoken of in this nonverbal, textural way across cultures and countries and language barriers, those that are common to the human condition, the symbols of friendship, death, love, peace. In her *Collectors Guide to Quilts*, Suzy McLennan Anderson identifies many of these symbols used across cultures in quilts. A goose, for instance represents providence or vigilance, a willow tree, death (158). Young adults could identify the symbols in our culture which are relevant to them and write about them or use them in their own quilt squares or clothing to create more powerful works, yet to be discovered.

In identifying the similar symbols used by peoples across

cultures young adults can discover the satisfaction of seeing the many expressions of one truth, and the many truths of one expressive form. They can see how elemental knowledge common to the human condition is echoed from one culture to another, at once unique to that culture and at one with the whole human story. They could compare and contrast the arpilleros, the story quilts of the women from the Andes in South America, with quilts coming out of the Russian immigrant's experience, for instance. Patricia Polacco's delightful book, *The Keeping Quilt*, for younger children tells the story of a quilt which becomes, for a Russian Jewish family of immigrants, a family heirloom and talisman, and offers pictures which could well be used for a study like this. *Quilting the World Over*, by Willow Ann Soltow, would be a marvelous resource for any group comparing quilting styles from different countries. She introduces quilting techniques from many countries, such as Japanese Sashiko, African Dahomey and Indian Shisha appliqué, the Hmong patchwork from Laos, and tifaifai from Tahiti. This is a lucid, pleasing book, with good resources listed in the Notes at the end of each section. The many projects would make it a useful resource when working with young people, and there is a recommended reading list on each indigenous group. Soltow herself says of this book: "it is offered as a modest exercise in global thinking . . . as a bridge between . . . cultures; between our time and those to come. . . . After all the needle was invented to bind things together." (1)

It is exciting to identify these common threads of our destiny and our past. The flying geese motif, for instance, is used in many different cultures and is frequently identified with freedom. It would be fascinating to study with a group of young adults the symbols of flight in story quilts, what they mean to each culture, to the human condition in general, to see how different cultures view the same natural entities such as birds or air, and weave them into their stories. In "North African Bird Lore: New Light on Old Problems," James Bynon speaks of many Berber stories about birds, some quite fantastic, such as those of birds that suckle human infants secretly in the night. Some of the bird motifs used by the women in their quilts serve as charms to protect their infants from the harm which these suckling birds can cause which is variously spoken of as sickness, weakness, or even death. He also identifies a tantalizing scrap of a story and song which seem to link the wren and the robin of European folktale with similar birds in Northern Africa. Such a study of bird symbols might include a reading of *Silent Dances* by Crispin O'Malley, a science fiction novel depicting two societies who value quilting, one which is made up of great, intelligent, bird-like beings of haunting beauty. For the many uses of birds and flying in African-American quilts, see *Signs and Symbols* (Wahlman), and for mid-nineteenth century American quilts with bird motifs, see *Baltimore Album Quilts* (Sienkiewicz). The study of African-American quilts with symbols of flying could accompany the reading of Virginia Hamilton's fine collections such as *The People Could Fly* or *Many Thousand Gone*.

It is the oneness which fascinates. In a society where fragmentation is everywhere, where families are divided, tradition forgotten, relationships splintered, a deep yearning for wholeness arises. It takes many forms. People, especially adolescents and those in their early twenties, seek new spiritual paths, or reconnect with the old ones. They search for roots, their own and those of others. Ultimately all peoples are mixtures and come from multiple heritage. In this fractured society perhaps it becomes all the more important to identify from whence we come. Story is a powerful tool for doing this whether written, quilted, or spoken.

INVESTING TIME

It is not a romanticized nostalgia that sends us back in time with our young companions to discover how our ancestors represented in quilting stories what was important to them, but a desire to know from whence we came, so that we and they may bring the knowledge gained along the way with us into our daily lives and carry it into our future. We need to remember also that although and "possibly because they embodied the voices of women, quilts have not been accepted as avant-garde . . . their history reveals them to have been quite radical" (New Jersey State Museum, 48).

Some of us begin to realize that the very technological advances which are supposed to improve our lives, and which can give us access to one another, contribute to fragmentation and lack of stability in our lives. There was a time when this was not the case, when travel was slow and laborious, when there were no machines to speed up life. In these times there were troubles in plenty, but there was also a rooted, connected aspect of life for which many of us now hunger. Hence the fascination with "folk art", the art which grows out of a stable community existing in one place for a long time, long enough to build a history and develop unique ways of expressing that history. This art can then be carried with the people, and influenced by new traditions of another area. But *it takes time* to build it initially, and time is what seems to be swallowed up in so many peoples' lives today. This is something those of us who work with young people can give to them, the knowledge that taking time to create a community project such as a quilt is valuable and enjoyable.

I recently worked with two girl scout troops over the space of several weeks, making patchwork quilts to be donated for use with babies who are HIV positive, many of whom live in hospital settings, not necessarily because they are ill but because there is no home for them to go to. The girls ranged in age from nine to thirteen years, and spanned the usual wide range in terms of skill level, and attention span. They worked in groups cutting blocks, drawing designs with fabric crayons, pinning fabric together, and sewing patches and strips together. The younger ones generated more crayoned squares than we could fit into the quilts, but these we had them frame off with fabric scraps to take home with them. The older girls were more interested in finishing the quilts, and did not need to take anything home with them to feel fulfilled. The whole group worked in harmony together for hours at a time, and spoke most earnestly among themselves about the babies who would receive the quilts, their hopes and dreams for them. I am sure the loving, optimistic vibrations stitched into these offerings must have been beneficial to the little ones who finally rested under them, and they created a nice space within which to work with the young people. More important, this project gave the girls an opportunity to do something positive in the face of a national tragedy.

INTEGRATION

This is important work. Humans are essentially artists and need to express this in order to be whole, especially when confronted by situations which are puzzling, frightening, or simply sad. The creative process can help one make sense of senseless situations and rise above pain. Examples of how people have responded to these types of situations by creating story quilts can be found in *Story Quilts, Telling Your Tale in Fabric*, by Mary Mashuta. For instance, there are two quilts illustrated there which are responses to the horror and heartbreak experienced when Japanese Americans were interned by our government. One of them tells the story of a woman who experienced the pain as a small child observing the rounding up of her friends who were Japanese Americans. The other tells the touching story of two Japanese American children who were incarcerated. Naoko Anne Ito, now a grown woman, tells in her quilt "Letting Go" how she and her brother released the bird they had hoped to keep as a pet when they realized they were separating it from its mother and making it a captive, like themselves. While it is a moving metaphor for the years of her imprisoned youth, there is a great sense of joy and liberation in her quilt. Another example is of course the incredible AIDS quilt project, which attempts to remember and cherish the thousands of Americans dying in this epidemic.

In our compartmentalized and success-driven society, we forget the value of taking time to express these creative, sensitive aspects of ourselves. We forget also that it does not have to be the *best* to be valuable. To express our story, or that of another, is healthy in and of itself. It is to be celebrated. It does not have to be the most important; it can just be a part of who we are, a written/spoken/or handcrafted item that speaks of the creator. For young adults this is especially true since they are questioning society, and seeking a meaningful place for themselves in their world. In *Hands All Around*, Judy Robbins and Gretchen Thomas validate that the process is what matters when they give examples of cooperative quilts for all occasions, such as weddings, babies, new houses and old, cultural heritage, for families and institutions, and communities large and small, whether village, city, county or country. Many schools, both elementary and upper grades, have discovered the value of creating quilts together. Usually it is a celebration of one of life's passages. Sometimes, it is a class project to go along with a unit. Often each child is represented in the quilt, with a picture created by them, or a symbol chosen by each child. Robbins and Thomas chronicle celebrations of human connection, laments over the past, such as the Hiroshima quilt which attempts to bridge gaps and forge new ways of relationship. They show quilts made by people of all ages. Essentially a guide book on how to successfully quilt cooperatively, it also has information interesting to those exploring the folklore aspect of quilting. And it affirms that it is the act of creation which is important as much as the resulting beauty.

In the textural stories we see this faith expressed, that what the creator did with the scraps of cloth or beads or threads had intrinsic meaning by virtue of her desire to create. As Suzy McLennan Anderson so aptly puts it in *Collectors Guide to Quilts*, "The endurance of art in any form is, by its nature, a reflection of the inherent dignity of the human spirit. Quilting, like other art forms, illuminates our will to create, to speak out, to embellish and improve the world in which we mysteriously find ourselves. They were, at the time of their creation, as they are now, an answer to the question of who we are, who we were . . ."(4). Young adults, who are coming to a new awareness of their own dignity, welcome ways of improving the world in which they find themselves.

The satisfaction of knowing and expressing one's story can add a dimension of safety and meaning to one's existence. Mary Chiltoskey knows this. She quilts to tell a story and to teach about her Cherokee culture and history. She made the Smokey Mountain Child's Quilt in 1988 to present the legends, history, nature, and geography of the Qualla Indian Boundary, home of the eastern Cherokees.

SKILL BUILDING

Another advantage to young people of the "time-taking" aspect of quilting is that skills are built while they are engaged in the process. Not only the obvious skills, such as sewing, but more subtle, deeply needed skills, such as communication, character building, negotiating, a sense of timing, tolerance, and self-control are developed. A social worker I know, who works with young inner city mothers at risk for abusive behavior, describes the reasons she began to quilt with these young adults. She notes that there are many skills not generally valued or learned during the course of growing up in this society. These are skills which in an earlier era would have been learned automatically while performing the necessary daily household tasks. Because these young women have not learned that things take time, they want immediate response, especially from their children. They need to learn a sense of tolerance, timing, history, control of anger. Through quilting they learn to take time, to take steps which gradually build towards a goal, to take pride in a process and in the finished product. She has found that in working on a quilt they recreate an arena where some of these skills can be learned and, she hopes, eventually applied to child-rearing skills. Some of them resisted the process at first, but the other young women encouraged them and pushed them to participate. Of these initial reluctant quilters, all now quilt joyfully; one enjoyed her first square so much that she went on to make five more!

Most of the mothers are under 22 years old, some as young as 16. They desperately want friendships that have weight. The social worker speaks with feeling of the support experienced as the young women gather around one another, working on a common goal. There are many levels of communicating, and while they rarely know the specifics of each other's situations, they are able to be supportive on a wordless level. One woman found the process so moving that she sat and quilted with tears streaming down her face, and the teenagers to each side of her moved wordlessly closer and touched her hands, her shoulder in sympathy. It is the age-old model of women nurturing one another while engaged in work, mitigating individual pain through corporate venture. It seems highly fitting that it should be a craft form which allowed many of these young women's ancestors the opportunity to sustain themselves, to express their creativity in the midst of oppression, that now offers their descendants a means to learn the skills which might enable them in some measure, to escape from the vicious cycle of victim becoming abuser and perpetuating the abuse. As the contemporary writer Alice Walker has said, slave and later free black women kept their creativity alive through quilts. As the only medium available to them, it enabled them to order the universe in a personal image of beauty.

TRIUMPH OF THE HUMAN SPIRIT

The slaves who worked on the plantations, the indentured servants, those who worked in the mills, the women, black and white, who designed old quilts were able to rise above the indignities thrust upon them by expressing some small measure of the beauty of their spirits in these fragments of cloth. I think of that lovely picture book for middle readers, *Sweet Clara and the Freedom Quilt*, based on a true story of a resourceful young slave woman who made a quilt "map" showing the way from her plantation to the first stop on the underground railway, thus earning freedom for herself and many others. I think also of Harriet Powers, born a slave in 1837, and creator of some of the most powerful and spirited story quilts ever made. It is important for young adults to know that the art forms their ancestors created are valued and given a place of honor in our society. Harriet Powers' quilts are treasured by the Smithsonian Institution and the Museum of Fine Arts in Boston. For more information on Harriet Powers see *Stitching Stars, the Story Quilts of Harriet Powers*, a book in the series African-American Artist and Artisans, by Mary E. Lyons. It is a juvenile biography, but one which is written and illustrated so beautifully that its appeal becomes ageless. Young adults, struggling for their own voice, seeking their own place in the world, can be strengthened by examples of how others have done this, often against great odds.

A study of women's struggles to achieve equality belongs naturally in the curriculum of young adults, consumed as they are by issues of personal freedom and justice. The stories of women struggling to recognition as full human beings can rightly be placed beside those of other marginalized peoples, all through history and throughout the world. The recognition of the stories encapsulated in the household items that these women created adds a dimension of reality to the study of their lives. Rather than being facts on a page, they can be experienced as the real valiant humans they were. The names of quilt patterns frequently reflected the political issues of the times, and women renamed them to indicate their political opinions. Jacob's Ladder was renamed Underground Railroad during the abolitionist movement. Robbing Peter to Pay Paul was renamed Drunkards Path when the Women's Christian Temperance Union, established in 1874, began to use quilts as banners for their cause. Many quilts showing intolerance of alcohol were made during this period, frequently using blue and white, the WCTU's colors. Although some of the suffragettes denounced the needle and thread as a major force in their subjugation they did raffle off handmade quilts to raise funds for their cause. As with the Hawaiian quilts, this art has frequently reflected women's social or political statements when they were not given the right to speak out publicly or vote. For instance, there is a quilt made by a Deborah Coates, of Lancaster County, Pennsylvania, around 1840. Right in the very center, the heart, of this quilt is a small triangle on which is seen the figure of a slave with upraised arms, and the text, "Deliver me from the oppression of man." (Ferrero, 71–72).

THE PROCESS

The social worker I spoke of earlier involves as many of the young mothers as possible in the quilting process from the very beginning. She thinks the young women have always viewed the project favorably because she began with something from their own history. They all had memories of quilts in their backgrounds. She herself was raised Amish and remembers helping with many quilts as a child. They talk about the characteristics of the fabrics, using analyzing and categorizing skills. In a somewhat unorthodox fashion, from a quilter's point of view, each person chooses fabric she likes and creates at least one square (the more common practice is to plan the quilt before the squares are made!). Then they meet as a group to decide how to put the squares together into a quilt. This can be quite a challenge, as the squares sometimes vary widely in size and even in shape. Great excitement is generated and political and negotiating skills are developed during the spirited discussions which ensue, where everyone tries to explain her vision and convince the others to side with her views!

This process would work equally well with other groups of teenagers. The decision making process could include some discussion of personal taste, style and preferences just as the social worker does. A perusal of some of the very fine book collections of quilts from different cultures could help the young adults decide on a style that matched either their own heritage or character, or both. There are hundreds of books on quilting, some better than others. I would suggest *A Gallery of Amish Quilts*, *Japanese Quilts*, *African Images in African-American Quilts*, and *Quilts from Appalachia*, as likely to inspire the creation of more cloth creations. In addition *Quilts of Illusion* by Laura Fisher might be especially intriguing to young adults. She has gathered together an impressive selection of optical illusion quilts. They are visually exciting and different, with lots of movement and Escher-like tiers of designs which are a joy in and of themselves. One can only stand in awe of the mathematical genius of these women who had no formal training yet were able to design these intricate geometric eye/brain teasers. Another one which is really special is Mary Mashuta's *Story Quilts, Telling Your Tale in Fabric*. She answers many of the questions which first-time story quilters might ask, and illustrates several story-quilts created by herself and by her students in her story-quilt classes. She calls it a book about creative problem solving, about how to create a narrative quilt where fabric, design and color combine to tell a story. Like Robbins and Thomas, she emphasizes that what is important is the process, not the product, though many of the products are still things of great beauty.

We can help young people to see that the fantasies of any group form the basis of its culture, that this is where we search for common ground, in the fantasy, or story of a people. For if play is story in action, and story telling is play put into narrative form, then each time we discover a new way of telling or interpreting a story we are learning to "play" a new way and are enriched corporately and individually. Young adults, balanced on the cusp of childhood and adulthood, have the capacity to play, still know that play is story acted out, and yet are developing their critical faculties at the same time. This gives their story telling a special quality, and means that they are capable of working through important issues by working with their hands and hearts in story making.

IN RESPONSE TO OPPRESSION

Young adults need to know that the stories of a people are part of everything they do. They are not compartmentalized into one section of their lives, just the written or just the oral. The stories are woven into every thing they make, sometimes unconsciously, sometimes deliberately, as when this is a joyful celebration of the symbols of their history, or a concerted effort to pass the stories on, frequently when other avenues of expression are being suppressed by an outside oppressor. On the other hand, the need to express a story can simply grow out of that wholeness of one's experience. Native Americans, forced to speak only English and punished for their heritage, expressed their traditions and stories in visual ways, through their craft, in cloth, beadwork, and textiles of different kinds. There is an exquisite quilt example of this illustrated on page 67 in *Hearts and Hands*. Made of deer skin and strung with delicate beading, like paths of cobweb glittering with sunlit dew, it is an obvious expression of love for the maker's Sioux traditions. And in Erica Wilson's *Quilts of America* on pages 64–65 there is a picture of a striking Seminole Indian quilt by Gayle Dixon, where traditional Seminole patchwork motifs gleam in polished cotton against a rich dark background to make a bold and powerful expression of her pride in her own heritage. It was out of the experience of oppression that Hawaiian women responded in 1893 to the American invasion of their country. They were forbidden to fly their flag over their country and quilters responded by making flag quilts called "Ku'u Hae Aloha" which means "My beloved flag". And Hawaiian women also make another type of quilt, celebrating their history, depicting their gods, stories and patriotic themes in stylized figural motifs. They use appliquéd shapes that almost look at times like abstract depictions of oriental dragons, or fire, or flowers, while at others they recall the formal Norwegian snowflake patterns of the kind knitted into sweaters. More information on the unique art of Hawaiian quilting can be found in several books such as *American Quilts* by Jennifer Regan.

Young adults need to know that a people's story is their power. The Jewish people have always known this and have guarded their written story as sacred, deeming it the "Word of the Lord" or the Torah. Other peoples have known this too and preserved their stories in any way they can. These are the stories of particular interest, the ones written not in words but in symbols and signs. In certain West and Central African cultures woven and appliquéd textiles are used to encode various writing systems, as well as to act as protective charms. According to Maude Southwell Wahlman at least three such pre-European ideographic writing systems are known. In her fascinating book, *Signs and Symbols*, she connects the images found in African-American quilts with their sources in Africa. Karl-Ferdinand Schaedler speaks of similar patterns in *Weaving in Africa*, such as those done on a background called mamponhemmaa, meaning "queen mother of mampon". Who is she? Whoever she is, the gorgeous quilt celebrating her is crammed with symbols. Many of them are geometric, yet reminiscent of flowers or stars evolving into flowers; some are so female that they remind one of Georgia O'Keeffe's flower paintings. The whole pattern is bound together by intricate borders of diagonal lines and stripes, so that a sense of harmony and strength emanates from this piece.

Another example of how art grows out of oppressive conditions comes from Southeast Asia where the Hmong textile traditions go back to the period when the Hmong lived as a minority group in southern China. Under Chinese rule they were forbidden to speak their own language. There was no written language, and the women were concerned that their language and cultural tradition would be lost. They used appliqué and cross-stitch to preserve and pass on their history and legends. An account of their journey may be found, along with samples of their exquisite quilts, in Jennifer Regan's *American Quilts, A Sampler of Quilts and Their Stories* beginning on page 17. They are some of the many unique story-quilts she chronicles with faithful attention to detail. She speaks of personal visions, journeys and emerging faces, among the other things that are portrayed by quilting women across many cultures. Another good reference work on the Hmong textiles is Anthony Chan's *Hmong Textile Designs* in which he makes the annotated designs the main body of the work. The bittersweet quality of such stories speaks to young adults. They are beginning to notice the injustices abounding in our world, and need examples of how the human spirit has repeatedly triumphed over the evil which human corruption continually creates. Examples of this kind of victory can help young adults come to terms with the duality of human nature, and to maintain faith in the ultimate triumph of the positive powers of the universe. They are themselves full of personal visions, making their own journey and discovering their emerging faces. They frequently have a deep fascination with stories of oppression, because they themselves feel like "strangers in a strange land". Studying other people in that situation can be deeply affirming for them while it places their own angst in perspective.

At some time around the end of the Civil War, a wounded discharged soldier made a quilt in order to soothe his shattered nerves. It is a poignant mixture of symbols both of war and of domesticity, beautifully balanced in color, shapes and patterns. Multicolored soldiers march and ride horseback on wide panels around a harlequin field which in turn frames the central large square, in which women, men and animals converge on a star-like flower. The soldiers on horseback have the look of medieval characters while the foot soldiers seem to foreshadow the helmeted men of World Wars I and II. It is rather like the ancient Scythian chieftain's quilt. Some stories get told over and over again. In this case he has told a story not only of the past, but sadly of the future. One only hopes that the process was healing to this particular soul; viewing the result is certainly inspiring to ours. It would be an enriching addition to the study of the Civil War by any group, including young adults. They could be given assignments, such as "reading" the quilt for meaning, telling stories inspired by the quilt, inventing character studies of the maker and/or the characters depicted, and so on. It may be seen in Anderson's book, *Collector's Guide to Quilts.*

STORIES INSPIRED BY QUILTS

Quilts are not only wonderful presenters of stories, they can also provide the inspiration for and be used in stories. Several books on every level, from picture books to adult fiction, have used them either as the theme or talisman. The Appalachian picture book, *The Rag Coat*, about a little girl who needs a warm coat, uses patchwork as a metaphor for healing. Her mother's friends join together to make her a patchwork coat, which becomes more than a warm garment, for it changes her mean-spirited companions into allies when she tells them how all the stories behind the patches come from their lives. The unifying principle is her shining spirit. Another story for younger readers which is rather fun is "The Tatty Patchwork Rubbish Dump Dancers" in Margaret Mahy's *The Chewing-Gum Rescue*. It is about a resourceful little girl and her grandmother who create their own high-spirited form of patchwork comfort and joy while living at a rubbish dump, and in true fairy tale style, end up transforming the life of a bored king. Two young adult novels weaving quilts throughout their plots are *Nell's Quilt* by Susan Terris, and *Crazy Quilt* by Jocelyn Riley. *Nell's Quilt* is a rather dark, somewhat puzzling story, where the quilt seems to suck the power and life out of a young woman on the verge of a difficult marriage. It might make for interesting discussions on will and personal power. In *Crazy Quilt* Jocelyn Riley uses the quilt in a more traditional and satisfying way, as a metaphor for integration. Her young heroine deals with a mother's mental instability and other difficulties in her life with courage, and ultimately comes to a sense of peace with herself. Riley ends the book with this passage: "A quilt never starts as one piece, but, in the dream, by the end there was a beautiful quilt made into a whole—pieced out by what was broken or spoiled. The edges were smoothed, stray ends sewn down. And the quilt lay flat and smooth, ready to warm and ready to please." (215)

Finally, there is an adult work of fiction which is too wonderful not to include in any discussion of quilt-based stories. *How to Make an American Quilt*, by Whitney Otto is the *New York Times* best seller, which the reviewers correctly called "radiant", and "intensely thoughtful". Otto owes her debt to the writers of

Hearts and Hands, which she recommends as strongly as I do. Her novel works because of the clever way she uses quilting as the framework. She lifts us with compelling artistry into a world where the patterns of her quilts are echoed in the stories of her characters' lives.

The stories I have found are more those associated with the art of quilting than the ones represented by the symbols. For example, Ruth Finley tells a lovely swashbuckling romance of a story in her book *Old Patchwork Quilts.* It seems that there was a certain young lady working on an "Oak Leaf" pattern quilt while imprisoned in her attic room by her father, who did not think that the young whaling master she had chosen was good enough for their family. It was 1828 in Long Island, and this was common practice for fathers of obstreperous daughters, but after two weeks the young lady abruptly surrendered to her father's wishes and became engaged to the man of his choice. It was during a clamming party when the newly betrothed couple was on the shore with the other young people of the village, that suddenly a ship dropped anchor close to the shore and a dory manned by several husky sailors quickly rowed to shore. The obstreperous maiden was abducted from under her friends' noses and ran away to sea with her beloved. An eye-witness account has it that there was a path of gold made by the setting sun all the way from the shore to the sailing vessel (52–54). I can imagine the fun a group of young adults would have making a play out of that story, and the unfinished "Oak Leaf" pattern quilt left behind to jog the memories of the family.

Yes, stories I have found in plenty, stories of those who made the quilts, and used them, stories of those who created the fabrics, spun the thread, picked the cotton, planted the seed. There are narratives about the quilts themselves, how they grew, the ofttimes passionate causes underlying their creation. In many ways the whole story of quilting in America becomes the history of the nation. Though it is not "his" story so much as "hers". A reading of the previously quoted *Hearts and Hands,* or a viewing of the video by the same name, will show you what I mean by this. In this book, three women bring together hundreds of examples of how quilting has played an integral part in the forming of America. They celebrate the accomplishments and

contributions of women to the history of our country. They
point out issues we may not have always realized, such as the
fact that nineteenth century women not only quilted in patterns
called Monkey Wrench, Carpenter's Square, Compass, or Anvil;
they also knew how to use these tools, and made use of their
knowledge of carpentry and building design when designing
their quilts. This book could be used to augment the study of
history or to inspire an English class, or just as an enjoyable
read. The authors have gathered together an impressive amount
of information, and pieced it skillfully into a whole which flows
from subject to subject as gracefully as the colors on some
Amish quilts flow from light to dark and back again. It is a tender, inspiring and fascinating "take" on United States history,
and one which puts women in their rightful place as integral
movers and shapers of this country's destiny.

POSSIBILITIES; SOME WAYS TO ENRICH STUDY

Young adults do not have to actually do the quilting for quilts to
enrich their lives, although I would certainly encourage it. They
can study and be inspired by the quilts themselves, and by their
place in history. They can design quilts on paper if time and/or
inclination do not permit the real thing. Creating a fantasy quilt
which is meaningful to the person involved is valuable; it is
encouraging storytelling in a visual way, and calls on the right
brain's powers over symbol and intuition, creativity, and spatial
design. Young adults could be given assignments of many kinds
based on a piece of textile symbolism such as a quilt. They could
be told to write a story with the quilt as the talisman or the central theme, or as the turning point of the plot. They could be
asked to write a story inspired directly by the quilt, just by looking at it and absorbing the piece before they begin to write, and
see what happens. Of course one would want to use the very
finest story quilts in order to give them some real substance to
work from and with. Harriet Powers' quilts or Faith Ringgold's
or one of the many exquisite offerings illustrated in *Japanese
Quilts* would be fine examples. And one would want to offer
books wherever possible to round out the experience and offer
more information. Robyn Montana Turner has written a delight-

ful biography for young people, *Faith Ringgold*, with full-color photographs of many of Ringgold's most beautiful works. One in a series on notable women artists, it is a celebration of Ringgold's unique talent, and shows how she maintains her artistic integrity and establishes her work as being rooted in her African-American heritage. One can sense when viewing her powerful quilts of art, that Faith Ringgold, as a feminist, has made a conscious decision to wed her politics to the female art of quilting, because of all it represents in terms of the bedroom, and its social history. (New Jersey Museum, 48–49.)

One beautiful textile could become the unit, a Navajo blanket or an exceptional quilt available for careful and constant scrutiny. Display the item, and ask the young people to discover as much as possible about it, and report back to a central coordinator. It could encourage independent study, initiative, a sense of connection with the roots of a particular community and increase appreciation for that cultural group.

Such a quilt could become the focal point for research into the meaning and origin of the symbols, or the story of the creator, or the materials used, the dyes, threads, and fabrics. A reading of Katherine Paterson's fine young adult novel *Lyddie* would accompany such a study. And information from *Hearts and Hands*, making the connection between the slave trade and the weaving of cotton in the mills could be included. The young people with their penchant for the dark marker of intensity would relate to such poems as this powerful one by Lucy Larcom, quoted in *Hearts and Hands*; it begins with this verse:

> "I weave, and weave, the livelong day:
> The woof is strong, the warp is good:
> I weave, to be my mother's stay;
> I weave to win my daily food:
> But ever as I weave" saith she,
> "The world of women haunteth me."

. . . and ends with this verse:

> "And how much of your wrong is mine,
> Dark women slaving at the South?

Of your stolen grapes I quaff the wine;
The bread you starve for fills my mouth;
The beam unwinds, but every thread
With blood of strangled souls is red."

Lucy Larcom, Poems
(Boston: Fields, Osgood, & Co., 1869), 134–137

I have concentrated here on quilting as a means of extending the literary experience for young adults. Any other textural art form would work as well. To thoroughly explore the production, means, process, symbols used, and conditions surrounding the creation of Turkish carpets or Navajo blankets, for instance, would yield equally satisfying learning and an expanding awareness of the strengths and weakness not only of those being studied, but also of those engaged in the study. This is especially true when a part of the learning process is the participation in the creation of one of these textile art forms, to as great an extent as is practical. However, quilts are very special for Americans in that they are a particularly American art form, and exhibit characteristics in one way or another, of almost every ethnic group which has come to make up this vast "melting pot".

CONCLUSION

I hope I have induced you to think about using quilts with young adults in some fashion. I hope you now have an inkling of the myriad possibilities and ways in which this might make sense. Each group is unique, and it always works best with adolescents to begin with an established interest and expand the horizons from there. I think the implications of projects such as the social worker's with the at-risk group of young women, are tremendously exciting. There are any number of other at-risk groups with which such a project might work, within schools, detention centers, rehab programs, and anywhere that a focused activity is needed in order to create a context for healing dialogue. Quilting projects could enliven a homeschooling environment, be used as a cross-generational activity, or unite people in a neighborhood. The possibilities are endless, limited only by imagination. I hope you will take the idea and put it to use with the young adults in your life, whoever they may be, and may it be fun, and satisfying, and may you feel connected with the rich history and creative people who have led the way in piecing together the threads of their lives and our heritage.

We have a challenge to take up with young people: to identify and translate into the spoken/written word again the stories which came from the wisdom and strength of peoples long ago. It is only a beginning, and the major portion of work remains yet to be done. But the process they used is available to us in our search, and if the search is satisfying, if we discover ourselves in the process, perhaps this is what really matters. I hope that this will serve as a catalyst for the reader to explore further the fascinating world of quilt stories, the physical embodiments of traditional tales produced by oppressed yet triumphant peoples. These stories so captured the imagination that they permeated every aspect of the lives about them, and were echoed in song, dance, household craft and textile design; they were the strength and hope of the people, that which formed and made them unique, fascinating and one.

WORKS CITED

Anderson, Suzy McLennan. *Collectors Guide to Quilts*, Radnor: Wallace-Homestead, 1991.

Bascom, William R. *Contributions to Folkloristics*. Sadar, India: Archana, 1984.

Bishop, Robert, and Elizabeth Safanda. *A Gallery of Amish Quilts, Design Diversity from a Plain People*. NY: Dutton, 1976.

Brommer, Simon J. *Creativity and Tradition in Folklore, New Directions*. Logan: Utah State UP, 1992.

Brooks, Vicki, and Linda Stokes. *The Quilter's Catalog, A Complete Guide to Sources and Supplies*. Pittstown: Main Street P, 1987.

Bynon, James. "North African Bird Lore: New Light on Old Problems" *Folklore*, Vol 98. ii, 1987. 152–171.

Chan, Anthony. *Hmong Textile Designs*. Owings Mills: Stemmer, 1990.

Crispin, A. C., and Kathleen O'Malley. *Silent Dances*. New York: Ace Books, 1990.

Dewhurst, C. Kurt, Betty Macdowell, and Marsha Macdowell. *Religious Folk Art in America, Reflections of Faith*. NY: Dutton (in assoc. with Museum of American Folk Art) 1983.

_____. *Artists in Aprons, Folk Art by American Women*. NY: Dutton, 1979.

Ferrero, Pat, Elaine Hedges, and Julie Silber. *Hearts and Hands, the Influence of Women and Quilts on American Society*. San Francisco: Quilt Digest P, 1987.

Finley, Ruth E. *Old Patchwork Quilts and the Women Who Made Them*. Newton Centre: Manufacturers Trust, 1970.

Fisher, Laura. *Quilts of Illusion*. Pittstown: Main Street, 1988.

Granick, Eve Wheatcroft. *The Amish Quilt*. Intercourse: Good Books, 1989.

Hamilton, Virginia. *Many Thousand Gone, African Americans from Slavery to Freedom*. NY: Knopf, 1993.

_____. *The People Could Fly, American Black Folktales*. NY: Knopf, 1985.

Hopkinson, Deborah. *Sweet Clara and the Freedom Quilt*. NY: 1993.

Kresge Art Center Gallery and Maude Wahlman. Ceremonial Art of West Africa. East Lansing: Kresge Art Center, 1979.

Khin, Yvonne M. *The Collector's Dictionary of Quilt Names and Patterns*. Washington DC: Acropolis, 1980.

Liddell, Jill and Yuko Watanabe. *Japanese Quilts*. NY: Dutton, 1988.

Lipsett, Linda Otto. *Remember Me, Women and Their Friendship Quilts*. San Francisco: Quilt Digest P, 1985.

Lyons, Mary E. *Stitching Stars, The Story Quilts of Harriet Powers*. NY: Scribner's, 1993.

Mahy, Margaret. *The Chewing Gum Rescue*. Woodstock: Overlook P, 1991, 77–85.

Mashuta, Mary. *Story Quilts, Telling Your Tale in Fabric*. Lafayette: C & T, 1992.

Mills, Lauren. *The Rag Coat*. Boston: Little, 1991.

Miner, Patricia MacNeal, and Maude Southwell Wahlman. *Quilts from Appalachia*. University Park: Penn State UP, 1988.

Mori, Kyoko. *Shizuko's Daughter*. NY: Holt, 1993.

Museum of the Confederacy. *Before Freedom Came, African-American Life in the Antebellum South*. Charlottesville: UP of Virginia, 1991.

New Jersey State Museum. Alison Weld, Curator. *Dream Singers, Story Tellers: An African-American Presence*. Japan: Yoshida Kinbundo, 1993.

Nunley, John, and Judith Bettelheim. *Caribbean Festival Arts*. St Louis: St. Louis Art Museum, 1988.

Orlofsky, Patsy, and Myron Orlofsky. *Quilts in America*. NY: McGraw Hill, 1974.

Otto, Whitney. *How to Make an American Quilt*. NY: Ballantine, 1992.

Paterson, Katherine. *Lyddie*. New York: Dutton, 1991.

Polacco, Patricia. *The Keeping Quilt*. NY: Simon & Schuster, 1988.

Regan, Jennifer. *American Quilts, A Sampler of Quilts and Their Stories*.

NY: Gallery Books, 1989.

Riley, Jocelyn. *Crazy Quilt*. NY: Morrow, 1984.

Rinaldi, Ann. *A Stitch in Time*. NY: Scholastic, 1994.

Robbins, Judy, and Gretchen Thomas. *Hands All Around*. New York: Prentice Hall Press, 1986.

Schaedler, Karl-Ferdinand. *Weaving in Africa, South of the Sahara*. Munchen: Paterra, 1987.

Sienkiewicz, Elly. *Baltimore Album Quilts*. Singapore: General Printing Services Pte, 1990.

Soltow, Willow Ann. *Quilting the World Over*. Radnor: Chilton, 1991.

Terris, Susan. *Nell's Quilt*. NY: Farrar, 1987.

Turner, Robyn Montana. *Faith Ringgold*. Boston: Little, 1993.

Wahlman, Maude Southwell. *African Images in African-American Quilts*. NY: Studio Books (in association with American Folk Art Museum), 1993.

Wilson, Erica. *Quilts of America*. Birmigham: Oxmoor House, 1979.

CHAPTER ELEVEN

Establishing Roots: African-American Images, Past and Present

Farris J. Parker

Images of African-Americans, past and present, are becoming more and more available to young people today. With the current concern for multicultural diversity, that beautiful mosaic of people of different cultures, languages, and nationalities and their contributions to the American way of life presents young people with alternative ways of knowing about their world and its history. In this chapter, I have examined the contributions of artists beginning with a brief discussion of a few outstanding illustrators of contemporary picture books who present strong images of African-American people and culture for young children. This is followed by an historical account of images of African-Americans in art, often inseparable from Native-American art in its early history, that presents and values the roots from which contemporary images have grown. Such images are critical in laying the groundwork for young people of all races, colors, and ethnicities to appreciate the contributions of those who, throughout history, were often overlooked or blatantly and completely ignored. In the discussion of early black artists, I have included biographical information to demonstrate some of the relationships between these artists and their positions in the society in which they lived. Although my concern is with young adults, it is clear that efforts to help these young people get in touch with the roots of African-American art draw upon both children's picture books and art books for adults.

Today literature regarding ethnicity and the contributions of various ethnic groups is increasingly important in schools and libraries. Libraries are addressing this issue through the purchasing of books, videos, and periodicals, by instituting committees, seminars and programs to answer the needs of users throughout the community. Perhaps this is partly due to the recognition by local libraries and schools of the need to provide the youth of their communities with a clearer picture of the contributions by their ancestry. It is also due in part to the nationwide outcry to improve the quality of education in America and to instill within the youth of America a vested interest in the survival of their country. Self-esteem and pride in one's beginnings are critical as young people learn to value themselves and others and what they have to offer for the good of society.

This chapter is directed at parents, teachers, and librarians who guide and share information with children and young adults. African-American fine artists and illustrators of children's books can make a profound difference in the projection of positive images, reflecting a more diverse representation of America. Knowing the heritage of black images and of black artists in this country adds a sense of connectedness as young people examine and build a personal self-image. Although the African-American is the vehicle for this venture, the central theme deals with the sensitive treatment of all those who, despite being discriminated against, have contributed to our society. Whether we are referring to ethnic groups, women, or those who are physically challenged, inclusiveness is a broad-based issue, and educators will continue to play a key role in defining and re-defining it. Understanding and appreciating the contributions of all peoples is important both in the intellectual and the aesthetic growth of young people.

The term African-American will be used in conjunction with and as the culmination of previous terms throughout history, such as Negro, Afro-American, and Black people. Not so long ago in the post-bellum rural south, when an African-American child was born, the description of the child's race was indicated on the official birth certificate as being that of *colored*, a derogatory term, which was the official designation at that time. Negro is simply a term derived from the word Negroid, which is one of the four root terms to describe the different races of the world, that is, Caucasoid, Negroid, Mongoloid, and Polynesian. "Afro-American" and "Black People" were terms African-Americans adopted for themselves during the Civil Rights unrest during the 1960s and 1970s to express the pride, beauty, and determination found within themselves. In the 1990s the concern is to be politically correct; thus, the phrase African-American is used. Terminologies referring to African-Americans are important because of the classification and indexing schemes found in libraries. Information regarding African-Americans can be retrieved in indexes under the terms: Black People, Afro-American, Negro, and African-American.

AFRICAN-AMERICAN CHILDREN'S BOOK ILLUSTRATION

There are many contemporary illustrators of African-Americans whose target audience is children. Children's books and their themes reflect one of the first contacts young children have in developing their own self-images, their views of the world around them, and expectations of social interactions with one another. There are certain illustrators whose characters and themes encompass multicultural diversity and are fine examples of sensitivity to the developing self-image of children. It is important to note, however, that those professionals who interact with young adults should also take interest in picture book illustration. Older youngsters can also benefit from familiarity with this work and may be instrumental in sharing these images with younger children.

I have selected only a small sampling of those illustrators who are my personal favorites and whose art work has been inspirational in their treatment of story content. The collaboration between a husband and wife team, Leo and Diane Dillon, has produced many beautifully illustrated children's books, and the Dillons have received numerous awards for their illustrations. *Why Mosquitoes Buzz in People's Ears*, a Caldecott Award winner, is a retelling of a West African folktale by Verna Aardema, published in 1975. The Dillons describe their artistic insights, mental projections, and imagery in depicting the story in *Something About the Author*:

> *Mosquitoes* is a repetitive tale in which the events are interpreted
> by different animals, each with a distinct point of view. We found
> ourselves concentrating on the play between the animals. People
> often ask us if we have spent time in Africa. We have not,
> although we would love to. People have said that we have 'cap-
> tured African light,' for example. But you know, if you look up at
> the sky anywhere in the world, you see the same sunsets, the
> same clouds. You get the same feeling of wonder (63).

Leo and Diane Dillon painstakingly compose and illustrate
each page of a story as though it were an independent work of
art. The techniques the Dillons incorporate in the illustration of
a story carry a wide range of diversity in color, line, and composition. One noticeable and distinctive aspect of their style has to
do with the methods they employ to frame the illustrations on
each page of the story. Their range of colors can vary from a full
color palette to a limited monochromatic treatment. Themes can
range from fairytales and folklore to the most sensitive social
story of family love between a boy and his great-great-aunt as
found in *The Hundred Penny Box*. This story was illustrated in the
medium of watercolor with a limited palette of earth tones
(monochromatic). The style is distinctive with softened edges of
the figures and background, in which the Dillons employ a
direct narrative in terms of imagery to guide the reader or
viewer through the story. Also, the Dillons have incorporated a
few illustrations in which they simulate "memory and recollec-
tion," through combining a collection of images from the past
with the central image, which is the present time. Thus, the Dillons have illustrated stories that encompass both remembered
time and history, as found in the beautifully executed *Aida*. This
is a tragic and romantic opera, the story set during a war between Egypt and Ethiopia. It is also a story of the love between a
young Ethiopian, Aida, and Egyptian general, Radames. From
the beginning their love is doomed, and, in the end, it claims the
lives of the heroine and hero. The Dillons have adorned each
page of the story with elaborate decoration and ornamentation.
Beautifully illustrated, the story is a fascinating array in full
color palette of design and draftsmanship. *Aida* is a must read, a

classic display and showcase of superb illustrative techniques. Their illustrations leave the reader or viewer with a sense of mystery and wonder and appreciation which can be shared by young and old. They also create images that complement and enhance the author's intent. Children are excited by the pictures they see and are highly motivated to read the story.[1]

Tom Feelings, notable author and illustrator of children's books, primarily focuses on African and African-American subject matter. His use of line and color is subtle but deliberate in its execution, creating beautifully composed illustrations that leave a lasting effect on the reader. His subject matter and themes convey a sense of pride and dignity directed towards the young reader. Feelings has traveled extensively back and forth to Africa, illustrated numerous children's books, and has also received a prestigious array of awards and honors. Throughout his life and work, Feelings has tried to demonstrate, through his illustrations, the strength and beauty of the black people. As Feelings writes in *Something About the Author*:

> I strive to intensify the reality, to tell the truth about the past, even if it hurts now in the present (55).

It is interesting that Feelings chose to briefly chronicle his life in his children's book, *Black Pilgrimage*. In this children's book, Feelings tells of his trials and tribulations of growing up in New York and his struggle to gain entry into the field of illustration. His experience is also intertwined with the black experience and black identity. Eventually, he traveled to Ghana, Africa. It was there that he spent several years and found his true calling as a children's illustrator. It is through his attempt to capture an inner glow that Feelings fashions his artistic approach for his illustrations. He creates bright and fused depictions of limited color and a somber mood. Ultimately Feelings' illustrations are not just about who's black or who's white; they have more to do with the human condition and human dignity.[2]

Tom Feelings' illustrated *Soul Looks Back in Wonder*, a Coretta Scott King award winner, is a miraculous compilation of images, thoughts, and ideas. The cover depicts silhouettes of a young girl and boy looking inward, linked by a narrow yellow band or stripe connecting their spirits. Suspended vertically is the "key of hope." The key is positioned downward, just above books of knowledge. Symbolically, the image conveys the idea that knowledge and education unlock doors and overcome obstacles, giving credence and rise to dreams, hopes, aspirations, and the pursuit of happiness. Throughout the illustrations in this book, Feelings engages viewers with his use of somber earth tones, bright colors, and dramatic compositions to provide a quiet intensity to the mood of the book. All of the illustrations appear to have been done with a deep concern for their positive impact on African-American children.

The first image, accompanying Margaret Walker's "Mother of Brown-Ness, Earth Mother," shows tightly clasped hands and arms; a mother's embracing and caressing arms showing strength, love, and security. The hands and arms are all encompassing, reaching around the world and graceful, as demonstrated by the display of the arm bracelets. The hands and arms also convey a sense of past, present, and trial. The woman as the central subject is looking on in quiet reflection, pondering the journey as a traveller or voyager riding a bus or train, observing the landscape as it speeds by. Her facial expression in profile is pensive, resigned to the task at hand. The circular colors of her earring on her ear lobe represents the colors of the African-American flag, her heritage. The viewer also gets the impression that the artist himself has been on a quest or hero's journey, seeking means and ways of expressing himself through artistic pursuits. This can best be explained to viewers, by taking a closer look at another of Tom Feelings' earlier works, *Daydreamers* authored by Eloise Greenfield.

Jerry Pinkney works primarily in watercolor with a strong emphasis on contoured line and overlapping perspective, an illustrative technique that creates the illusion of distance by overlapping one shape over another shape. Working with both primary and secondary colors in transparencies, Pinkney is able to model his subjects through the use of line, paying attention to detail, mood, and subtle nuances.

Pinkney, as a draftsman, works carefully not to overstate the obvious in his illustrations; he provides readers or viewers with just enough information to keep them turning pages. Pinkney's illustrations for *The Patchwork Quilt* by Valerie Flournoy is a fine example of his illustrative narrative technique. He sets the stage through the cover illustration of a young African-American girl seated on the arm of a chair next to an elderly woman wearing glasses. One may deduce that the woman is the young girl's grandmother. In the woman's lap is a quilt, and the girl and the woman seem to be in discussion over the quilt. This image and the title immediately make the quilt the focal point of the story. The cover also projects a sense of family togetherness, a link between the past and present, between young and old. As readers and viewers progress through the story, Pinkney's illustrations reinforce this concept of family unity.[3]

Brian Pinkney, or Jerry Brian Pinkney, is the son of Jerry Pinkney. Brian Pinkney's work, like that of his father, is rooted in a concern for positive images of African-Americans in fiction and non-fiction. Brian Pinkney works primarily in scratchboard, fashioning his figures and compositions by scratching and carving away excesses with a pointed stylus or wedged instrument. An interesting result that can be achieved through this technique is a linear effect or scribbling which follows the contours of the forms, giving the impression of motion and rhythm, a distinctive characteristic that denotes Pinkney's work. Brian Pinkney also employs overlapping perspective in the creation of his subjects and background scenes. His background scenes are limited, and his use of colors is also limited, restricted to primary and secondary colors.

In describing Brian Pinkney's work, one notes its poetic nature and the flow of movement across the pages with action and momentum. The illustrations for *Alvin Ailey*, authored by Andrea Davis Pinkney, his wife, illustrate this point. Here Brian Pinkney captures the feeling and essence of the times and a young man's aspirations to become a dancer. He incorporates a series of off angle compositions to attract and move the viewer or reader through the narration of the story. The illustrations are dramatic and heroic in their depictions.[4]

It would be useful to explore possibilities and alternatives by examining a wide range of talent representative of diverse ethnic and gender backgrounds. For example, Floyd Cooper has illustrated a variety of books from the poetry collection *Pass It*

On to *Grandpa's Face* to *Chita's Christmas Tree*. The above are African-American artists, but those of other races have also illustrated picture books with sensitive and strong portrayals of African-Americans. Patricia Polacco has brought a wonderful sense of movement in *Chicken Sunday*. Trina Schart Hyman has illustrated *The Fortune-Tellers* in densely packed pictures. Other illustrators such as Faith Ringgold, Jacob Lawrence, James E. Ransome, John Steptoe, Ann Grifalconi, Vera Williams, Bernie Fuchs, and Carole Byard have all portrayed African, Caribbean, and African-American images for young children that inspire a sense of self-awareness and connected identity.

HISTORICAL IMAGES OF BLACK PEOPLE AS PAINTED BY WHITE ARTISTS

It is especially important for young adults to be familiar with our country's history and with the artistic images that recorded and preserved that history. There are some excellent adult sources that can contribute to young people's understanding and appreciation of the contributions of African-Americans to this history. Ellwood Parry's, *The Image of the Indian and the Black Man in American Art* is an historical account, beginning in 1590, of the first publishing of images of Native Americans and black people in the New World. No other races or racial groups ever came to symbolize the North American continent in the same way that Native Americans, who were discovered here, and the black slave, who was brought here to work the fields. These two groups defined the land that is now the United States.

Images of Native Americans and black people have been standard elements in the iconography of the New World for several centuries. Ellwood Parry's work contains prints of comparatively authentic views of people and places along the eastern coast of North America. These images appeared as engravings which were presented as first-hand information, available to large numbers of readers one century after the initial voyage of Columbus. The engravings of 1590 had an important influence on later artists. Parry's work indicates that no complete documentation has ever been compiled for the period 1590–1900.

During the seventeenth century, for example, pictures of Black slaves or servants in America were virtually non-existent. At the end of the eighteenth century, a few American painters working in London, managed to incorporate Black figures into semiheroic compositions or history paintings. Negroes were usually forced to play comic parts in American genre scenes and political cartoons well into the 1800s. It was not until the 1850s that images of Black people began to change drastically in content as they multiplied rapidly in number (xiii).

The Image of the Black in Western Art, From the American Revolution to World War I, Vol. 4, by Hugh Honour, is part of a four-volume set which chronicles images of black people throughout the world. Volume 4 focuses particularly on the African-American leading up to and at the turn of the century, highlighting the artworks of white artists, such as, Thomas Eakins and Winslow Homer. It was through the works of Eakins and Homer that the heroic and humanistic positive portrayal of the African-American in America was finally realized in image, highlighting the African-American's participation and contributions to American society during the mid-1800s.

Thomas Eakin's painting of a black woman titled: *Portrait of a Black Woman* (1867–1869), is profiled in a semi-three quarter view, from head to upper torso, with the left side of the figure cast in shadow or darkness, presenting a subtle and ominous atmosphere to the viewer. The painting conveys the sentiment and plight of black people in America. The woman's expression is one of being resigned to her dilemma and to the circumstances of her situation. A beautifully executed painting by Eakins, this work also projects a haunting, unmistakingly sad, and pensive reflection of an aspect of America's dark history, surrounding slavery and the post-bellum period.

A watercolor, also painted by Thomas Eakins a decade later, titled: *Negro Boy Dancing*, initially entitled: *The Negroes* (1878), depicts three African-American figures engaged in a mesmerizing scene that was often popularized in early American paintings of black people. It is a stereotypical image of a young man seated playing a banjo, an older man standing and looking on, and a young boy dancing to the music. Once again, Eakins's mastery of realism and exacting details reveals an underlying social comment about white perceptions of the role of black people in America.

Honour focuses primarily on the musical characterizations of the banjo player and the boy dancer and the intense concentration conveyed among the three figures. Although I am not in complete disagreement with Honour and his description of the scene, I find that Eakins's concerns were much more complex and involved than the surface musical depiction of a banjo player and dancer. The boy dancer appears detached from his surroundings; his facial expression seems unemotional, and his dance movements mechanical and automatic, as though he is being trained and prepared for a life of second-class citizenship.

In a painting by Homer titled: *A Visit from the Old Mistress* (1887), Honour refers to the scene as being directly from the post-bellum situation in the South. He states:

> It is not a polemical work. The black women are neither obsequious nor rebellious, though obviously free and self-confident in their stance. The old mistress, just as sure of herself, neither ingratiating nor commanding, eyes her former slaves across a gulf of incomprehension (190).

Homer's painting is indeed worth discussion and examination, particularly as to the artistic techniques applied, and as to what is actually taking place in the scene depicted. It is interesting that the old mistress (white) enters the composition or picture from the right side of the painting. Many compositions are composed so that the viewers read from left to right, the normal pattern of reading text. Although rules are made to be broken, I believe Homer's suggestion is that it was an unannounced visit, in which the old mistress suddenly appears. As the scene progresses in the opposite direction, from right to left, there is a gradual darkening of the picture plane. This painting is a five figure composition, comprised chiefly of four women, and one small female child being held in the arms of her slave mother. The child's gender is clear by the bonnet she wears. I am fascinated by the fact that Homer focused primarily on four women and one child in this composition, as suggested by Honour, either among the women who are slaves or the old mistress. As indicated earlier in my discussion, the picture plane moves from right to left, and from light to dark. At the left side of the painting number five figure (slave woman in the composition) is seated in darkness. This image seems to project a strong sense of the uncertain, not knowing what to expect or what the future holds. Freedom is a state of mind, provided that you have a strong sense of what freedom means to you intrinsically. These women who for all of their lives were slaves suddenly find themselves free, and have yet to reconcile between no longer being in bondage and now being free. I do agree somewhat with Honour in his observation that this is not a controversial painting, but it should not be assumed that there is not an uneasy tension in the painting. There most certainly is. The black women and white woman in this composition fully comprehend the dilemma of their situation and are resigned to the circumstances, but they seek to find a common ground as women.

A leading white artist of his time, John Singer Sargent, demonstrated through his magnificent painting ability an image of a black man titled: *Nude Study of Thomas McKeller* (1917). In an article for *Arts Magazine*, Trevor Fairbrother describes Sargent's painting as a bravura ability in which the artist renders

> highlights or shadows with a single, long dramatic brushstroke, and they possess the kind of richly worked paint surface at which he excelled (57).

Fairbrother conveys to the reader a clear understanding as to Sargent's expertise, but does not delve at length into the psychological underpinning of Sargent's painting. Thomas McKeller was Sargent's principal Boston model, and Sargent posed McKeller in a position that is quite telling. The representation is of a black male nude, completely stripped of self-ownership, semi-seated, legs spread somewhat back as though chained, and arms also positioned rigidly as though chained. The model's head is positioned looking upward, defiant, and yet hopeful. Sargent painted this work when he was in his early sixties. He never exhibited the painting, and it remained obscure and unknown for years, until it was discovered in his Boston studio after his death. (Fairbrother, 56–63)

HISTORICAL IMAGES OF BLACK PEOPLE

Guy C. McElroy's work, *Facing History, The Black Image in American Art 1710–1940*, is an excellent example of a compiled work that not only documents the contributions of African-Americans in representational artforms but also provides insights into the behind-the-scenes concerns and interests of the artists that motivated and impacted on the creation of various works.

> Prosperous collectors created a demand for depictions that fulfilled their own ideas of blacks as grotesque buffoons, servile menials, comic entertainers, or threatening subhumans; these depictions were, for the most part, willingly supplied by American artists. This vicious cycle of supply and demand sustained images that denied the inherent humanity of black people by reinforcing their limited role in American society (xi).

McElroy's book tracks the early injustices perpetuated and directed at African-Americans through images in terms of the *Jim Crow* mentality, followed by indignities and lies which America adopted as truths and half truths. This volume reveals what actually occurred historically. The readings and images demonstrate the evolution, through various artists of different ethnic groups, of presentations of African-Americans in a more positive, truthful, and humanistic light. The talents and technical skills of these artists were highly advanced and they contributed greatly to more realistic perceptions of African-Americans. Among the artists responsible for bringing about this change at the turn of the century were: George Wesley Bellows, Robert Lee MacCameron, Robert Henri, John Sloan, Wyman Adams, John Stewart Curry, James Chapin, Edward Kimble, Augusta Savage, Charles Burchfield, Reginald Marsh, Thomas Hart Benton, Archibald J. Motley, Jr., Ben Shahn, and Jacob Lawrence.(xi)

SHARING TRADITIONS AND THE BLACK LEGACY

Five African-American artists are highlighted in the work, *Sharing Traditions, Nineteenth-Century America*, by Lynda Roscoe Hartigan. Hartigan describes the black racial situation and climate of America in the 1800s as an era of identity sorting for African-Americans. Many African-Americans could trace their ancestry back over a hundred years in America. Unfortunately, a continuing problem in the United States has been that African-Americans were, and even now are, treated as though they were invisible in their own homeland. It was out of this period of African-Americans seeking their own identity and attempting to establish a foothold and their own place in America that five key African-American artists emerged: Joshua Johnson, Robert Duncanson, Edward Mitchell Bannister, Edmonia Lewis, and Henry Ossawa Tanner. These five African-American artists were to set the course and pave the way for future black artists on the American art scene. About Joshua Johnson, Hartigan wrote:

> Johnson's life and art were lost in historical oblivion. Rediscovered in the late 1930s, Johnson is now recognized as one of the South's most intriguing portraitists of the early nineteenth century; he is among only about a dozen Afro-Americans known to have worked as painters prior to 1840. (39)

Before an examination of Joshua Johnson's style, work, and painting technique, there has to be a brief insight into the man as artist. In many of the records regarding Johnson, it would appear that Johnson was a man of mystery. There is no documented evidence, as of yet, that has been uncovered as to the date and place of Johnson's birth. Essential dates regarding his life achievements are unknown. It can be ascertained that the most productive years of his life took place between the years 1796–1824. Although it is known that Johnson immigrated from Haiti to the United States, records are somewhat obscure as to whether he entered the United States as an indentured servant, slave, or freeman. Many of the years of his life were spent in and around the city of Baltimore, Maryland, a port city for seafarers. Johnson was a self-taught painter and artist who derived many of his commissions for portraits from Maryland's leading civic, military, and mercantile families. Johnson may have been a light skinned black (mulatto), able to speak English with a degree of competency, but he also spoke French fluently. As a black man living in Baltimore, Maryland, he was required to carry papers indicating that he had freeman status. This is also highlighted by the fact that his name was listed in the city directory; no slave would have been granted such a consideration. Although most scholars agree that Johnson's background can be considered as that of a slave, his early beginnings are unknown. As he was owned by the John Moale family, he was possibly also owned by several other families in Baltimore. It is thought that he earned his freedom through his artistic ability.

Another factor that may have had an influence which impeded recognition and acknowledgments of Johnson's fame had to do with the incorrect spelling of his name. The city directory revealed that often his name would appear as Joshua Johnston. Johnson did not sign his artwork, and better known painters often received the credit for that work. Quite recently two portraitures were discovered bearing Johnson's signature, titled: *Sarah Ogden Gustin* (1805) and *Mrs. Thomas Everette and Her Children* (1818). Based on the finding of these two paintings and on records of the court and the Catholic church, it would appear that Johnson was the correct spelling of the artist's name. It is also through Catholic church records that Johnson's family members are identified: Sarah his wife, and his three children George, John, and Sarah (daughter). Johnson and his family moved frequently about Baltimore in his efforts to establish himself as a painter of portraits.

In regard to Joshua Johnson's painting technique, it can be said that he was an American Primitive or Folk painter. His figures were highly stylized with a flat appearance which was the accepted painting style of the early American period. Interiors or background information and props relating to the environment were extremely limited. The poses of the figures were stagnant and facial expressions taut, particularly around the mouth.

For example, in a family portrait study titled: *The James McCormick Family* (1804), Johnson poses the family in a stoic seating arrangement on a settee. The children are positioned in the center of the composition, parents are at opposite ends of the settee, the mother to the left of the picture plane, the father to the right. The scene is designed to convey an idyllic, and upright posture of the family. Three of the figures, a daughter and son, together with their father appear to have blank gazes or stares, looking off in different directions, with no discernible expressions. The mother on the other hand, appears to look directly at the viewer or artist depicting the scene, with a slight pensive smile. This I believe is an interesting point of subjective observation, pertaining to the mother and lady of the house. Her gaze is not for the eventual viewer of the portrait, but for the artist painting the portrait, not suggesting intimacy, but a look of friendship and affection. The females are dressed in white flowing dresses, indicating dainty and delicate natures, while the father and son are in black coats. The son's left hand touches his father's chest area, and his right hand touches his father's left hand, where the father is holding a letter.

The father's arm is posed around the boy, on the back of the settee, encompassing his son. In the father's right hand there is an envelope, indicating a mutual connection of male bonding, signifying men of letters. To the left of the painting, the mother is seated with her left arm and hand resting around her youngest daughter, and on her daughter's left shoulder, indicating access to her daughter, but not her son. The youngest daughter's right arm and hand is resting on the mother's left shoulder, indicating soothing or a giving of comfort. A curious feature concerning the youngest daughter pertains to her left arm and hand, where the small child is pointing to her mother's lower abdominal area, suggesting that her mother may be pregnant. Of course, these findings and perceptions are subjective observations and determinations, but it does demonstrate the power of an image, its implications, and its lasting impact on the viewer. Beauty, ugliness, and the discerning of an image is in the eye of the beholder; but it also depends upon the clarity of the image.

Many of Johnson's subjects were wealthy white socialites who afforded Johnson and his family a comfortable living style. The simulation of distance in Johnson's paintings was achieved through what is called overlapping perspective, an artist's technique which was commonly used in early American painting. Although an acceptable artistic technique, overlapping perspective could be somewhat limiting in its delivery of an image, depending on the subject matter. Instead of giving the illusion of a three dimensional composition, subject matter in images using overlapping perspective can appear as flat and rigid. Johnson painted in a direct and straightforward manner with an emphasis on modeling and detail.

A noticeable trait or signature pertaining to Johnson's subjects was the holding of an item which conveyed their station or position in the family or their social status. As outlined in the "James McCormick Family Portrait," subjects such as males may hold such items as letters, charts, and mechanical instruments. Women, on the other hand, hold books, flowers, and gloves. For instance, the child at the center of the McCormick painting, holds a basket of cherries. Johnson's work was never exhibited during his lifetime except in private homes. Today his work can be viewed in the Maryland Historical Society, the National Gallery of Art, the Baltimore Museum of Art, and in private collections.

Robert Scott Duncanson was a renowned muralist, a still-life painter, a painter of portraits and genre themes, and a photographer. He was most revered for his landscape paintings. Duncanson's biography, like Joshua Johnson's, is meager and sketchy in details. No portrait or photograph of Duncanson has ever been located.

> The artist was born in Seneca County, New York in 1821 or 1822. The son of a free black or mulatto mother and a Scottish-Canadian father. . . . Little more is known about Duncanson's life until 1841. (Hartigan 51–52)

Duncanson settled in Cincinnati, Ohio, where he embarked on a career as a landscape painter. Like Johnson, Duncanson was self-taught, but he excelled in his artistic abilities commercially and financially. With all his fame and the acknowledgments of the quality of his art, Duncanson was plagued by internal and external strife relating to the color of his skin, and he was unable to reconcile the turmoil within himself. Duncanson was a light skinned black, accepted in the white artists' community as an accomplished painter but ridiculed in the black community as a black man attempting to pass for white, a charge which was unfounded. This was the climate in which Duncanson found himself. It is an interesting dilemma in which societal problems set the stage to destroy a person of merit. Duncanson eventually succumbed to mental illness and was treated for approximately three months at the Michigan State Retreat facilitie.

Duncanson died on December 21, 1872. The cause of his death is unknown, but it can be speculated that his inter-racial background was assuredly a social and personal factor. Duncanson's versatility and range regarding subject matter was so broad and all-encompassing that to explain his artistic techniques in these various subject themes would require extensive explanations as to his diverse style. For the purpose of this chapter, the focus is primarily on his landscape painting. Duncanson had a clear and profound understanding of the beauty of the great outdoors. Through the use of one-point and two-point perspective, Duncanson would engage the viewer by transplanting the mind's eye into scenes of serenity and calm. He created atmosphere in landscape painting that would give a sense of time, distance, and space. One-point and two-point perspective has to do with the horizon line. In other words, imagine if you were in a car on a stretch of roadway, the windshield would become your picture plane, the area in which you would wish to draw or paint a picture. Looking straight ahead, you have a horizon line at your eye level. Imagine also a row of fences, telephone lines and posts on both sides of the roadway. Select a middle point or vanishing point on the horizon line, and notice how everything is either to a right-angle or left-angle of the picture plane. Everything seems to converge to this middle point you have selected; this includes the roadway, telephone lines and post, and fences. This is the principle surrounding perspective drawing: things are wider as they are closest to you; they become smaller or diminish as they are farthest from you. The same principle also applies to two-point perspective; the difference is that you have two vanishing points on the horizon, but at opposite ends of the picture plane, widening and intersecting as the right and left angles approach the foreground of the picture plane. Other forms and techniques in regard to perspective drawing can also be mentioned here, such as aerial perspective, ground or ant perspective, overlapping perspective, diminution, foreshortening and convergence. To discuss a few of these varying aspects of perspective drawing would require more detailed information, which is not necessary for the purposes of this chapter. The central and essential principle to keep in mind is the horizon line, vanishing point, left and right angles. Duncanson's draftsmanship and brush-work were sharp and rich in detail, capturing the subtle nuances found in hills, valleys, and rivers; and his colors were vibrant and representative of nature. He was truly a master of landscape painting. One such painting which is a fine example of one-point perspective, and of Duncanson's skill in landscape, can be found in the painting titled: *Mountain Pool* (1870). Duncanson not only incorporates one-point perspective to simulate distance, but he also uses overlapping perspective for the rock formations in the foreground of the painting to draw the viewer into the scene. The scene depicts two slopes with trees to the right and left of the painting. The point at which these two slopes meet is slightly off center; a waterfall pours down into a lake. In the immediate foreground are the overlapping rock formations with two or three lone figures in the foreground. It is important to note that Duncanson also emphasizes a feeling of distance through his painting technique by creating atmospheric conditions of haze or fog in the background. Duncanson may have selected landscape painting as his forte because of his love of outdoors, but it may also have been the neutrality of landscape and still life painting which attracted him. Landscape and still life painting depend on the degree of the finished look and are more acceptable artforms to the general public. Thus, landscape painting would insure Duncanson a successful career in art, neither rupturing nor stirring public opinion or creating controversy. Duncanson's view of himself made him a successful artist, but, unfortunately, may have impacted on his true identity.

Many artists, black or white, select landscape or still life scenes as a possible avenue for success in the fine art community. The majority of those artists, however, probably choose such themes based on their passion for the subject matter. One such black artist was Edward Mitchell Bannister. He was a deeply religious man whose landscapes were spiritually inspired by the beauty of the countryside and the French Barbizon tradition or style of painting. The French Barbizon tradition was the forerunner of Impressionist and Post-Impressionist painting. Bannister was a mulatto black who, unlike Duncanson, was able to freely move among blacks and whites socially without succumbing to the racial stereotypes perpetuated against dark skinned blacks and mulattos.

> Bannister was born in November 1828 in St. Andrews, Canada. His father originally from Barbados, died in 1830. His mother, Hannah Alexander Bannister, whose racial origin has not been determined, was a native of St. Andrews. Executing his first drawings and a watercolor by the age of ten, Bannister credited his interest in art to his mother. (Hartigan, 70)

Between the years 1863 and 1865, Bannister attended Lowell Institute for evening drawing classes. This was also the opportunity for Bannister to learn anatomy and to draw from live models under the tutelage of his mentor, William Rimmer, sculptor and physician. Bannister is credited with being one of the few African-American artists afforded the opportunity to receive artistic training during the nineteenth century. He married Christiana Carteaux on June 10, 1857. She was born in 1822, in North Kingston, Rhode Island and may have been descended from the Narragansett Indians. Christiana Carteaux owned a hairdressing salon which catered to Boston's elite patronage. Her prosperous business contributed significantly to Bannister's success as an acknowledged painter in the Boston and Rhode Island area. Bannister also won a major first-place medal in 1876 at the Philadelphia Centennial Exposition which grounded and enhanced his popularity.

In discussing Bannister's work, it is important to focus on his devout spiritual beliefs. He embraced the rural landscape as God's way of affirming harmony and spirituality in all things creative. Edward Mitchell Bannister's painting titled: "Seaweed Gatherers" (1898), is a scene which depicts a man pushing a wheelbarrow from right to left in the picture plane, set in an open field. The wheelbarrow is filled with seaweed; on top of the seaweed is a small size pitchfork standing upright in a diagonal position used for gathering the seaweed. The subject matter is one of the simple country life of work and toil. Bannister also incorporates a dominating pyramid shape, which grounds the overall composition, conveying a sense of power and strength with a series of diagonal and verticle lines, that are the underlining and underpinning of the composition. It is also evident of

Bannister's training and devotion to the Barbizon school of thought; his use of somber and muted colors, coupled with brushstroke manipulation, fuses together soft tonal values, creating a solemn and quiet mood. Bannister's colleagues described him as a poetic painter whose concerns were with the natural order of things in nature. The mood of his paintings reflected and exemplified this belief. He died on January 9, 1901. It is difficult to access the production of his paintings between 1850 and 1860, due to the fact that so few have survived. In the last ten years of his life, Bannister produced twenty-seven paintings dated up to the 1890s which are on exhibit at the Museum of Art, Rhode Island School of Design.

Edmonia Lewis (sculptor) was born in 1843 or 1845, perhaps in Ohio or near Albany, New York. It was also proposed that she was born on July 4, 1845, in Greenbush, New York. The exact date of her birth is somewhat obscure.

> Lewis noted that her father was a full-blooded black gentleman's servant and her mother a Chippewa Indian 'of copper color' and with 'straight black hair.' Orphaned before she was five, Lewis followed the wandering life of her mother's tribe until she was about twelve years old. Lewis entered Oberlin College in Ohio in 1859. The college promoted co-education since its founding in 1832 and admitted Afro-Americans since 1835. . . . Emerging as a sculptor during the Civil War, Lewis modeled medallion likenesses in clay and plaster. (Hartigan 86–88)

Edmonia Lewis was a self-sufficient and determined artist. She relied totally and completely on her own talent, self-awareness, and self-worth as an artist and human being. Lewis was a woman descended from two cultural backgrounds, Black and Native American. She attributed a large part of her innate talent and ability to her mother and her Native American people. Although she did not disassociate herself from her black heritage, she felt that her Native American people chose to take a stand against the white establishment, as opposed to being subjugated into slavery and servitude as black people had. In her efforts to escape American stereotypes, Lewis decided to travel to Europe to study sculpture, where she eventually settled in Rome during the winter of 1865–66. She worked primarily in marble, creating exquisitely beautiful sculptures of a neoclassic tradition. Edmonia Lewis's sculpture, *Forever Free* (1867), is a nineteenth century sculpture done in the neoclassic tradition. The figures are of a black male and a female whose race is not quite discernable; both figures appear to have been released from slavery and captivity. The black man is standing with his left hand raised in triumph, with a shackle and broken chain dangling from his wrist. The woman is kneeling with her hands clasped in prayer. On her left ankle there is a shackle and broken chain. The heads and expressions of both figures are raised in hope. The sculpture is delicate and a refined piece of detailed artwork. Lewis also incorporated and fused into her sculpture her own personal heritage as an African-American and Native American, coupled with social commentary relating to the treatment of her people in the United States. Lewis neither sought nor accepted art criticism or guidance concerning her work. She learned various sculptural techniques from the works of the old masters, by copying and imitating. It was also through her own tenacity that she was able to acquire recognition, acknowledgment, and commissions for her work.

As a young woman, Lewis's work reflected a refinement and accuracy found in the works of artists well into their years. Unfortunately, only forty-six different sculptural compositions were located after her death in Rome in 1911. Many of her works can not be found. Not much information has been documented concerning the final decades of her life. The date and place of her death remain unknown.

Henry Ossawa Tanner is possibly the most significant African-American artist of the five artists discussed. He set the standard for artistic excellence for African-American artists to follow.

> Henry Ossawa Tanner (painter) was born on June 21, 1859, in Pittsburgh, Pennsylvania, of English, African, and Indian ancestry. (Hartigan 99)

As Tanner developed into a young man, he became keenly interested in pursuing a career as a painter. Tanner's parents at first were not sold on the idea of their son becoming an artist. His father's hopes were that his son would follow in his footsteps as a minister. Benjamin Tucker Tanner also hoped that his son would consider working in a flour business belonging to a family friend. As a child Tanner was stricken with a childhood illness, and the work in the flour business proved to be too much for the young Tanner, aggravating his already fragile health. Tanner's parents, realizing their error in judgment, decided to finance their son's interest in becoming a painter. Tanner enrolled in the Pennsylvania Academy of the Fine Arts in 1880 where he was introduced to his teacher, friend, and mentor, Thomas Eakins.

It was through his association with Eakins that Tanner developed many of the artistic disciplines necessary to become an accomplished painter. Although Tanner enjoyed the close association and instruction of his mentor, Eakins, he was saddened and dismayed by the taunting and physical humiliation from his fellow students. He eventually left the Pennsylvania Academy in 1882, after only two years. Tanner then struggled for the next six years to establish himself as a painter. Philadelphia at the time was not very supportive of the city's artists, particularly its African-American artists. Because of this climate of non-support and racial discrimination, Tanner exhibited and sold his work only infrequently. Although Tanner did achieve some degree of success in Philadelphia, eventually he decided to relocate to Atlanta, Georgia to open a photography business. Tanner concluded at the time that the additional training he had received from Eakins in photography would prove invaluable in starting his business. Unfortunately, the business proved to be unsuccessful and provided him little opportunity to paint. It was at this time that Bishop Joseph Crane Hartzell, a well known Methodist Episcopal clergyman and his wife purchased many of Tanner's paintings to help finance his trip abroad. Tanner traveled to Europe on January 4, 1891. At first his intentions were to study in Rome; but, after a brief stay in Paris, he changed his mind and settled there. Tanner enrolled at the Academie Julien in Paris where he studied painting throughout the balance of the 1890s. During Tanner's studies in Europe, his artistic concerns focused primarily on human dignity. He painted sensitive depictions of African-Americans in genre type American scenes such as *The Banjo Lesson* (1893) and *Old Couple Looking at a*

Portrait of Lincoln (1892–1893). It was also at the Academie Julien, under the influence of his principal teachers, Jean Joseph Benjamin-Constant and Jean Paul Laurens, that Tanner developed a strong and poignant interest in historical and biblical scenes. As Tanner progressed in his art instruction, his intent was to deal primarily with humanitarian themes; thus, he was led back to his family roots grounded in religion. It was through his personal experiences that Tanner began to create religious scenes after 1895. He never again returned to genre American scenes involving African-Americans. His spiritual paintings earned him instantaneous recognition. The first large such painting was *Daniel in the Lion's Den,* which was exhibited at the Salon of 1896 and won an honorable mention. *Daniel in the Lion's Den* is an extraordinary painting in which Tanner depicts the scene in a blue and green color scheme. Tanner orchestrates the scene by transplanting a man unjustly accused of a crime into a den of lions. There are two sources of light, that appear to come from open areas above the den. Daniel, the central character is partly seated and posed leaning against the wall of the den, with his head and shoulders in shadow. Moving about the den are five adult lions, curious and fascinated by the lone human figure that has invaded their space and territory. Daniel's arms are crossed in front of him, and he appears docile and passive before his captors. It is an ominous scene, that is made even more compelling, when one of the lions moves closer as his head appears in the light, to investigate and taunt the unwelcomed visitor. The following year Tanner won a third-class medal for the *Raising of Lazarus* (1897), purchased by the French government for its Luxembourg Gallery. It must have been quite an irony for Tanner to have the Philadelphia Academy of the Fine Arts buy and exhibit his painting titled: *Christ and Nicodemus on a Rooftop.* This was his first significant honor in America.

In time Tanner met Jessie Macauley Olssen (1874–1925), a young American studying operatic singing in Europe. Tanner and Olssen married in 1899. They had one son named Jesse, born in 1903. During the course of their life together, Jessie and their son Jesse frequently modeled for Tanner's paintings. For example, they were models for *Christ Learning to Read* (1910–1911) and *The Annunciation* (1898). Tanner eventually received the highest notable award that could be bestowed on a notable individual, the Chevalier of the Legion of Honor (1923). On September 8, 1925, Jessie Tanner died of a fatal lung disease. The death of his wife completely devastated Tanner, making him unable to work for two years. Tanner eventually recovered and resumed painting. Throughout the balance of his life, he was periodically visited by young black artists who regarded him as the Dean of Painters. Tanner died May 26, 1937 quietly in his sleep. In his quiet demeanor he stood against all odds; and through his work he expressed hopes, dreams, salvation, freedom, and peace for all mankind.[5]

AGAINST THE ODDS

An important work by Gary A. Reynolds and Beryle J. Wright, titled: *Against the Odds, African-American Artists and the Harmon Foundation*, discusses this foundation that brought together a pool of African-American artists and supported the artists in their pursuits. Two leading philanthropists, William E. Harmon and Andrew Carnegie, played key roles in insuring the exhibiting of African-American artists' work. Harmon provided the necessary funding which allowed the artists to study and travel abroad. Carnegie's generous support of various ventures opened the door for African-American artists to exhibit their work. Carnegie's particular contribution was the establishment of public libraries throughout the United States. He supported a special program for building libraries in black communities as part of the general library building program. These libraries, as well as an expanding network of YMCA buildings, created the opportunity to give black artists the exposure they needed. Prior to the involvement of Carnegie and Harmon, African-American artists were shut off from exhibiting their works in American galleries and museums. This period between 1928 to 1933 was known as the "New Negro Movement."

> While exhibition opportunities were generally limited for contemporary artists at that time, the added race barrier prevented African American artists from participating in gallery and museum exhibitions and artists societies that could have furthered their careers. For this reason, artists societies and exhibitions

whose primary objective was to provide opportunities to show the work of black artists were usually supported by institutions whose purpose bridged social and artistic interests. Promotion of the work of visual artists was generally undertaken by these organizations that had the space to mount public exhibitions. The erection or expansion of public libraries and Y.M./Y.W.C.A. buildings in Harlem, as well as in other black communities around the country, provided the necessary facilities. (Reynolds and Wright 15 and 17)

A number of important African-American artists surfaced through the Harmon Foundation during this time, one of whom was William H. Johnson. He, like Tanner, became an expatriate and went to live in Denmark for some years. Johnson was originally from South Carolina; his life was a tragic one. He gained some recognition during the course of his lifetime but later died in a mental institution in obscurity. It is only recently that he and his work were rediscovered identifying him as an important artist on the American scene.[6] Johnson's work is difficult to pigeonhole into a category; it is an eclectic body of work. Johnson began as a representational painter; but, while in Europe, he studied a variety of artistic schools of thought, ranging from the representational to the modern abstract expressionistic style. Eventually, later in his career, he seemed to focus primarily on a more simplified stylized depiction of rural African-American life. At whatever school of thought of Johnson's assimilation of artistic techniques you choose to examine, it is evident that Johnson was a master and genius.

Two Centuries of Black American Art by David C. Driskell, with catalog notes by Leonard Simon, is a rich volume of information on black artists. This book details the evolvement of the African-American artist across the ancestry of his or her interest and self-expression through painting, sculpture, and constructivism. The word struggle when referring to African-Americans implies an ongoing attempt to achieve a deserved rightful goal or acceptance into American birthright.

And so it is not mere skin color that gives this survey a unity, although it is true that many of the artists underwent uniquely personal torments because of a majority of society's prejudices.

Some escaped through exile: Edmonia Lewis to Rome, Henry O. Tanner to Paris, and William H. Johnson to Denmark. But a larger number did not or could not. One revelation of this present assemblage is that the human creative impulses can triumph in the face of impossible odds, and at times perhaps even because of them. (Driskell 9)

Seventeen Black Artists by Elton C. Fax is an anthology in which each chapter is devoted to a particular artist's narrative account of his or her early beginnings as an artist. The significance of these personal accounts is made even more poignant by the racial conflicts they endured. Young adults would find their stories engaging, provided they are introduced through a sense of shared and ongoing intergenerational experiences. Artists included in this work include: Elizabeth Catlett, John Wilson, Lawrence Jones, Charles White, Eldzier Cortor, Rex Goreleigh, Charlotte Amevor, Romare Bearden, Jacob Lawrence, Roy De Casava, Faith Ringgold, Earl Hooks, James E. Lewis, Benny Andrews, Norma Morgan, John Biggers, and John Toffes.

Some years ago I had the pleasure and honor of referring to one of these seventeen artists, Rex Goreleigh, as my teacher and later my friend. Professor Goreleigh taught for one semester in the early 1980s at Montclair State College, New Jersey. During that time, his counsel was enlightening to me as one of his students. His stories of his travels through Europe as a young artist and his brief friendships with such artists as Braque and Picasso were for me, as his student, an enriching experience. An aspect of Rex Goreleigh's subject matter dealt with the rural South having to do with labor and work in the fields. He particularly focused on a project titled "The Planter's Series" in which the activity of the representational figures, males, females, and children, was the seasonal planting and harvesting, a natural order of things. Goreleigh chose for his medium for this theme printmaking (Seriographs). He never settled on one or a few images as a way of expressing this activity. His reasons for carrying the subject over into multi-prints had to do with "processes and progressions," which were his concerns. Some time ago my wife Linda had the pleasure of interviewing him as part of her coursework at Montclair State College. After the conclusion of the interview, he gave her seven wonderful 18x24 prints

(Tobacco Series). She immediately had them matted, glassed, and framed they are now a welcomed addition to our home, as well as being a treasured memory of a gifted and talented, quiet and soft spoken genius.

These artists' narratives of their experiences give credence and hope to those who are willing to read or listen. As Elton G. Fax states,

> Travel and contact have taught me that man's experience is universal and that no human experience dwells in a vacuum. Artists, like all other human beings, neither feel, nor see, nor think alike. They shouldn't. And if one is to survive as a truly creative force, he dares not seek to silence or obscure from view other artists who do not see as he sees. The role of the artist is creative rather than destructive. His knowledge of life teaches him that one man's exposure to adversity will drive him to look inward toward those strengths that proclaim his manhood to him. Another man, under the same stimulus, will be driven to seek escape from that which is inescapable, even as he recognizes the futility of his flight. Knowing this, the true artist, surely one of the freest of individuals, will not seek to violate the freedom and individuality of others. (Fax ix–x)

Fax's work is an excellent accumulation of thoughts of notable African-American artists who made an indelible impression on the art community. I do have one contention with Fax's study. Of the seventeen artists selected, only four women are included. This book and all of the works discussed in this chapter contribute to young people's understanding and appreciation of African-American images, experiences, and viewpoints depicted through the years in the fine arts.[7]

CONCLUSION

The purpose of this chapter is to provide parents, teachers, and librarians with information and materials relating to artistic images of African-Americans from both an historical and a contemporary perspective. These images can have a profound and lasting effect on the way young people perceive themselves and their perceptions of others in the world. Aesthetic ways of knowing, through the arts, have always been important companions to scientific or intellectual knowledge. Through the appreciation of artistic images and the understanding of the lives of those who created them, children and young adults can grow both aesthetically and intellectually. Equally important, young people, regardless of their ethnicity, need to encounter works of art that promote the development of their own self-esteem and their respect for others in our culturally diverse world.

NOTES

1. The following are exemplary of the works illustrated by Diane and Leo Dillon: Paterson's *The Tale of the Mandarin Ducks*; Walker's *Brother to the Wind*; and Hamilton's *The People Could Fly, American Black Folktales*.

2. Additional suggested book titles illustrated by Tom Feelings are: *Tom Traveler in the World of Black History*; Muriel Feelings *Jambo Means Hello, Swahili Alphabet Book*; Muriel Feelings *Moja Means One, Swahili Counting Book*.

3. Other examples of Pinkney's work authored by Julius Lester are *The Tales of Uncle Remus, The Adventures of Brer Rabbit; More Tales of Uncle Remus, Further Adventures of Brer Rabbit, His Friends, Enemies, and Others; The Misadventures of Brer Rabbit, Brer Fox, Brer Wolf, the Doodang and Other Creatures*. Jerry Pinkney's concern with civil rights and multi-cultural diversity, has also compelled him to illustrate books relating him to African-Americans, and their contributions to American history in such books as *Mary McLeod Bethune* by Eloise Greenfield. Jerry Pinkney has illustrated *Mirandy and Brother Wind, The Green Lion of Zion Street* and *Half a Moon* along with many other stories.

4. Other examples of Brian Pinkney's work include: *Sukey and the Mermaid* by Robert San Souci and *The Ballad of Belle Dorcas* by William Hooks.

5. Additional readings that chronicle Tanner's life include works by Mathews and by Mosby and Sewell. There is also a video available on Tanner's life and times narrated by Julian Bond and titled: *Henry Ossawa Tanner: Great American Artist/African American Legend* and a video on Tanner's close friend and teacher titled: *Thomas Eakins: A Motion Picture*.

6. Johnson's life and achievements are chronicled in a work by Powell. There is also a video on his life and work by Powell.

7. I would also recommend Cedarholm, a companion source for young adult reference, which alphabetically lists African-American artists in the fine arts, a biographical dictionary that provides brief artists' biographies.

WORKS CITED

Aardema, Verna. *Why Mosquitoes Buzz in People's Ears*. illus. Diane Dillon and Leo Dillon. New York: Dial, 1975.

Alexander, Lloyd. *The Fortune-Tellers*. illus. Trina Schart Hyman. New York: Dutton, 1992.

Cedarholm, Theresa Dickson. *Afro-American Artists, A Bio-bibliographical Dictionary*. Washington, DC: Boston PL, 1973.

"Diane Dillon, and Leo Dillon," in *Something About the Author, Facts and Pictures About Authors and Illustrators of Books for Young People*. ed. by Anne Commire. Vol. 51. Detroit: Gale, 1988, 47–64.

Dragonwagon, Crescent. *Half a Moon*. illus. Jerry Pinkney. New York: Macmillan, 1986.

Driskell, David C. *Two Centuries of Black American Art*. Los Angeles: Museum of Art/Knopf, 1976.

Everett, Gwen. *John Brown: One Man Against Slavery*. illus. Jacob Lawrence. New York: Rizzoli, 1993.

Fairbrother, Trevor J. "John Singer Sargent's 'Gift' and His Early Critics." *Arts* 61 (February 1987): 56–63.

Fax, Elton C. *17 Black Artists*. New York: Cornwall, 1971.

Feelings, Muriel. *Jambo Means Hello: Swahili Alphabet Book*. illus. Tom Feelings. New York: Dial, 1976.

_____. *Moja Means One: Swahili Counting Book*. illus. Tom Feelings. New York: Dial, 1971.

Feelings, Tom. *Black Pilgrimage*. New York: Lothrop, 1972.

_____. *Soul Looks Back in Wonder*. New York: Dial, 1993.

_____. *Tommy Traveler in the World of Black History*. New York: Black Butterfly, 1993.

"Tom Feelings," in *Something About the Author, Facts and Pictures About Authors and Illustrators of Books for Young People*. ed. by Donna Olendorf. Vol. 69. Detroit: Gale, 1992, 54–58.

Feelings, Tom, and Eloise Greenfield. *Daydreamers*. New York: Dial, 1981.

Fields, Julia. *The Green Lion of Zion Street*. illus. Jerry Pinkney. New York: McElderry, 1988.

Greenfield, Eloise. *Grandpa's Face*. illus. Floyd Cooper. New York: Philomel, 1988.

Grifalconi, Ann. *The Village of Round and Square Houses*. Boston: Little, 1986.

Hamilton, Virginia. *The People Could Fly: American Black Folktales*. illus. Diane Dillon and Leo Dillon. New York: Knopf, 1985.

Hartigan, Lynda Roscoe. *Sharing Traditions, Five Black Artists in Nineteenth-Century America*. Washington, DC: Smithsonian, 1985.

Henry Ossawa Tanner (1859–1937), Great American Artist/African American Legend. Videocassette. narr. by Julian Bond. Tanner Film Group Pix, 1991, 17 min.

Honour, Hugh. *The Image of the Black in Western Art from the American Revolution to World War I, Vol. IV*. Houston: Menil Foundation, 1989.

Hooks, William H. *The Ballad of Belle Dorcas*. illus. Brian Pinkney. New York: Knopf, 1990.

Howard, Elizabeth Fitzgerald. *Chita's Christmas Tree*. illus. Floyd Cooper. New York: Bradbury, 1989.

Hudson, Wade, comp. *Pass It On: African-American Poetry for Children*. illus. Floyd Cooper. New York: Scholastic, 1993.

Johnson, Angela. *The Girl Who Wore Snakes*. illus. James E. Ransome. New York: Orchard, 1993.

Lawrence, Jacob. *The Great Migration: An American Story*. New York: Museum of Modern Art/ Phillips Collection/Harper, 1993.

_____. *Harriet and the Promised Land*. New York: Simon, 1993.

The Life and Times of William H. Johnson. Videocassette. Prod. by Richard Powell/National Museum of American Art/Smithsonian. Powell Pix, 1991, 30 min.

McElroy, Guy C. *Facing History, The Black Image in American Art 1710–1940*. Washington, DC: Corcoran Gallery/Bedford Arts, 1990.

McKissack, Patricia. *Mirandy and Brother Wind*. illus. Jerry Pinkney. New York: Knopf, 1988.

Mathews, Marcia M. *Henry Ossawa Tanner, American Artist*. Chicago: U of Chicago P, 1969.

Mathis, Sharon Bell. *The Hundred Penny Box*. illus. by Diane Dillon and Leo Dillon. New York: Viking, 1975.

Mitchell, Margaree King. *Uncle Jed's Barbershop*. illus. James E. Ransome. New York: Simon, 1993.

Mosby, Dewey F., and Darrel Sewell. *Henry Ossawa Tanner*. New York: Philadelphia Museum of Art/Rizzoli, 1991.

Musgrove, Margaret. *Ashanti to Zulu: African Tradition*. illus. Diane Dillon and Leo Dillon. New York: Dial, 1976.

Parry, Ellwood. *The Image of the Indian and the Black Man in American Art, 1590–1900*. New York: Braziller, 1974.

Paterson, Katherine. *The Tale of the Mandarin Ducks*. illus. Diane Dillon and Leo Dillon. New York: Dutton, 1990.

Polacco, Patricia. *Chicken Sunday*. New York: Philomel, 1992.

Powell, Richard J. *Homecoming, The Art and Life of William H. Johnson.* Washington, DC: Smithsonian, 1991.

Price, Leontyne. *Aida*. illus. Diane Dillon and Leo Dillon. San Diego: Harcourt, 1990.

Reynolds, Gary A., and Beryle J. Wright. *Against the Odds: African-American Artists and the Harmon Foundation*. Newark: Newark Museum, 1989.

Ringgold, Faith. *Aunt Harriet's Underground Railroad in the Sky*. New York: Crown, 1993.

_____. *Dinner at Aunt Connie's House*. New York: Hyperion, 1993.

_____. *Tar Beach*. New York: Crown, 1991.

Schroeder, Alan. *Ragtime Tumpie*. illus. Bernie Fuchs. Boston: Little, 1989.

Steptoe, John. *Mufaro's Beautiful Daughters: An African Tale*. New York: Lothrop, 1987.

Thomas Eakins: A Motion Picture. Videocassette. Dir. by T. W. Timreck. Timreck Pix, 1986, 60 min.

Thomas, Joyce Carol. *Brown Honey in Broomwheat Tea*. illus. Floyd Cooper. New York: Harper, 1993.

Walker, Mildred Pitts. *Brother to the Wind*. illus. Diane Dillon and Leo Dillon. New York: Lothrop, 1985.

Williams, Sherley Anne. *Working Cotton*. illus. Carole Byard. San Diego: Harcourt, 1992.

Williams, Vera B. *Cherries and Cherry Pits*. New York: Greenwillow, 1986.

CHAPTER
TWELVE

Why Angels Fly: Humor in Young Adult Fiction

Janet Kleinberg
and Lynn Cockett

H umorous fiction for young adults is important, for there is wisdom in the adage that angels fly because they take themselves lightly. Humor allows one to distance oneself from problems, to objectify rather than personalize them, "so that they become temporarily part of the non-self, objects to be toyed with" (Goldstein 110). Whether reading a comic novel like J. Clarke's *Al Capsella Takes a Vacation* or a realistic novel infused with humor such as Ron Koertge's *The Arizona Kid*, teens need the opportunity to laugh. They benefit from the perspective that humor affords. The development of a sense of humor is important to the evolution of a fully realized personality (Jalongo 113).

IS HUMOR A GENRE?

In order to understand the place occupied by humorous novels for young adults in the canon of literature for youth, it is important to first understand the nature of genre literature. In fact, it is difficult to discern if humor is a species of its own as in genre literature or a thread that can run through any novel. Not everyone agrees. Sally Estes edited *Genre Favorites for Young Adults*, a publication of *Booklist*, that includes a list of humorous books. The Young Adult Library Services Association (YALSA) of the American Library Association also defines humor as a genre. However, Betty Rosenberg and Diana Herald, in their book, *Genreflecting*, do not. They are outstanding champions of genre fiction who inspire librarians to look closely at what their patrons are reading and to respond accordingly with collections that reflect recreational reading needs. The absence of humor as a category in their book illustrates its elusive nature.

Often publishers' ad copy or genre designations on book jackets lead readers to believe a book will be funny when it is simply a realistic novel with a few funny lines. Sometimes humor is the paramount element, the defining characteristic; sometimes it is subordinate. "Humor is a slippery subject. Put simply, humor is the comic quality in a person, experience, or idea that makes one laugh" (Schwartz 281). This begs the question: what is that comic quality and from where does it come? With the young adult members of an interpretive community, we explored this question. What follows is a description of that community and its exploration of humorous fiction.

AN INTERPRETIVE COMMUNITY

Conventional wisdom once taught "that a mythical 'perfectly informed' reader could extract full meaning from [a] text" (Vandergrift, "Meaning-Making and the Dragons of Pern" 27). However, reader-response criticism has led to an enlightened view of meaning-making and considers the reader to be the most important element in that process. "Meaning is made as much from what one brings to a text as from what one takes from it. Thus, different readers decoding the same text may actually be 'reading' very different stories and the same reader may read that text quite differently at different times" (27).

Stanley Fish, author of *Is There a Text in This Class?: The Authority of Interpretive Communities*, defines reader-response theory. While previously the most important question to ask in literary criticism was "what does this mean?," now Fish defines the most important question to be "what does this do?" (3). This question, according to Fish, empowers the reader as the maker of meaning. "If meaning is embedded in the text, the reader's responsibilities are limited to the job of getting it out; but if meaning develops . . . in a dynamic relationship with the reader's expectations, projections, conclusions, judgments, and assumptions, these activities . . . are not merely instrumental, or mechanical, but essential, and the act of [describing meaning] must both begin and end with them" (2).

METHODOLOGY

In a spirit encompassing reader-response theory in an interpretive community, we brought together six young adults who met once a week over a five week period at the Nutley, New Jersey, Public Library to read and discuss humorous books. Nutley, New Jersey, is a 3.3 square mile town with a middle class population of approximately 27,000 in the greater New York metropolitan area.

Participants

Five girls and one boy were chosen at the conclusion of a summer reading program in which young adults used reference materials, searched for current events, and read books—fiction and information. Four participants for this study were chosen based upon the number and quality of books they read during the summer reading program. Two of the young adults were chosen because they had been on last year's youth advisory board and were hard working and reliable. All the young adults chosen were likable youngsters whom I found interesting and engaging.[1]

Cristina, age 12, is a quiet, mature seventh grader who indicated that during the school year she reads more than one book a week outside of her school assignments. She uses the public library for studying and for locating interesting books for leisure reading. Her interests are sports oriented.

Marisa, also 12 and also a seventh grader, is one of Cristina's best friends. Marisa's reading habits are similar to Cristina's, but her interests are mostly scientific. Her extracurricular activities include tennis, Interact (the youth division of the Rotary), and singing. Realistic fiction is her reading preference.

Mark, 12, is an active and talkative young man. My observations during the summer reading program revealed that he is well-liked and kind. He spoke freely during summer reading program meetings to me and to boys and girls alike. He plays the drums and is a confident young man. He attends a large evangelical church in the area and participates in their scout organization. For leisure reading Mark enjoys realistic fiction.

Dolina, age 12, is a voracious reader. Each week I gave her more books to read than the others, and each week she completed all of them before our next meeting. Dolina is intellectually sophisticated and reads all sorts of fiction. She read more books than any other participant, and I could always rely on her to take the more challenging books and anything that I asked her to read. She is interested in drama and photography.

Aja is 14 and was the oldest of the participants. She is a freshman in high school and has been a member of the library's youth advisory board. She takes voice and acting lessons and models. She is the picture of a confident, well-adjusted adolescent. Aja is an officer in her school's Interact club. She loves to be the center of attention but is patient and gracious as a participant in discussion. She prefers to read nonfiction, mysteries, and humorous novels.

Kathy at 13 is a confident eighth grader who also serves on the library's youth advisory board. She makes friends easily and is comfortable with adults. She is always agreeable. At Youth Advisory Board meetings, Kathy was the leader, directing others and taking responsibility. She reviews fiction for the Public Library's young adult newsletter. As an example of her literary taste, Kathy read Francesca Block's punk, gothic, young adult fairy tales *Weetzie Bat* and *Witch Baby* last year and loved them. She tells her friends about them now. She also did a school project in which she played Harriet Hemings after reading *Wolf by the Ears*. Ann Rinaldi's book is a fictionalized account of the life of Sally Hemings, Thomas Jefferson's slave and the alleged mother of several of his children. Any time I want a young adult opinion about a book, I ask Kathy who reads the book and reports back within days.

How the Books Were Chosen for the Pool

All of these young adults agreed to read at least four books. They were to choose from a pool of twenty-nine books. Appendix A lists these titles with full bibliographic information.

Books chosen for the pool were selected in a number of ways. We started with *Genre Favorites for Young Adults*, edited by Sally Estes and published by *Booklist*, and the Young Adult Library Association's (YALSA) humor genre list. Both of these publications were recent, but were composed of books both old and new. We could not locate a number of the books after searching the shelves at two public libraries with total collections of over 100,000 volumes, and a trip to a book super store. Those books that were unavailable were disregarded. Our rationale for this decision was to use books readily available to young adults and librarians.

The humor lists published by both YALSA and *Booklist* included adult books for young adults. We left all but two of these books out of our pool. We wanted to know about the literature written specifically for a young adult audience, and were less concerned with adult literature. We did include, however, two adult books as controls in the study. We wondered what the responses to these books would be, how those responses would differ from those to young adult books, and if they would be chosen at all. Douglas Adams' contemporary classic, *The Restaurant at the End of the Universe*, and *The Secret Diary of Adrian Mole, Age 13 3/4* by Sue Townsend were the two adult novels that made our list. Townsend's book, first published in England, was reprinted in the United States by Grove Press. Grove has only one list, choosing not to separate adult from young adult or children's books, but in response to our inquiry, stated that they consider *Adrian Mole* to be an adult book. Like Salinger's *The Catcher In the Rye*, it is an adult novel with a young adult protagonist. We chose these two books because of the enormous popularity of Adams' books and because of the setting and age of the main character in the *Adrian Mole Diaries*.

Later, we came to learn that Houghton Mifflin, publisher of *Motel of the Mysteries* by David Macaulay, includes this book on both their children's and adult lists. Young adult readers, whose comments are included later in the chapter, illuminated for us the wisdom and marketing prowess of the people at Houghton Mifflin. This book works on many levels, making it a perfect example of an intergenerational piece. Our readers enjoyed the concrete humor of Macaulay's book, but the abstract elements eluded them.

Next, we compiled a list of the books we knew to be funny. Our professional experience and knowledge of the literature for young adults dictated these decisions. We also included books recently published by authors with reputations as humorous writers. Examples include Daniel Hayes, whose first two books about Tyler and Lymie, *The Trouble with Lemons* and *Eye of the Beholder* were well received by both librarians and young adults. We chose his newest book, *No Effect*. Also new and not yet on any genre lists was *Al Capsella Takes a Vacation* by J. Clarke. Clarke's two previous books about Al and his friend Lou were, like Hayes' books, also well-received.[2]

How Participants Chose Books to Read

Each week I met with the young adults at the public library. We set the pool of books out on a table and looked them over for a few moments. Participants read jacket descriptions and talked about the books. Perhaps the age of the participants (12–14) contributed to the fact that the books they chose most often were those with humorous premises. These included: David Macaulay's *Motel of the Mysteries* in which someone from the future comes to earth to look objectively at the objects that are a part of our everyday lives; J. Clarke's *Al Capsella Takes a Vacation* in which two sixteen-year-old boys take their first vacation alone and end up with surf boards in Scutchthorpe, Australia—a town with a leech infested lake; and Stephen Manes' *The Obnoxious Jerks*, a story about a group of high school boys who buck the system.

Next I talked about the books, summarizing plots. My greatest concern at this time was to give enough information about the stories without revealing my enthusiasm or distaste for a title. Examples of the brief booktalks include the following:

One Fat Summer by Robert Lipsyte.

This book is about a guy who always gets made fun of because he's fat. His best friend's name is Joanie and she has an enormous nose. They've been thrown together by fate and their undesirable body parts. During the summer, Bobby gets a job cutting the lawn for a doctor who could double as a dictator, and Joanie gets a nose job. The book is primarily about the changes they go through in their selves and in their friendship.

The Ghost Belonged to Me by Richard Peck.

This book takes place in the early 1900's but is not bogged down with history. The main action of the story centers on a boy named Alex and his tomboyish friend named Blossom Culp. Alex sees a ghost in his barn loft one night and believes it's just Blossom playing one of her usual tricks on him. Alex tries to convince his family and neighbors that he's really seen a ghost, but of course no one believes him. Later, Alex's great uncle shows up and tells a story about a woman named Inez Dumaine. Everything the uncle says about the woman answers the ghost's riddles that have plagued Alex through the story. People who previously thought he was lying are now convinced that what he saw was really Inez's ghost.

Enter Three Witches by Kate Gilmore.

Bren is a high school student who lives with his mother, grandmother, and a tenant named Louise. Bren meets Erica and starts going out with her. Throughout the novel, he tries to keep Erica away from his apartment because all the of the women in his house are witches, and he doesn't want Erica to know. Erica believes Bren is embarrassed about her because she thinks he's trying to hide her from his mother. The story is about their relationship and a school production of Macbeth *that they're both working on in which Erica plays nothing other than a witch.*

After the students listened to the descriptions, they chose books based on the stories they found most interesting. Often they disregarded books with uninspired cover art. Examples include *Phone Calls* by R. L. Stine that is on YALSA's list. Only one young adult picked up the book, and she put it back, commenting that it would be too young for her. The cover on the edition that we used showed two girls talking on the phone. It is done in tones of pink with green accents giving it a treacly appearance. The dominating figure is a close up of a young girl's head and shoulders.

The paperback cover of Bruce Stone's *Half Nelson, Full Nelson* is a cartoon. It features a boy sporting a very dated hair cut, leaning out of a yellow van talking to a girl whose clothes reflect the style of the mid-eighties. No one took it.

Another unappealing cover was that of Ron Koertge's *The Arizona Kid*. The cover illustration on this book is a cartoonlike picture of a kid in cowboy boots and a ten gallon hat standing by a split rail fence with horses around it. The "picture book" art of the front cover misrepresented the content of the book and deterred readers.

Peripheral to the study, but also important, was an incidental discovery. A young adult's positive or negative comment about a book had a great impact upon its being chosen or ignored for subsequent readings. This only validates what we already know about peer influence and the power of peer comment. Cristina was the first to read *The Obnoxious Jerks* by Stephen Manes. After reading it she described, in our discussion, that she not only felt it was *"stupid"* and that the boys in the book acted like *"jerks,"* but that she was offended by the way they treated girls. *"It wasn't funny at all. The author tried to make it too funny, and it wound up being stupid; kind of cutesy. I don't think anybody would think it was funny. I didn't finish it because it was boring."* After that, I had to ask others to read the book to see if they would feel the same way. Marisa, the next reader, agreed with Cristina and could not finish the book.

The opposite happened to *The Secret Diary of Adrian Mole, Age 13 3/4*. After I talked briefly about it, Dolina was excited to read it since it is British, and she has spent time in England. I was surprised that any of the youngsters would want to read it, given its setting and its cover art that sports white letters in a traditional font on a dark green field with no illustration. The book did not impress her as funny, but her explanation of its diary format persuaded Aja to take the book home the following week. Aja responded positively to the book's humor, and she agreed with Dolina that its diary format was appealing.

By far the most successful book was David Macaulay's *Motel of the Mysteries*. Mark was its first reader. *"I liked the way the pictures showed the scientist doing stupid things like on pages 30 to 32."* What Mark described was the incongruity that results from the juxtaposition of scientifically written text with an illustration depicting a scientist, on the brink of his greatest discovery, stopping to make shadow figures on the wall. Mark's enthusiasm worked its way through the entire group. Three of the six participants read this book—the only one read that many times. Each week participants had to compromise if they weren't the one to receive the book.

Table One is a graphic representation of all the books read over the course of this project. Readers' opinions are included both in numeric and narrative form. A numeric value of "1" means that a reader judged a book to be funny. A "2" defines a book as poised somewhere between funny and not funny, and a "3" labels a book not at all funny. Readers' ages appear directly under their names.

"Laughter and humor are commonly assumed to be primarily social phenomena" (McGhee 178). This concept informed our decision to create a group project rather than simply to interview individual readers. Reading is a solitary activity. Discussion is a social interaction. The fusion of these two enabled participants to clarify meaning and further relish humor where they found it. This encouraged readers to share with the group specific passages and language that would support their opinion about a particular book. Their comments and opinions add a practical dimension to our theoretical definition of the literary nature of humor, discussed later in this chapter.

Knowledge of the nature of our discussions is essential for full appreciation of the importance of this kind of work. A sustained group interaction, even as brief as five weeks, is important and has impact upon the kind of thinking young people do. The letter outlining instructions for group members is included as Appendix B. In it, participants were asked to write their reactions to the humor in the books they read. Later, during our first meeting, I also encouraged them to mark the pages they could refer back to as textual examples of their opinions.

At each meeting, students described books they read and shared their opinions. They were each given as much time as desired to talk about the humor in what they had read, and to read to the group examples of things they found funny and, in some cases, not funny. The first two meetings included less discussion because readers had not yet read the same books. After that, I began encouraging specific kids to read books that others

TABLE 1. Readers' Responses to Humorous Novels

	AJA (14)	CRISTINA (12)	DOLINA (12)	KATHY (13)	MARISA (12)	MARK (12)
Adams. Restaurant at the End of the Universe			1 Very funny			
Block. Weetzie Bat				2 The names and the plot were funny		
Clarke. Al Capsella Takes a Vacation		1 Funny because I relate to it			1 Lots of good jokes	
Conford. Genie with the Light Blue Hair		2 Good story but not hilarious			2 Sort of funny	
Danziger. Cat Ate My Gymsuit					.	
Gilmore. Enter Three Witches		2 Only funny in spots. It started to get funny every time you wanted to put it down			2 The Black witch made it funny, the way she talked	
Koertge. Arizona Kid	3 Wasn't funny. More serious					3 If this book was funny, I'd hate to see funny

Book						
Koertge. *Mariposa Blues*						
Lipsyte. *One Fat Summer*	3 There was no turning point			2 More realistic than funny		2 Well written, interesting
Macaulay. *Motel of the Mysteries*		2 Some parts were funny			1 Imaginative and creative	1 Funny
Manes. *Obnoxious Jerks*		3 Not funny at all. Boring			3 Childish	
Mazer. *I Love You, Stupid!*		3 Stupid. Didn't make sense			3 I think he thought it'd make people laugh, but it didn't	
Peck. *Ghost Belonged to Me*				3 Not funny		
Townsend. *Secret Diary of Adrian Mole*	1 Like a soap opera. Adrian's thoughts were funny		3 I thought it was just there			
Zindel. *Undertaker's Gone Bananas*			2 Kind of weird, but that's what made it funny in situations			

had either liked or disliked in order to glean second opinions and to have more intense discussions at group meetings. This provided for better interactions among participants.

By the fifth and final meeting, group members had become relaxed and comfortable with one another and had done a great deal of thinking about humor and things humorous. At that meeting, I asked each young adult to think about the most memorable book they read during our project. Next, I asked them to answer the questions that Vandergrift uses in her article "Meaning Making and the Dragons of Pern." [3] These questions elicited from group members their memories and thoughts about a book. The most interesting thing about this exercise was that almost every book chosen was one that had not been discussed previously at length.

DIFFICULTIES FOR READERS

In early meetings, readers chose to talk about difficulties they encountered in their reading. These difficulties arose out of two fundamental sources: heightened expectations from book jackets and pre-reading perceptions that were not met upon reading and contextual void. Kay Vandergrift defines contextual void as "gaps" in prior knowledge, life experience or understanding of literary conventions ("Exploring the Concept of Contextual Void: A Preliminary Analysis" 352).

Both of Ron Koertge's books left readers frustrated when stories did not meet their expectations for humor. About *Mariposa Blues*, Dolina said that it was *"generally a little bit funny but nothing specific. It was more realistic. I could really imagine that this is what someone's life would be like."* She indicated that she liked the book but failed to find much humor in it. Mark and Aja both read *The Arizona Kid*. Aja commented that it was more serious than funny and that she was surprised by how often the characters used foul language. Mark said that *"if this book was supposed to be funny, I would hate to see not funny."* While each reader liked the books they read, Koertge's books were considered decidedly unfunny.

Many books that caused these problems went unfinished based upon our ground rule: If you don't like a book, put it down. Kathy began the project while she was on vacation and, therefore, missed the first two meetings. She took with her Gordon Korman's *A Semester in the Life of A Garbage Bag*, and *Howl's Moving Castle* by Diana Wynne Jones. She read approximately half of Korman's book, and though she considered the last part of the first chapter funny, the rest of the book was less amusing to her. I encouraged her to keep notes for herself while she was away so that she would remember what she wanted to tell me when she got home. Her note about Korman's book stated, "*I didn't want to finish it but I always force myself to finish a book, even when I don't like it. I guess that comes from school assignments and always having to read books no matter how you feel about them. After I quit reading this book, I was glad.*"

The second difficulty evident in some of the readers' reactions was what Vandergrift refers to as the concept of contextual void. In some cases this contributed to readers' decisions to abandon books before completing them. Mark had problems with Korman's *A Semester in the Life of a Garbage Bag*. The book's main action centers around two high school juniors, Sean and Raymond, who choose an obscure poet about whom they will do a semester-long independent project. When their search for information yields nothing, the students fabricate information based on Sean's grandfather, hoping no one will find out what they've done. Mark's comment about the book, "*There was no point to it in the beginning, you barely understood it,*" is evidence that a project like the one described did not resonate for him as a seventh grader who has not yet had this kind of academic experience.

A second example of contextual void was evident in our readers' inability to recognize satire. Satire derides society and its ills or an individual and their foibles through the use of sarcasm, irony, and ridicule. Some modicum of life experience is necessary for satisfied appreciation of this form of humor. Although everyone who read it agreed that *Motel of the Mysteries* was funny because of its mildly scatological elements (for example, illustrations of explorers worshipping a toilet bowl), not one young reader mentioned the fact that Macaulay's book is essentially a satire of the methods used in early archeological explorations of ancient Egypt. Perhaps upon subsequent readings,

especially later in life, these students will fully realize the satirical premise and more completely appreciate the humor. Interestingly, while young adults liked this book, they all agreed that
it was probably intended for a *younger* audience and that fourth,
fifth or sixth graders might like it even better. *"It was really quick
reading and easy to get through. I think younger kids would like it
because of all the pictures,"* Marisa said. Most people are conditioned to believe that if a book contains illustrations, it must be a
children's book.

MEANING-MAKING IN A GROUP

As group members began reading some of the same books, meetings became livelier—more like discussions and less like oral
reports. A certain rapport had been established among group
members, and between the group and myself as intermediary.

Readers revealed that they sometimes recognized an author's
humorous intentions but that, even so, the subject at hand had a
different meaning for them within the context of their own lives
and, therefore, was not funny to them. This surfaced during a
discussion of *The Obnoxious Jerks.* Marisa pointed out a scene in
the book in which a girl was manipulated into doing work for a
group of boys. Marisa recognized that this part of the book
might be funny to someone else, but to her it felt like discrimination. Cristina responded to the same passage stating, *"It isn't
funny because it doesn't fit well with other passages in the book, and
it's sexist."*

Next Cristina used an example from *I Love You, Stupid!* She
referred to a passage in the book where the narrator describes
Marcus' feelings toward Bev. "She was one of a dozen girls he
would have liked to know better . . . know bed-der . . . much
bed-der . . ." (Mazer 5). Cristina specifically said, *"I know the
author put that in there to make me laugh, but it didn't."* It was
not funny to Cristina because she identified with Bev and didn't
want to be thought of as a sexual object. Kathy discussed Richard Peck's *The Ghost Belonged to Me.* In it, Alexander, Uncle
Miles and Blossom Culp must go to New Orleans to return the
remains of Inez Dumaine to her rightful place among her family.
Along the way they foil a less-than-legitimate reporter who

attempts to steal her body for a sensational story. He ends up with an empty coffin. Kathy perceived this macabre trickery as mean rather than funny even though she recognized Peck's humorous intent.

Each week, student readers met to discuss the book(s) they had read. They were asked to rate a book as 1) funny; 2) funny in parts; or 3) not funny. Other instructions directed readers only to complete those books which they liked and could finish over one week's period and to take brief notes while reading so that they could refer to specific passages during our discussions. Readers were encouraged to talk openly about what they liked as well as what they did not like.[4] Our greatest concern was in eliciting various interpretations of the books to learn if books that librarians and publishers considered humorous were in fact considered so by their intended audience. We were also concerned with the meaning a reader brought to a text and how that affected the meaning they took from it. This understanding of the meaning-making process was most evident when girls read books with sexist or chauvinist language and situations. A reader's negative opinion about a book caused others not to choose it for subsequent readings.

THEORIES OF HUMOR

E. B. White wrote that "humor can be dissected, as a frog can, but the thing dies in the process. . . . It has a certain fragility, an evasiveness, which one had best respect. Essentially it is a complete mystery" (qtd in Cart 131). No one really wants to witness the dissection of a favorite joke. However, scholars, philosophers and scientists in many disciplines have stubbornly grappled with the need to understand and explain the ubiquitous and fundamentally enigmatic nature of humor. People laugh for a number of reasons. We define humor as consisting of two elements: superiority (an effect of humor) and incongruity (an inherent quality).[5]

Superiority

Thomas Hobbes is credited with originating the superiority

theory of humor in the seventeenth century. This theory suggests that a human being's feelings of superiority are proportionate to their perception of inferiority in others. Hence, the racist or sexist joke, the slur, the put-down.

Often, that feeling of superiority grows out of one's positive reference group. Group identification is, therefore, an important ingredient in the superiority element. Examples in young adult literature abound. Harry Mazer's *I Love You, Stupid!* is an excellent model of how something funny only works for a particular group—in this case, a gender group. Early in the novel, Marcus meets Bev and is instantly taken by her good looks. Mazer's use of language play is intended to cause a chortle, as he writes "She was one of a dozen girls he would have liked to know better . . . know bed-der . . . much bed-der . . . . He could see the freckles through her blouse. Was she freckled all over, and would she unbutton her blouse if he had the nerve to ask?" (Mazer 5). Female young adult readers agree that this device was probably created to make them laugh, but it simply served to offend them. Cristina, age twelve, commented after reading *I Love You, Stupid!* that *"some of the things that were supposed to be funny weren't."* Marisa read this passage to support her opinion that *"it was like [sic] stupid what he was thinking. I think he [Mazer] thought that was going to make people laugh, but it didn't."*

Sexist humor seems to lead the pack as the most pervasive group-oriented humor in young adult books. A second example of such humor in young adult fiction is Stephen Manes' *The Obnoxious Jerks*. This novel is infused with sexist language, ideology, and humor. The book's protagonists are a group of eleventh grade boys who call themselves "The Obnoxious Jerks" and do crazy things to show the rest of the student body and administration at their school just how ridiculous school rules and social mores are. The boys organize "jerk outs"—major attacks on school policy. The most elaborate and daring one comes at the end of a school year when they decide to wear skirts to class to protest a rule forbidding boys to wear shorts. The group, which until this point in the novel, denied membership to a girl, now enlisted her help in buying and altering skirts for each member. As a reward, she would be allowed an honorary membership. Female readers were offended by the actions and attitudes of these boys. Twelve-year-old Marisa said that it was *"childish. Maybe some boys would have to read it because of what they did to girls. It kind of like [sic] offends me."*

Female characters throughout the history of American humor have "function[ed] as negative stereotypes in masculine humor. Undoubtedly [this] has contributed . . . to perpetuating the assumption that women lack, or ought to lack, a capacity for humor and wit . . ." (Dresner 138). Further, as members of a male-dominated society in which women have been conditioned to be submissive rather than assertive, we have been encultur-ated to perceive humor through the filter of a masculine bias. However, the twelve-year-old female readers quoted above have either benefited from a more contemporary societal order or have developed their own world views that overcome earlier influences.

A third example of superiority-related humor prompted a great deal of discussion. Robert Lipsyte's *One Fat Summer* was agreed by all to be an excellent book, filled with funny situations and language. In it, Bobby Marks wins the hearts of readers as he struggles through a summer vacation at his family's lake home, taking a new job and fighting off his weight and his cruel neighbors. Bobby takes eating very seriously and discusses it in great detail as narrator of the story. The following passage illus-trates Bobby's love for food: "Peanut butter and ice cream are two of my favorite foods, but you've got to be careful eating them. They can hurt you. The only thing worse than a peanut butter strangle is an ice cream headache. A few times in my life I've had both at the same time and that's murder" (Lipsyte 103). Everyone laughed when we read this passage aloud. Aja said that the reason she thought it was funny was due to Bobby's obsession with food and his assumption that this is how every-one else must feel. She said that at first it just seemed humorous, but later she realized that she was laughing at Bobby the way she would if she were making fun of him. Others in the group agreed upon reflection that they too were essentially mocking Bobby. This suggestion resonated for group members. We all realized that even though we might not overtly ridicule others, the superiority element of humor is a powerful and seductive one.

Positive group identification and feelings of superiority over others feed a person's self-esteem. This makes self-esteem the second ingredient in the superiority element. Self-worth is diminished by put-down humor. The butt of a joke loses self-esteem while the joker feels an increase in self-respect. In this model, there appears to be no place for self-deprecating humor.

However, many people engage in self-deprecating humor as a way of saving face. When one recognizes and exploits the humor in a personal flaw or foible, it preempts the opportunity for others to ridicule (Zillmann 155). These devices serve basically as damage control. People who make fun of themselves may realize that exposing their personal humiliations might not increase their appeal to others, but might at least minimize personal depreciation.

Many characters in young adult literature use self-disparaging humor in the ways just described. Adolescence is a period of life in which body image and physical beauty are very much at the center of consciousness. Characters whose looks in particular do not conform to the expected norm are often outsiders and pariahs. Chris Crutcher paints this kind of character with empathy and sensitivity. "A Brief Moment in the Life of Angus Bethune" is a short story collected in *Athletic Shorts*. In it, Angus is a very overweight teenage boy whose divorced parents are each remarried to people of their own genders. As a joke, Angus's classmates select him for an honor similar to homecoming king. He is placed opposite one of the most fabulously beautiful girls in school and made to dance with her before the entire student body. While dancing, Angus and his "date" begin to talk about her bulimia. When she asks him if he knows what bulimia is, Angus responds "I'm a fat kid with faggot parents who's been in therapy on and off for eighteen years. . . . Yes, I know what that is. It means when you eat too much, you chuck it up so you don't turn out to look like me. . . . Actually . . . I even tried it once, but when I stuck my finger down my throat, I was still hungry and I almost ate my arm" (22).

The self-disparaging humor Angus employs illustrates a number of points. Readers laugh when they hear the way he talks about himself. They also find him charming. Interestingly, Angus's references to his size and his parents as "faggots" illustrate the ease with which one can joke about his or her own positive reference group. Those terms coming from someone outside either of Angus's two positive reference groups would be both cruel and hurtful. Why is a disparaging joke funny when it comes from within a group rather than from outside? Perhaps the answer lies in the incongruity of the situation. It just is not expected.

Incongruity

Most theorists recognize incongruity as the fundamental cornerstone of humor. The incongruity theory "emphasizes the occurrence of two or more illogical or incongruent events, often eliciting the double-take or puzzled look before the laughter" (Coleman 270). It works when there is expectation based upon the assumption of a norm, an established convention or pattern, and this expectation is upturned.

From birth, children learn culturally determined patterns and their boundaries. Incongruity, however, is a relative concept. Something is only illogical according to one's experiences or orientation. David Macaulay's *Motel of the Mysteries* is a satirical look at the iconography of contemporary life as seen through the eyes of a visitor from the thirty-ninth century. The visitor is baffled by such banal objects as a television remote control and a toilet. The main part of the story is what the visitor makes up about the unfamiliar objects he/she sees. The book is funny because it shakes up the taken-for-grantedness of everyday life by enabling the reader to see common objects from an alien perspective.

Young adults who read this book agreed that it was funny. However, an interesting discussion about its format revealed the maturity of the readers and their individual tastes and levels of sophistication. Readers were divided about a labeled picture at the beginning of the second section. The picture illustrates a house and numbers all the objects that are later outlandishly described. While Marisa and Mark were convinced that the picture was necessary to carry the story, Cristina was the only young adult who had reservations about its humor. She thought that the *"diagram took away the element of surprise. If [Macaulay] didn't use it, you could have used your imagination to figure out what they were describing, and when you found out, it would have been even funnier."* What Cristina relates discloses her level of cognitive development and prior knowledge. As children mature they find humor in intellectually challenging materials. Cristina would have preferred to decode the information herself because reading the descriptions without the diagram would have allowed her to do the work for herself. Since she had the diagram to start out with, there was no surprise in the revelations. The delight of the incongruity was lessened for her because of the absence of surprise.

Irony occurs when the literal meaning is in opposition to the intended meaning. By definition it is incongruous. In *Al Capsella Takes a Vacation* Al and Lou intend to have a wild vacation at a hot resort called Scutchthorpe surfing, dancing, and meeting girls. The two arrive only to find that Scutchthorpe is in the middle of nowhere. The premise of two sixteen-year-olds taking their first vacation alone, only to be foiled, is what drives the humor in this story. In spite of themselves, Scutchthorpe begins to grow on the boys. Readers used textual descriptions to point out the irony in the story. Both young adults who chose to read this novel did so based on a description of the plot and both agreed, after reading it, that the plot was indeed funny. What they found most amusing, however, was Al and Lou's sharp wit. Al's description of his math teacher resonates for young adults. "Everyone knows he did the counting, not because he's a telltale or has a thing about school uniforms, but because he's the only teacher on the staff who'd be able to concentrate on something as boring as that and really find it interesting" (Clarke 2). *"The way these kids reacted to seeing their teacher outside of school reminds me of how I react when seeing my teachers outside school."* And, *"Describing the way their teacher was when they saw her in the grocery store was exactly the way I acted when I saw my teacher in the store. I didn't recognize her till she started to talk to my mom. 'Oh, my God! Where's the blackboard?'"*

Macaulay's and Clarke's books are intrinsically incongruous. Kate Gilmore's *Enter Three Witches* is a third example of incongruity at work in a humorous story, but in this case the incongruity comes through in the personality of a character. Bren is a teenage boy whose purpose throughout this novel is to keep his new girlfriend from learning that his mother, his grandmother, and their tenant are all witches. This becomes increasingly difficult as Erica's interest in witches grows after she lands the part of one of Macbeth's three witches. A turning point occurs when Erica stops by Bren's apartment and meets all three witches. Louise is an African American who practices black magic. In this scene her comments, rendered in Black Vernacular English, drive the humor. "Hey, Erica, you a fine witch, girl. . . . Who would have thought it? You miss your calling for sure" (Gilmore 196). Marisa pointed out the incongruity when she said, "*The Black witch made it funny—the way she talked. I just thought a witch would only talk like the ones in fairy tales.*" The humor comes out of her ethnicity because readers expect a witch to be a generic witch who talks like a character from *The Wizard of Oz* or *Macbeth*, not a member of an ethnic group. Surprise and incongruity combine to create a very funny character.

CONCLUSIONS AND RECOMMENDATIONS

At the last meeting of the young adult discussion group, each participant was asked to answer two questions in addition to the ones discussed earlier. First, they were asked to define humor; next, they were asked if their opinion of the nature of humor had changed as a result of the thinking they had done about it over this summer.

Most participants still could not define humor beyond describing it as something that makes a person laugh. Nevertheless, using textual examples rather than their own words, the young people involved in this project did communicate an understanding of the literary nature of humor and of meaning-making in different people. Marisa said that the definition of humor is different for everyone depending upon what or how a person thinks. She felt, after reading a variety of humorous books over one summer, that there are many types of humor and that each type appeals to a different kind of person. To illustrate this theory, Marisa used *I Love You, Stupid!* She said that to someone with ideas or values different from hers, this book would definitely have been funny.

Marisa's ability to articulate through example was important. By using *I Love You, Stupid!* she showed, rather than told, exactly how she felt and what she had learned over the course of five short weeks. Frank Smith argues a similar point in his book *To Think*. He says that each of us has a story of our lives. It is made up of our values and beliefs, derived from myriad places, experiences and persons—a mosaic, to borrow from this book's title. Because each of us has our own unique story, we make meaning in unique ways, and we understand in different ways. Whether in experience, thought, or word, each idea that we encounter is held up to a personal narrative. A piece of information is easily accepted, rejected, or ignored when an individual understands and adheres closely to a personal narrative.

For young adults, these narratives are just beginning to take shape. At the tender age of twelve or thirteen, many of the elements that make up a person's story are those things that have been handed down by their parents or community. This is the period in the life course when young adults begin to call into question those values and attitudes which until now they had accepted from their parents and peers. Marisa's statement, that each person must have a different opinion of what is funny based upon what they personally believe, is smart. She went further, then, to articulate her own beliefs and described that, as a girl, she thought the passage early in the book was chauvinistic.

Marisa, along with Mark and Kathy, also described a change that occurred in her thought processes during the summer. Each of these young people said that before this summer they never thought much about what humor was, or about what was funny and why. Mark and Kathy said that they enjoyed our project because they were asked to read books that someone gave them, saying *these books are funny*. Had no one told them this, they might never have read as closely and would not have enjoyed the books for the pleasure of reading for meaning. Mark said that his idea of what was humorous had *"changed because when you see that something is supposed to be funny, you're expecting something that might not be there or something that often is very different from what's there."*

The interpretive community that we formed also helped young people to refine their tastes. Each young person said at the end of the summer that they never thought much before about what they liked or disliked, vis-à-vis literary humor. Previously, they would choose books almost randomly, but now they had definite criteria they knew to be helpful in finding books they liked. Cristina said that before the project began she thought she would never be able to enjoy a book that was supposed to be funny. But after reading for humor all summer she felt that she had a new perspective on herself and on literature. The change that occurred in Cristina helped her to begin to mature as she pieces together the narrative that will become her own. Dolina defined humor as *"something enjoyable."* She went on to say that the book she found least humorous was *The Secret Diary of Adrian Mole* because, although she liked it, *"it had no plot,"* indicating that for her, humor grows out of story.

The subjectivity inherent in an individual's encounter with humor makes it difficult to pin down. Because the participants in this group were young and because they listened to their friends expressing ideas and opinions very different from their own, they began to understand the nature of subjectivity. They also began to question whether humor is a genre after all. Kathy articulated it this way: *"You can know right away if something is horror or science fiction, but funny books can be anything."* Kathy is absolutely right.

The literary nature of humor is elusive, and this quality caused the young adults in our group to think more critically. They knew that they were to be looking for humor in the books they read, so if they did not find it immediately they had only two options: put the book down or dig deeper inside themselves to think about why someone else might consider a particular story to be funny.

This short-term study with six adolescents has provided us with some important understandings about thinking, learning, reading, and growing. First, this experience validated once again that group interaction is beneficial to young adults because it helps them to think and to approach material in different ways. It helps them to listen to others and feel a sense of trust in the group's willingness to hear them out without making judgments about what they are saying.

Some might argue that group interaction would dilute an

individual's thoughts, forcing that person to defer to the group's opinion. Because meaning-making is a moment in time, our participants were encouraged to engage in silent generation, wherein each young adult wrote down their reactions to and thoughts about a book during and immediately after reading it. They were also asked to write individual responses to a series of questions. These notes enabled readers to return to their original opinions and reactions to a text. The group discussion helped them to continually refine what they thought while maintaining the integrity of their own intellect.

Perhaps a diluted effect would be evident if students were asked to come to consensus. Our group was not striving for that, but rather for the affirmation of the interaction between reader and text as well as among readers. In stressing to the young adults that no one had to agree with any other person's opinion, an atmosphere of discovery through exploration was created. These young adults felt comfortable sharing their opinions and perceptions, even knowing that others might disagree. This was evident in our earlier example concerning *Motel of the Mysteries*. Readers did not agree about the necessity of one element in the book but did agree that the story was, indeed, funny. Discussion about that book encouraged readers to examine more closely why they laughed and what was actually the source of the book's humor.

Second, we witnessed during the course of this project, the development of intellectual skills through experiencing literature. Many of us feel the pressure of serving the adolescent population because adolescence is a brief and volatile time of rapid and dramatic change. A young adult librarian typically serves twelve- to eighteen-year-old library users. Young adult literature, however, rarely appeals to adolescents over the age of fourteen or fifteen.[6] This means that anyone working with young adults must possess a knowledge of and familiarity with the resources and literature for a broad range of maturity levels.

The young adults who were chosen for this project were at the youngest end of the continuum called young adulthood. Four out of six were preadolescents, on the cusp of many changes—physical, emotional, and intellectual. While inclusion of older teens in the group might have led to an understanding of a broader spectrum of young adult perceptions of humor, we believe that our group offered interesting insights of their own that might have been quelled by the presence of older participants.

Children just entering middle school are in the beginning stages of finding the pieces in order to create the "story" that will be their own. This story is a mosaic—a picture created by bits of other stories and pictures, by experiences. At the beginning of adolescence, we gave these six young adults an opportunity to think for a moment about one complex question: "what is humorous in literature?" In so doing, their lives were, for at least five weeks, changed while they pondered what they read and searched for just the right passages and words to illustrate their feelings and thoughts about a text. They were not asked, for example, if Uncle Wes, the gay character in Koertge's *The Arizona Kid* was stereotypical or if he was positively or negatively drawn. They were not asked to think about the myriad issues that could have been discussed in relationship to the books they read. Instead, they were asked to focus on just one thing, honing their skills in critical reading and thinking. In doing so, these young adults made some important distinctions about how humor can affect people and what humor itself is. It was a delight to see this change come about in the young people involved and to know that this experience will become a piece in the mosaic of their lives.

SUGGESTIONS FOR FURTHER STUDIES

The study outlined in the pages of this chapter was beneficial to all involved. It is, however, a microcosmic study and reveals much about six individual adolescents. A similar study should be undertaken and sustained over a longer period of time with a wider age range of participants reading the same books simultaneously. This would yield a number of positive results that were impossible to attain over a five-week period with six young adults ranging in age from only twelve to fourteen.

Adding older readers would yield more information about the controls in the study. We included two adult books in the pool of available books. Our interest in including these books was twofold. We wanted to see if young adults would choose adult books at all, and if so, how they would respond to the humor in comparison to that in the young adult books. As stated earlier in the chapter, these two books were *The Restaurant at the End of the Universe* and *The Secret Diary of Adrian Mole, Age 13 3/4*. Older readers' opinions of these books might add a new dimension to our study. *Adrian Mole*, while popular with both young adult readers, was only considered funny by Aja, the oldest participant. Aja commented that this book evoked from her *"laughter and sympathy."* She viewed Adrian as a victim of school and society. An older reader might be somewhat more astute at recognizing the satiric nature of this piece. Even the book's cover quotes a *New York Times* book review saying that *Adrian Mole* is "part Woody Allen, part a kindred spirit to the heroes of Philip Roth's early novellas. . . ." Adult or older young adult readers who know either Allen's or Roth's work will immediately draw a picture of who this character is. Upon reading Adrian's diary and discovering that he calls himself an intellectual, these readers will see the humor in this declaration, particularly for a fourteen-year-old who worries about his pimples.

Adrian Mole was chosen twice in this group. This was interesting to us because we had hypothesized that no one as young as our participants would care to read it. Yet the setting, format, and age of its main character attracted both Dolina and Aja.

Our second adult book, *The Restaurant at the End of the Universe*, was read and loved by one young adult. Dolina read it because her older brother has all of Adams' books. She was interested to learn just what was so funny. After she read it, Dolina commented that it was the best book she had read in a long time. Despite her enthusiasm, others did not read it. None of our participants identified themselves as science fiction readers. This could have been a deterrent to their choosing this book. Understanding Adams' humor requires some foreknowledge of science fiction and its conventions because his books are essentially parodies of that genre.

A similar study extended over a longer period of time would allow all participants to read the same books. This would bring us closer to consensus about which books are funny for young adults. More readers for each book would make discussions livelier. During our discussions we did our best to describe books and read important passages to one another, giving others as full a description as we could. If all of us had read the same book each week, less time could have been spent describing story. Describing stories in the manner that we did meant that each of us chose elements to share that were important to us personally. Although it is perfectly valid to share information like this in a reader-response community, it means that listeners do not have as full an understanding of a text as they would if they had read it themselves. Had we all read books together, discussions might have elicited greater understanding, both corporately and personally.

Finally, we remind other librarians and teachers that a project such as the one described herein is quite a simple thing. Carrying out our mission of bringing books and young people together is enriched when we add to that combination an element of community. The young adults who participated in this study *did* learn how to take themselves more lightly, and began to see their own concerns as less formidable. As Cristina said, *"Some of the things that I relate to became funny to me."* This is why angels fly.

NOTES

1. As a young adult librarian in a public library, Lynn had access to a young adult population throughout the summer. Throughout this section, the "I" narrator refers to Lynn.
2. Clarke's previous books are *The Heroic Life of Al Capsella* and *Al Capsella and the Watchdogs*.
3. Vandergrift's questions, included in "Meaning Making and the Dragons of Pern," are as follows: *Content: What [is the] story about? What key words or phrases describe the stor[y]? Are any of these words or phrases actually used in the books? Feelings: What, if anything from these books prompted strong emotions? Why does this affect you as it does? Beliefs: Did particular beliefs surface as you read? What brought them to the surface? How did these beliefs affect your response? Memory: Were you aware of any connections between text and your memories? What were the similarities and differences between your reading and your memories? Sharing: What from your reading would you like to share with others?*
4. Appendix B includes a letter sent to each participant explaining the

project and including instructions for our work together.

5. Theories of humor are many and varied. Our definition grew out of an examination of a wide selection of these theories. Interested readers are encouraged to explore the following authors listed in our works consulted: Cantor, Chapman, Coleman, Goldstein, Jalongo, LaFave, Mintz, Nilsen, Schwartz, Willoughby, and Zillmann.

6. At the American Library Association's Miami Beach conference in June 1994, the Young Adult Library Services Association sponsored a preconference in which a panel of publishers spoke about young adult publishing and YA books. Richard Jackson, of Richard Jackson Books, a division of Orchard, declared with assuredness that his audience for young adult publishing stops at age fourteen.

WORKS CITED

Bennett, John E., and Priscilla Bennett. "What's So Funny? Action Research and Bibliography of Humorous Children's Books—1975–80." *Reading Teacher*. 35.8 (1982): 924–927.

Cantor, Joanne R. "What Is Funny to Whom?: The Role of Gender." *Journal of Communication*. 26.3 (1976): 164–172.

Cart, Michael. "What's So Funny?: Humor in the Writing of Walter R. Brooks." *The Lion and the Unicorn*. 13.2 (1989): 131–140.

Chapman, Antony J., and Nicholas J. Gadfield. "Is Sexual Humor Sexist?" *Journal of Communication*. 26.3 (1976): 141–153.

Coleman, J. Gordon, Jr. "All Seriousness Aside: The Laughing-Learning Connection." *International Journal of Instructional Media*. 19.3 (1992): 269–276.

Dresner, Zita. "Women's Humor." *Humor In America: A Research Guide to Genres and Topics*. Ed. Lawrence E. Mintz. Westport: Greenwood, 1988. 137–162.

Estes, Sally, ed. *Genre Favorites for Young Adults: A Collection of Booklist Columns*. Chicago: Booklist-ALA, 1993.

Fein, Linda Abby. "Laughlines: The Role of Humor in Children's Books." *Catholic Library World*. 59.2 (1987): 67–72.

Fish, Stanley. *Is There a Text in This Class?: The Authority of Interpretive Communities*. Cambridge: Harvard UP, 1980.

Goldstein, Jeffrey H. "Theoretical Notes on Humor." *Journal of Communication*. 26.3 (1976): 104–112.

Humor Genre List. Young Adult Library Services Association. American Library Association, 1993.

Jalongo, Mary Renck. "Children's Literature: There's Some Sense to Its

Humor." *Childhood Education*. 62.2 (1985): 109–114.

Klein, Amelia. "Storybook Humor and Early Development." *Childhood Education*. 68.4 (1992): 213–217.

LaFave, Lawrence, and Roger Mannell. "Does Ethnic Humor Serve Prejudice?" *Journal of Communication*. 26.3 (1976): 116–123.

McGhee, Paul E. "Sex Differences in Children's Humor." *Journal of Communication*. 26.3 (1976): 176–189.

Nilsen, Don L. F. "Incongruity, Surprise, Tension, and Relief: Four Salient Features Associated with Humor." *Thalia: Studies in Literary Humor*. 11.1 (1989): 22–27.

Rinaldi, Ann. *Wolf By the Ears*. New York: Scholastic, 1991.

Rosenberg, Betty, and Diana Tixier Herald. *Genreflecting: A Guide to Reading Interests in Genre Fiction*. 3rd edition. Englewood: Libraries Unlimited, 1991.

Salinger, J. D. *The Catcher in the Rye*. Boston: Little, 1951.

Schwartz, Alvin. "Children, Humor, and Folklore." *The Horn Book*. 53.3 (1977): 281–287.

Smith, Frank. *To Think*. New York: Teachers College, 1990.

Vandergrift, Kay E. "Exploring the Concept of Contextual Void: A Preliminary Analysis." *Library Education and Leadership: Essays in Honor of Jane Anne Hannigan*. Ed. Sheila Intner and Kay E. Vandergrift. Metuchen: Scarecrow, 1990. 349–363.

_____. "Meaning-Making and the Dragons of Pern." *Children's Literature Association Quarterly*. 15.1 (1990): 27–32.

Willoughby, Bebe. "Humor Tells the Truth in Children's Books." *Journal of Youth Services*. 1.1 (1987): 57–64.

Zillmann, Dolf, and S. Holly Stocking. "Putdown Humor." *Journal of Communication*. 26.3 (1976): 154–163.

APPENDIX A:
Humorous Young Adult Fiction

Adams, Douglas. *The Restaurant at the End of the Universe*. New York: Harmony, 1980.

Anthony, Piers. *Ogre, Ogre*. New York: Del Rey-Ballantine, 1982.

Block, Francesca Lia. *Weetzie Bat*. New York: Harper, 1990.

Clarke, J. *Al Capsella Takes a Vacation*. New York: Holt, 1992.

Conford, Ellen. *Genie with the Light Blue Hair*. New York: Bantam, 1989.

Crutcher, Chris. "A Brief Moment in the Life of Angus Bethune." *Athletic Shorts: Six Short Stories*. New York: Laurel-Dell, 1989.

Dahl, Roald. *Boy*. New York: Penguin, 1984.

Danziger, Paula. *The Cat Ate My Gymsuit*. New York: Delacorte, 1974.

Gilmore, Kate. *Enter Three Witches*. New York: Scholastic, 1990.

Hayes, Daniel. *No Effect*. Boston: David R. Godine, 1994.

Jones, Diana Wynne. *Howl's Moving Castle*. New York: Greenwillow, 1986.

Koertge, Ron. *The Arizona Kid*. Boston: Joy Street Books-Little, 1988.

_____. *Mariposa Blues*. New York: Flare-Avon, 1993.

Korman, Gordon. *Losing Joe's Place*. New York: Scholastic, 1990.

_____. *A Semester in the Life of a Garbage Bag*. New York: Scholastic, 1987.

Levitin, Sonia. *The Mark of Conte*. New York: Atheneum, 1976.

Lipsyte, Robert. *One Fat Summer*. New York: Ursula Nordstrom-Harper, 1977.

Macaulay, David. *Motel of the Mysteries*. New York: Scholastic, 1983.

Manes, Stephen. *The Obnoxious Jerks*. New York: Bantam, 1990.

Mazer, Harry. *I Love You, Stupid!* New York: Crowell, 1981.

Myers, Walter Dean. *Fast Sam, Cool Clyde, and Stuff*. New York: Viking, 1975.

_____. *The Young Land Lords*. New York: Viking, 1979.

Peck, Richard. *The Ghost Belonged to Me*. New York: Viking, 1975.

Pinkwater, Daniel. *The Snarkout Boys and the Avocado of Death*. New York: Signet-Penguin, 1983.

Stine, R. L. *Phone Calls*. New York: Archway-Pocket Books, 1990.

Stone, Bruce. *Half Nelson, Full Nelson*. New York: Harper, 1987.

Thompson, Julian F. *Simon Pure*. New York: Scholastic, 1987.

Townsend, Sue. *The Secret Diary of Adrian Mole, Age 13 3/4*. New York: Avon, 1987.

Zindel, Paul. *The Undertaker's Gone Bananas*. New York: Bantam Starfire, 1979.

APPENDIX B

Dear Young Adult,

Thank you for agreeing to help with *Mosaics of Meaning: Enhancing the Intellectual Life of Young Adults through Story.* I am working on a chapter about humorous books for young adults, so your input will help me a great deal. The book will be published in 1996 by Scarecrow Press, and other librarians will read it in order to better serve young people where they work.

Here are the things I need you to do.
1) Read as many books from the special collection as you can.
2) Read for only a week. If you didn't have time to finish it in a week, you didn't like it enough. Be sure to return them right away.
3) As you think of it, write down your reactions to the book based on how funny you think it is.
4) After you're finished reading the book, give it a rating of:
     1—funniest
     2—kind of funny
     3—not funny.
5) Have fun. If for any reason, you decide you don't want to do this anymore, please let me know.

Also, please fill out the attached permission form. I would like your parents to sign it as well. This gives me permission to reprint your comments in my book chapter, and use only your first name.

Thanks again,

Lynn Cockett
Young Adult Librarian

---

93 Booth Drive, Nutley, New Jersey 07110–2782   Phone: 201-667-0405

Letterhead reproduced from stationery used in 1913

APPENDIX B. *Continued*

I, _____, give my permission for my statements to be quoted and my first name and age only to be used in *Mosaics of Meaning: Enhancing the Intellectual Life of Young Adults through Story* (Scarecrow Press, 1996).

Signature _____

Printed Name _____

Parent / Guardian _____

Printed Name _____

CHAPTER THIRTEEN

Foul Play, Fair Play— Gender Awareness in Movement Education: Research, Resources, and a Model for Change

Linda A. Catelli

> Catholic schoolgirls once played intramural basketball all winter long, and though it was with a smaller ball and slacker rules than the boys used—and though I traveled more often than I ever scored—it gave me a visceral feeling for the nonpareil grace, skill and teamwork of the sport. Not to mention that glow in your chest when the ball leaves your hands, arcs through the air with all eyes following, and falls almost inevitably through the hoop. Yessss. . . . There's a moment when the ball arcs perfectly downward to the waiting web of the net—or when the words lie down just right on the page—that makes you feel as if you could live forever. (Quindlen 1992, p. 3H)

Yessss . . ." as Anna Quindlen, *New York Times* columnist, has so wonderfully remarked in recapturing a meaningful and powerful sport moment in her life. Unfortunately, too few girls and young women even today have ample opportunities to have such moments in their lives—moments from which they may experience the joy of movement and the confidence of their bodies through some form of physical activity. The importance of such moments is that they can shape young girls' lives dramatically. They can shape their image of themselves, their potential and their future. In a society that struggles at every turn to define itself in a fair way for human freedom, expression and dignity, girls and women have relentlessly struggled to remove cultural barriers, attitudes and behavioral patterns that have prevented them from exploring freely their nature and abilities as participants in physical activities. Hindered by stereotypical remarks, stigmas and policies, girls and young women have not been able to freely and fairly participate in sports, physical education classes, fitness and recreational physical activities. Their movement education and education about their bodies and capabilities have been skewed by past medical theories and current unfair practices.

This chapter focuses on gender awareness in girls' and young women's movement education and a proposed working model for change in a postmodern era. The model suggested serves a dual purpose: One, it sets forth a view of gender awareness and a process for creating change and a new and fairer reality for girls' and young college women's movement education; and two, it provides the organizational schema of the content of this chapter. Drawing from history, recent research and personal experience, gender-biased behaviors and existing inequities for girls and young women are explained within a working model. Related to the process of change and incorporated within the model is the selection of readings that not only supports each section of the chapter but also serves as resources for readers. A curriculum of resources is identified in the Appendix and serves as a critical component to the change process. The chapter begins with a proposed view of gender awareness in girl's and young women's movement education and a model for change.

PROPOSED VIEW AND A WORKING MODEL FOR CHANGE

What is fair? I may have some problem at times defining this, but I have very little difficulty in telling you what is foul. It is all around me and has been ever since I was a young high school girl in the early 1960s and told by the New York City public school officials that I and my female classmates were not permitted to have an interscholastic basketball team like the boys. Girls . . . as they began to give their rationale . . . were not physically able nor emotionally capable of dealing with vigorous competition. It's difficult for some young college women I converse with to relate to the response given by the school officials or the fact that it occurred in 1964. Title IX, a federal law (Public Law 92–318) passed in 1972 prevented any discrimination based on sex by federally funded institutions. The law helped girls and young women gain access to athletics and it significantly increased their participation in competitive sports in high schools, colleges and on community leagues.[1] And yet if you look more closely today, not enough has changed: Especially, when I see a young female of six in 1994 receive a trophy for her karate competitive accomplishments with a male figure placed at the top. Or when a female sports journalist is sexually harassed in a locker room of the New England Patriots and told in essence that she has no right being there (Quindlen 1993, 63; Rubarth 53–54). Or when a nationally-recognized collegiate female coach is paid less than her male counterpart in the same sport at the same institution. Or when intercollegiate scholarships are fewer for females than males (Hill 49; Arrigo 6). These are not isolated instances of gender bias or inequities. They are linked to past thinking about gender roles and a current socialization process for girls and boys. And they are linked to a hierarchical power structure that is controlled by a dominant group that is reluctant to redefine femininity or change a patriarchal view of females as being the weaker sex, inferior and physically frail. Sport and other forms of physical activities that take place in schools, health clubs and community centers are reflections of the norms of the society. The often cited report by the American Association of University Women and the Wellesley College Center for Research, *How Schools Shortchange Girls* has dramatically demonstrated the inequities for girls in the realm of education. Such reports on inequities and gender-biased behaviors may be found in all areas of the culture.[2] If females in this society are to grow intellectually, physically and emotionally in a holistic way, then much of what they see, hear, read and do has to be examined for the built-in biases, inequities or foul play. Our challenge is to empower girls and young women to freely explore and achieve all that is rightfully theirs and change what is foul in order to construct a new reality.

To make sweeping societal changes and alter norms and values will on one level mean that more females in the movement arena will have to test the law in court in order to level the playing field. But laws do not legislate people's thinking nor do the results of lawsuits substantially change practices of institutions or individuals. At another level, and one more complex, change lies in an awareness and an understanding of the factors that influence a girl's image of her body. It is an awareness of those situational events and contextual factors that shape a girl's confidence in her body and herself as a participant in physical activities. It is an awareness that translates into a willingness to take action to eradicate that which is negative, damaging and oppressive. And it is an awareness and understanding arrived at by females in concert with a supporting cast of significant others with whom they interact and model. My contention is that girls' and young women's movement education is multifaceted and takes place in three intricately related contexts: home, school and the society at large. Girls and young adult women are greatly influenced by their relationships with their mothers. What messages are sent, what is encouraged, what gets supported and promoted by mothers determines to a large extent what young girls will think and act upon. In school, their teachers, coaches, and the curriculum, individually and collectively, impact their futures. And in society, the cultural norms and values promoted by the mass media—television, newspaper articles, books, movies and home videos—all play a part of a total process in which girls and young women define themselves and construct their knowledge about the world and their place in it. My intent is not to examine all three contexts in depth. But rather it is to illuminate from relevant research and personal experience some of the unfair practices and behaviors in each context that influence females' movement education and identify a curriculum of resources for empowering females. And it is to assist individuals in constructing a new reality. My overall purpose is to set forth a working model and process to bring about "awareness" and "change." A model from which individuals may operate in order to develop a different and fairer reality for the physical-intellectual lives of girls and young women in a postmodern era. Figure 1 presents the proposed working

FIGURE 1. A Working Model for Change: Girls' and Young Women's Movement Education

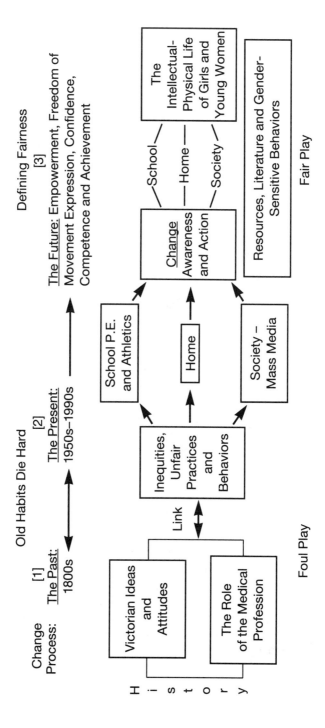

model for change. An important first step in the process is a solid understanding of the "past" and how it relates to present practices and attitudes. Historically, the 1800s and medical doctors played a profound role in dictating many biased behaviors of the present. Present-day habits, attitudes and behaviors against women are deeply ingrained in and linked to the Victorian era and the medical profession. In order to move forward and break habits that tie us negatively to the past, an understanding of the origins of biased attitudes toward women in their movement education is absolutely crucial. A second step in the change process is an awareness and an acknowledgment of "recent" inequities and unfair behaviors within the context of the home, school and society. This step is most important if one is to tackle comprehensive, meaningful and effective change. And finally, critical to the process is a third step which is the act of defining what is "fair" and engaging in a curriculum of resources from which one can interact with others and act from. The premise here is that change is initiated and supported by reading and taking action. The working model identifies the factors which influence gender awareness in a female's movement education and serves as a guide for change as well as a guide through the chapter. My hope is to bring about an "awareness" on the part of educators, librarians, parents, girls and young women—an awareness that leads to actions that will turn foul into fair.

OLD HABITS DIE HARD

Much of what is unfair today with regard to a female's movement education and her participation in physical activities can be traced back to a time when society and, in particular, the medical profession, held erroneous theories, Victorian ideas of and attitudes towards women. Those past theories and attitudes, promoted by a powerful few, formed intractable patterns of biased behaviors, habits and practices that have remained with us today.

THE PAST: THE HISTORICAL LINK
TO THE MEDICAL PROFESSION

In a book entitled *Out of Bounds*, author and researcher Helen Lenskyj has written a scholarly historical account and an analysis of women, sport, and female sexuality. Spanning a period of time from the 1880s to the mid 1980s, Lenskyj has convincingly made the connection between women's sport participation and the control of female sexuality. In Lenskyj's well-supported analysis, "control" is the major issue. It is control of female sexuality—inclusive of women's reproductive functions, sexual expression and, by extension, their participation in sporting activities—by a dominant group of white upper-class males (12). Supported by erroneous theories and attitudes held by nineteenth century experts in medicine, science, and religion, this controlling upper-class group constituted a powerful societal force which determined to a large degree a woman's nature and lifestyle.

In the first two chapters, Lenskyj explains how the medical profession profoundly influenced what was to be considered "appropriate" and "safe" for females' physical participation. Many of the medical experts' pseudo theories, Victorian ideas, and faulty interpretations of the physiological and anatomical differences between males and females were used to define femininity. They were used to determine a female's role in society and to reinforce a view of women as being subordinate and inferior to men. For example, as Lenskyj explains, in the latter part of the nineteenth century, professed notions of females being physically and intellectually inferior to males were supported by medical doctors citing that females had smaller brains and lighter bones (18). Physiologically, it was thought that, because women had fewer red corpuscles in a millimeter of blood than men, they were capable of less and should be restricted in their activities (Park and Hult 35–36). Also, the science of craniology, popular at the time, measured cranial size of persons and promoted the theory that brain size correlated with intelligence. The larger the skull, the larger the brain, and the retore the more intelligent the person (Sadker 1994a, 29–30). These unsupported theories were used against women and fueled prejudicial beliefs that males were intellectually superior. According to medical professionals, women's anatomy and physiology, designed uniquely for childbearing, relegated them to the primary role of mother and wife. As pronounced by the experts, it was women's responsibility and even their moral obligation to "preserve" what was called "vital energy" for childbearing (Lenskyj 18). Thus, vigorous sport competition and participation in strenuous physical leisure activities were to be avoided as they were thought to drain or deplete the body of this vital energy needed for a woman's special role. This, along with a Victorian view of women as being passive, timid, and dependent, contributed to a definition of femininity that placed females subordinate to men and portrayed them as frail. Clearly, sports that required physical exertion, strength, and aggression were taboo for woman. Those women who challenged prevailing views by participating in vigorous physical activities were considered unfeminine, masculine, or labeled derogatorily as "tomboys" (13). Women were restricted to certain activities that developed grace, balance, flexibility—such as rhythmic gymnastics and synchronized swimming. These activities were considered safe and appropriate. They were safe in that they posed no danger to a woman's reproductive function or to her anatomy and physiology. They were appropriate in that they conformed to a male definition of femininity. Vigorous activities that required speed, strength and endurance were not compatible with a woman's "nature" as construed by males (36–37, 139–141). It was determined that women's goals were to focus on reserving energy for childbearing, childrearing, and on becoming attractive enough to capture the interest of the males who might marry them.

As explained by Lenskyj, all this converged and then emerged as medical principles and advice to school programs, college athletic programs, and community health programs. Medical principles influenced institutional practices and, in some cases, they were translated into two different systems of game rules for men and women along with long lists of culturally differentiated manly and womanly sports e.g., hunting, fishing, boxing—manly sports; gymnastics, dance—womanly activities (28, 358, 140–143). Doctors were the appointed voices of authority on female sexuality and their sporting activity. Their advice greatly impacted institutional policies and it influenced what mothers would do in structuring their daughter's upbringing and in providing them with guidance for their daughters' development.

The medical profession's dominance of women's general health issues, restrictive lifestyle, and sporting participation was traced to the theories of "vitalism" prevalent in nineteenth-century physiology. As Lenskyj explains:

> Vitalism held that energy for the human organism was derived from a "vital force," which, being limited and non-renewable, should therefore be expended only in the service of family, god or country. (19)

What is most disturbing is that even though references to vitalist theories were difficult to find in the medical literature by the 1900s, they were still evidenced, as Lenskyj notes, in the popular culture and appeared as late as 1935 in some medical publications. As an example, Lenskyj cites an article focusing on the dangers of girls' basketball published in the American Medical Association publication *Hygeia*. She excerpts and quotes an explanation that appears in the article:

> In some cases, basketball can make too heavy a demand on the organic vitality of a growing girl . . . a great deal of the excess energy is needed for the physical changes which are naturally taking place. (19)

Other related concerns were reiterated in medical advice to mothers not to have their daughters participate in exercise during menstruation and to avoid certain physical activities such as jumping. Jumping was thought to cause injury to a woman's uterus (28–30). In fact, at the 1930 Olympic the broad jump was eliminated from women's competition because of the so-called danger it posed to the displacement of the uterus; and the shot put was eliminated because it was "excessively strenuous" (30).

In summary, much of what was poorly researched and empirically unsupported got translated into rationales for placing medical and cultural restrictions on women for participating in sports. Women's and girls' freedom to explore the full range of their potential in human movement was stifled and scientifically manipulated to support biased beliefs and prejudices. Their knowledge of their bodies was skewed and their understanding of their female nature was distorted and controlled by the dominant sex. It is important to note that there were many women who defied and challenged what was culturally and medically dictated.[3] As pioneers, these women caused tremendous breakthroughs for females in the movement arena. However, in the final analysis, nineteenth-century beliefs regarding a woman's physical and intellectual inferiority, her wife-mother role in society, and her construed physical limitations prevailed and were unfortunately carried well into the twentieth century. Deeply rooted in Victorian ideas and under the profound influence of medical professionals, prejudices and faulty medical theories permeated all facets of the culture including journalism, literature, education, government, and politics. Under the guise of what was natural, medically right, and culturally appropriate for women, biased notions became a way of thinking. They became standard operating behaviors on the part of politicians, administrators, teachers, coaches, and families in the twentieth century. The pseudo medical theories conforming to a male image of a woman dictated what women should participate in and at what levels (110). Entrenched in the society and transformed as habits and patterns of behaviors, they became twentieth-century discriminatory practices by institutions and individuals. They have shaped the way boys and girls interact with one another. They have shaped what mothers thought right to encourage or discourage daughters from doing. And they have shaped a girl's image of herself and her confidence in her movement abilities and athletic expression.

THE PRESENT: WHAT IS FOUL—
ONE, TWO, THREE STRIKES YOU'RE OUT!

There is little doubt about the major role the medical profession has played in the origins of today's discriminatory practices— practices that have so powerfully structured a female's movement education. Pseudo theories and Victorian ideas have remained with us in some cases as unintentional habits and in other cases as concerted efforts to maintain the status quo. They die hard. Current literature is riddled with factual information about the existing inequities and gender-biased behaviors covering all areas of girls' and women's lives. For girls and young women their education in the context of school, home, and society through the mass media affects who they are and what they become. We have made progress since the 1800s; and we, as a society, today are becoming more aware of the gender-biased behaviors embedded in each context. Not to change and make advances in all three is to strike out girls and young women. It is to strip them of their rights and their future. Change in one without the others will not produce the substantive advances that are needed to shed the past. In this component of the model and the second step of the process, some of the more recent inequities and unfair practices in each context are presented. The context of school—physical education and athletics—is examined first from the 1950s to the 1990s. Subsequent sections focus on the home and then society's role in influencing a female's movement education through the mass media. Although the sections on the home and society's role are shorter than the one on physical education, they serve to provide readers with a few of the more powerful unfair practices influencing girls' and young women's movement education.

School Physical Education and Athletics

Carried almost intact from the past and flying often in the face of twentieth-century 'hard' scientific evidence, the physical education curriculum in schools prior to 1972 and Title IX:

- Had girls and boys in separate classes.
- Offered separate programs of sports and activities to boys and girls.
- Supported financially more sport athletic teams for boys.
- Provided more and better equipment and facilities for boys' programs and teams.
- Had separate high school departments and faculties, with boys' departments usually receiving more monies.
- Hired more male coaches to coach boys' teams with salaries that were higher than female coaches in the same school, for the

same sport and for the same sport season (e.g., basketball). (AAHPERD March 1992; AAHPERD March 1993; Vertinsky 1992)

During the 1950s and 1960s the girls' curriculum in physical education included and emphasized 'feminine' sports—dance, calisthenics, gymnastics, volleyball, and "soft" ball. Boys' programs offered baseball, soccer, football, and wrestling. Basketball was popular in both programs. However, the rules and procedures for girls' basketball were substantially different than those for boys. Girls were not permitted to cross the middle line of the court and they were only allowed three bounces to advance the ball. Girls were still thought not to be capable of the physical endurance needed to play full court. In many programs females were encouraged to develop nonaggressive, lady-like behaviors and be supportive of the boys' teams. Becoming a cheerleader ensured popularity. Girls were encouraged to look like movie stars and to develop a body that would have all the physical attributes society considered attractive. For example, I can remember one of my physical education teachers in the early 1960s conducting an exercise with the class involving the arms and upper body that supposedly would lead to increasing the size of our busts. If you were fortunate to find a girls' team to play on outside of school, which I did, and if you were highly skilled, which I was, you would have inevitably heard the comment, "she plays like a boy." Conservatism and traditionalism prevailed. As Patricia Vertinsky has aptly coined a phrase appropriate here, it was the "institutionalization of sexist physical education practices" right down the line (376–80). Barriers to girls' participation in sports were formidable. All too often in the 1950s and 1960s girls and young women were still restricted from experiencing the full range of the movement capabilities. Worse, they believed the misinformation fed to them about their bodies. For example, many girls did not want to participate in activity during menstruation and would ask to be excused from their physical education class period. A large number of girls still thought "sweating" was bad and that taking a bath while menstruating was medically dangerous and wrong. And many girls bought into the idea that they must look like fashion models or movies stars of the day (Wolf 1991).

During the 1950s and 1960s professional philosophies differed significantly between male and female physical educators. This was due in part to their rather divergent teacher preparation programs. Men believed in a professional sports model philosophy of competition: a "winning isn't everything, it's the only thing" attitude along with the "opponent is the enemy" thinking. And they promoted a ladder system for the elite athlete that was to lead to success, fame, and professional play. Women emphasized character development through sport, cooperation, and fair play (Hill 50–51). Intellectual and emotional tensions were evident between the two sexes. And in many college and university departments interactions between male and female faculty led to fierce battles that are still fought today. Also, at the time, most high school and college athletic programs were dominated by men who were in powerful administrative positions making most of the decisions.

By the late 1960s the cry for equal opportunity for and by women became stronger. This was not only the case in physical education and athletics but in all other areas of the society as well. Thus, in 1972 Title IX of the Education Amendments was passed. Title IX states:

> No person in the United States shall, on the basis of sex, be excluded from participation in, be denied the benefits of, or be subjected to discrimination under any education program or activity receiving federal financial assistance.

As applied to physical education, Title IX mandated equal opportunities in physical education programs and athletics for males and females at all schools and colleges receiving federal funds. Many institutions resisted implementation of the law and many also complied. In a large number of schools, coeducational physical education classes were instituted for the first time. Did coed classes increase girls' and young women's participation? As reported by Vertinsky, surprisingly, the research on coeducational physical education revealed that:

> . . . girls were often less actively involved than in gendered settings and performed less well;
> . . . boys actively harassed girls, monopolized available space

and limited girl's participation in game activities;

. . . the behaviors and role play of boys and girls became more rather than less polarized with boys dominating leadership roles and girls accepting a subservient one;

... game rules [modified] in a coeducational strategy . . . [sent messages] . . . to the girls that they were not competent enough or strong enough to compete with boys without special assistance, and to boys that playing with girls implied accepting extra rules and constraints;

. . . teachers consistently gave more attention to boys than girls . . . [They] spent over two thirds of their time with boys who comprised less than half the class, or they consistently rewarded boys for their effort and good performance, while praising girls for neatness and criticizing them for being assertive,... [and] explaining their achievement as luck rather than hard work. (378–380)

By the middle 1970s and well into the 1980s girls receded into the walls of the gymnasiums. Teachers, unprepared to adequately teach coeducational physical education, professed that "coed-phys. ed." is a disaster. Many male physical educators did not like or want to teach girls who they had assessed as being poorly skilled and not interested in sports. And many men had not learned to analyze skill development well enough to effect sport skill development. Also, many women avoided teaching boys who they felt were unruly, aggressive, and not interested in learning from a female teacher. Some women physical educators, having conducted lessons that focused on cooperation and participation, sometimes at the expense of skill development, were not prepared to teach highly skilled boys. Boys, throughout their early lives, had had more experiences than girls in the motor skills needed to play team sports. Thus, boys had more opportunities to become skilled. As a result of this discrepancy, girls were often sneered at by boys—disappointing to have on a team according to boys. Choosing sides for teams was embarrassing for girls. Even if teachers selected a boy and girl captain, boys usually ended up taking charge of the team from the girl captain. Girls' levels of confidence were at an all-time-record low, and those boys who were not well-skilled were often recipients of such derogatory comments by peers and male teachers as "you throw like a girl'" or "you play like a sissy."

Unfortunately, many male physical educators and athletic directors still assumed a patriarchal and protective attitude toward female participation in sports—holding on to the frailty myth. I remember a lecture given at Columbia University in the early 1970s by a famous physical educator and women's rights advocate Dorothy Harris. When at one point in her talk she vigorously urged the audience to enforce Title IX and increase female participation in traditionally "male" sport activities and coed activities, many men in the audience voiced their concerns regarding the potential risk of injury to a young woman's breasts. Such participation, they protested, would be too rough. Her response stopped them cold when she said "no more than what occurs in healthy foreplay." Fears were expressed loudly by both male and female physical educators and biased attitudes in heated discussions came through loud and clear. The bottom line was that teachers and administrators were not adequately prepared to institute coeducational physical education, and many were unwilling to give up past attitudes.

Twenty years after the passage of Title IX a series of articles in a special feature section of the March 1992 *Journal of Health, Physical Education and Recreation* (AAHPERD) was published focusing on the effects of Title IX. Editor, Connie Fox, remarked in the introduction that Title IX had an effect on individuals and on institutions in that it provoked them to re-examine their policies, practices, curriculum, facilities, and budgets (34). No one would deny that it certainly opened doors for young women in intercollegiate and interscholastic sport competition. It is true that today we do have many more girls participating in athletics than we did in the past. In fact, Karen Hill notes that since Title IX, "Participation in girl's interscholastic sports has increased more than 500 percent . . . with nearly two million high school girls playing sports" (49). However, it is also true that we do not have nearly enough girls participating in physical education classes. Nor do we have substantial numbers of females participating in recreational and fitness activities to derive the physical as well as the psychological benefits from such activities. All total, the gains are relatively small in relation to the entire picture. For example, according to the Women's Sports Foundation only 36% of all high school athletes are girls even though females make up 50% of the high school enrollment. And as reported by Karen Hill:

- While over 50 percent of college students are female, only about 30 percent of college athletes are women.
- Women receive only 33 percent of collegiate scholarship dollars and less than 20 percent of athletic budgets.
- Coaches of women's teams are paid significantly less than 99 percent of their male counterparts coaching men's sports.
- The ranks of women coaches have decreased from more than 90 percent in 1972 to less than 50 percent in 1991. (49–50)

Ironically, Title IX led to fewer women coaches and athletic directors today than before. Researchers J. Vivian Acosta and Linda Carpenter have studied the problem extensively. Their research provides insight as to why this has occurred and cites from one study "old boys club network," "lack of support systems for females," and "female burn out" as three of five identified causes for the underrepresentation of females (AAHPERD-JOPERD, March 1992, 37). Today, women are still expected to do most of the childrearing, housework, and other domestic chores in addition to their new twentieth-century roles. Coaching requires many hours of intense work after school in addition to an individual's teaching responsibilities. Many women find that they simply cannot afford the time. Other women hit the glass ceiling when it comes to being assigned to or hired for an administrative athletic position. Thus, on both counts, girls and young women do not have role models nor do they have women directing athletic programs serving their needs and capabilities.

With regard to sporting participation, Fox reported that—when a sizeable number of women attending a national conference on issues in girls' and women's sports were asked to identify the current problems or changes needed, they listed the following repeatedly: ". . . access to facilities, better practice time, lack of programs (or dropping programs) for girls, poor schedules for games (lack of priority), no administrative support, inadequate budget, low salaries for women coaches and for coaches of girls and women, poor equipment, and lack of adequate transportation" (34). Fox commented that these, unfortunately, were the same problems that existed twenty years ago. The point is well made that substantial change has not yet occurred, even with a federal law.

Today, in 1995 while there are many excellent and educationally sound physical education programs, there are still far too many around the nation that have inequities. And most unfortunately today we find too many school programs in urban settings that continue to promote gender-role stereotyping in their class structure, instructional style, and physical activity offerings. From my own extensive work in schools (Catelli 1990a; 1990b; 1992a; 1992b; Catelli and Nix 1992) I have observed this to be true. For example, I still see a number of teachers and students preparing to become teachers who will not put a boy on a balance beam or assign girls as frequently as boys as captains of teams. Terminology such as "man-to-man" defense rather than "player-to-player" or "one-on-one" defense is persistently used by teachers of coed classes. In many sport books selected by teachers and librarians, girls are still either portrayed in stereotypical roles or they are totally absent from photos illustrating performance techniques. And in a large number of urban-school programs that I have observed, coeducational classes are rare. Classes of physical education are separated according to sex. Boys are taught by male faculty and girls by female faculty with traditional male and female sporting activities. What is most sad is that in the 1990s when health care and prevention has taken a priority position on our nation's agenda, girls in elementary, middle, and high school are scoring lower than boys on health-related fitness tests, e.g., cardiovascular endurance, muscular strength and endurance (AAHPERD 1987; Simmons-Morton, et al. 1987; Gutin, et al. 1990; Wughalter 1990). National surveys (AAHPERD 1985; 1987) have revealed this as well as my own research with an urban middle school population (Catelli, et al. 1992). In fact, the health-fitness standards that are set for girls by the medical and health professions are lower than for boys. Kay Williamson has commented that the different standards are inherently sexist and that we should use one criterion for both boys and girls (20–21). The fact is that girls have not been encouraged nor given sufficient opportunities to be physically active and thus reach higher levels of performance.

Perhaps what is most revealing and convincing are the voices of girls and young women. In Myra and David Sadker's book, *Failing at Fairness: How America's Schools Cheat Girls*, the authors report on a survey conducted by *Glamour* magazine in which readers were asked if they had had "a teacher who was biased against females or paid more attention to boys." Seventy-four percent of the respondents said they did. In identifying subjects, physical education was ranked second as an area in which they saw inequities. Math was ranked first, with 58%of the respondents selecting it and science was ranked third, with 47% of the respondents (8). Also, in a Michigan survey, 1,100 girls and boys were asked to write an essay about "what life would be like if they experienced a gender change." Many of the girl respondents expressed extremely favorable statements about being male, while 95% of the boys related that it was a disadvantage to be a girl citing physical abilities in sports as the loss. Overwhelmingly, boys made contemptuous statements about being a girl (84–86).

As we approach the twenty-first century we have not successfully rid our education system of the inequities or the gender-biased behaviors against girls and young women. We have not severed ties from our past. And we have unfortunately continued to perpetuate a society that is male oriented and dominated. The past has profoundly dictated the present and programmed a limiting and an unjust future for girls and young women. This is also true in other school subjects [4] and, as we have seen, in physical education and athletics. Taken together, general education has defined and structured girls' and young women's intellectual education and movement education. For females, the negatives in their school experiences have dramatically impacted their self-image, self-esteem, their confidence and competence. The unfair practices in education constitute a significant strike against girls and young women. But all of which is foul does not originate from nor happen only in school. Home is where it all begins.

Movement Education in the Home

From day one parents, and in particular mothers, dramatically structure and affect their daughters' movement education. Through their expectations and often inadvertent choices of psychological and physical environments for girls, parents dictate what is appropriate and culturally desirable for their daughters to do. They tell them in subtle and overt ways what they are supposed to be like and how they are supposed to act. Starting in the days after birth right into the early years of life, girls are handled, nurtured and developed differently than boys. For example, it has been found in studies reviewed by Judy Mann (1994) and Myra and David Sadker (1994) that:

> Girls are still dressed in pink, have pink rooms (connoting soft and cuddly); boys still have the color blue in dress and decor (connoting perhaps, blue ribbon-first place winners) (Mann 20; Sadker 255).

> Boys are greeted with more enthusiasm and expectation—"he might be president"; girls are welcomed into the world with less "fanfare." In fact world wide it is still a majority of couples that want boys as their first born (Mann 20).

> Infant girl cries are interpreted as one of sadness; infant boy cries are interpreted as anger (Mann 20–21).

> Girls are spoken to with words that express more warmth and emotion; adult interactions with boys convey and encourage more activity, motion, aggressiveness (Sadker 254).

> Girls are described and rated by their parents right after birth as "fine-featured," "soft," "delicate"; boys are described as "large-featured," "big" and "attentive" (even though the infants surveyed were of equal height, weight and "robustness") (Mann 21).

> Girls are more protected, held close to the body or on the lap and they are complimented on their appearance; boys are rough-housed and thrown up in the air. Boys are encouraged to participate in physical activity, to explore, seek adventure and risk; girls are not (Mann 22–23; Sadker 255).

> Girls are told by their mothers to be nice, polite, not to make waves or be confrontational; they are encouraged to be sensitive, caring—more so than boys. And it is accepted and expected by both mothers and fathers that daughters are more emotional than their sons (Mann 24–25).

Thus, the early messages that are sent by parents are strongly biased toward programming a girl for a traditional female role in society. Such messages program a female for traits that constrain her potential for developing physical and intellectual abilities that have been reserved for males (e.g., strength, endurance, assertiveness and leadership abilities).

The choice of toys for girls significantly affects their later competence in academic skills and in physical skills leading to sport activities not selected by females in high school and college. For example, Canadian researchers in visiting the homes of young children in 1990 found ". . . boys' rooms filled with sports equipment, toy vehicles, tools and building kits [and] . . . girls' rooms [filled with] children's furniture, kitchen utensils and lots of dolls" (Sadkers 255). Spatial skills that are developed by manipulating building blocks and transportation toys of "motion" are forerunners of competence in math, science, and in team sports such as soccer (Mann 22–24). Lower percentages of girls select sports that rely on spatial abilities. Depriving girls in early years impacts their motor development and limits their motor skill competency dramatically. No one wants to engage in an activity they may have very little chance of succeeding in.

Mothers and their daughter's bodies! One of the most fascinating areas to explore is the nature of the mother-daughter relationship and the changes that take place over time with regard to mothers' messages to their daughters about their bodies. During early and late adolescence such messages contain information about bodily and hormonal changes, bodily function and care, sexual activity, appearance, and physical movements. This information, usually reserved for mothers to communicate to daughters either verbally or by example, can unintentionally play a constraining role. For example, mothers often send confining messages to their daughters about the style of their bodily movements and posture. I can vividly remember hearing my mother's voice as an adolescent repeatedly instructing me to sit, stand, and walk like a lady. "Keep your legs together, not spread apart; sit with your legs crossed; keep your arms close to your body; walk in a straight line—put one foot directly in front of the other," she would say. In other words, I was to assume a posture and movement style that was confined to an imaginary "midline" running vertically through my body from head to toe. I was not to "spread open" like a male's style of movement and posture. Have you ever tried to teach females, who are characteristically "midline," the forehand stroke in tennis? As an instructor, I have, and it is physically and psychologically traumatic for them to spread apart their arms and legs in a stance and motion appropriate to the sport technique. They are rigidly stuck in a closed midline position. Studies of body motion and suppositions by educator-philosophers have noted that females acquire what it means to be a girl through their social training. In this case they are given information about how a female should move which often connotes fragility and again perpetuates the frailty myth (Lenskyj 117). What develops during the early years in many females is a "style of movement that lacks 'fluid and direct motion'—the motion is concentrated in one body part and . . . tends not to reach, extend, lean, stretch, and follow through, . . ." (Young 143–4 qtd. in Lenskyj 117). As Lenskyj comments, this is a movement pattern frequently observed in girls' "throwing," [hence the phrase 'he throws like a girl'] and in "hitting a ball and running" (117). Much of this occurs, motorically, well before females even begin kindergarten or nursery school and continues through the young adult years. This physical-psychological conditioning detracts from girls' confidence in their physical abilities to select and successfully participate in sporting activities requiring similar forms of movement patterns. Thus, many mothers inadvertently place restrictions on their daughters' participation in physical activities. They often do not provide their daughters with the necessary prerequisite experiences they need to achieve a level of success in sports or a level of confidence that is needed to venture out and experience sport.

Finally, from research studies reviewed by Maureen Weiss and Susan Glenn (1992) and those reviewed by Cathy Lirgg (1992), we know that a girl's self-confidence is shaped in early life and that mothers can play a significant role in either being supporters or detractors of a girl's involvement in sporting activities. We know that girls who have supportive parents are more likely to continue their participation in sport than those girls for whom support is lower (Weiss and Glenn 142). Also, we know that the degree to which adolescent girls maintain involvement in physical activity is positively related to the type and amount of influence received from mothers and other significant others in their lives (Weiss and Glenn 142). And we know that a girl's self-confidence and future achievement in sport performances is affected by verbal feedback by parents (Lirgg 164–170). Thus, home experiences and the mother-daughter relationship in particular provide a crucial piece of the total picture for a young woman's movement education. However, the home is not alone in being responsible for shaping a girl's movement education. It has become increasingly clear that society's role through the mass media can dominate, reinforce or even at times override totally what happens at home.

The Role of the Mass Media

In a recent newspaper interview with Martina Navratilova, the champion tennis player commented on how the media has unfairly treated female athletes—"treatment" that is different than what males receive. Her main point, which was communicated at a 1994 press conference at Wimbledon and later reiterated in the interview was that most reporters will simply "protect" male athletes ". . . whether they hit their wives or hit on other men" (Stains 5). Her comments never appeared in newspapers—proving to some extent her point. She also remarked that while reporters will persist in questioning the sexuality of female athletes who are suspected of being lesbian, male football athletes who are gay will be left untouched and unannounced by the media (Stains 5).

Newspapers, television, films, books, magazines, and commercial ads collectively reflect and direct society's cultural norms and values. Most assuredly, the media has played a major role in shaping and defining a female's image of her body and her sporting participation. Gender stereotyping and existing inequities for girls and women in all facets of the media, not just in the sporting arena, have proven enormous and alarming. For the most part, women are discriminated against, trivialized, underrepresented, and often placed in non-achieving, stereotypic roles (Weiss and Glenn 1992; Lirgg 1992; Rubarth 1992; Miner 1993). For example, ponder some of these media facts:

- Women receive less than 3.5 percent of newspaper print sport coverage and 5 percent of television coverage. (Miner 45)
- The lowest average percentage of references to women on the front pages (8%) of newspapers was found in the *New York Times* and the *Los Angeles Times*. (WAC 35)
- Ninety-two percent of the televised news time is focused on men's sports, while women's sports comprise 5 percent of the time and gender-neutral topics comprise 3 percent of the time. (Weiss and Glenn 140)
- Commentators refer to women athletes as "girls" or use their first names, while male athletes are referred to as "men" and their last names, a sign of respect, are used. (Women's Sports Foundation)
- Fewer than 50 women work as sportscasters at the 630 network affiliate stations around the nation and . . . no woman [except during the Olympics] does a play-by-play commentary. . . . (Rubarth 53)
- Ninety-one percent of the voice-overs on television commercials are male and of the 49,088 roles cast in Screen Actors Guild film and TV projects in 1989 only 13.9 percent were female leading roles. (WAC 35–36).
- On *Sesame Street*, the educational children's television program, the ratio of male to female characters for fifteen observed episodes was 2:1; male characters were assigned primary roles more often than female characters; and for the fifteen televised episodes reviewed, female characters exhibited a total of 1,256 stereotypical attributes in comparison to only 228 non-stereotypical attributes. (Abelli, et al.)
- And finally, an analysis of school curriculum materials and books revealed that the ratio of boy-centered stories to girl-centered stories was 5:2; adult male characters to adult female characters was 3:1; male biographies to female biographies was 6:1; and whereas men were portrayed in picture-books in 150 different work positions, women were portrayed as house-wives. (Sadker 69–70)

This media reality sends powerful messages to girls and young women about their role in society and what they are expected to become, be like, and participate in.

The world of commercials has significantly influenced the last two generations of youth. In an essay that examines the postmodern youth culture and secondary school physical education, Richard Tinning and Lindsay Fitzclarence have remarked on how TV's Coke and Reebok sneaker commercials have created visual images that promote distorted ideas about the body. TV ads flashing images of desirable bodies of both males and females engaged in stimulating, emotionally charged "fun" activities have created "expectations" and concerns by youth about how one's life ought to be "styled" and if one's body measures up to the one projected by the media (293). Health club ads show slender, sexually seductive and appealing females exercising and enjoying a fabricated version of and an illusionary view of the "good life." Often times the health, fitness and psychological benefits of exercise are traded off for pushing forward with a more sexual message—promoting thinly shaped, cleavage and curved female body images that are used for "seductive" appeal. Whether it is an ad for a health club or for swim suits, sneakers or jeans, girls and women are too often placed in positions that reflect a media constructed view of the female body. The consequence of which points squarely to the fact that many girls become anorexic and bulimic in their quest to match the projected image and reach the expectation. Too often the female body is situationally manipulated and distorted by media images for purposes of economic profit. This permeates the visual lives of youngsters and greatly influences their definition of the world and what they have come to believe is relevant and meaningful. What disturbs me greatly is the fact that, in a class I teach of college men and women preparing to become physical education teachers, only one student could find anything objectionable with a recent swimsuit issue of *Sports Illustrated*. The projected subordinate position of the female and demeaning aspects of the photo image were not seen at all. In general, the media has promoted women in sport primarily as a means to making them appear more physically attractive and not for their achievement in skill (M. Jane Miner 45).

In a review of popular video tapes of films found in video rental stores, I was astonished at the large number of recent films that cast a male character in a sport to the exclusion of any female main character or lead role. For example, *Rudy, Rookie of the Year, School Ties, Field of Dreams, Karate Kid, Searching for*

Bobby Fischer, The Natural, and *Hoosiers* are all films that feature males involved in sport. The only films I could find where females and sport were the main topic or at least part of the story line were *Personal Best, A League of Their Own,* and a new film release soon to be on video, The Next *Karate Kid.* If, in the past, women and sport were portrayed in film, it was either in a traditional female sport or movement forms such as ice skating, swimming or ballet e.g., *The Turning Point.* What does this tell a young girl? What limited, constrained meaning is conveyed?

Recently, however, in the last year or so as I conducted my research for this chapter, it was refreshing to see more girls and women represented in major newspaper articles. Interviews (e.g., Stains 1994), success stories (e.g., Blais 1993; Hershenson 1993; Lombardi 1993; Hamill 1994; Couples 1994) and articles discussing major problems and issues facing females (Orenstein 1994a; Sadker 1994b; Lewin 1993; Gross 1992; Matthews 1992) have all appeared as feature articles in the Sunday *New York Times* and *Daily News.* Today, we are beginning to see more women's magazines (e.g., *Working Woman*), sporting magazines (e.g., *Women's Sports & Fitness*), biographies and articles focused on women in politics (e.g., Cook 1993; Kunin 1994), the Senate (e.g., Milligan 1994) and sport (e.g., Navratilova with Vecsey 1985, 1992): all counterpoints to what has existed in the recent and distant past. In summary, it is critical to recognize that the social context and the media are powerful influences in shaping girls' and women's movement education. Undoubtedly, the task in instituting change is to understand society's role through the media and how it can be used effectively to alter gender-biased beliefs, redirect females' movement education, and heighten their opportunities to reach their intellectual-physical potential and career dreams.

DEFINING FAIR PLAY

What is fair play? Fair is females having control of their bodies and having a larger say in their destiny. Fair is having equal monies spent in medicine for researching the female body. Fair is having equal scholarship monies for females as for males. Fair is encouraging employment of women coaches and administrators for athletic programs and departments of physical education. Fair is creating opportunities for increasing the numbers of high school and college students participating in sports and other forms of physical activity. Fair is insisting on girls' and women's rights and demanding that institutions comply with Title IX. Fair is selecting books that have female protagonists that are strong and wise. Fair is selecting books and films where girls and women are portrayed in nontraditional roles. Fair is fulfilling needs for both boys and girls. And finally, as Roberta Bennett has said so well, fair is having young women and men ". . . come together as equals respecting, honoring and celebrating all their differences . . ." (63). What girls and young women want is a level playing field; one where their differences are valued and their skills and talents are elevated to that of males (Mann 1994). Complicated issues abound as to whether equal is fairer or whether separate programs for girls would provide girls with a "fairer" chance to develop skill. Or is it that we need to create new physical and sporting activities, thus eliminating the types of physical aggression that are present in some. Judgment is an essential element in making such decisions that will institute change. But judgment relies on being aware of the unfair practices and their origins and having an understanding of the factors that influence girls' and young women's movement education. My purpose in this last section of the chapter and step three of the change process is to outline what I am promoting as an essential aspect of what change will entail for constructing a new reality for the intellectual-physical life of girls and young women in the future. It is the component of the model that focuses on a curriculum of resources that impacts females and aids them in their way of "knowing." That is a type of knowing that is intimately related to, contextually derived from, and developed by what young women read, do, hear, and see. A type of knowledge that Jane Hannigan and Hilary Crew have commented on in their analysis of Belenky and others' *Women's Ways of Knowing*, referred to as "constructed knowledge." It is labeled as such to mean, ". . . a way of thought that does not split self-knowledge from other knowledge" (Hannigan and Crew 30) and a way of thought, as I am proposing here, that does not separate the physical from the intellectual. The two are intertwined. In this model, the body and mind are one. In this schema, societal change and the enhancement of personalized meaning for the intellectual-physical lives of females relies heavily on the combined participation of young women and men. It relies on those individuals who are responsible for providing guidance and education for girls in the contexts of home and school. And it relies on the participation of those who may influence a young women's movement education through the mass media. The resources identified are for use by and for girls as well as for boys. They are for high school and college students. They are for educators, parents, librarians, and students preparing to become teachers—all of whom prepare worlds and interact as significant others for girls and young women. The resources identified in Appendix A are arranged according to the groups mentioned above and the steps of the change process. They constitute a "preliminary curriculum." As a preliminary curriculum of resources, it serves as a supporting structure for the development of units of instruction, lessons, courses of study or self-study endeavors in gender awareness in girls' and young women's movement education. The curriculum includes carefully selected books, videos, and readings from journal essays, newspaper and magazine articles, along with the identification of relevant national organizations and associations. Such resources are associated with the components of the model for change and are intended to be used in conjunction with this chapter. They support the basic ideas presented in sections of the chapter and assist individuals in engaging in the overall proposed three-step process for change.

For example, the book *Out of Bounds* (Lenskyj) and the article "Women as leaders in physical education and school-based sports, 1865 to the 1930s" (Park and Hult) present excellent and encompassing historical accounts and examinations of women's sporting activity and movement education. *Out of Bounds* is appropriate in step one for all groups to read in order to gain insight about the links to the past and the influence of the medical profession. For high school students who are particularly interested in the history of women, the books *Women in Baseball: The Forgotten History* (Berlage) and *When Women Played Hardball* (Johnson) portray women's historical participation in the sport of baseball, their problems, issues, obstacles, and triumphs. *When Women Played Hardball* reads like a novel capturing the experiences, stories, and memories of twenty-six women who played for the 1950 Rockford Peaches and Fort Wayne Daisies teams. The video *A League Of Their Own*, about the All-American Girls Professional Baseball League formed in 1943, is a perfect adjunct to the two readings. For college students, *Coming On Strong: Gender and Sexuality in Twentieth-Century Women's Sport* (Cahn) delivers a social history as well as a contemporary examination of women in sport, including an analysis of the interactions of race and class. For educators, especially physical educators, the first section of Patricia Vertinsky's *Reclaiming Space, Revisioning the Body: The Quest for Gender-Sensitive Physical Education* relates information about the past specific to physical education. Thus, all these works provide a historical perspective while identifying clearly the obstacles, social attitudes, prejudices, and barriers preventing females from experiencing physical activity. They foster in step one a critical analysis of the past and provide an awareness and understanding of the origins of contemporary biased attitudes and practices and how we are tied to them. They, as well as other readings listed in section "A" of the curriculum for each group, are suggested as a critical first step in the process of change. They are intended to aid readers in not only achieving an "awareness" and an "understanding" of the past but also in dismantling old negative habits, attitudes, and thinking.

If one is to transform one's thinking and truly tackle meaningful and effective change, then an awareness and an understanding of "recent" inequities and unfair behaviors within the contexts of home, school, and the society at large is proposed as the second step of the model for change. The resources to achieve this purpose are listed for each group in section "B" entitled "The Present."

For example, for an awareness of current gender bias against females and social attitudes, the book *Failing at Fairness: How America's Schools Cheat Girls* (Sadker) and The AAUW Report *How Schools Shortchange Girls* provide the most comprehensive view in the realm of education, including school physical education and athletics. They are based on research and should be read by all groups. The book by Judy Mann, *The Difference: Growing Up Female in America*, especially the first four chapters, is an important one for parents to read in that it will supply them with insights about subtle, biased interactions with their daughters during the earlier years. College students will gain a sociological-psychological understanding of attitudes and sexism from *The Stronger Women Get, The More Men Love Football: Sexism and the American Culture of Sports* (Nelson). From the article "Girls Talk; Boys Talk More," (*The Harvard and Education Letter*) and the research of Catherine Krupnick, college students learn that higher education classroom discourse is dominated by and biased toward males. Essays by Anna Quindlen, "Foul Play" and "Offensive Play" offer poignant and recent editorials for college students on sport, sexism, and sexual harassment. And for high school students Quindlen's "Cement Floor" comments on the social injustice and abuse to women baseball umpires. For educators, a series of featured articles by AAHPERD entitled, "Title IX at Twenty—Mature Programs or Still Toddling?" and "Women in Sport Leadership: The Legacy and the Challenge," the research of Pat Griffin, and an essay by Juan-Miguel Fernandez-Balboa, read as a set, will adequately inform educators of the current inequities, unfair practices in physical education, sport and athletics as well as providing facts about Title IX.

High school girls and college women need to understand how society's cultural values and popular practices may discriminate against them and profoundly affect their image of their body, self-esteem, and confidence in physical and intellectual capabilities. Naomi Wolf's *Beauty Myth: How Images of Beauty Are Used Against Women* for high school girls and Susan Faludi's *Backlash: The Undeclared War Against American Women* for college students are particularly good for accomplishing this purpose. In order for parents to gain an understanding of the current research in this area, Cathy Lirgg's "Girls and Women, Sport and Self-Confidence," Maureen Weiss and Susan Glenn's "Psychological Development and Females' Sport Participation," Catherine Steiner-Adair's "When the Body Speaks: Girls, Eating Disorders and Psychotherapy," and Peggy Orenstein's book *Schoolgirls: Young Women, Self-Esteem, and the Confidence Gap* are all suggested. These readings include information about the parents' role in the development of girls and how experiences in the home may impact females. Also, some of the readings provide insight and research specific to the mother-daughter relationship, e.g., *Women, Girls and Psychotherapy: Reframing Resistance* by Carol Gilligan, et al. and the video *The Joy Luck Club*.

All of these readings, as well as others listed in sections "B," achieve the objective of the second step of the change process. They supply readers with research findings, analyses, and editorials on current inequities and unfair practices as they exist in the home, school, and society. Many speak to the role of the mass media and how it has negatively served to shape a female's image of herself. The resources in section "B" for each group are intended to bring about not only an awareness of the recent past, but also a sobering acknowledgment of what exists today that is discriminatory and damaging to females. Of course, it should be mentioned that readings identified for individuals of one group may certainly be read by others as well. My selection of resources for groups was based on an educational appraisal of what I believed to be appropriate for the age level, level of development, and interests of the individuals making up the groups in relation to the concepts presented in the model for change. Some readings have been deemed appropriate for all and thus have been listed for each group.

As a final and most critical third step of the change process, section "C" for each group includes resources that are intended to provide new meanings and understandings and to assist individuals in creating new and fairer worlds for females. They are resources aimed at breaking with tradition, sparking imaginations and thoughts of girls and young women. Some will identify new and non-traditional possibilities for females. Others provide knowledge and ideas for individuals involved in creating a better intellectual-physical existence for females in a postmodern era. And still others demonstrate creative writings by females. This last step contributes significantly to defining fairness in the 21st century. It provides a foundation and serves to usher in a new era for females and their movement education. It is a future for girls and women defined by empowerment and freedom of movement.

Sections "C" of the curriculum for high school and college students include poems, essays, novels, articles, non-fiction books, and videos. Some examples for high school students are "Wait Till Next Year" a poem by Lillian Morrison, and one by Georgeann Eskievich Rettberg entitled, "Women in the Pits"; the book *Golden Girls: Time Stories of Olympic Women Stars* by Carli Laklan; and, although about a young eighth-grade girl-athlete who starts a school football team, the novel *Zanballer* by Knudson is a good choice. All will spark imaginations. For college students, the novel *Squeeze Play* by Jane Leavy, and a short story "Jogging at the V.A." by Sharon Weinstein, are exemplars of the section. The video *Women of Courage: The Story of Women Pilots of World War II* I found particularly inspirational and quite informative about the physical capabilities and leadership qualities of women. A wonderful book of poems, short stories, essays and excerpts from novels on baseball, all by women writers and edited by Elinor Nauen, is *Diamonds Are a Girl's Best Friend*. I highly recommend this book for both high school and college students. Also listed for both groups is an excellent video, *In the Game* with a companion instructional booklet, and *Aethlon: The Journal of Sport Literature* (formerly *Arete*), published by the Sport Literature Association, which contains poems, essays, and other literary works by male and female authors.

In shaping the future, it is extremely important for young female athletes to see that they too can make headlines and be a featured story in magazines and prestigious newspapers. For high school students, the article featured in the magazine section of the Sunday *New York Times* "They Were Commandos: A Season in the Lives of the Amherst Hurricanes," about the members of the Amherst Regional High School girls' basketball team and their quest for the state championship and "Somewhere Over the Goal Post a Girl's Dreams Lies" by Kate Lombardi are good examples. For college students, a brief newspaper article appearing in the *Daily News* by and about Deborah Couples the only woman to have competed in polo's prestigious East Coast Open, and one by Laurence Stains, "Martina's Final Volley" are both true-life success stories.

For parents, and in particular mothers, I have included readings that will provide a deeper understanding of the mother-daughter relationship and that will hopefully assist them in guiding their daughters toward positive, active and healthy futures. Examples are Elizabeth Debold's "The Body at Play," Rose Glickman's *Daughters of Feminists*, and *Mother Daughter Revolution: From Betrayal to Power* by Elizabeth Debold, Marie Wilson and Idelisse Malave.

And lastly, for educators, the listing of resources is directed at providing knowledge, ideas, and strategies for developing and conducting instructional environments that promote gender awareness and change for females' movement education. Such environments may include seminars in gender awareness conducted by librarian-educators for parents, teachers, college and high school students. These seminars may be offered for each population separately or for what is today referred to as "intergenerational seminars," enrolling high school students, parents, and grandparents. Other instructional environments include teacher education courses in colleges, classes or courses conducted by educators in high schools and universities, and clinics for coaches and physical educators.

The resources of this preliminary curriculum are to be interacted with and from along with other ideas and gender materials from other disciplines. Included in the curriculum is a series of questions[5] for discussions, readings and essay assignments that may be used with some of the resources identified or used for assignments that necessitate additional resources and further investigations. They are offered to aid educators in their development of lessons and unit of instructions for course work and seminar discussions.

CONCLUSION

Finally, the resources of the curriculum range from those works that are personalized, based on experience, to those that are instructive and based on empirical research or historical accounts. Some are consciousness-raising, challenging tradition. Many are contemporary, insightful, and from a feminist point of view as well as promoting gender-sensitive behaviors. They are works that hopefully will have the potential force to empower girls; to provide them with ideas and knowledge that will lead to freedom of movement expression, confidence, competence and achievement. They include literary works which will hopefully serve as Kay Vandergrift has said as ". . . a vital source of vicarious experiences and alternative meanings that help young people imagine potential futures for themselves and for their worlds" (24). My premise in proposing the model for change is that awareness and the action needed for turning foul into fair is initiated and supported by reading, participating, interacting, and providing gender-sensitive environments for girls and young women. Thus, the resources included in the curriculum as well as those cited in sections of the chapter are envisioned as tools for change and a curriculum for creating a new reality for women in a postmodern era.

NOTES

1. See the March 1992 issue of the Journal of Physical Education, Recreation and Dance (*AAHPERD-JOPERD*) for a series of articles that discuss the effects of Title IX, twenty years after its passage.
2. A book entitled *WAC STATS: The Facts about Women* includes statistics concerning the inequities confronting women in this culture. The statistics were drawn from numerous surveys, reports and research studies. Information ranging from data on abortion to inequities in the media is identified. WAC is an acronym for Women's Action Coalition.
3. Throughout the book *Out of Bounds,* author Helen Lenskyj identifies women who defied the status quo. The reader is also referred to the March 1992 and 1993 issues of *JOPERD* for the identification of women who are recognized as leaders.
4. The reader is referred to Myra and David Sadker's book, *Failing at Fairness: How America's Schools Cheat Girls* and the American Association of University Women's Report, *How Schools Shortchange Girls* for an in-depth examination of the existing inequities and unfair practices in education.
5. The list of questions included in the curriculum was adapted from a list formulated by Daryl Siedentop from a book entitled *Introduction to Physical Education, Fitness and Sport.*

WORKS CITED

AAHPERD—American Alliance for Health, Physical Education,

Recreation and Dance. "Breaking with Tradition—Women and Outdoor Pursuits." *JOPERD* [Special Feature Articles] 63.2 (February
1992): 49–64.

_____. "Dance Dynamics—Gender Issues in Dance Education." JOPERD
[Special Feature Articles] 65.2 (February 1994): 25–48.

_____. "The National Children and Youth Fitness Study I." *JOPERD*
56.1 (1985): 45–50.

_____. "The National Children and Youth Fitness Study II." *JOPERD*
[Special Feature Articles] 58.9 (November/December 1987): 49–102.

_____. "Title IX At Twenty—Mature Programs or Still Toddling?"
JOPERD [Special Feature Articles] 63.3 (March 1992): 33–64.

_____. "Women in Sport Leadership: The Legacy and the Challenge."
JOPERD [Special Feature Articles] 64.3 (March 1993): 33–64.

Abelli, Richard, Russell W. Jones, and Donna M. Abelli. Ratio of Male
to Female Characters and the Incidence of Gender Stereotyping in
the Children's Television Program Sesame Street. 1994 NEERO Conference, Thursday, April 21, 1994.

Acosta, J. Vivian, and Linda J. Carpenter. "As the Years Go By—Coaching Opportunities in the 90s." *JOPERD* 63 (March 1992): 36–41.

American Association of University Women. *The AAUW Report: How
Schools Shortchange Girls*. Washington: American Association of University Women Educational Foundation, 1992.Arrigo, Mary. "Donna
Lopiano: Executive Director, Women's Sports Foundation." *Networking: Newspaper for Women* [Remsenburg, New York] July, 1994: 6–8.

Belenky, Mary Field, Blythe McVicker Clinchy, Nancy Rule Goldberger,
and Jill Matuck Tarule. *Women's Ways of Knowing: The Development of
Self, Voice, and Mind*. New York: Basic, 1986.

Bennett, Roberta. "Dismantling the Master's House—A Tale Told in
Affirmation of Diversity." *JOPERD* 64.3 (March 1993): 49–52, 63.

Berlage, Gai Igham. *Women in Baseball: The Forgotten History*. New York:
Praeger, 1994.

Birell, Susan, and Cheryl Cole, eds. *Women, Sport, and Culture*. Cham-
paign: Human Kinetics, 1994.

Blais, Madeline. "They Were Commandos: A Season in the Lives of the
Amherst Hurricanes." *New York Times Magazine* 18 April 1993, Sec. 6:
24–30.

Brown, Jennifer. "Reasons for the Selection or Nonselection of Physical
Education Studies by 12 Girls." *Journal of Teaching in Physical Education* 11.4 (July 1992): 402–410.

Brown, Lyn Mikel, and Carol Gilligan. *Meeting at the Crossroads:
Women's Psychology and Girls Development*. Cambridge: Harvard UP,
1992.

Cahn, Susan. *Coming on Strong. Gender and Sexuality in Twentieth-*

Century Women's Sport. New York: Free, 1994.

Catelli, Linda A. Against All Odds: "A Holistic Urban School/College Partnership: Project SCOPE." *Action in Teacher Education* 14.1 (1992a): 42–51.

_____. "Fair Play: Gender Awareness in Middle School Physical Education." *Connection* 18 (1992b): 16–17, 21.

_____. "Physical Education in the 1980s: A Guide for Developing Children's and Young Adult Collections." *Collection Building* 5.4 (Winter 1984): 7–22.

_____. "School-College Partnership: Development of a Working Model for the Louis Armstrong Middle School Curriculum in Physical Education." *Middle School Journal* 21.4 (1990a): 36–39.

_____. "School-University Partnerships: The Transference of a Model." *Leadership in Library Education: Essays in Honor of Jane Anne Hannigan.* Eds. Shelia S. Intner and Kay E Vandergrift. Metuchen: Scarecrow, 1990b.

Catelli, Linda, and Wanda Nix. "Project SCOPE: An Urban Partnership Venture—Descriptions and Predictions." *Collaboration Between Researchers and Practitioners, An International Dialogue.* Eds. George Graham and Margaret Jones. Atlanta: AIESEP/NAPEHE, 1992.

Catelli, Linda, Bonnie Mongiello, and Ken Moskowitz. "A Longitudinal Study of Individual and Group Change in the Health-Related Fitness Performances of an Urban School Student Population—Report of Preliminary Findings." New York: Center for the Improvement of Education, Queens College, 1992.

Cook, Alison. "Lone Star." [Ann Richards] *New York Times Magazine* 7 Feb. 1993, Sec. 6: 23–26, 27, 38, 42, 47.

Couples, Deborah. "She Reigns in a Sport of Kings." *Daily News* 18 Sept. 1994, Sunday Forum: 74.

Debold, Elizabeth. "The Body at Play." *Women, Girls and Psychotherapy.* Eds. Carol Gilligan, Annie Rogers and Deborah Tolman. New York: Harrington-Haworth, 1991.

Debold, Elizabeth, Marie Wilson, and Idelisse Malave. *Mother Daughter Revolution: From Betrayal to Power.* Reading: Addison, 1993.

Dewar, Alison. "Would All the Generic Women in Sport Please Stand Up? Challenges Facing Feminist Sport Sociology." *QUEST* 45.2 (1993): 211–229.

Eckart, Joyce, and Tracy Dyanne. "Gender Socialization in Schools: A Course for Change Agents." *Teaching Education* 5.1 (1992): 59–64.

Faludi, Susan. *Backlash: The Undeclared War Against American Women.* New York: Crown, 1991.

Fernandez-Balboa, Juan-Miguel. "Sociocultural Characteristics of the

Hidden Curriculum in Physical Education." *QUEST* 45.2 (1993): 230–254.

Field of Dreams. Video. Dir. Phil Alden Robinson. Universal–MCA Home Video, 1990. 106 min.

Fox, Connie. "Title IX At Twenty—Mature Programs or Still Toddling?—Introduction." *JOPERD* 63.3 (March 1992): 34–35.

Gasperini, Kathleen. "Beauty, Sports and Power Feminism." [Interview with Naomi Wolf on beauty, sports and empowerment]. *Women's Sports & Fitness* March 1994: 24–25.

Gilligan, Carol. "Women's Psychological Development: Implications for Psychotherapy." *Women, Girls and Psychotherapy*. Eds. Carol Gilligan, et al. New York: Harrington-Haworth, 1991.

Gilligan, Carol, Anne G. Rogers, and Deborah L. Tolman, eds. *Women, Girls and Psychotherapy: Reframing Resistance*. New York: Harrington-Haworth, 1991.

Glickman, Rose. *Daughters of Feminists*. New York: St. Martin's, 1993.

Griffin, Pat. "Assessment of Equitable Practices in the Gym." *CAHPER/ACSEPL Journal* 55.2 (1989): 19–22.

Gross, Jane. "Does She Speak for Today's Women?" [Patricia Ireland, President of NOW] *New York Times Magazine*, Mar. 1992, Sec. 6: 16–19, 38, 54.

Grossman, Herbert, and Suzanne H. Grossman. *Gender Issues in Education*. Boston: Allyn, 1994.

Gutin, Bernard, et al. "Blood Pressure, Fitness and Fatness in 5- and 6-Year-Old Children." *Journal of the American Medical Association* 264 (1990): 1123–1127.

Hamill, Denis. "Diamonds are a girl's best friend." *Daily News* 13 April 1994: 13.

Hannigan, Jane Anne, and Hilary Crew. "A Feminist Paradigm for Library and Information Science." *Wilson Library Bulletin* 68.2 (1993): 28–32.

The Harvard and Education Letter. "Girls Talk; Boys Talk More." [Published by the Harvard Graduate School of Education in association with Harvard UP, Cambridge] Jan./Feb. 1991: 6–8.

Hershenson, Roberta. "In Archers' World, She's the Whizzz Kid." *New York Times, Sunday* 10 Oct. 1993, Sec. 13:1, 6.

Hill, Karen. "Women in Sport: Backlash or Megatrend." *JOPERD* 64.9 (November-December 1993): 49–52.

Hoosiers. Video. Dir. David Anspaugh. Hemdale-HBO Video, 1986. 115 min.

In the Game. Video. [Including a Study Guide containing questions for discussions and essay assignments.] Dir. Becky Smith. Smith

Productions, 1994. 55 min.

Jewett, Shay. "Free Throws." *Aethlon: The Journal of Sport Literature* [Formerly *Arete*] 7.1 (Fall, 1989): 31–39.

Johnson, Susan. *When Women Played Hardball.* Seattle: Seal, 1994.

The Joy Luck Club. Video. Dir. Wayne Wang. Hollywood Home Video-Buena Vista Pictures,1993. 139 min.

Karate Kid. Video. Dir. John G. Avidson. RCA–Columbia, 1984. 126 min.

Karnes, Frances, and Suzanne Bean. *Girls and Young Women: Leading the Way—20 True Stories about Leadership.* Minneapolis: Free Spirit, 1993.

Knudson, R. *Zanballer.* New York: Delacorte, 1972.

Krupnick, Catherine. "Women and Men in the Classroom: Inequality and Its Remedies." *On Teaching and Learning: Journal of the Harvard Danforth Center* Spring 1985.

Kunin, Madeleine. *Living a Political Life.* New York: Knopf, 1994.

Kyvallos, Lucille. "Queens College: Success with No Frills." *A Century of Women's Basketball: From Frailty to Final Four.* Eds. Joan Hult and Marianna Trekell. Reston: AAHPERD, 1991.

Laklan, Carli. *Golden Girls: Time Stories of Olympic Women Stars.* New York: McGraw, 1980.

A League of Their Own. Video. [Including a documentary on real-life women's baseball league, formed during World War II]. Dir. Penny Marshall. Columbia TriStar. 127 min.

Leavy, Jane. *Squeeze Play.* New York: Doubleday, 1990.

Lenskyj, Helen. *Out of Bounds: Women, Sport and Sexuality.* Toronto: Women's, 1986.

Lewin, Tamar. "A Feminism that Speaks For Itself." [Hillary Rodham Clinton] *New York Times* 3 Oct. 1993, Sec. 4:1, 3.

Lirgg, Cathy. "Girls and Women, Sport, and Self-Confidence." *QUEST* 44.2 (1992): 158–178.

Lombardi, Kate Stone. "Somewhere Over the Goal Post a Girl's Dream Lies." *New York Times, Sunday* 26 Sept. 1993, Sec. 13:1, 14.

Luke, Moira, and Gary Sinclair. "Gender Differences in Adolescents' Attitudes Toward School Physical Education." *Journal of Teaching in Physical Education* 11.1 (Oct. 1991): 31–46.

Mann, Judy. *The Difference: Growing up Female in America.* New York: Warner, 1994.

Matthews, Anne. "Rage in a Tenured Position." [Carolyn Heilbrun] *New York Times Magazine* 8 Nov. 1992, Sec. 6: 46–47, 72–75, 83.

McHugh, Clare. "The Prophet of Power Feminism: Is Naomi Wolf the Gloria Steinem of Her Generation?" *New York* 29 November 1993: 44–50.

Milligan, Susan. "House work—Senate, too." Sunday *Daily News* 6 Mar.

1994, Special Report: 30.

Miner, M. Jane. "Women in Sport—A Reflection of the Greater Society?" *JOPERD* 64.3 (March 1993): 44–48.

Morrison, Lillian. "Wait Till Next Year." *Aethlon: The Journal of Sport Literature* [Formerly *Arete*] 6.2 (Spring 1989): 136.

NAPEHE—National Association for Physical Education in Higher Education. "Girls and Women in Sports and Physical Activity: Psychosocial Perspectives." *QUEST* [Special Feature Essays] 44.2 (August 1992): 135–265.

The Natural. Video. Dir. Barry Levinson. RCA–Columbia Home Video, 1984. 134 min.

Nauen, Elinor ed., *Diamonds Are a Girl's Best Friend.* Boston: Faber, 1994.

Navratilova, Martina with George Vecsey. *Martina.* New York: Fawcett Crest, First Edition 1985, Seventh Edition (Paperback), 1992.

Nelson, Barton Mariah. *The Stronger Women Get, The More Men Love Football: Sexism and the American Culture of Sports.* New York: Harcourt, 1994.

The Next Karate Kide. Dir. John G. Avildsen. Columbia, 1994.

Orenstein, Peggy. "Children Are Alone." *New York Times Magazine* 24 July 1994a, Sec. 6: 18–25, 32, 40, 44.

_____. (In Association with AAUW). *Schoolgirls: Young Women, Self-Esteem, and the Confidence Gap.* New York: Doubleday, 1994.

Park, Roberta J., and Joan S. Hult. "Women as leaders in physical education and school-based sports, 1865 to the 1930s." *JOPERD* 64.3 (1993): 35–40.

Personal Best Video. Dir. Robert Towne. Geffen Co., 1982. 126 min.

Quindlen, Anna. "Birthday Girl." *New York Times* 21 Nov. 1993, Week in Review, OP-ED: E 17.

_____. "The Cement Floor." *Thinking Out Loud: On the Personal, the Political, the Public and the Private.* New York: Random, 1993.

_____. "Feeling Fully 40, Ex-Ballplayer Exults in Dream Team's Excellence." *Columbus Dispatch* 12 July 1992: 3H.

_____. "Foul Play." *Thinking Out Loud: On the Personal, the Political, the Public and the Private.* New York: Random, 1993.

_____. "Offensive Play." *Thinking Out Loud: On the Personal, the Political, the Public and the Private.* New York: Random, 1993.

Rettberg, Georgeann Eskrevich. "Women in the Pits." *Aethlon: Journal of Sport Literature* [Formerly *Arete*] 7.2 (Spring 1990): 86.

Robinson, Christine. "Working with Adolescent Girls: Strategies to Address Health Status." *Women, Girls and Psychotherapy.* Ed. Carol Gilligan et al. New York: Harrington-Haworth, 1991.

Rookie of the Year. Video. Dir. Daniel Stern. Fox Video, 1993. 103 min.

Rubarth, Lisa. "Twenty Years After Title IX: Women in Sports Media. *JOPERD* 63.3 (March 1993): 53–55.

Rudy. Video. Dir. David Anspaugh. Columbia-TriStar, 1994. 112 min.

Sadker, Myra, and David Sadker. *Failing at Fairness: How America's Schools Cheat Girls.* New York: Scribner's, 1994a.

_____. "Why Schools Must Tell Girls: 'You're Smart, You Can Do It'." *Daily News* 4–6 February 1994b, USA Weekend Magazine Section: 4–6.

School Ties. Video. Dir. Robert Mandel. Paramount, 1992. 110 min.

Searching For Bobby Fischer. Video. Dir. Steve Zaillian. Paramount, 1994. 111 min.

Sherr, Lynn, and Jurate Kazickas. *Susan B. Anthony Slept Here.* New York: Times, 1994.

Shortchanging Girls, Shortchanging America. Video. American Association of University Women, 1991. 15 minutes.

Siedentop, Daryl. *Introduction to Physical Education, Fitness, and Sport.* Mountain View: Mayfield, 1990.

Simmons-Morton, B. et al. "Children and Fitness: A Public Health Perspective." *Research Quarterly for Exercise and Sport* 58 (1987): 295–302.

Smith, Barbara. "In Balance." *Arete: The Journal of Sport Literature* [Now *Aethlon*] 5.1 (Fall, 1987): 72.

Stains, Laurence. "Martina's Final Volley." *Daily News* 26–28 Aug. 1994, USA Weekend: 4–6.

Steiner-Adair, Catherine. "When the Body Speaks: Girls, Eating Disorders and Psychotherapy." *Women, Girls and Psychotherapy.* Eds. Carol Gilligan et al. New York: Harrington-Haworth, 1991.

Tave, Isabelle. *Not Bad for a Girl.* New York: Evans, 1972.

Tinning, Richard, and Lindsay Fitzclarence. "Postmodern Youth Culture and the Crisis in Australian Secondary School Physical Education." *QUEST* 44 (1992): 287–303.

Tobey, Charles. "The Loneliness of the Woman Athlete." *NYSAHPERD Journal* Winter (1993–94): 7, 24.

The Turning Point. Video. Dir. Herbert Ross. Twentieth Century Fox-Magnetic Video, 1977. 119 min.

Valens, E. G. *The Other Side of the Mountain—The Inspiring Story of the Skiing Star, Jill Kinmont.* New York: Harper, 1988.

Vandergrift, Kay E. "A Feminist Research Agenda in Youth Literature." *Library* 68.2 (1993): 23–27.

Vertinsky, Patricia A. "Reclaiming Space, Revisioning the Body: The Quest for Gender-Sensitive Physical Education." *QUEST* 44.3 (1992): 373–396.

Weinstein, Sharon. "Jogging at The V.A." *Aethlon: The Journal of Sport*

Literature [Formerly *Arete*] 6.1 (1988): 79–80.

Weiss, Maureen, and Susan Glenn. "Psychological Development and Females' Sport Participation: An Interactional Perspective." *QUEST* 44.2 (1992): 138–157.

Williamson, Kay. "Is Your Inequity Showing? Ideas and Strategies for Creating a More Equitable Learning Environment." *JOPERD* 64.8 (October 1993): 15–23.

Williamson, Kay, and Jacqueline Williams. "Promoting Equity Awareness in the Preparation of Physical Education Students." *Teaching Education* 3.1 (1990): 117–123.

Wolf, Naomi. *Fire with Fire*. New York: Random, 1993.

_____. *The Beauty Myth: How Images of Beauty Are Used Against Women*. New York: Morrow, 1991.

Women in Sport. 3–Video set. Program One: Our Social Selves; Program Two: Our Inner Selves; Program Three: Our Physical Selves. Human Kinetics, 1989. 69 min.

Women of Courage: The Story of the Women Pilots of World War II. Video, Documentary, K. M. Prod., 1992. 1 hour.

Women's Action Coalition. *WAC STATS: The Facts about Women*. New York: New Press, 1993.

Women's Sport & Fitness. Women's Sports Foundation. Boulder, CO 80302

Working Woman. 230 Park Ave., New York 10169.

Wughalter, Emily. *Executive Summary Report: New York City—Youth Fitness Study, 1989 and 1990*. New York City: American Heart Association, New York City Affiliate, 1990.

APPENDIX A
SAMPLE CURRICULUM RESOURCES

Turning Foul into Fair:
A Preliminary Curriculum of Resources

Resources for High School Students

A. THE PAST [1]*:

American Association of University Women. *The AAUW Report: How Schools Shortchange Girls.*
Berlage, Gai Igham. *Women in Baseball: The Forgotten History.*
Johnson, Susan. *When Women Played Hardball.*
A League of Their Own. Video [Including a documentary on real-life women's baseball league, formed during World War II].
Lenskyj, Helen. *Out of Bounds: Women, Sport and Sexuality.*

B. THE PRESENT [2]:

Quindlen, Anna. "The Cement Floor."
Sadker, Myra and David. *Failing at Fairness: How America's Schools Cheat Girls.*
Wolf, Naomi. *The Beauty Myth: How Images of Beauty Are Used Against Women.*
Women's Action Coalition. *WAC STATS: The Facts about Women.*

C. THE FUTURE [3]:

AAHPERD. "Breaking With Tradition—Women and Outdoor Pursuits."
In the Game. Video.
Karnes, Frances and Suzanne Bean. *Girls and Young Women: Leading the Way—20 True Stories about Leadership.*
Knudson, R. *Zanballer.*
Laklan, Carli. *Golden Girls: Time Stories of Olympic Women Stars.*
Morrison, Lillian. "Wait Till Next Year."
Nauen, Elinor, Ed. *Diamonds Are a Girl's Best Friend.*
Navratilova, Martina with George Vecsey. *Martina.*
Rettberg, Georgeann Eskrevich. "Women in the Pits."
Sherr, Lynn and Jurate Kazickas. *Susan B. Anthony Slept Here.*

*Numbers refer to the three-step change process of the working model.

Smith, Barbara. "In Balance."
Tave, Isabelle. *Not Bad for a Girl.*
Valens, E. G. *The Other Side of the Mountain—The Inspiring Story of the Skiing Star, Jill Kinmont.*
Women in Sport. 3-Video set. Program One: Our Social Selves; Program Two: Our Inner Selves; Program Three: Our Physical Selves.

NEWSPAPER AND POPULAR MAGAZINE ARTICLES:

Blais, Madeline. "They Were Commandos: A Season in The Lives of the Amherst Hurricanes."
Gasperini, Kathleen. "Beauty, Sports and Power Feminism."
Hamill, Denis. "Diamonds are a girl's best friend."
Hershenson, Roberta. "In Archers' World, She's the Whizzz Kid."
Lombardi, Kate Stone. "Somewhere Over the Goal Post a Girl's Dream Lies."

Resources for Young College Students

A. THE PAST [1]:

American Association of University Women. *The AAUW Report: How Schools Shortchange Girls.*
Cahn, Susan. *Coming on Strong. Gender and Sexuality in Twentieth-Century Women's Sport.*
Lenskyj, Helen. *Out of Bounds: Women, Sport and Sexuality.*

B. THE PRESENT [2]:

Birell, Susan and Cheryl Cole, eds. *Women, Sport, and Culture.*
Faludi, Susan. *Backlash: The Undeclared War Against American Women.*
The Harvard and Education Letter. "Girls Talk; Boys Talk More."
Krupnick, Catherine. "Women and Men in the Classroom: Inequality and Its Remedies."
Kyvallos, Lucille. "Queens College: Success with No Frills."
NAPEHE. "Girls and Women in Sports and Physical Activity: Psychosocial Perspectives."
Nelson, Barton Mariah. *The Stronger Women Get, The More Men Love Football: Sexism and the American Culture of Sports.*
Personal Best. Video.
Quindlen, Anna. "Foul Play."
Quindlen, Anna. "Offensive Play."
Rubarth, Lisa. "Twenty Years After Title IX: Women in Sports Media."

Sadker, Myra and David Sadker. *Failing at Fairness: How America's Schools Cheat Girls.*

Tobey, Charles. "The Loneliness of the Woman Athlete."

Wolf, Naomi. *Fire with Fire.*

Women's Action Coalition. *WAC STATS: The Facts about Women.*

C. THE FUTURE [3]:

In the Game. Video.

Jewett, Shay. "Free Throws."

Leavy, Jane. *Squeeze Play.*

Morrison, Lillian. "Wait Till Next Year."

Nauen, Elinor, ed. *Diamonds Are a Girl's Best Friend.* (Poems, Essays, Stories).

Weinstein, Sharon. "Jogging At The V.A."

Women of Courage: The Story of the Women Pilots of World War II. Video.

NEWSPAPER ARTICLES:

Couples, Deborah. "She Reigns in a Sport of Kings."

McHugh, Clare. "The Prophet of Power Feminism: Is Naomi Wolf the Gloria Steinem of Her Generation?"

Stains, Laurence. "Martina's Final Volley."

Resources for Parents

A. THE PAST [1]:

AAHPERD. "Women in Sport Leadership: The Legacy and the Challenge."

Lenskyj, Helen. *Out of Bounds: Women, Sport and Sexuality.*

Vertinsky, Patricia A. "Reclaiming Space, Revisioning the Body: The Quest for Gender-Sensitive Physical Education."

B. THE PRESENT [2]:

American Association of University Women. *The AAUW Report: How Schools Shortchange Girls.*

Brown, Lyn Mike, and Carol Gilligan. *Meeting at the Crossroads: Women's Psychology and Girls Development.*

Gilligan, Carol, Annie Rogers, and Deborah Tolman. *Women, Girls and Psychotherapy: Reframing Resistance.*

Hill, Karen. *Women in Sport. Backlash or Megatrend?*

The Joy Luck Club. Video.
Lirgg, Cathy. "Girls and Women, Sport and Self-Confidence."
Mann, Judy. *The Difference: Growing up Female in America.*
Orenstein, Peggy. *Young Women, Self-Esteem, and the Confidence Gap.*
Sadker, Myra and David Sadker. *Failing at Fairness: How America's Schools Cheat Girls.*
Steiner-Adair, Catherine. "When the Body Speaks: Girls, Eating Disorders and Psychotherapy."
Weiss, Maureen, and Susan Glenn. "Psychological Development and Females' Sport Participation: An Interactional Perspective."

C. THE FUTURE [3]:

Debold, Elizabeth. "The Body at Play."
Debold, Elizabeth, Marie Wilson, and Idelisse Malave. *Mother Daughter Revolution: From Betrayal to Power.*
Glickman, Rose. *Daughters of Feminists.*
Miner, M. Jane. "Women in Sport—A Reflection of the Greater Society?"

Resources for Educators: Librarians, Teachers, Teacher Educators and Preservice Education Students

A. THE PAST [1]:

AAHPERD. "Women in Sport Leadership: The Legacy and the Challenge."
AAHPERD. "Dance Dynamics—Gender Issues in Dance Education."
Lenskyj, Helen. *Out of Bounds: Women, Sport and Sexuality.*
Vertinsky, Patricia A. "Reclaiming Space, Revisioning the Body: The Quest for Gender-Sensitive Physical Education."

B. THE PRESENT [2]:

AAHPERD. "Title IX At Twenty—Mature Programs or Still Toddling?"
American Association of University Women. *The AAUW Report: How Schools Shortchange Girls.*
Brown, Jennifer. "Reasons for the Selection or Nonselection of Physical Education Studies by 12 Girls."
Fernandez-Balboa, Juan-Miguel. "Sociocultural Characteristics of the Hidden Curriculum in Physical Education."
Griffin, Pat. "Assessment of Equitable Instructional Practices in the Gym."

The Harvard and Education Letter. "Girls Talk; Boys Talk More."

Hill, Karen. "Women in Sport. Backlash or Megatrend?"

Kyvallos, Lucille. "Queens College: Success with No Frills."

Luke, Moira, and Gary Sinclair. "Gender Differences in Adolescents' Attitudes Toward School Physical Education."

NAPEHE. "Girls and Women in Sports and Physical Activity: Psychosocial Perspectives."

Sadker, Myra, and David Sadker. *Failing at Fairness: How America's Schools Cheat Girls.*

Shortchanging Girls, Shortchanging America. Video.

Tinning, Richard, and Lindsay Fitzclarence. "Postmodern Youth Culture and the Crisis in Australian Secondary School Physical Education."

C. THE FUTURE [3]:

AAHPERD. "Women in Sport Leadership: The Legacy and the Challenge."

Catelli, Linda. "Fair Play: Gender Awareness in Middle School Physical Education."

_____. "Physical Education in the 1980s: A Guide for Developing Children's and Young Adult Collections."

Dewar, Alison. "Would All the Generic Women in Sport Please Stand Up? Challenges Facing Feminist Sport Sociology."

Eckart, Joyce, and Tracy Dyanne. "Gender Socialization in Schools: A Course for Change Agents."

Gilligan, Carol, Anne G. Rogers, and Deborah L. Tolman, eds. *Women, Girls and Psychotherapy: Reframing Resistance.*

Grossman, Herbert, and Suzanne H. Grossman. *Gender Issues in Education.*

Hannigan, Jane Anne, and Hilary Crew. "A Feminist Paradigm for Library and Information Science."

In the Game. Video.

Robinson, Christine. "Working with Adolescent Girls: Strategies to Address Health Status."

Sadker, Myra and David Sadker. *Failing at Fairness: How America's Schools Cheat Girls.*

Vandergrift, Kay E. "A Feminist Research Agenda in Youth Literature."

Williamson, Kay. "Is Your Inequity Showing? Ideas and Strategies for Creating a More Equitable Learning Environment."

Williamson, Kay and Jacqueline Williams. "Promoting Equity Awareness in the Preparation of Physical Education Students."

ORGANIZATIONS AND ASSOCIATIONS:

American Alliance for Health, Physical Education, Recreation and Dance. 1900 Association Drive, Reston, VA 22091.

American Association of University Women. 1111 Sixteenth Street, N.W. Washington, DC 20036.

National Association for Girls and Women in Sport. (NAGWS). 1900 Association Drive, Reston, VA 22091.

Sport Literature Association, San Diego State University, San Diego, CA 92182.

Women's Sports Foundation. Eisenhower Park, East Meadow, NY 11554.

QUESTIONS FOR DISCUSSIONS, READINGS AND ESSAYS

• How is the image of girls and young women in sports been changed by television and film?
• Has the media promoted a damaging stereotyped image of girls who are athletic?
• How has Title IX changed a female's participation in sports and in other physical activities?
• Does competition mean something different to girls than it does to boys? To young women than to young men?
• How does "feminist philosophy" interpret sport literature?
• What does fair play mean to girls—to boys? What should it mean?
• How do young women's and men's philosophy about sport and sporting participation differ?
• How do they differ with regard to fitness activities?
• How are girls and young women portrayed in films that emphasize a "sport" theme?
• How is a sport heroine treated in sport fiction?
• How are a young woman's failure and success treated in sport novels?
• What ideas about girls and young women are being expressed in sport poems, fiction?
• What role does sport play in fiction that focuses on adolescent development?
• To what extent is a film's characterization of a sports-woman true?
• How are girls discriminated against in physical education class?

CHAPTER FOURTEEN

Sex Education in an Age of Sexual Epidemic: Overcoming Discursive Limits

Nancy L. Roth

This is an era of sexual epidemic. It is an historical moment when not only has HIV/AIDS reached pandemic proportions, but sickness and health have come to be the dominant metaphors of the times. Other sexual "viruses" and "cancers" including teenage pregnancy and sexual violence have also come to be called "epidemic" (Singer).

YOUNG ADULTS AND THE SEXUAL EPIDEMIC

Young adults are at great risk in this era of sexual epidemic. More than half of American women and three quarters of American men report having had intercourse by the time of their 18th birthday. Seventy-four percent of women who had intercourse before the age of 14 and 60% of those who had sex before age 15 report having had sex involuntarily (Alan Guttmacher Institute 29).

While teenage contraceptive use at first intercourse has increased dramatically in recent years, teen pregnancy rates are still high. Each year more than one million teenagers become pregnant, most of them unintentionally; approximately 416,000 have abortions (Henshaw and Van Vort), 472,000 give birth (National Center for Health Statistics) and the remainder miscarry. It is estimated that 3 million adolescent men and women get a sexually transmitted disease (STD) each year—and young people account for 25% of all new STD cases annually (Alan Guttmacher Institute 38).

Young adults are particularly vulnerable in the HIV/AIDS epidemic. It is estimated that from 1987 to 1991, one of every four people newly infected with HIV was younger than 22 (Rosenberg et al., 789). By July 1994, 1,768 cases of AIDS among 13–17 year olds had been reported to the Centers for Disease Control and Prevention; 15,204 cases were reported among those aged 20–24. Because of the long period between infection with HIV and diagnosis with AIDS, most 20–24 year olds with AIDS were probably infected while in their teens (CDC).

PREVENTING THE SPREAD OF SEXUAL EPIDEMIC AMONG YOUNG ADULTS

As society struggles to find interventions to stem the spread of sexual epidemic, attention is increasingly focused on young adults. Several sources are available to them to learn about prevention of sexual epidemic. Informal sources such as parents, churches, peers, the media, and printed materials may help some to make informed decisions about sexual behavior. However, many argue that formal sources such as classroom education can help to meet some of the education needs that are not met by informal sources (Timmreck, Cole, and Butterworth 24–28). In the United States Surgeon General's (1988) controversial report on HIV/AIDS, he suggested that sex education should begin as early as 3rd grade. Sex education is also offered as a method for preventing teen pregnancy, sexual violence, and the spread of other STDs.

Formal sex education has the potential to enhance knowledge and such skills as communication and decision making that are essential for adolescents who confront sexual situations (Strouse and Fabes). Research shows correlations between classroom education about contraception and birth rates in several segments of the population (Kirby 421–424), and that education about variant lifestyles is associated with increased acceptance of single parent families and homosexuality (Timmreck, Cole, and Butterworth). While formal sex education in the classroom has been linked by some researchers with efforts to stem the sexual epidemic, increasing rates of sexually transmitted diseases including HIV as well as continued high pregnancy and violence rates among the targeted population suggest that current educational techniques should be reviewed.

SIECUS performs some of this review function. Their *Guidelines for Comprehensive Sexuality Education: Kindergarten Through 12th Grade* suggests a series of 36 topics at age-appropriate levels that might comprise a comprehensive sexuality education program. Unfortunately, by focusing on topics, rather than the discourses used in explaining the material, the SIECUS guidelines might lead one to choose a text that covers the appropriate topics in a manner that is less effective.

In this chapter, I suggest that the textbooks used in ninth grade health education classes, a primary formal source of sexuality and sex information for adolescent students, may be limited in their effectiveness due to the way they use language. I argue that in discussing sexuality, they construct three primary discourses: 1) "body mechanics"—the physiology of sexual behavior and human reproduction, 2) "dread diseases"—the biology and transmission of sexually transmitted diseases, and 3) "don't get carried away"—admonitions concerning how to date without getting pregnant or sick. If formal sex education is limited to these circumscribed discourses, it precludes the possibility of engaging students in meaningful discussion of their everyday experience in ways that will help them to make informed choices about their own behaviors. I offer recommendations of alternative ways to address adolescent sexuality issues in formal classroom settings that allow a wider range of discourses to emerge.

TOPICS AND DISCOURSES OF SEX EDUCATION TEXTBOOKS

Texts Reviewed

To identify the discourses used in sex education textbooks, I reviewed 15 ninth grade health education textbooks adopted for use in the state of Texas for the years 1956 to 1993. During each of the adoption periods (1956–1966, 1966–1973, 1973–1980, 1980–1986 and 1987–1993), Texas selected three to five health education textbooks among which schools in the state could select for classroom use. I randomly selected three books from each time period; they are listed in the references for this chapter. I chose to use texts adopted in the state of Texas because such texts are often used widely throughout the United States. Texas' narrow selection and large population provide it with a great deal of power to influence the type of books that are offered on the market elsewhere.

Range and Depth of Topics Addressed

The range of topics and the depth to which they are covered have increased dramatically in the last 40 years. I determined this by first searching the tables of contents and indexes to identify sections where sex-related topics are addressed. Three major topic areas were identified: sex and human reproduction, sexually transmitted diseases, and dating. Using the standardized measure "column inch" to correct for variations in text format, I then measured the amount of space the text devoted to each primary topic. Table 1 displays the average column inches for each topic and the subtopics addressed during each of the textbook adoption periods.

As the table indicates, the range of subtopics found in each content area increases markedly between the first and third adoption periods, and remains fairly constant between the third and fifth periods. In addition, the amount of space devoted to each of the content areas increases markedly between the first and third adoption periods, decreases somewhat in the fourth period and increases again in the fifth time period. The general trend was toward devoting more space to more sex-related topics over time.

Increases in the breadth and depth of topics covered is evident in treatment of all three of the content areas: sex and human reproduction, sexually transmitted diseases, and dating. For example, a 1955 text, adopted for use in Texas from 1956–1966, devotes a total of 10.5 column inches to the first two topics and does not address the third. It discusses gonorrhea in a

Table 1. Topics Addressed and Space Allocated to Sex-Related Topics in 9th Grade Health Texts Adopted for Use in Texas 1956–Present

Adoption Period → Content Area ↓	1956–1966 Column Inches	1956–1966 Subtopics	1966–1973 Column Inches	1966–1973 Subtopics	1973–1980 Column Inches	1973–1980 Subtopics	1980–1986 Column Inches	1980–1986 Subtopics	1987–1993 Column Inches	1987–1993 Subtopics
Sexually Transmitted Diseases	5.5	Gonorrhea (eye infection) Neurosyphilis	15.13	Gonorrhea Syphilis STDs in general	20.17	Syphilis Gonorrhea STDs in general	16.75	Syphilis Gonorrhea STDs in general Herpes Prevention Vaginitis	37	Syphilis Gonorrhea Herpes Chlamydia Vaginitis Chancroid Vaginal Warts AIDS NGU
Sex and Human Reproduction	4.3	Reproductive Hormones	3.88	Reproductive Hormones Reproductive System	8	Male/ Female Development Beginning of Life	13	Reproductive Hormones Menstruation Male/ Female Development Beginning of Life	37.7	Male/ Female Development Disorders Fertilization
Dating	1.16	Adolescent Pastimes	15.38	Maturity Adjusting to Opposite sex Control of impulses	40.34	Developing Understanding of Sexuality Family Plan Violence and Pornography Homosex. Dating/Petting Premarit. sex Nocturnal Emissions	17.6	Dating Responsibility for Sexual Behavior Family Planning Masturbation Homosex. Violence Child Abuse	19.5	Dating Attraction Teen Pregnancy Abortion Homosexuality
Total Column Inches	10.96		34.39		68.51		47.65		94.2	

section devoted to eye disease because babies born to infected mothers may develop eye infections. Syphilis is addressed as a neurodisorder because in the late stages, it can lead to insanity. Discussion of the reproductive system is limited to glands that secrete male and female hormones.

Discussion of dating and relationships appears to have peaked in texts written in the late 1960's and early 1970's and adopted for use from 1973–1980. Topics expand to encompass not only dating, going steady and control of impulses but also homosexuality, premarital sex, nocturnal emissions, violence and pornography. Texts devote an average of more than 40 column inches to dating and relationships in addition to the more than 28 column inches devoted to other sex-related topics during this period.

Texts published in 1987 and adopted for use through 1993 greatly expand the range of sexually transmitted diseases discussed from only gonorrhea and syphilis to include chlamydia, AIDS, vaginitis, chancroid, venereal warts and other STDs. However, sexual abstinence is the only preventive measure mentioned. In addition to describing the form and function of the reproductive organs, reproductive disorders are discussed at length. Discussion of dating and relationships is enlarged to include mention of contraception and in one case abortion, though details about available contraception options are not provided. In contrast with the 1955 text which allocated only 10.5 column inches to all sex-related topics, the most recent books present an average of 95 column inches of sex-related information.

This analysis shows an expansion in the range of topics covered and the amount of space devoted to them over time. However, it gives little indication of the manner in which these topics are addressed. Insight into how key topics are addressed is provided by a discourse analysis.

Discourses

While the range and depth of topics covered increased dramatically over time, the discourses used to construct sexuality did not change significantly. Each of the three major topic areas identified in my review of the depth and breadth of text content is characterized by its own discourse. Discussions of sex and human reproduction are characterized by a discourse of "body mechanics," sexually transmitted diseases by a discourse of "dread diseases" (as well as the "body mechanics" discourse), and dating by a discourse of "don't get carried away." One of the most significant features of the texts is that the discourses used to discuss sex and human reproduction and STDs are so different from those used to address dating—particularly along the dimension of emotional content. Discussions about the former are devoid of emotional content while discussions of the latter are emotionally laden, and they are found in chapters that are removed by hundreds of pages from each other.

Body Mechanics. "Body mechanics" discourse is characterized by descriptions of body structures and functions and the use of scientific terminology. Discussions of sex and human reproduction in the texts studied present two primary types of information. In earlier texts, they are limited to addressing "the hormones of the reproductive organs." A representative example from those texts is found in Otto, Julian, and Tether, 1955:

> Cells in the reproductive organs secrete sex hormones. Cells in the male reproductive organs produce *androgen* (an-droh-jen). Cells in the female reproductive organs secrete *estrogen* (*es*-troh-jen) and *progesterone* (proh-*jes*-ter-own).

> Sex hormones have a powerful influence on the body. They produce the secondary sex characteristics which develop during adolescence. They lie behind the deepening of the boy's voice as his larynx grows, the broadening of his chest, the rapid lengthening of his arms and legs, and the growth of his beard. In the girl, they cause the hips to broaden, the abdomen to become more slender, the breasts to develop, and menstruation to begin. Along with these come important mental and emotional changes.

In later texts, "body mechanics" discourse is used to describe "the male and female reproductive systems" and "the beginning of life" instead of or in addition to discussions of the sex hormones. A typical example of such discussions is found in Getchell, Pipin, and Varnes:

The female reproductive organs are shown in Figure 16–8. The largest sex organ is the uterus (YOO *tur us*), which has the function of protecting and nourishing a developing baby. The uterus is also called the womb. It is a muscular organ located in the pelvis about in the center of the body.

The bottom third of the uterus is called the cervix. Normally the opening to the cervix is smaller than a zero in this book. When a baby is born, the cervix stretches to allow for the size of the baby. The cervix opens into the vagina. The vagina is a hollow tube that connects the uterus to the outside opening of the body. The vagina is also called the birth canal. It serves as a passageway for the baby during childbirth.

In such discussions, neither sexual pleasure nor the emotions associated with sexuality are mentioned. In fact, the diagram that accompanies the above text does not include a depiction of the clitoris, though it does highlight such details as the labia minora and majora, the urethra, and the "tiny" cervix. Discussion of male erection and ejaculation in another text from the same adoption period (Merki and Merki) similarly avoids any mention of pleasure or emotion—the discourse continues to be one of "body mechanics":

The urethra passes through the penis, a tube like organ, which is normally soft and hangs downward from the front of the body at the groin area. The penis is made up of a spongy tissue that, when filled with blood, causes it to become enlarged and erect. When the penis is in its erect state, semen is able to leave the body.

The lower trunk muscles provide the force that ejects the semen from the body. When these muscles contract, they cause an ejaculation (ee-jak-yuh-lay-shun). In the small amount of semen that leaves the body, there are about 300 to 400 million sperm.

"Body mechanics" discourse also characterizes the discussion of "the beginning of life." In the Getchell, Pippin, and Varnes text, it is addressed as follows:

The development of a new individual begins when a sperm and egg cell unite. Even though these tiny cells are much smaller than a period on this page, they contain all the information needed to make a new person.

The joining of an egg and a sperm is called fertilization (*fur til ih ZAY shun*). Fertilization takes place in the mother's Fallopian tubes. Three conditions are necessary for fertilization to occur. First an egg must be present in the Fallopian tube. The egg will be in the Fallopian tube for approximately two days after ovulation. Second, sperm must also be in the Fallopian tube. Sperm swim into the Fallopian tube after they have been deposited in the woman's vagina.

The third event that actually leads to fertilization is the joining of the egg and the sperm. . .

In these examples as well, there is no mention of the pleasure or emotion associated with the bodily functions described. Nor is there any discussion of what might occasion the penis to become erect. Finally, there is no discussion of how the sperm might have come to be deposited in the woman's vagina in the first place.

Dread Diseases. Discussion of sexually transmitted diseases (STDs) is also characterized by the "body mechanics discourse" found in discussions of sex and human reproduction. However, another attribute characterizes the discourse used to discuss such diseases (it is only found in [rare] discussions of sex and human reproduction where unwanted teenage pregnancy is addressed): dread. STDs are represented as dangerous, potent, and having the potential to make people very sick while the "body mechanics" discourse used to discuss sex and human reproduction goes to great lengths to describe the bodily changes that characterize adolescence as normal.

In the earlier texts, discussions of STDs are limited to brief segments grouped together with other diseases. For example, in Otto et al., 1955, gonorrhea is discussed in a section devoted to eye diseases because babies born to infected mothers may develop eye infections. Syphilis is addressed as a neurodisorder because it can lead to insanity in its later stages. In Goldberger and Hallock, diseases are organized by the nature of their causative agents: gonorrhea is discussed under gonococci and syphilis under spirilla.

In later texts, STDs are grouped together as diseases that are associated with close bodily contact, venereal diseases, or STDs.

Regardless of how they are labeled, the discourse used to discuss them includes characteristics of the "body mechanics" discourse with the addition of "dread." The following examples from Gmur et al. exemplify first the use of "body mechanics" discourse in discussion of STDs and then the use of "dread disease" discourse.

> Syphilis is caused by a spirochete, a form of bacteria. The organism is delicate and is easily destroyed by drying or by soap and water. It survives only a short time outside the human body. As a result, the only mode of transmission is by direct, intimate bodily contact with someone who has the disease. This contact usually occurs in sexual intercourse (either heterosexual or homosexual) and rarely through other means such as kissing. The main exception to this mode of transmission is the passing of the disease from the infected mother to her unborn child during pregnancy. There is no evidence of the transmission of the disease through toilet seats, drinking glasses, towels, or other inanimate objects.

> Syphilis and gonorrhea are major health problems. They are among the leading communicable diseases in the United States. They cause a great deal of suffering, both emotional and physical.

"Dread disease" discourse is replete with discussions of suffering, warnings that the diseases can cause permanent damage if left untreated, and that they represent a serious threat to the health of young adults. Combined with "body mechanics" discourse, "dread" highlights the causes and consequences of sexually transmitted diseases without addressing the feelings of young adults who contract them, and without discussing the emotions that accompany the sexual behaviors that might transmit them. Devoid of any emotional content but the preachy dread, these discussions bear little resemblance to the lived experience of young adults.

Don't Get Carried Away. "Don't get carried away" discourse is characterized by recognition that young adults may feel deep emotions when they develop close relationships and admonitions to avoid situations where such emotions might arise. Therefore, readers are urged to conduct social activities in groups rather than pairs, and to avoid "going steady" which might lead to uncontrollable emotions. This discourse is replete with references to young people's emotions that were entirely absent from the discourses of "body mechanics" and "dread diseases." This passage from Diehl, Tsumura, et al. is typical:

Boys and girls share the responsibility for their sexual behavior. If you have a special affection for another person, it is easy to get carried away by your feelings. A physical attraction can be very strong. Think ahead about sensible limits to set in expressing affection. This will help you to stay out of situations that could lead to uncomfortable feelings, unwanted pregnancy, or other serious problems. It is hard to make sound decisions on the spur of the moment. In the end, it is up to you to decide about sexual activity on a date. . .

An excerpt from Getchell et al. addresses the issue of group dating:

Dating often begins as a group activity. Attending sports events, dances, parties, or movies with other individuals of both sexes is a form of group dating. Many young people feel more comfortable in this group type of setting.

Surveys show that most young people prefer to date several different individuals before picking out one special partner. But sooner or later, many young people choose one person for a special relationship and go steady. Going steady means that each person will date only the other person. Couples can develop a strong friendship and sense of loyalty to each other. However, steady relationships may develop problems.

This quote from Haag addresses the issue of "going steady":

There are decisions that need to be faced by the young man and woman who go steady. When their relationship becomes strong, there may come a time when they may feel that they need other ways to express their affections besides kissing, a hug, or an embrace. Each time the young man and woman are together, it may become more and more difficult to exercise self-control. Heavy petting may occur with physical contacts producing sexual stimulations and desires. When these desires are not fulfilled, strong frustrations result. The young couple becomes irritable and upset with each other. The young man and woman realize

that they are building up relations that will end in sexual intercourse or that their affection for each other must be expressed in
ways that do not lead to heavy petting.

 If premarital sexual relations occur between the young man and
woman, it may damage their relationship. Pregnancy can also
result. A marriage may be forced upon a young man or woman
for which neither of them is ready.

Interestingly, such admonitions are often followed with discussions of courtship, engagement and marriage as they are in
the above text. How readers are to negotiate the move from
group activities to courtship is not spelled out. Neither is there
much guidance offered concerning how to deal with strong
emotions when they do arise.

DISCOURSE CRITIQUE

If formal sex education is limited to the circumscribed discourses described above, it may not contribute greatly to stemming the sexual epidemic. It would seem that some primary
goals of such formal education is to raise issues that are difficult
to talk about in other settings in a way that allows students to
relate them to their own lives and to make informed decisions
about their behavior. The discourses described above, however,
are not likely to help educators reach such goals.

Body Mechanics

The "body mechanics" discourse is replete with tedious descriptions of body parts, their locations and functions. This "thigh
bone connected to the knee bone" type of presentation is an
invitation to students to memorize which gland secretes which
hormone without thinking about how such secretions might
influence their emotions and behaviors. Another key feature of
this discourse is its use of technical terminology. The texts often
offer little more than pronunciation guides to long medical
terms along with their definitions. This dispassionate "the act of
placing the penis in the vagina is called intercourse or coitus"
representation of sexual activity may be so distant from young

adults' experience that they fail to recognize the relationship between their lived experience and what they are reading in the text.

Both the location/function discussion of body parts and the technical jargon can serve a distancing function. They allow both students and teachers to read and discuss the texts without experiencing any discomfort—the discomfort that might arise with recognition of experience. They remove everything from the text that might be considered to be "sexy," and in so doing, make discussions that might otherwise hold great student inter-est—boring.

Of course, it is highly likely that the texts were carefully crafted to avoid being "sexy." If they were to describe what hap-pened to people's bodies when they become aroused and the accompanying feelings, the authors might be accused of produc-ing pornography. It is surely difficult to balance the need to address students' everyday experience with the need to remain inoffensive.

Dread Disease

"Dread Disease" discourse warns of the horrible scourges that will be visited upon young adults who participate in the placing of penises in vaginas. Such discourses may have little influence on young adults, as some research suggests that the egocentrism of youth may lead them to be overly optimistic—while sexual behavior may lead to disease in some people, I will not be so affected (Elkind; Enright and Lapsley). Other research suggests that people, regardless of age, see themselves as less likely to develop disorders than others, even if they engage in behaviors associated with such disorders more frequently than others. For example, people who do not floss their teeth regularly perceive themselves as less likely than the average person to develop gum disease, and those who do not wear seat belts see them-selves as less likely than the average person to die in an auto accident (Weinstein 498).

As a result, young adults may perceive the texts as being "preachy" because they predict dire consequences from which students perceive themselves as being more or less invulnerable.

Such perceptions may, like the use of tedious description and technical jargon, serve to create distance. While such distancing may reduce discomfort with difficult topics, it may also impede young people from using information to make informed decisions.

Don't Get Carried Away

"Don't get carried away" discourse constructs emotions as things that cannot be controlled but rather must be avoided to avoid the consequences of intimate caresses that can stimulate sexual appetite and lead to sexual intercourse which can lead to unwanted pregnancy. Such discourse suggests that rather than learning healthy ways to address emotions that arise, young adults should try to avoid situations in which such emotions might occur. It further implies that once young people encounter such feelings, they are overwhelmed and unable to stop themselves.

Such implications are quite dangerous because they send a message that may be counter to the one intended. They suggest an all or nothing view of sexuality. Sexual feelings are to be avoided at all costs and if they are not avoided, all is lost. Young people have no responsibility for sexual behavior once feelings are encountered because the feelings are so strong, they are helpless to stop.

The limited discourses of formal sex education found in 9th grade texts may preclude the possibility of engaging students in meaningful discussion of their everyday experience in ways that will help them to make informed choices about their own behaviors. They distance students from their experience and provide them with an excuse for engaging in the behaviors such education is designed to discourage. Alternative ways of delivering sex education that use an expanded repertoire of discourses are outlined in the following section.

EXPANDING THE RANGE OF
FORMAL SEX EDUCATION DISCOURSES

My review of sex education texts suggests that while the range and depth of topics covered has expanded over the years, the range of discourses used to convey the material has remained limited. It is possible that expanding the array of discourses used might serve to make small changes in the norms surrounding how sex-related topics can be addressed in text books. For example, a study of safer sex brochures suggests that by using other discourses that were available within the constraints of acceptability, safer sex educators were able to change some of the norms about how sexuality could be addressed in such pamphlets (Roth and Goyo-Shields).

Employ Different Texts

The most apparent way to expand the range of discourses would be to employ text books that use more or different discourses. Educators, parents, and others concerned about how formal sex education is provided to young adults should employ similar critical skills to those used in this chapter to analyze not only the topics covered but also the discourses used to address them. Texts that emphasize such skills as:

- dealing with emotions
- making informed decisions
- balancing pleasure and consequences
- taking the position of a person who is at risk

provide a range of discourses not available in those analyzed.

SIECUS provides a *Resource Guide of Recommended Curricula and Textbooks* that indicates the extent to which the texts meet the SIECUS guidelines. The guidelines include "personal skills" such as decision-making. To obtain a copy of the Resource Guide or Guidelines contact SIECUS at: 130 West 42nd Street, Suite 2500, New York, NY 10036, 212/819-9770.

Replace or Complement Texts with Trade Books

In recent years, a number of trade books have been published that present material about sexuality using discourses not seen in the textbooks reviewed. Many of these books would make excellent complements to existing texts—or could be used to replace texts in school districts where that is possible. Parents or counselors might wish to employ these books when discussing sexuality issues with young adults. I would highly recommend three such books that cover a wide range of sexuality issues.

Organized around questions that sound like the ones real young adults might ask, Jean and Hal Fielder's *Be Smart About Sex: Facts for Young People* provides responses that are a wonderful mix of emotions and mechanics. The text meanders a bit—as real conversations about sex tend to do. It is very readable; the language is accessible and the presentation makes sex sound interesting.

How Sex Works, by Richard Fenwick and Richard Walker, makes the link between mechanics and emotions in sections that discuss body sensuality, sexual enjoyment, and relationships and emotions—all topics that were neglected in the texts reviewed above. A lovely layout and color pictures add to the text's attractiveness. However, the book has been criticized for not having greater multicultural representation in graphics. Librarians report that they cannot keep it on the shelves—a good indicator that young adults find it to be informative.

Dr. Ruth Westheimer interweaves basic information with personal stories and black and white illustrations in her book, *Dr. Ruth Talks to Kids: Where You Come From, How Your Body Changes, and What Sex Is All About*. The personal stories make the text interesting and readable. I particularly liked her anecdote about dealing with having been a large breasted, but tiny adolescent.

In addition to the books that cover a wide range of sexuality issues, some recent books cover specific topics. I recommend the following three which address HIV/AIDS.

Earvin (Magic) Johnson's *What You Can Do to Avoid AIDS* is HIV specific, but covers more general sexuality topics too. It is nicely designed—uses a variety of type styles, boxes, drawings to set off text. The language is very accessible and includes some stories and personal references.

In *Risky Times: How to Be AIDS-Smart and Stay Healthy, a Guide for Teenagers* Jeanne Blake presents HIV/AIDS information in a painless style that makes the book read like a documentary. It begins with a "girl next door has AIDS" story. Several pictures of real people who are affected and infected, personal stories, and questions and answers round out the book.

An excellent edited compilation of essays about AIDS-related issues from a variety of perspectives is Lynn Hall and Thomas Modl's *Opposing Viewpoints: AIDS*. Librarians report that young adults love this series—it provides material that allow them to form their own opinions about current issues. The reading level may be challenging for some ninth graders.

Finally, I would recommend one book that addresses the issue of date rape. Francis Shuler-Haine's *Everything You Need to Know About Date Rape* presents the story of a date rape situation, then provides analysis from both participants' perspectives. This book is provocative reading.

Use Texts Differently

Some people concerned with sex education of young adults may have limited choices as to texts used. Limits may be imposed by text selection as is the case in Texas, by text availability as is the case in much of the US due to the influence of Texas selections on the range of texts available, or by personal desire to avoid texts that present material in ways that the person making the selection finds objectionable. Educators and others in this position may find it possible to expand the available discourses by using limited texts creatively.

Some theories suggest that people reading the same texts will develop different interpretations (Fish, 1980; Iser, 1979; Rosenblatt, 1978). If this is the case, it is possible that students will interpret the text differently than the teacher, or than I did in this chapter. Therefore useful class exercises might include:

- asking students what they believe to be the underlying message in each chapter
- asking students how such messages relate to their experience or understanding of the topic
- asking students to identify the discourses used to convey the material in each chapter
- asking students to develop their own discourses for conveying the information to peers, parents, and partners

Such exercises might encourage students to think critically about what they are reading as well as provide the opportunity for a wider range of discourses to be used in discussing sex-related topics.

Use Other Media

A wide range of media are available to parents, teachers and others who wish to discuss sex-related topics with young adults. Sex-related issues are addressed in young adult novels, television shows, movies, and popular songs. Teachers might wish to use such popularly available media as the basis of their discussions. One way to do this would be to ask all of the students to read, view, or listen to the selected text and ask them to write their impressions of it. They might be asked to consider several issues found in Vandergrift (1990):

- Content: What are these texts about? What key words or phrases describe them?
- Feelings: What kinds of feelings did the text evoke? Why?
- Beliefs: What beliefs surfaced when viewing the text? What made them surface?
- Memories: Were you aware of connections between the text and memories? What were the similarities and differences between what was in the text and your memories?
- Sharing: Would you like to share something about your text with others? What?

Such exercises might encourage critical thinking about popular texts and provide a wider range of discourses for discussion of sex-related issues.

CONCLUSIONS

In this era of sexual epidemic among young adults in the United States what and how we teach young people about sex-related topics becomes an increasingly important issue. The texts available for conducting formal sex education employ a limited range of discourses, and may in some cases contribute to, rather than ameliorate the problem. I have outlined some of the texts' limitations and have provided recommendations for overcoming them.

Brandt (1987) admonishes those concerned about sexual epidemic not to depend upon medical science to develop a "magic bullet" to eradicate sexually transmitted diseases. Even the discovery of penicillin has not kept people from dying of the effects of syphilis. The effort to stem the spread of STDs, teen pregnancy, sexual violence, HIV, and other "viruses" that characterize the sexual epidemic will require a wider range of available discourses as well as medical miracles. Efforts to expand the discourses available in formal sex education may indeed be a more powerful tool in stemming sexual epidemic than any medical magic bullet.

An earlier version of this essay was prepared while the author was a visiting Research Fellow at the University of New South Wales, National Centre in HIV Social Research, Sydney, Australia. Many thanks to Beth M. Wescott and Veronica Thomas of the CDC National AIDS Clearinghouse, Bonnie Kunzel of the New Brunswick Public Library, and Dena Leiter who assisted in conducting background research for this project. I also wish to acknowledge Rod Hart who inspired the original version and Karen Foss, Michael Ross, and Kay Vandergrift who read and commented upon earlier drafts of this manuscript.

WORKS CITED

The Alan Guttmacher Institute. *Sex and America's Teenagers.* New York: The Alan Guttmacher Institute, 1994.

Althaus, Ruth A., Merita Thompson, Nora Walker, and William B. Zuti. *Health.* Glenview: Scott, 1987.

Blake, Jeanne. *Risky Times: How to Be AIDS-Smart and Stay Healthy, a Guide for Teenagers.* New York: Workman, 1990.

Brandt, Allan M. *No Magic Bullet: A Social History of Venereal Disease in the United States Since 1880.* New York: Oxford UP, 1987.

Centers for Disease Control. *HIV/AIDS Surveillance Report* 6(1), Mid-year Edition, 1994.

Diehl, Harold S., and Anita D. Laton. *Health and Safety for You.* New York: McGraw, 1954.

Diehl, Harold S., Anita D. Laton, and Franklin C. Vaughn. *Health and Safety for You.* New York: McGraw, 1964.

Diehl, Harold S., Ted K. Tsumura, Lorraine J. Henke, and Thomas W. Bonekemper. *Health and Safety for You, Fifth Edition.* New York: McGraw, 1980.

Elkind, David. "Egocentrism in Adolescence." *Child Development* 38 (1967): 1025–1034.

Enright, Robert D., Daniel K. Lapsley, and Diane G. Shukla. "Adolescent Egocentrism in Early and Late Adolescence." *Adolescence* 14 (1987): 687–695.

Fenwick, Richard, and Richard Walker. *How Sex Works*. London: Dorling Kindersley, 1994.

Fielder, Jean, and Hal Fielder. *Be Smart About Sex: Facts for Young People*. Hillside: Enslow, 1990.

Fish, Stanley. *Is There a Text in This Class? The Authority of Interpretive Communities*. Cambridge: Harvard UP, 1980.

Getchell, Bud, Rusty Pippin, and Jill Varnes. *Health*. Boston: Houghton, 1987.

Gmur, Ben C., John T. Fodor, L. H. Glass, and Joseph J. Langan. *Making Health Decisions*. Englewood Cliffs: Prentice, 1970.

Goldberger, I. H., and Grace T. Hallock. *Understanding Health*. Boston: Ginn, 1955.

Haag, Jessie H. *Health Education for Young Adults*. Austin: Steck-Vaughn, 1965.

Hall, Lynn, and Thomas Modl (Eds.). *Opposing Viewpoints: AIDS*. San Diego: Greenhaven, 1988.

Henshaw, Stanley K., and Jennifer Van Vort. "Patterns and Trends in Teenage Abortion and Pregnancy." *Teenage Pregnancy in the United States: The Scope of the Problem and States' Responses*. New York: The Alan Guttmacher Institute, 1989.

Iser, Wolfgang. *The Act of Reading: The Theory of Aesthetic Response*. Baltimore: Johns Hopkins UP, 1979.

Johnson, Earvin (Magic). *What You Can Do to Avoid AIDS*. New York: Times Books/Random, 1992.

Jones, Evelyn G., Betty L. Wright, and Reuben D. Behlmer. *Living in Safety and Health*. Philadelphia: Lippincott, 1966.

Kirby, Douglas. "Sexuality Education: A More Realistic View of Its Effects." *Journal of School Health* 55(10) (1985): 421–424.

Lawrence, Thomas G., Jessie W. Clemensen, and R. Will Burnett. *Your Health and Safety*. New York: Harcourt, 1963.

McClendon, Edwin J., Wanda H. Jubb, Robert G. Norred, and Geraldine Moore. *Healthful Living for Today and Tomorrow*. River Forest: Laidlaw Brothers, 1978.

Merki, Mary B., and Don Merki. *Health: A Guide to Wellness*. Mission Hills: Glencoe, 1987.

National Center for Health Statistics. "Advance Report of Final Natality Statistics." *Monthly Vital Statistics Report* 37(3) (1986): Supplement, 1988.

Otto, James H., Cloyd J. Julian, and J. Edward Tether. *Modern Health.* New York: Holt, 1955.
_____. *Modern Health.* New York: Holt, 1963.
_____. *Modern Health.* New York: Holt, 1971.
Otto, James H., Cloyd J. Julian, J. Edward Tether, and Janet Z. Nassif. *Modern Health.* New York: Holt, 1980.
Rosenberg, Philip S., Robert J. Biggar, and James J. Goedert. "Declining Age at HIV Infection in the United States." *New England Journal of Medicine* 330(11): (1994). 789–90.
Rosenblatt, Louise M. *The Reader, the Text, the Poem: The Transactional Theory of the Literary Work.* Carbondale: Southern Illinois UP, 1978.
Roth, Nancy L., and Raul Goyo-Shields. "Gender, Sexuality, and Sexual Behavior in an Age of Sexual Epidemic." Ed. Lou Diamant and Rick D. McAnulty. *The Psychology of Sexual Orientation, Behavior, and Identity: A Handbook.* Westport: Greenwood (in press).
Shuler-Haines, Francis. *Everything You Need to Know About Date Rape.* New York: Rosen, 1990.
Singer, Linda. *Erotic Welfare.* Ed. Judith Butler and Maureen MacGrogan. New York: Routledge, 1993.
Strouse, Jeremiah, and Richard A. Fabes. "Formal Versus Informal Sources of Sex Education: Competing Forces in the Sexual Socialization of Adolescents." *Adolescence* 78 (1985): 251–263.
Timmreck, Thomas C., Galen E. Cole, Gordon James, and Diane D. Butterworth. "The Health Education and Health Promotion Movement: A Theoretical Jungle." *Health Education* Oct.–Nov. 1987: 24–28.
Vandergrift, Kay E. "The Child's Meaning-Making in Response to a Literary Text." *English Quarterly* 22(3/4) (1990): 125–140.
Vaughn, Franklin C. *Health and Safety for You.* St. Louis: McGraw, 1969.
Weinstein, Neil D. "Unrealistic Optimism About Susceptibility to Health Problems: Conclusions from a Community-Wide Sample." *Journal of Behavioral Medicine* 10(5) (1987): 481–500.
Westheimer, Ruth. *Dr. Ruth Talks to Kids: Where You Come From, How Your Body Changes, and What Sex Is All About.* New York: Macmillan, 1993.

CHAPTER FIFTEEN

To Boldly Go . . .
Science Fiction
(A Personal Odyssey)

Bonnie Kunzel

Fans of the genre know that reading science fiction can be a rich and rewarding experience, intellectually stimulating and challenging at the same time. Since the science fiction world is in a constant state of flux, each new invention, discovery, or technique in the real world leads to ever greater flights of fancy in the realm of the imagination. Young people with the desire to stretch the boundaries of their everyday existence gravitate towards science fiction works as naturally as rockets go up and meteorites fall down. It is vital that we as adults encourage such explorations, for their inquisitive minds can only be strengthened with each new venture into the unknown.

Unfortunately, the reverse is what teens usually experience. Instead of being encouraged and guided in their exploration of the science fiction universe, they are left to find their own way. Adult readers, who are frequently not familiar with the genre, do not understand or appreciate the rewards gained by those who are willing to suspend their disbelief and boldly go wherever the authors lead them. They do not realize how much teen fans can benefit from the challenge each new work presents, especially when different ways of knowing both themselves and their universe are the result of such a satisfying reading experience.

Science fiction fans come in all ages, sizes, and sexes. This genre is particularly rewarding for the teen reader, however, because of the nature of adolescence. At a time when teenagers are questioning who they are, what life is all about, what their place in it is, and what the future will be like, they are presented with a body of work that assures them of a future completely different from present experience. Even if they encounter familiar problems, situations, and concerns, such as coming of age, belonging, fitting in, being accepted, or feeling different, finding someone who really understands them, etc., the "trappings" will be different, as far-flung and fanciful as the minds of the author and receptive reader can make them. On the other hand, they may encounter the strange, the weird, the truly bizarre, and, being teens, will love every minute of it. In this instance, science fiction allows the reader to "know" vicariously what could not be "known" in real-life, thereby expanding horizons and providing ultimately another way of "knowing."

Orson Scott Card has an explanation for why teen readers are drawn to science fiction. In fact, in his book *How to Write Science Fiction and Fantasy,* he has put into words exactly how I felt when I began reading such works and was drawn to the strangeness, to the surprise elements, and to how different these stories and novels were from anything else I had ever read. "Speculative fiction [his term for science fiction]) by definition is geared toward an audience that wants strangeness, an audience that wants to spend time in worlds that absolutely are *not* like the observable world around them" (20). So teen readers, according to Card, come to science fiction for its strangeness and its sense of surprise and wonder.

SCIENCE FICTION SETTINGS

In contemporary fiction, the world is already there for the reader. In science fiction, it must be built, following believable scientific principles. The author must provide extensive details of the setting and background, in addition to character development. Because of this attention to the setting, the place can become an integral part of the story, almost another player so to speak. Certainly, with so much effort being devoted to world building, it is understandable why so many authors revisit their worlds time and again.

Pern

Years ago Anne McCaffrey created Pern, a planet with a popu-
lace that lives at a low level of technology and that is devastated
periodically by the fall of "thread" from the sky. This "thread" is
a truly inventive creation, an omnivorous organism that burns
its way through anything organic, destroying all living things in
its path. The feudal society of the planet could not have survived if it weren't for its dragonriders, individuals who have
bonded with fire-breathing dragons and are carried by them
into battle to destroy the "thread" before it reaches the ground.
McCaffrey has visited Pern a number of times in novels written
specifically for adults: *Dragonflight, Dragonquest, The White
Dragon, Moreta, Dragonlady of Pern, Dragonsdawn, Renegades of
Pern, All the Weyrs of Pern, The Chronicles of Pern: First Fall*, and
The Dolphins of Pern. She has also written a trilogy set on Pern
for younger readers: *Dragonsong, Dragonsinger*, and *Dragondrums*.

Darkover

Another planet with a highly-structured medieval society is
Marion Zimmer Bradley's Darkover. When Terrans first land on
the planet, they discover a primitive civilization that, nevertheless, has an extremely sophisticated form of science, one that is
based on mind control, telepathy, and telekinesis. After the Terrans build a spaceport, the authorities on Darkover do everything they can to see that the influence of Earth stops at its
boundaries. Political intrigue, the clash of disparate cultures,
and sophisticated hardware confronted with sword and sorcery
abound in novels that are noted for their edge-of-the-seat suspense. In addition to Darkover anthologies written by her loyal
followers, such as *Towers of Darkover* and *Sword and Sorceress I*
through *XI*, this prolific author has written a number of well-
crafted novels set on this strange dark planet. A representative
sampling of my favorites include: *The Bloody Sun, Star of Danger,
The Forbidden Tower, The Shattered Chain, The Heritage of Hastur,
Thendara House, Hawkmistress!, Two to Conquer, The Heirs of Hammerfell, City of Sorcery*, and *Darkover Landfall*.

Barrayar

Space opera makes an amazing and well-deserved comeback in Lois McMaster Bujold's novels involving the planet Barrayar, in particular the adventures of one individual from that planet, Miles Vorkosigan. The son of the planet's Prime Minister and a Betan warrior/scientist, Miles is damaged in utero by a poison gas attack directed at his father and pregnant mother. As a result, the dwarf-sized Miles is born with brittle bones but an extremely high I.Q. His determination to make it on his own merit in the militaristic society of Barrayar leads to a series of unbelievable adventures that are full of non-stop action and tongue-in-cheek humor. The first book about Miles, *The Warrior's Apprentice*, appeared in 1986, followed in rapid succession by *The Vor Game*, *Brothers in Arms*, *Borders of Infinity*, *Shards of Honor*, *Barrayar*, and her first hardcover science fiction novel, *Mirror Dance*.

The Galactic Empire

The universe of Isaac Asimov's Foundation novels has become a science fiction classic, introducing Hari Seldon and his concept of future history. Hari Seldon is a genius whose new theory of prediction, called psychohistory, winds up threatening the emperor and changing the course of the Galactic Empire. The novels in this popular series include: *Foundation*, *Foundation and Empire*, *Second Foundation*, *Foundation's Edge*, *Foundation and Earth*, and *Prelude to Foundation*.

Starbridge

A. C. Crispin created Starbridge Academy as a vehicle for bringing about cooperation among sentient beings. Starbridge is a dream come true, an educational institution for the young of *all* sentient species. Its goal is to promote greater understanding through increased knowledge of one another, starting with the very young. The ultimate result to be achieved in this way, if successful, is peaceful coexistence. She began this series in 1989 with *Starbridge*, followed by novels written with other authors, including *Shadow World* with Jannean Elliott, *Serpent's Gift* with Deborah A. Marshall, and *Silent Songs* with Kathleen O'Malley.

Dune

Frank Herbert's monumental *Dune* introduced a desert world where the sands gave birth not only to monstrous worms but also to a new religion that took the galaxy by storm. Young Paul Atreides was fighting for his life when he led a successful revolt against representatives of an interstellar empire. In the process, he discovered how to use the "spice" peculiar to the planet, which had far-reaching consequences not only for Paul, but also for the people who came to regard him as their messiah. Enormously popular, this first in the series led to the following sequels: *Dune Messiah, Children of Dune, God Emperor of Dune, Heretics of Dune,* and *Chapterhouse: Dune.*

Merchanter

C. J. Cherryh's Merchanter universe depicts influential families in control of fleets of spaceships. These families battle with one another, with independent ship owners, with pirates, and sometimes even with the law-enforcement representatives of the fleet, all in the name of profit. Her Chanur series is perhaps the best-known of these novels, which features the members of the cat-like Hani race as the protagonists: *The Pride of Chanur, Chanur's Venture, The Kif Strike Back, Chanur's Homecoming,* and *Chanur's Legacy.* Another example is her *Faded Sun Trilogy: Kesrith, Shon'jir,* and *Kutath.* In these, as well as novels such as *Downbelow Station,* she details the intricacies of alien/human interaction. Her speciality, as *The Cuckoo's Egg* reveals, is the human who must learn to be an alien and carve out a special niche in order to survive. Thorn is offered no special treatment or consideration, and under the most adverse circumstances imaginable, strives to be accepted through his own efforts.

Real-world fiction has a comfortable, knowable setting. Science fiction, on the other hand, as the preceding examples have shown, takes place in a world that is originally "unknowable." That world becomes knowable, however, to those readers willing to make the effort and face the challenge of the unknown. For, as Card reminds us, not only must every science fiction story challenge the reader's experience and learning, it also has to create a strange world and introduce the reader to it" (23). Reading science fiction, then, is an activity that should be encouraged because teens willing to become immersed in this new way of knowing will be richly rewarded for their investment of time and energy. Furthermore, those lucky enough to connect up with the "right" books (for them) will be exposed to some of the most intellectually-stimulating and unique fiction being written today.

PERSONAL ODYSSEY

I have been reading science fiction since I first encountered the genre in grade school, and I'll never forget the impact that first novel had on me. Several years ago I was appointed to the American Library Association's Science Fiction Genre Committee, and I re-read that first science fiction novel while considering books to suggest to today's young adult readers. After all these years I was delighted to discover that *Star Beast*, one of the juveniles by Robert Heinlein that had just been reissued, was a novel that I could still recommend to today's teen readers. (The members of the 1992 Science Fiction Committee felt the same way, and Heinlein's *Star Beast* is one of the twenty titles that we selected for that year's list.)

The "sense of wonder" that characterizes science fiction struck me in this novel with the metamorphosis of the beast, a young teen's amiable pet, into an alien from outer space, a stowaway who was taken to Earth by mistake. When his formidable parents arrived in a spaceship with demands for his return, just in time to save him from being destroyed by the authorities, I was on the edge of my seat. I remember the "WOW" effect that I felt when I got to the end of the story. I wanted *more* books just like that one, and I set out to find them.

I'm still finding them today, an absolute wealth of them. Browsing the science fiction section of a bookstore reveals a wide variety of paperbacks with bright, attractive covers, promising flights of fancy that are infinitely appealing to fans.

According to the 14th edition of Bowker's *The Reader's Advisor*, science fiction is one of the most popular literary genres, so it is understandable that bookstores will have so many titles to choose from, attractively displayed. What I find fascinating is that so many of the authors and titles on display are ones that I grew up with, popular years ago and still popular with teen readers today. Brief introductions to some of my favorites follow.

Robert A. Heinlein

As a teen myself, I devoured all of Heinlein's "juveniles," so-called because they had young protagonists, not because they were specifically written for a teen audience. I struggled for the preservation of the Earth with *Starship Troopers*, fought my way up from slavery to a position of power and influence with *Citizen of the Galaxy*, was kidnapped by aliens in *Have Spacesuit, Will Travel*, and travelled instantaneously to other worlds in *Tunnel in the Sky*, to name just a few of this prolific author's output. Even younger teens can enjoy these and his other juveniles. Then science fiction and Heinlein grew up in the sixties, with the appearance of *Stranger in a Strange Land*. Suitable for older teens and adults, this is a book that deals with adult themes, including sexual situations. Widely read at the time, it became something of a cult classic and continues to be read today.

Arthur C. Clarke

Heinlein was only one of the major science fiction writers who contributed to my early development as an undying fan of the genre. Arthur C. Clarke produced works that were both intellectually stimulating and emotionally involving. In *Childhood's End*, aliens appeared in the skies of Earth and refused to let mankind continue to destroy itself with its implements of war. I still have a vivid image of the last bullfight on the planet—it seems that audiences quickly lost interest when they began actually feeling the pain and terror of the exhausted bull. Clarke's short stories are also remarkable, in particular, "The Sentinel." This story features a strange monolith left behind by other, more powerful, races and cultures, an idea he used again in *2001: A Space Odyssey* and its sequels. And I defy anyone to read "The Star" and remain detached, as its Jesuit narrator, chief astrophysicist on a spaceship, discovers the devastation wrought by the star that shone over Bethlehem. Clarke is still writing science fiction, and his *Rama* novels, *Rendezvous with Rama*, *Rama II* and *Garden of Rama*, have quite a following.

Isaac Asimov

I first met Isaac Asimov through his robot stories. *I, Robot* hooked me from the very beginning, followed by the adventures of Lucky Starr on various planets in the Solar System. *Fantastic Voyage*, in which a submarine and crew is miniaturized and injected into a scientist, gave me a whole new outlook on the internal workings of the human body. He is perhaps best known, however, for his three robotic laws, which explain why it is impossible for a robot to ever deliberately injure a human, and for his *Foundation* series in which Hari Seldon becomes the most dangerous man in the Empire when he begins using his new science of psychohistory to predict the future.

Andre Norton

Andre Norton, the acknowledged Grande Dame of Science Fiction and Fantasy, drew me into her *Witch World* initially, but kept me hooked with her immense variety. One of my personal favorites is *Catseye*, with its telepathic hero and that wonderful human-like cat. Norton creates wonderful animal protagonists who frequently have more appeal than their human counterparts. Telepathic abilities and mind-control techniques are also an important part of her stories. She has created several memorable series, including action-packed adventures involving *Time Traders*, *Space Merchants*, and the denizens of *Witch World*. Recent works by Norton include *Redline the Stars*, a new entry in the *Solar Queen* series, and *Firehand*, a new *Time Traders* novel, both co-authored with P. M. Griffin. In *Brother to Shadows*, which was selected by the New York Public Library for inclusion in its annual publication entitled *Books for the Teen Age*, her characters are once again involved in a search for the mysterious Forerunners and the artifacts they left behind. Communicating telepathically with a lovable, furry, peace-giving little alien, her protagonist becomes enmeshed in a struggle with members of the Thieves Guild. The result is an action-filled page-turner in which the contrast of alien cultures is vividly depicted.

A. E. Van Vogt

A. E. Van Vogt's picture of persecution and the agony of being different is as vivid today as it was when I first read *Slan* years ago. In this novel he relates the struggles of mutants to stay alive in the face of hostility on the part of the "normals" they live among. This is particularly effective for teen readers, who can so easily relate to the aliens among us because that is frequently exactly how they feel. And it is an even more powerful message for those who not only feel different, but also in some way actually look different, due to a physical handicap or because of their ethnic background. I was equally intrigued by his *Weapons Shop* works, a fascinating concept in which people are given the tools to help them stop being victims.

Anne McCaffrey

It was in the pages of *The Hugo Winners, Volumes I and II*, edited by Asimov, that I first made the acquaintance of Anne McCaffrey. The Hugo is the award voted every year by science fiction fans for, among other categories, their favorite novels, novellas, and short stories. Her novella, "Weyr Search," won the Hugo in 1968 and was my introduction to Lessa and the Dragonriders of Pern, detailing the plight Lessa was in when dragonriders "rescued" her and took her back to their lair in time for the hatching of the next Queen dragon. I couldn't wait to continue my acquaintance with McCaffrey's work, and she has yet to let me down. In fact, all these years later, she is still exploring the familiar landscape of Pern and its genetically-engineered dragons that are both fire-breathing and telepathically-gifted. She doesn't limit herself to Pern, however. As is the case with so many prolific authors, she explores other worlds and characters.

Dinosaur Planet depicts human settlers investigating a planet where dinosaurs roam. Mankind meets Hrrubans, cat-like aliens who have a lot in common with humanity, in the novels set on *Doona*. Space pirates bite off more than they can chew when they encounter *Sassinak* and its sequels: *The Death of Sleep* and *Generation Warriors*. But my favorite is *The Ship Who Sang*, introducing a universe in which severely damaged bodies do not keep active brains from contributing to society. Spaceships are driven by "shellpersons," who explore the universe from inside their titanium columns, with the assistance of capable "brawn" partners to do the legwork for them. The result is a fascinating symbiotic relationship which frequently demonstrates the fact that a whole can be greatly enhanced by the fusion of its disparate parts.

After a hiatus of many years, McCaffrey began writing more novels in the universe of *The Ship Who Sang*, this time with a variety of co-authors. With Margaret Ball she wrote *Partnership*, in which the "shellperson" Nancia uncovers and foils a plot to take control of the known universe. *The Ship Who Searched*, co-authored with Mercedes Lackey, is perhaps the most poignant and moving treatment of this theme. In this instance, the "shellperson" was exposed to an alien virus as a young child, which left her completely paralyzed. Late entry in the special training program for "shellpersons" is the only hope for her, and the obstacles she must overcome before she can get on with her life are truly daunting. War comes to the universe of the "shellpeople" in the next entry in the series, *The City Who Fought*, co-authored with a specialist in military science fiction, S. M. Sterling. For the first time, the "shellperson" is a male, Simeon, who is in control of a mining and processing space station. He gets a new "brawn," a female scientist, and before they have a chance to adjust to each other, he is battling an invading force for the continued existence of his space station. *The Ship Who Won*, co-authored with Jody Lynn Nye, involves fantasy gaming for the first time. The "brawn" is a Knight Errant, the "shellperson" is his Lady Fair, and the planet they land on gives them a chance to play these roles for real in a first contact mission that turns into a life and death struggle.

McCaffrey also deals with the challenges faced by the

physically-handicapped in her novel *Pegasus in Flight*. In a future where overcrowding is a fact of life, with only one legal child allowed per parent and sterilization accepted as a method of birth control by the authorities, humanity has become aware of the need for "psychically"-talented individuals who can help with the construction of a space station. The director of the Parapsychic Center is constantly on the lookout for new "wild" talents, and one of the most powerful ones she has ever encountered turns out to be a young boy whose spine was severed in an accident. He has compensated by being able to tap into electric energy and move anything, including himself, while in an out-of-body state.

Frank Herbert

For an example of world building of an incredibly high order, it is hard to beat Frank Herbert's *Dune*. The unforgettable adventures of young Paul Atreides on the barren desert planet his family was forced to move to marked the beginning of an extremely popular series. Life on this waterless world, which produced both the immortality drug *Melange* and a strange religion involving a new messiah, is depicted in riveting detail. I can still feel the heat, taste the grit, experience the dryness, and face the heart-pounding attacks of the giant sand worms.

Douglas Adams

Who could forget *The Hitchhiker's Guide to the Galaxy*? Certainly not the many fans who have joined Douglas Adams on his irreverent journey in a science fiction spoof that is loaded with zany characters, bizarre settings and situations, and lots and lots of humor. Teens have been reading *The Hitchhiker's Guide* and its sequels: *The Restaurant at the End of the Universe, Life, the Universe and Everything, So Long,* and *Thanks for All the Fish,* and *Mostly Harmless: The Fifth Book in the Increasingly Inaccurately Named Hitchhiker's Trilogy* in droves, ever since the first one appeared, and they continue to do so.

Marion Zimmer Bradley

Marion Zimmer Bradley is the creator of *Darkover*. Telepathic families are the prime movers and shakers here, particularly when they interact with random adepts, who are a danger to everyone until they have learned the proper techniques for controlling their wild talents. In spite of all efforts by the authorities to keep the influence of Terra at a minimum, representatives of both cultures work together towards a future that promises to be much brighter for the planet, provided they survive the present.

David Brin

David Brin has also contributed a post-holocaust classic in his novel *The Postman*. Who would have thought that wearing the uniform of a postal carrier could trigger a resurgence, slow, painful, often dangerous and bloody, but eventually leading to the successful regrowth of civilization? And then there's *Startide Rising* with its talking dolphins and space-faring races in a battle for a lost technology, winner take all. In the sequel, *The Uplift War*, neo-chimps have already been uplifted. What species will be next? Finally, his *Glory Season* is a remarkable treatment of clones in a rich, complex, female-dominated society in which male and female roles have been turned upside down.

Orson Scott Card

Orson Scott Card's *Ender's Game* is a contemporary classic, a novel that is still powerful and moving today. Young Ender is too bright for his own good, which means that the government has plans for him. Forcibly removed from his family, he is put into special training with other gifted youths who are being taught the art and technique of war. After playing endless games against each other, they eventually tackle an alien invading force—only no one tells them that these games are for real. In addition to two other works about Ender (*Speaker for the Dead* and *Xenocide*), Card has written numerous other science fiction novels, including *Seventh Son*, *Red Prophet*, and *Prentice Alvin*, an alternative history of the American frontier in which magic and religion are closely intertwined. An omniscient computer plays a pivotal role in his five-volume *Homecoming* series, which has many of the elements that made *Ender* such a popular and powerful work for teens. In volume one, *The Memory of Earth*, 14-year-old Nafai, the youngest son of an influential trader and clan chief on the planet Harmony, is contacted by the sentient computer known as the Oversoul. By keeping the planet at a low level of technology, the computer has been protecting humanity from following the same destructive path experienced on Earth centuries ago. Unfortunately the computer needs repairs and, therefore, help in getting back to Earth. Nafai discovers that there is a price to pay in being known as the one who can talk to the gods; and, before the novel ends, civil war has broken out in his city of Basilica. In *The Call of Earth* (Volume II), conditions in the city degenerate, and dreams plague those "chosen" by the Oversoul. These dreams may be messages from the Master Computer, known as the Keeper of the Earth, as he calls his children home. Nafai and his family and friends have no choice but to follow the dictates of the Oversoul, striking out into the desert on the first leg of their long journey back to Earth. Cultures clash in *The Ships of Earth* (Volume III) as the women on the trek through the desert, representatives of a strong feminist society, are forced to make temporary concessions in status due to the need for strong male leadership on their journey. Also, a third generation is born during these years of travel, children who will have an important role to play when the spaceships they discover at journey's end actually lift off for the next stage of their return to Earth. This is science fiction with a soul, written by a master who understands the conventions and can bring his characters to life.

Lois McMaster Bujold

Lois McMaster Bujold burst upon the science fiction scene and quickly won two Hugos and a Nebula (the award voted on by the science fiction *writers*—a tribute to the craftsmanship, rather than the popularity, of the author). She received her first Hugo for *The Vor Game*, the second novel detailing the adventures (and misadventures) of the irrepressible Miles Vorkosigan, the son of the Prime Minister of warlike Barrayar. His mother, a scientist from the planet Beta, had also been trained in armed combat, training that came in handy when she had to fight to keep her infant son alive. There is no room on the planet Barrayar for the weak or the damaged, and Cordelia literally had to fight for the life of her son, seeing that he received the very latest in medical treatment from Betan scientists, while using armed force to keep Barrayaran hotheads from destroying the fetus. He lives to grow up and eventually shows the entire Barrayaran aristocracy what a true son of his father can do. Miles is not a mutant, even though he looks like one, and he proves that looks can be deceiving in every book devoted to his adventures, taking the reader on a roller-coaster ride of fast-paced action, lively dialogue, and laugh-out-loud humor. The unstoppable Miles refuses to give an inch to his physical deformities, managing to carve out a niche for himself in Barrayaran society by the strength of his will, his considerable intelligence and an incredible amount of luck, as can be seen in the very first novel about him, *The Warrior's Apprentice*. As a member of the Barrayaran aristocracy, Miles is expected to enter the military academy. Unfortunately, his brittle bones can not make it through the obstacle course every applicant must complete. Flunked out of the academy, Miles is sent to visit his grandmother on Beta, and while just trying to be helpful, buys a spaceship, breaks Betan law, helps out in a rebellion, and accidentally acquires a Mercenary Force several thousand strong, an offense punishable by death on his home world. Miles is nothing if not fast on the uptake and this wheeler-dealer has soon created an alternate ego, Admiral Naismith of the Dendarii Mercenaries, to cover all of his so-called indiscretions. Bujold received her second Hugo for another novel about Miles, *Barrayar*, which tells the story of the events leading up to his birth.

Bujold began her career writing original paperbacks, but that changed with the publication of *Mirror Dance*, her first Miles Vorkosigan adventure to appear as a science fiction hard cover. A character introduced by Bujold in *Brothers in Arms* re-enters Miles' life, with a vengeance. In that earlier novel, a clone of Miles was created by his enemies and trained to be his thankfully-unsuccessful assassin. Brother Mark, who has avoided Miles since his older brother helped him to escape his tormentors two years ago, has decided to take revenge on those specialists at creating clones, the laboratories of Jackson Whole. He impersonates Miles and leads a detachment of Dendarii Mercenaries on a mission to rescue the new crop of brain-transplanted clones before they are exterminated. In the heat of battle, everything that can go wrong does, and when Miles comes to the rescue, he is shot in the chest, dies, and is placed in a cryo-unit for later rejuvenation by quick-thinking mercenaries. Unfortunately, the cryo-unit is lost before they reach the safety of their ship, and Mark must impersonate Miles on Barrayar while frantically looking for some trace of his missing brother. The trail eventually leads him back to where he least wants to go, to Jackson Whole and its clone factories. Bujold's speciality is action-filled science fiction adventures that are solidly-grounded in a carefully-thought out universe, which in turn is peopled by complex, believable characters. In addition to episodes of "good clean violence," her works are characterized by humor, romance, and a strong sense of advocacy for those who are different, like the Quaddies in her unusual novel *Falling Free*. These are genetically-altered mutants, people who have been given four arms, instead of two arms and two legs. They were created by Galtech and specially trained to work in freefall. But when a new Betan gravity device makes them obsolescent, they are slated for destruction, until the engineer hired to train them decides to undertake a rescue mission instead.

Other Authors in Brief

The list of science fiction authors who made an impression on me goes on and on:

Alfred Bester's *The Demolished Man* introduced a criminal who had to face his own past while a detective was in hot pursuit.

Ray Bradbury's *Martian Chronicles* and *The Illustrated Man* are two short story collections which I read and re-read. Combining elements of horror with science fiction themes, the former is an account of the exploration of the red planet, while the latter features an individual adorned with writhing tattoos that come chillingly to life. These stories demonstrate the high literary quality of Bradbury's writing while at the same time leaving the reader breathless with their rapid-fire pacing and edge-of-the seat suspense. His *Fahrenheit 451*, in which censorship is taken to a fiery extreme, has some of the same elements and has become a modern classic.

Zena Henderson's *The People: No Different Flesh* and *Pilgrimage: The Book of the People* demonstrate the care that must be taken in the use of telepathic powers, along with the dangers inherent in being different. I read these novels again and again, and was struck by how very human her people were, especially the children.

Pat Frank's *Alas, Babylon* and Neville Shute's *On the Beach* are two different treatments of the same theme—what happens after the bombs fall. Both are gripping recreations of an all-too-possible future and are still available and being read today.

H. G. Wells did time travel like no other, and his *Time Machine* led to any number of variations on the theme, backwards and forwards, and in the case of Robert Silverberg's *Project Pendulum*, even both directions at the same time.

SCIENCE FICTION TOPICS AND THEMES

When I started reading science fiction, I had the primary requisites: a highly-developed sense of wonder and an extremely willing suspension of disbelief. I read initially for the "Wow" effect, but I kept on reading and enjoying science fiction because I loved having reality shaken up, opening a door and stepping through into an entirely new universe, going for a spaceship ride and investigating new worlds, exploring mental telepathy, psi abilities, telekinesis, and dream worlds that become more real than what we experience while awake. Reading science fiction, in my opinion, gives a whole new meaning to the phrase, "a book is a friend to take us miles away." I immersed myself totally in each new reading experience and unconditionally accepted each situation, conflict, and other-worldly setting.

Speculative Fiction

Among the labels applied to science fiction are phrases such as "speculative fiction," the literature of the great "What If . . . ?" and "the literature of infinite possibilities"—possibilities because it is science fiction. These are stories, situations, and characters with a scientific foundation, with a basis, however tenuous, in fact. They contain events that could conceivably have happened (in an alternate time line), be happening right now, or perhaps may happen at some time in the future. This is the intriguing aspect, the unique quality that drew me to science fiction in the first place and that keeps me reading. In its infinite variety science fiction can be anything at all. It can be a mystery like Harry Turtledove's *The Case of the Toxic Spell Dump* or a hardboiled detective story like Jonathan Lethem's *Gun, with Occasional Music*, in which private investigator Conrad Metcalf tries to keep a client from being sent to the freezer by solving a murder. Unfortunately, his investigation gets him involved with the local Inquisitors, who are as dangerous to him as the gun-toting kangaroo that has been following him (further proof that evolution therapy is not necessarily a good idea). Works of science fiction can be set in a past that never was, resulting in alternate history works like Turtledove's *Worldwar: In the Balance*, or Ben Bova's *Triumph*, in which World War II ends in quite a different manner. Suppose President Roosevelt stopped smoking, does not have a fatal stroke, and remains healthy and fully in charge, all the way to the bitter end. At the same time, Winston Churchill, foreseeing the dangerous beast that Stalin would become, takes steps to eradicate him before the end of the war. And suppose Patton pushes through to Berlin before the Russians can get there. The result is an America that is the only game in town, a worldwide empire that will not *allow* any other nation to acquire atomic weaponry.

Space Opera

An early, and still popular, form of science fiction is that of "Space Opera," from the space battles depicted in E. E. "Doc" Smith novels to the action/adventure ride Robert Asprin takes the reader on in his riotous *Phule's Company* and its sequel *Phule's Paradise*. Timothy Zahn has continued the tradition with his *Star Wars* trilogy: *Heir to the Empire, Dark Force Rising,* and *The Last Command*. These novels begin years after the movies end, with Han and Leia married and expecting twins. Meanwhile, Luke has become involved in a search for the clone of a master Jedi, and the evil Empire is once again up to its old tricks. The characters, including Chewie, Lando, and those inimitable robots, R2D2 and C3PO, are brought to life with the same breezy dialogue, crackling, fast-paced battle scenes, and exotic, other-world settings found in the movies. The author, who is an expert at military science fiction, has captured the spirit and the personalities of these well-known movie figures perfectly.

B.E.M.s (Bug-Eyed Monsters)

In addition to Space Opera, early science fiction was known as the literature of the B.E.M.s (bug-eyed monsters, to the uninitiated). Examples can be found in works such as H. G. Wells' *War of the Worlds*, the Orson Welles radio broadcast of which led to mass hysteria as fiction became reality to an all-too-gullible public. On October 30, 1938, an adapted version of the novel was broadcast as an on-the-spot news report, describing aliens from Mars landing in New Jersey and attacking unarmed citizens. Wide-spread panic was the result, in spite of on-the-air disclaimers that this was a work of fiction. The same basic premise is behind the vicious vegetation of John Wyndham's *Day of the Triffids*, and the mechanical tripods with their mind-control helmets in John Christopher's *The White Mountains, The City of Gold and Lead, The Pool of Fire,* and *When the Tripods Came*, the prequel to the trilogy.

Space Exploration

Space exploration is natural to science fiction writers, but each brings a unique vision to what happens once the spaceship lands. Take, for example, the treatment of the planet Mars by various authors. In his *Mars*, Ben Bova presents us with an account of an early expedition to that planet that reads with the immediacy of the evening news. Greg Bear's *Moving Mars*, on the other hand, addresses the issue of tension between Earth and its colony on Mars, resulting in armed conflict that eventually forces the inhabitants of the red planet to take a drastic step for their survival. What it would take to make Mars habitable is the subject of Kim Robinson's trilogy about the colonization and resulting terraforming of the planet: *Red Mars*, *Green Mars*, and *Blue Mars*. The military mindset can cause problems in space exploration novels like the ones McCaffrey set on the planet Doona: *Decision at Doona*, *Crisis on Doona*, and *Treaty at Doona*. When human colonists landed on the planet, they were not aware that cat-like Hrrubans already lived there. Once the two races discovered each other, it took the young of both species to bring about a peaceful compromise and an eventual treaty. Gordon Dickson's *Soldier, Ask Not*, on the other hand, makes us grateful that the military mindset is still around, particularly since his *Dorsai* warriors are so adept at protecting the human race. Sometimes it is the spaceship ride itself that is the focus of a novel, like the one in Greg Bear's *Anvil of Stars*, or a similar theme, the discovery that your world is actually a spaceship, which is what happens to the children in Pamela Sargent's *Earthseed*.

Computers

For those interested in computers, but wanting something different, there is Orson Scott Card's *Lost Boys*. A computer expert moves his family to a small town in North Carolina, only to discover that someone in the neighborhood is killing young boys. The horror strikes close to home when he discovers that his seven-year-old son has some new imaginary friends, young boys who just "happen" to have the same names as the missing boys. Experimenting with virtual reality games is a relatively recent motif in science fiction, one that is masterfully handled in Piers Anthony's *Killobyte*, featuring a new action/adventure game that is so seductive because its entire premise is based on the concept of kill or be killed. A player sits at a terminal, wrapped in plastic and literally plugged in—helmet, gloves, boots, all of which provide an adrenaline surge when someone is killed, as well as the pain of death when your player is zapped. Two players meet in the confines of the game, a high school senior contemplating suicide and a paraplegic ex-policeman who can walk and run again, courtesy of the game. Then Phone Phreak, a psychotic teenage hacker, enters the picture, and their game struggles become ominously real. The same concept is given a different twist in Gillian Rubinstein's *Space Demons* and its sequel *Skymaze*. A seventh-grade boy receives a pirated copy of a Japanese computer game with no instructions, but a deceptively simple method of initiating play. What Andy doesn't realize is that the game feeds on hate, and once the space demons are strong enough, they can leave the confines of the game and appear in real life. This is a wonderful picture of the addictive attraction of zapping monsters, and how violence and anger breed more of the same, particularly in the tumultuous adolescent years. *Skymaze* is the next generation of the Space Demons game, this time actually requiring the teen players to physically enter the maze, where only their cooperation and interdependence can save the Earth. For those eager to ride the cyber waves, the place to start is the seminal cyberpunk novel, William Gibson's *Neuromancer*, a dark work depicting a society devoted to getting high on alcohol and drugs, except for the "Cowboys," who get high on computer interaction, interfacing or wiring themselves into a terminal and riding the electronic pathways.

Social Issues

Contemporary "mainstream" fiction sometimes uses a stream of consciousness technique to deal with problems, including the use of drugs, alcohol and indiscriminate sex. A New Wave struck science fiction towards the end of the sixties with the publication of Harlan Ellison's trailblazing *Dangerous Visions*, an anthology of science fiction stories that were so different they were not considered eligible for publication in science fiction magazines. (Gunn, p. 429.) The authors in this collection were very concerned with style, using some of the techniques of "mainstream" fiction while, at the same time, not being afraid to tackle previously untouchable issues. Another recent concern of science fiction is the state of the ecology, rather than the economy. For a look at the ecological disasters in store for us, take a trip on the wonderfully-inventive space beast ship Evangeline depicted in Megan Lindholm's *Alien Earth*. Or learn the startling secret revealed in Pierre Boulle's *Planet of the Apes*. What about society's many woes? Take a look at the incredible solution to the problem of overcrowding faced by the characters in Harry Harrison's *Make Room! Make Room!*, which Hollywood turned into the movie *Soylent Green*. Far more acceptable to this problem are the solutions that the psychically-gifted are able to come up with in McCaffrey's *Rowan* novels: *The Rowan, Damia, Damia's Children*, and *Lyon's Pride*. The Rowan's psychic abilities are incredibly strong, so much so that she can move any amount of materials from the Tower she operates to their destinations throughout known space. Her daughter, Damia, and her eight grandchildren have inherited her psychic abilities, which is fortunate because their powers are essential in the battle against the warriors of the alien Hive ships. Society takes many different forms in science fiction novels, from the big brother is watching you of George Orwell's *1984*, to the role of religion in a post-holocaust world like the one depicted in Walter Miller's classic *A Canticle for Leibowitz*. A grim, bleak future is in store for us if current trends continue, at least that's the premise of Octavia Butler's *The Parable of the Sower*. But then, traveling back into the past at the time of the bubonic plague can also be a frightening experience, especially when another plague is threatening the world of the future, as is the case in Connie Willis's award-winning *Doomsday Book*.

WOMEN AND SCIENCE FICTION

A significant development in contemporary science fiction is the rise of women authors and strong female protagonists. In fact, in all my years of reading science fiction, this is one of the most remarkable changes that I have observed. In the early "Golden Years" of science fiction, if a woman submitted something to an editor, she needed to use a masculine name, like Andre Norton or James Triptree, Jr. In keeping with advancements in so many other areas of society, female authors today have come a long way, both in the quantity of books produced each year and in the quality of their writing. I have already discussed a number of my favorites, but at this point I would like to mention a few others whose works mark this dramatic change in status, resulting in the prevailing rise of the feminine sensibility in the science fiction field.

Vonda N. McIntyre

Vonda McIntyre's *Dreamsnake*, which was published in 1978, won the Nebula Award and was also selected by the American Library Association for its Best Books for Young Adults list, and no wonder. It is a gripping picture of a post-holocaust future, in which primitive tribal groups are pitted against walled cities in a struggle for survival. Snake, the protagonist, is a young healer, culturing antitoxin and vaccine from her pet rattlesnake and cobra. Her most precious snake, however, is the small but deadly dream snake, which she uses to deaden pain or, when death is inevitable, to make it an easy one. When her dream snake is destroyed by the frightened parent of a sick child, she sets off on a quest to find another one, along the way making significant discoveries about herself and the society in which she lives.

Joan Vinge

A few years later, Joan Vinge published the first of her novels set on the planet Tiamat. *The Snow Queen*, which won the Hugo Award, was followed shortly afterwards by *World's End*. Not until 1991 did the long-awaited sequel appear, *The Summer Queen*. These novels represent the struggle between summer and winter, as periodic cyclical upheavals on the planet Tiamat lead to a summer that lasts 100 years, during which time all outsiders must leave the planet. But Tiamat is the only source of the immortality elixir; and, when the less-than-benevolent Hegemony tries to discover the secret behind its production, the new queen must do everything in her power to protect her planet from exploitation. In particular the sea-dwelling "mers," who have only recently been recognized as an intelligent species, are at risk because they are the source of the priceless elixir. In addition to her novels about Tiamat, Vinge also tackled the question of psi powers and the responsibility of those who possess them in *Psion* and its sequel *Catspaw*. Cat is an orphan from the slums whose half-alien parentage has given him a gift that the government can use, so he is forced into a psi research project that eventually leads to a telepathic confrontation for the fate of the universe.

Sheri S. Tepper

Sheri S. Tepper specializes in strong female characters, as is evident in works such as *Grass* and *The Gate to Women's Country*. In the latter, it is the women who control the civilized towns, with only nonaggressive males allowed to live with them there. The soldiers in the garrisons outside the walls may only visit under certain carefully-supervised conditions. In the former, a planet reminiscent of Dune, but with waving plains of grass rather than waterless sandy wastes, has a deadly secret that only Marjorie Yrarier, Lady Westriding, is equipped to solve. She and her family are sent to Grass to investigate the strange properties of the only planet that has not succumbed to a system-wide plague. Riding to the hunt is a passion of the planet's citizens; and, since she is a noted horsewoman, Marjorie goes along for the ride. To her horror, she discovers that the Hippae are not like horses but instead have a strange, hypnotic power over their riders; and, if these riders are young girls like Marjorie's daughter, they may sometimes disappear during a hunt. A further difference is in the hounds; these are not dogs, but beasts ready to turn on riders and tear away limbs during or after a hunt. As for the foxen, Marjorie soon learns that, unlike foxes, these are intelligent telepathic beings who have evolved from lower life forms on the planet. Before it's all over, Marjorie is involved in a struggle against ignorance, prejudice, and even religious intolerance for the salvation of mankind.

Janet Kagan

Janet Kagan is the author of *Uhura's Song*, recognized as one of the best of the Star Trek novels, a lyrical story of the quest for a life-saving vaccine, with only Uhura's memory of a forbidden song to lead the way. In 1991 Kagan wrote *Mirabile*, which took the concept of genetic mutations to a new height. Mirabile is a planet where all kinds of strange mutations keep popping up. Some, known as Dragon's teeth, are "friendly" and are kept as part of the gene pool. Some, on the other hand, are deadly and must be sought out and destroyed. That's the job of Annie Jason Masmajean, the head of the gene readers who are involved in trying to keep a record of what is mutating, when changes occur, and how to successfully preserve the safe mutations. The novel is actually a compilation of six related stories describing her adventures with challenges such as the Loch Moose Monster, the Kangaroo Rex, and Frankenswine (a cross between a boar and a mole). The novel is characterized by snappy dialogue, lots of humor, non-stop action, exotic animals, and a very human, strong-willed protector with a mind of her own to look after them.

Elizabeth Moon

Elizabeth Moon is the co-author with Anne McCaffrey of two of the latter's Planet Pirates books: *Sassinak* and *Generation Warriors*. Sassinak, who is captured by pirates as a young girl and eventually rescued by the fleet, becomes a dedicated military commander who is consumed with the need for vengeance on her enemies. *Generation Warriors* is the third volume in the trilogy, following *The Death of Sleep*, which McCaffrey wrote with Jody Lynn Nye. Now a commander, Sassinak and Dr. Lunzie Mespil, who appeared in the second volume, bring their battle against planet pirates to a close, while also protecting genetically-altered Heavyworlders from discrimination. Both authors blend their techniques and areas of expertise seamlessly in novels that include lots of fast-paced action. Moon continues to show her gift for rapid-fire pacing and edge-of-the-seat excitement in two novels she wrote independently involving a former fleet officer who is forced to go to work on a private spaceship. In *Hunting Party* Heris Serrano, who was unfairly forced out of the Regular Space Services, has no recourse but to accept command of the luxury space yacht Sweet Delight. Working for the aged Lady Cecilia turns out to be far more of a challenge than she had expected, however, as she takes a mediocre, lackadaisical crew and tries to forge it into a smoothly-functioning, efficient unit. While conducting a necessary overhaul, she discovers signs that the former captain was involved in a smuggling ring. And then there's the "royal pains," Lady Cecelia's spoiled young nephew and his five friends, all going fox-hunting with Cecelia. The fox-hunting turns into a man hunt, and soon Heris finds herself running for her life. In the sequel, *Sporting Chance*, Heris uncovers a plot on the life of the Crown Prince, but before she and Cecelia can do anything about it, the old lady has fallen into a strange coma that is blamed on her erstwhile captain. Heris has no choice but to dodge the authorities, while doing everything in her power to save her employer's life. Lots of action, including space battles and hand-to-hand combat, palace intrigues, and an ample dose of derring-do show her skill as a writer of military science fiction. Her lively dialogue is interspersed with wit and humor in a story that flows seamlessly from start to finish and is definitely fun to read.

Ursula K. LeGuin

No list of female writers and their contribution to the field of contemporary science fiction would be complete without the incomparable Ursula K. LeGuin. The variety and quality of her works alone provide incontrovertible proof of just how varied and all-encompassing the efforts of women writers have become. In her ground-breaking *The Left Hand of Darkness*, she addresses the issue of sexual identity by creating a society where individuals change sexes at certain predetermined intervals. Genly Ai, a visiting diplomat, gets caught in a web of political intrigue that leaves him fleeing for his life across the snow-bound wilderness of Gethen, accompanied by an official who had been one of his first contacts on the planet. How he relates to this official, particularly when Lord Estraven becomes a "she" as the cycles change, is an intriguing aspect of this unusual and complex novel. In addition to other adult novels like *The Dispossessed*, which addresses issues of the role of women in society, free will, and human rights, she has also written a series geared towards a much younger audience. *The Wizard of Earthsea Trilogy* is an account of how hubris leads to disaster for the young magician Ged and of the help he receives from a young priestess in training. *The Wizard of Earthsea, The Tombs of Atuan,* and *The Farthest Shore* comprise this classic trilogy which continues to be enjoyed by readers of all ages. Years later the author returned to Earthsea with *Tehanu: The Last Book of Earthsea,* a work in which the middle-aged Tenar is called upon once again to help Ged, now an Arch-mage, whose powers have been burned out in one final struggle against the forces of dark. This lyrical, thought-provoking fantasy is further proof of the author's masterful command of plot, story, and language.

THE NEED TO KNOW

As the previous discussion has demonstrated, many different themes and concepts have been the subject of top-notch works of science fiction. This is a genre that is changeable, multi-layered, and rich in variety, frequently represented by works that are intellectually challenging to read. Unfortunately, it is a much-maligned genre, in part because it is read by fans and teens, but all-too-often not by the teachers, parents, and librarians who interact with these teens. It requires an expenditure of time and effort to change reading tastes, but it is well worth making such an effort for the rewards involved, exposure to a rich, varied, complex, and satisfying reading experience. At first it may seem strange, even uncomfortable, to enter a world that is so different from everyday experience. Repeated exposure to such new worlds and different ways of knowing, however, will gradually make the unknown more comfortable and enjoyable. It is essential that the challenge of reading science fiction be accepted because it is the responsibility of those adults working with teens to become knowledgeable in areas that teens enjoy reading, whether they are initially comfortable in those areas or not. Reading science fiction can become an acquired taste, for those willing to work at it and give it half a chance. Those librarians who are unwilling or unable to make the effort still have a responsibility to provide teen readers with a collection that includes a variety of science fiction titles, representing both classic and current works. Reading reviews will help to a certain extent, but another way to get recommendations is to talk to teen fans themselves. Ask them what authors, titles, and types of books they like to read and then order a representative sampling for your collection.

YOUNG ADULT SCIENCE FICTION

Why should we as professionals be encouraging teens to read science fiction? What is the value of science fiction that is written specifically for the teen audience? An examination of select titles will answer such questions. In each of the following novels, a common science fiction concept is partnered with the more traditional themes found in young adult novels. Readers benefit on a dual level as a result, enjoying science fiction motifs within a framework that has been prepared for a typical teen problem novel.

Teleportation (Fathers and Sons)

Steven Gould's *Jumper* is an impressive first novel that tackles the concept of teleportation and how it is handled by an unsuspecting teen. Look at the length, the density of the prose, the challenging concepts presented, and the sheer fun involved in this science fiction approach to a typical teen problem novel. This is a classic plot of a young adult novel with a drunken, abusive father, a broken home, and a long-suffering son who finally gets fed up with being abused and runs away. But this particular runaway has something special going for him. He discovers that he can teleport, and once he masters the basic technique and learns how to live on his own in New York City, this 16-year-old has the world for his playground—literally. He finds and loses his mother, falls in love, plays keep away with members of the National Security Agency who want to exploit his gift, and undertakes a successful vendetta against Arab terrorists. The result is a fascinating action/adventure science fiction novel that is also a thoughtful look at the harm that can be caused by a dysfunctional family, until an independent teen takes his fate into his own capable hands and stops being a victim (assisted, of course, by his extraordinary gift for teleportation).

Ecological Issues (Peer Group)

Peter Dickinson's *Eva* is another example of why teens are (and should be) reading science fiction. Published in 1990, this book continues to be immensely popular among teen readers. The author grabs the reader from the very beginning, in which the protagonist wakes up in the hospital and discovers that her brain has been transplanted into the body of a chimpanzee. Once teens learn that she goes home from the hospital to live with her parents as a teenage girl in the body of a chimpanzee, they're hooked. This is not just any chimpanzee, however, but Kelley, a chimp that she has grown up with. In the severely overpopulated future depicted here, this is a member of the last extant group of chimps, a group that her scientist father has been studying. *Eva* is not only the story of this remarkable girl's adjustment to life in an animal's body, but also of her struggle to bring about a greater degree of freedom for the members of this group, known as "The Pool." Ecological issues are at the heart of this fascinating novel, as well as a plea for greater understanding and acceptance of the animals we share this planet with. Eva's mother wants her to be a girl, rather than a chimp, and treats her accordingly. Eva's father loves her, but at the same time is not averse to using her to further his own primate studies. Eva is the one who has to stand up for her animal nature, first by recognizing what it is and then by accepting the essential difference in her make-up.

Big Brother Is Watching (Sibling Rivalry)

Pogo said, "We have met the enemy and he is us." That is certainly the case in Thomas Baird's *Smart Rats*, which demonstrates what an overpopulated, severely polluted, government-controlled society has in store for those unneeded or unwanted "extras." The teen protagonist is aware of the injustice that is being done on behalf of the government; but when he finds himself caught in a no-win situation, his only recourse is to join up and become a part of the system he has been fighting against.

Post-Holocaust (Fear of Strangers)

Another example of a fine science fiction novel that is written for young adults can be seen in the richness of language and imagery found in Robert O'Brien's *Z for Zachariah*. After the bombs drop, only one 16-year-old girl is left alive in a valley that had been protected from radioactive fallout by strange weather inversions. Outside the valley, everything is barren, dead and sere. Inside, there's non-polluted water, green grass, and trees, even a few surviving animals. The title is from a picture book that Ann used in Sunday School, *The Bible Letter Book*. "A is for Adam," "B is for Benjamin," "C is for Christian," all the way to "Z is for Zachariah." She knew that Adam was the first man, and for a long time she had assumed that Zachariah must be the last man. Ann meets her personal Zachariah when a stranger makes it across the wasteland to the valley, wearing a green, radiation-proof, plastic suit. Ann has every reason to be afraid of this stranger's intrusion, and soon she is fighting for her life.

Time Travel (Friendship)

Grace Chetwin's *Collidescope* combines elements of time travel and space opera in a novel with likeable characters, believable science, and a satisfying conclusion. Hahn is a Humanoid Android for Hyperspace Navigation, a remote extension of his space ship and a conservationist looking for oxygen-type planets when he crash lands on Earth. He lands in Manhattan, but in order to avoid wholesale death and destruction, he is able to flash back in time before touching down, where he meets the Indian youth Sky-Fire-Trail. A trip back to modern times draws in Frankie, who is worried about the future of her planet and eager to help Hahn in his struggle to return home so that he can register the Earth, thereby saving it from planet robbers.

Greenhouse Effect (The Journey)

A very bleak future indeed is depicted in Monica Hughes' *The Crystal Drop*. The hole in the ozone layer and the greenhouse effect have led to prolonged periods of no rain, resulting in widespread drought. Thirteen-year-old Megan leads her ten-year-old brother away from their drought-stricken farm in search of their missing uncle, who left years ago to found a settlement in the West, a settlement that is supposedly near a waterfall. This is a novel that makes the reader appreciate water (the crystal drop) as well as the author's skill at scene-setting, character development, and the ability to paint an all too possible future in a manner that is relentlessly real.

Alien Contact (Being Different)

Paul Jacobs' *Born into the Light* is a gentle reflective tale of living with "aliens" among us. It has its frightening moments (the "monster" in the pond, for example), but basically it is a study in family love and the humanity of humanity, the cuckoo's egg concept, but without the harmful effects. The nestlings do not push out the true offspring; instead they grow up with them and make solid contributions to the advancements of science and society before their rapid aging leads to premature death. As they are assisted by their human friends to ultimately complete their mission, this becomes an engrossing and compelling psychological study of human beings' capacity for humanity.

Philosophical (Cooperation)

For philosophical science fiction, try Louise Lawrence's *Keeper of the Universe*. Music that soothes the savage beast is played throughout the universe, with the inhabitants of planets exposed to it becoming malleable and less violent, aggressive and antagonistic towards one another. In the process, however, they lose all self-will, originality, and creativity. Ben Harran is the only Galactic Controller who disapproves of this method of control. He believes in free will and non-intervention. Unfortunately, one of the planets he is responsible for literally blows itself up, and he is charged by the other controllers with genocide and culpable neglect. In an effort to exonerate himself, Harran conducts an experiment. He brings together a boy from Earth, a girl from the perfectly controlled world of Herra, and a savage barbarian queen from another non-controlled planet (like Earth). The purpose of the study is to see how well these three representatives of different races can adjust to being forcefully thrown together, and the result is a novel that is lyrical, philosophical, and intriguing.

Dystopia (Adolescent Idealism)

No discussion of science fiction written specifically for young adults would be complete without Lois Lowry's *The Giver*, winner of the 1993 Newbery Award. This incredible novel is a chilling look at a society that is a dystopia, rather than a utopia. When the novel opens, Jonas is a happy, productive member of his society, excitedly awaiting his Ceremony of Twelve. At that time he will cease to be a child and receive the assignment that will determine his life's work. His father is a Nurturer who works in the nursery, caring for each new child until the Ceremony of One, the Naming Ceremony, in which each baby is given to a carefully-selected family. Jonas' mother holds a prominent position at the Department of Justice; and, with the approval of the Elders, his seven-year-old sister rounds out the allowed family. At his Ceremony of Twelve, Jonas discovers that he has been selected (not assigned) to be the next Receiver of Memory, a position of great honor. The current Receiver picked the boy because he has the Capacity to See Beyond and can even see flashes of "Color" in his uniformly grey surroundings. As the old man becomes the Giver, passing his memories on to Jonas, the one who must protect the community in his place, the boy experiences glorious and wonderful moments, counterbalanced by episodes of excruciating pain. The true horror doesn't hit him until all the secrets of his community are revealed, and then his conscience determines the action he must take. This is a brooding, atmospheric novel that deals with heavy philosophical questions of guilt and responsibility, written in lyrical prose that is completely accessible to young readers and with an ending that is nothing less than stunning.

Pollution (Brothers)

Another bleak look at the future occurs in Kenneth Oppel's *Dead Water Zone*. Paul gets a telephone call from his brother Sam, who is weak physically but has a brilliant intellect. Sam has been doing research in the Dead Water Zone and wants Paul to meet him there; but when Paul arrives, Sam has disappeared. In his search for his brother, Paul encounters a strange young girl who offers to help him, avoids a couple of men asking questions, and is pursued by an unmarked helicopter that appears to be looking for him. It's a total mystery until he uncovers Sam's diskette with his research results and learns just what is going on in the Dead Water Zone. This page-turner has a setting reminiscent of the movie version of *Blade Runner,* and its complex plot, full of unexpected twists and turns, includes a meditation on the meaning of love and family responsibility that ends in a thoroughly satisfactory manner.

Back to the Basics (Absence of Adults)

Science fiction is combined with elements of Mark Twain in Caroline Stevermer's *River Rats.* It is fifteen years since the nuclear Armageddon known as the Flash. In the aftermath a group of orphans "liberated" the *River Rat,* an ancient Mississippi steam boat that had been used as an orphanage. Now they are the *River Rats,* living on the boat and working their way up and down the Mississippi River. The river itself is too polluted to drink from, but they are able to travel on it, delivering mail at towns along the bank and performing rock concerts at their regular ports of call. The one time they break their hard and fast rule to never take on passengers almost costs them their boat and their lives. The novel evokes the nitty gritty feel of a world beyond the edge of civilization, a fitting backdrop for a group of likeable teenagers with clear-cut personalities.

Sociological (Siblings)

A most unusual science fiction book written specifically for the teen audience is Nancy Farmer's *The Ear, the Eye and the Arm.* Set in Zimbabwe of 2194, it opens in the compound of one of that country's movers and shakers, General Amadeus Matsika. His three children, Tendai (13), Rita (11), and Kuda (4), have been cooped up behind barbed wire all their lives, closely guarded by a computer-animated automatic Doberman. They have never ridden on a bus, shopped in an open market or even seen the subway system. Until now, the Mellower, with his skillful use of praise-singing, has been able to keep things on a more or less even keel. But the children are chafing under all the restrictions and are able to convince the Mellower to help them get their father's unwitting permission to go on a Scout trip, an all day excursion in which they will be entirely on their own. With gatepass in hand, they head for the open market, where they are immediately kidnapped and sold to the great She Elephant, ruler of a former toxic waste dump that she has converted to a plastics mine. She plans to use the children as slaves for a while and then sell them to the infamous Masks; but they are able to escape, only to find themselves in even more danger than before. As the children go from the frying pan to the fire, the Ear, the Eye and the Arm are on their trail, mutant detectives who can see, hear, and sense the intent of those around them. The General is not allowed to offer a ransom, but his wife has no qualms about hiring detectives, and she employs a truly unique trio, who rely on hidden resources to bring their case to a successful conclusion. This ingenious novel is one of the most original young adult novels that I have read in a long time, wildly-inventive, witty, and wonderful.

Scientific Principles (Self-Reliance)

With regard to length, sentence structure, complex plots and multiplicity of characters, some of the challenging reads for young adults are frequently the science fiction works. Even the smooth-flowing, relatively lean prose of William Sleator can be used to express such challenging concepts as the chaos theory in *Strange Attractors*, black holes in *Singularity*, and radioactive pollution that has a most peculiar effect on those exposed to it in *Others See Us*. Two of his early science fiction novels, *Interstellar Pig*, in which a young boy finds himself playing a game for the fate of the universe, and *House of Stairs*, site of a series of sinister tests to which a group of orphan teens are subjected, continue to be widely read.

Series

One final reason to encourage a taste for science fiction among teens is the quality of the series in this market. First take a look at young adult series, not the literary trilogies (or longer), but the true series. Examine a sampling of Hardy Boys, Nancy Drew, and Sweet Valley High titles. Then take a look at the novels that have resulted from the Star Trek and Star Wars phenomenon. These are full-bodied novels, written by different authors, and set in a universe with fiercely-controlled scientific principles and details. Series books are immensely popular with teens— but which would it be better to encourage—formula fiction or the challenge of the unknown?

SEX IN SCIENCE FICTION

Sex in science fiction—be aware—it may be there. In the "Golden Age" of pulp fiction, especially under the aegis of John Campbell, there was no such thing as sex in science fiction. That is definitely no longer the case. Just as contemporary fiction has become bolder and more "with it," science fiction has entered the modern age with a vengeance. In a science fiction novel written for adults you may have strong language, sexual innuendo, bedroom scenes, and/or mature relationships engaged in by mature people. Controversial issues such as the depiction of gay and lesbian characters or homosexual relationships can also be an integral part of a story, accepted by readers with no thought of anything but how they fit into the narrative flow. In a novel written explicitly for young people, this is less likely to occur, although the depiction of mature themes and situations in books for younger readers is a growing trend. One of the truly remarkable things about science fiction is the fact that there is such universal and wide-ranging acceptance of issues that might be controversial in another format. In novels written both for an adult and a young adult audience, the richness of the language, the complexity of thought and the unique vision and unusual ideas are in the forefront, with controversial issues relegated to a position that is subservient to the progress of the story.

CONCLUSION

My advice to anyone looking for science fiction books to suggest to teen readers is "anything goes." Science fiction has been called "the books that science fiction writers write!" In other words, it can be about anything in or out of this world. For those who do not normally read science fiction, it is vital to sample a variety of titles before getting discouraged. Try sharing the ones you like with others, and most important of all, don't give up after just one or two titles. Reading and appreciating works of science fiction is an acquired taste. If you didn't start reading science fiction as a teen reader, it is not too late to start now, but you will have to work to develop a taste for it. The effort is well worth making, however, and the teens you work with will benefit from your open-minded acceptance as you venture into the worlds of the strange and the unknown.

In conclusion, science fiction as a genre is infinitely appealing in an infinite number of ways. Literature that is rich, complex, varied, challenging, intellectually-stimulating, and ultimately rewarding—that is what is in store for those who make the effort to read and appreciate science fiction. I have been boldly going in the science fiction genre for a number of years now, and I have no intention of stopping. The challenge is there, as well as the fun. Every book is so different. The universe is vast and there is always something new to discover in exploring its infinite possibilities. The new, the unique, the unusual are all a part of this rewarding genre.

WORKS CITED

Adams, Douglas. *The Hitchhiker's Guide to the Galaxy*. New York: Pocket, 1981.

_____. *Life, the Universe and Everything*. New York: Pocket, 1991.

_____. *Mostly Harmless: The Fifth Book in the Increasingly Inaccurately Named Hitchhiker's Trilogy*. New York: Harmony, 1992.

_____. *The Restaurant at the End of the Universe*. New York: Harmony, 1982.

_____. *So Long, and Thanks for All the Fish*. New York: Pocket, 1985. [Out of Print.]

Anthony, Piers. *Killobyte*. New York: Putnam, 1993.

Asimov, Isaac. *Asimov on Science Fiction*. Garden City: Doubleday, 1981.

_____. *Caves of Steel*. New York: Ballantine, 1986.

_____. *Fantastic Voyage*. New York: Bantam, 1988.

_____. *Fantastic Voyage II: Destination Brain*. New York: Bantam, 1988.

_____. *Forward the Foundation*. New York: Doubleday, 1986.

_____. *Foundation*. New York: Bantam, 1991.

_____. *Foundation and Earth*. New York: Ballantine, 1987.

_____. *Foundation and Empire*. New York: Ballantine, 1986.

_____. *Foundation's Edge*. New York: Ballantine, 1983.

_____, ed. *The Hugo Winners: Volumes One and Two*. Garden City: Doubleday, 1962 and 1971.

_____. *Lucky Starr & the Moons of Jupiter & Lucky Starr & the Rings of Saturn*. New York: Bantam, 1993.

_____. *I, Robot*. New York: Bantam, 1991.

_____. *Lucky Starr & the Oceans of Venus*. New York: Fawcett, 1982.

_____. *Prelude to Foundation*. New York: Bantam, 1989.

_____. *Second Foundation*. New York: Bantam, 1991.

Asprin, Robert. *Phule's Company*. New York: Ace, 1992.

_____. *Phule's Paradise*. New York: Ace, 1992.

Baird, Thomas. *Smart Rats*. New York: Harper, 1990.

Barron, Neil, Wayne Barton, Kristin Ramsdell, and Steven A. Stilwell. *What Do I Read Next?: A Reader's Guide to Current Genre Fiction - Fantasy - Western - Romance - Horror - Mystery - Science Fiction - 1993*. Washington, D.C.: Gale, 1994.

Bear, Greg. *Anvil of Stars*. New York: Warner, 1993.

_____. *Moving Mars*. New York: TOR, 1994.

Bester, Alfred. *The Demolished Man*. New York: New American, 1953.

Books for the Teen Age. New York: New York Public Library, 1994.

Boulle, Pierre. *Planet of the Apes*. New York: NAL, 1964.

Bova, Ben. *Mars*. New York: Bantam, 1993.

_____. *Triumph*. New York: TOR, 1994.

Bradbury, Ray. *Fahrenheit 451*. New York: Ballantine, 1987.

_____. *The Illustrated Man*. New York: Bantam, 1983.

_____. *Martian Chronicles*. New York: Bantam, 1984.

Bradley, Marion Zimmer. *The Bloody Sun*. New York: DAW, 1994.

_____. *City of Sorcery*. New York: DAW, 1988.

_____. *Darkover Landfall*. New York: DAW, 1987.

_____. *The Forbidden Tower*. New York: DAW, 1977.

_____. *Hawkmistress!*. New York: DAW, 1982.

_____. *The Heirs of Hammerfell*. New York: DAW, 1990.

_____. *The Heritage of Hastur*. New York: DAW, 1984.

_____. *The Shattered Chain*. New York: DAW, 1976.

_____. *Star of Danger*. New York: DAW, 1994.

_____. *Sword and Sorceress I* through *XI*. New York: DAW, 1986 to 1994.

_____. *Thendara House*. New York: DAW, 1983.

_____. *Towers of Darkover*. New York: DAW, 1993.

_____. *Two to Conquer*. New York: DAW, 1987.

Bretnor, Reginald, ed. *Science Fiction, Today and Tomorrow*. New York: Harper, 1974.

Brin, David. *Glory Season*. New York: Bantam, 1994.

_____. *The Postman*. New York: Bantam, 1986.

_____. *Startide Rising*. New York: Bantam, 1984.

_____. *The Uplift War*. New York: Bantam, 1987.

Bujold, Lois McMaster. *Barrayar*. New York: Baen, 1991.

_____. *Borders of Infinity*. New York: Baen, 1991.

_____. *Brothers in Arms*. New York: Baen, 1989.

_____. *Falling Free*. New York: Baen, 1988.

_____. *Mirror Dance*. New York: Baen, 1994.

_____. *Shards of Honor*. New York: Baen, 1991.

_____. *The Vor Game*. New York: Baen, 1990.

_____. *The Warrior's Apprentice*. New York: Baen, 1991.

Butler, Octavia E. *The Parable of the Sower*. New York: Warner, 1995.

Card, Orson Scott. *The Call of Earth*. New York: TOR, 1995.

_____. *Ender's Game*. New York: TOR, 1994.

_____. *How to Write Science Fiction and Fantasy*. Cincinnati: Writer's Digest, 1990.

_____. *Lost Boys*. New York: Harper, 1993.

_____. *The Memory of Earth*. New York: TOR, 1995.

_____. *Prentice Alvin*. New York: TOR, 1989.

_____. *Red Prophet*. New York: TOR, 1992.

_____. *Seventh Son*. New York: TOR, 1993.

_____. *The Ships of Earth*. New York: TOR, 1995.

_____. *Speaker for the Dead*. New York: TOR, 1994.

_____. *Xenocide*. New York: TOR, 1992.

Cherryh, C. J. *Chanur's Homecoming*. New York: DAW, 1991.

_____. *Chanur's Legacy*. New York: DAW, 1993.

_____. *Chanur's Venture*. New York: DAW, 1987.

_____. *The Cuckoo's Egg*. New York: DAW, 1985.

_____. *Downbelow Station*. New York: DAW, 1981.

_____. *The Faded Sun: Kesrith*. New York: DAW, 1978.

_____. *The Faded Sun: Kutath*. New York: DAW, 1980.

_____. *The Faded Sun: Shon'jir*. New York: DAW, 1979.

_____. *The Kif Strike Back*. New York: DAW, 1991.

_____. *The Pride of Chanur*. New York: DAW, 1982.

Chetwin, Grace. *Collidescope*. New York: Bradbury, 1990.

Christopher, John. *The City of Gold and Lead*. New York: Collier, 1988.

_____. *The Pool of Fire*. New York: Collier, 1988.

_____. *When the Tripods Came*. New York: Collier, 1988.

_____. *The White Mountains*. New York: Collier, 1988.

Clarke, Arthur C. *2001: A Space Odyssey*. New York: NAL, 1993.

_____. *2010: Odyssey Two*. New York: Ballantine, 1984.

_____. *2061: Odyssey Three*. New York: Ballantine, 1989.

_____. *Childhood's End*. New York: Ballantine, 1987.

_____. *Garden of Rama*. New York: Bantam, 1992.

_____. *Rama II*. New York: Bantam, 1990.

_____. *Rendezvous with Rama*. New York: Bantam, 1990.

Clute, John, and Peter Nicholls, eds. *The Encyclopedia of Science Fiction*. New York: St. Martin's, 1993.

Crispin, A. C. *Starbridge*. New York: Ace, 1989.

Crispin, A. C., and Deborah A Marshall. *Serpent's Gift*. New York: Ace, 1992.

Crispin, A. C., and Jannean Elliott. *Shadow World*. New York: Ace, 1991.

Crispin, A. C., and Kathleen O'Malley. *Silent Songs*. New York: Ace, 1994.

Dickinson, Peter. *Eva*. New York: Dell, 1990.

Dickson, Gordon R. *Soldier, Ask Not*. New York: TOR, 1993.

Ellison, Harlan. *Dangerous Visions*. New York: New American, 1975.

Farmer, Nancy. *The Ear, the Eye and the Arm*. New York: Orchard, 1994.

Frank, Pat. *Alas, Babylon*. New York: Harper, 1993.

Gibson, William. *Neuromancer*. New York: Ace, 1994.

Gillespie, John T., ed. *Best Books for Junior High Readers*. New Providence: Bowker, 1991.

Gould, Steven C. *Jumper*. New York: TOR, 1993.

Gunn, James E. *Alternate Worlds: The Illustrated History of Science Fiction*. Englewood Cliffs: Prentice, 1975.

Harrison, Harry. *Make Room! Make Room!*. New York: Bantam, 1994.

Heinlein, Robert A. *Citizen of the Galaxy*. New York: Ballantine, 1987.

_____. *Have Spacesuit, Will Travel*. New York: Ballantine, 1985.

_____. *Star Beast*. New York: Ballantine, 1991.

_____. *Starship Troopers*. New York: Ace, 1987.

_____. *Stranger in a Strange Land*. New York: Ace, 1991.

_____. *Tunnel in the Sky*. New York: Macmillan, 1988.

Henderson, Zena. *The People: No Different Flesh*. New York: Avon, 1968.

_____. *Pilgrimage: The Book of the People*. New York: Avon, 1980.

Herbert, Frank. *Chapterhouse: Dune*. New York: Ace, 1987.

_____. *Children of Dune*. New York: Ace, 1987.

_____. *Dune*. New York: Ace, 1990.

_____. *Dune Messiah*. New York: Ace, 1987.

_____. *God Emperor of Dune*. New York: Ace, 1987.

_____. *Heretics of Dune*. New York: Ace, 1987.

Hughes, Monica. *The Crystal Drop*. New York: Simon, 1993.

Immell, Myra, General Editor. *The Young Adult Reader's Adviser*. Volume 1. The Best in Literature and Language Arts, Mathematics and Computer Science. New Providence: Bowker, 1992.

Jacobs, Paul. *Born into the Light*. New York: Scholastic, 1988.

Jones, Patrick. *Connecting Young Adults and Libraries: A How-to-Do-It Manual*. (How-To-Do-It Manuals for Libraries, Number 19. Series Editor: Bill Katz). New York: Neal-Schuman, 1992.

Kagan, Janet. *Mirabile*. New York: TOR, 1992.

_____. *Uhura's Song*. New York: Pocket, 1987.

Lawrence, Louise. *Keeper of the Universe*. New York: Clarion, 1993.

Le Guin, Ursula K. *The Dispossessed*. New York: Gollancz, 1991.

_____. *The Farthest Shore*. New York: Atheneum, 1972.

_____. *The Left Hand of Darkness*. New York: Ace, 1969.

_____. *Tehanu: The Last Book of Earthsea*. New York: Bantam, 1991.

_____. *The Tombs of Atuan*. New York: Bantam, 1975.

_____. *The Wizard of Earthsea*. New York: Bantam, 1984.

Le Guin, Ursula K., and Brian Attebery. *The Norton Book of Science Fiction: North American Science Fiction 1960–1990*. (Karen Joy Fowler, Consultant). New York: Norton, 1993.

Lethem, Jonathan. *Gun, with Occasional Music*. New York: Harcourt, 1994.

Lindholm, Megan. *Alien Earth*. New York: Bantam, 1992.

Lowry, Lois. *The Giver*. New York: Dell, 1994.

McCaffrey, Anne. *All the Weyrs of Pern*. New York: Ballantine, 1991.

_____. *The Chronicles of Pern: First Fall*. New York: Ballantine, 1993.

_____. *Crisis on Doona*. New York: Ace, 1992.

_____. *Damia*. New York: Ace, 1993.

_____. *Damia's Children*. New York: Ace, 1994.

_____. *Decision at Doona*. New York: Ballantine, 1987.

_____. *Dinosaur Planet*. New York: Ballantine, 1984.

_____. *Dinosaur Planet Survivors*. New York: Ballantine, 1984.

_____. *Dragondrums*. New York: Bantam, 1980.

_____. *Dragonflight*. New York: Ballantine, 1986.

_____. *Dragonquest*. New York: Ballantine, 1986.

_____. *Dragonsdawn*. New York: Ballantine, 1989.

_____. *Dragonsinger*. New York: Bantam, 1983.

_____. *Dragonsong*. New York: Bantam, 1986.

_____. *Lyon's Pride*. New York: Ace, 1994.

_____. *Moreta, Dragonlady of Pern*. New York: Ballantine, 1984.

_____. *Pegasus in Flight*. New York: Ballantine, 1991.

_____. *Renegades of Pern*. New York: Ballantine, 1990.

_____. *The Rowan*. New York: Ace, 1991.

_____. *The Ship Who Sang*. New York: Ballantine, 1985.

_____. *The White Dragon*. New York: Ballantine, 1986.

McCaffrey, Anne, and Jody Lynn Nye. *The Death of Sleep*. New York: Baen, 1990.

_____. *The Ship Who Won*. New York: Baen, 1994.

_____. *Treaty at Doona*. New York: Ace, 1994.

McCaffrey, Anne, and Elizabeth Moon. *Generation Warriors*. New York: Baen, 1991.

_____. *Sassinak*. New York: Baen, 1990.

McCaffrey, Anne, and S. M. Sterling. *The City Who Fought*. New York: Baen, 1994.

McCaffrey, Anne, and Margaret Ball. *Partnership*. New York: Baen, 1992.

McCaffrey, Anne, and Elizabeth A. Scarborough. *Power Lines*. New York: Ballantine, 1994.

_____. *Powers That Be*. New York: Ballantine, 1993.

McCaffrey, Anne, and Mercedes Lackey. *The Ship Who Searched*. New York: Baen, 1992.

McIntyre, Vonda N. *Dreamsnake*. New York: Dell, 1986.

Miller, Walter M. *A Canticle for Leibowitz*. New York: Harper, 1986.

Moon, Elizabeth. *Hunting Party*. New York: Baen, 1993.

_____. *Sporting Chance*. New York: Baen, 1994.

Norton, Andre. *Brother to Shadows*. New York: Avon, 1994.

_____. *Catseye*. New York: Ace, 1961. [Out of Print.]

Norton, Andre, and P. M. Griffin. *Firehand*. New York: TOR, 1994.

_____. *Redline the Stars*. New York: TOR, 1994.

_____. *Time Traders*. New York: Ace, 1958.

_____. *Witch World*. New York: Ace, 1986.

O'Brien, Robert C. *Z for Zachariah*. New York: Collier, 1987.

Oppel, Kenneth. *Dead Water Zone*. New York: Little, 1993.

Orwell, George. *1984*. New York: Harcourt, 1949.

Pohl, Frederick. *Space Merchants*. New York: Ballantine, 1953.

Robinson, Kim Stanley. *Blue Mars*. Forthcoming.

_____. *Green Mars*. New York: Bantam, 1994.

_____. *Red Mars*. New York: Bantam, 1993.

Rosenberg, Betty, and Diana Tixier Herald. *Genreflecting: A Guide to Reading Interests in Genre Fiction*. 3rd Edition. Englewood: Libraries

Unlimited, 1991.

Rubinstein, Gillian. *Skymaze*. New York: Pocket, 1993.

_____. *Space Demons*. New York: Pocket, 1989.

Sader, Marion, series editor. *The Reader's Adviser*. 14th Edition. Volume 1. The Best in Reference Works, British Literature, and American Literature. New Providence: Bowker, 1994.

Sargent, Pamela. *Earthseed*. New York: Harper, 1983. [Out of Print.]

Shippey, Tom, ed. *The Oxford Book of Science Fiction Stories*. New York: Oxford UP, 1992.

Shute, Neville. *On the Beach*. New York: Ballantine, 1983.

Silverberg, Robert. *Project Pendulum*. New York: Bantam, 1989.

Sleator, William. *House of Stairs*. New York: Puffin, 1991.

_____. *Interstellar Pig*. New York: Bantam, 1986.

_____. *Others See Us*. New York: Dutton, 1993.

_____. *Singularity*. New York: Bantam, 1986.

_____. *Strange Attractors*. New York: Puffin, 1991.

Stevermer, Caroline. *River Rats*. New York: Harcourt, 1992.

Tepper, Sheri. *The Gate to Women's Country*. New York: Bantam, 1989.

_____. *Grass*. New York: Bantam, 1990.

Turtledove, Harry. *The Case of the Toxic Spell Dump*. New York: Baen, 1993.

_____. *Worldwar: In the Balance*. New York: Ballantine, 1993.

Van Vogt, A. E. *Slan*. New York: Garland, 1975.

_____. *The Weapon Shops of Isher*. New York: Ace, 1951.

Vinge, Joan D. *Catspaw*. New York: Warner, 1989.

_____. *Psion*. New York: Dell, 1985.

_____. *The Snow Queen*. New York: Warner, 1989.

_____. *The Summer Queen*. New York: Warner, 1992.

_____. *World's End*. New York: TOR, 1993.

Wells, H. G. *Time Machine*. New York: TOR, 1992.

_____. *War of the Worlds*. New York: TOR, 1993.

Willis, Connie. *Doomsday Book*. New York: Bantam, 1993.

Wyndham, John. *Day of the Triffids*. New York: Ballantine, 1985.

Zahn, Timothy. *Dark Force Rising*. New York: Bantam, 1993.

_____. *Heir to the Empire*. New York: Bantam, 1991.

_____. *The Last Command*. New York: Bantam, 1994.

CHAPTER
SIXTEEN

Alternative Meanings Through the World of Virtual Reality

Marlyn Kemper Littman

I magine sharing visual and auditory perceptive space with a dolphin in a virtual community, building a virtual city model with three dimensional (3-D) objects and images from around the globe, learning about geometric connections in a Post Euclidean walk-about, or participating in virtual interactive games.[1] These are but a few of the many new worlds of meaning already available to young adults through virtual reality or VR.[2]

Virtual reality is described as a technological revolution equivalent to the invention of movable type and the printing press. Remarkable improvements in the capabilities of computer systems, innovations in computer communications networks facilitating worldwide information transmission, and renewed interest in developing friendly user-machine interfaces are contributing to the excitement about emerging VR systems and applications.

VR is sparking widespread enthusiasm and debate in fields that include education, librarianship, entertainment, medicine, architecture, science, and the military. However, as noted by Durlach and Mavor (4), promises associated with the implementation of this powerful new medium are far outdistancing its current capabilities. Few people have, in fact worn instrumented gloves, put on VR goggles, and explored a virtual environment.

VR is a multidisciplinary field incorporating insights,

concepts, principles, and techniques from communications, computer science, engineering, physics, computer graphics, learning theory, music, and the performing arts. The creation of VR environments is complex. Benefits and limitations associated with VR enabling technologies, applications, devices, standards, and user interfaces are currently being examined.

The development of virtual worlds leads to questions such as the following:

- What is the meaning of virtual reality?
- What constitutes a virtual environment?
- What are potential harmful effects associated with the use of such VR devices as instrumented gloves, 3-D goggles, and head-mounted display (HMD) units?
- Will copyright be the major mechanism for maintaining intellectual property rights in VR applications?
- Can VR applications fulfill individual expectations and institutional requirements?
- Will VR implementations in the school and library be financially feasible?
- How will censorship at the local levels affect the use of VR in the school and library?
- Will walking, spinning, running, jumping, and/or flying through VR presentations contribute to meaningful learning experiences?
- Will displays of networked VR applications be reliable in distributed environments?

Most importantly here, will VR contribute significantly to the intellectual, social, moral, and aesthetic lives of young people in a technological society?

WHAT IS VIRTUAL REALITY?

There is no universally accepted definition of virtual reality. Various terms are used in the scholarly literature and popular press to describe the concept. VR is a catchword for everything from visually coupled systems, desktop virtual reality, artificial reality, and synthetic environments to artificial environments, information design, telepresence, and cyberspace. Virtual reality is also used to describe virtual worlds, microworlds, a "cartoon world you can get into," 21st century theater, and "anything that isn't real, but does a good job of faking it" (Larijani ix; Wodaski xix).

According to Machover and Tice (15–16), VR refers to an immersive, multisensory, interactive experience generated by a computer. Virtual reality is characterized by "the illusion of participation *in* a synthetic environment rather than external observation *of* such an environment" (Gigante 1993a, 3).

The major goal of VR is to induce a real world sensation by placing an individual in a virtual, or simulated, world. This process can be accomplished through the development of a synthetic, fully immersive setting in which a young adult can interact with computer generated objects as well as artificial or actual persons (Kalawsky 1993b, 2–3). A virtual environment can be an abstract form of an actual event or a computer generated representation of an actual situation. Through viewing stereoscopic images, listening to binaural sound, and manipulating objects in a three-dimensional computer generated world in real-time, a young adult can "step through the barrier of the computer screen" to experience new realities (Pimentel and Teixeira 67; Gradecki 7–9).

VR and multimedia applications are based on the integration of multiple media such as audio, text, video, still images, and full-motion video. VR is referred to as the ultimate expression of multimedia. As Pimentel and Teixeira point out, the main distinction between VR and multimedia is "the creation of environments versus the juxtaposition of existing media" (10). With a multimedia application, a young adult can use a PC to read an encyclopedia article about landing on the moon on half of the computer screen while watching a narrated video of the event on the other half of the screen. With a VR application, a young adult using a computer and appropriate VR gear can fly a virtual spaceship to the moon with Neil Armstrong and climb inside geological formations.

The quality of the VR experience is extremely important (Gradecki 4). The virtual experience must be believable in order to stimulate productivity and creativity.

VR ORIGINS

There is often a time differential between the initial exploration of a new technology and its general implementation. The fax machine was developed by Scottish clockmaker Alexander Bain in 1843 but took more than a century to gain acceptance. The technical foundations for the Internet were built in 1969 but did not achieve widespread popularity until the 1990s. VR is a new field but many of the underlying concepts have been explored over the past forty years. We are only now realizing the power of enabling technologies in facilitating the VR experience.

In 1956, cinematographer Morton Heilig created a simulator known as Sensorama (Gigante 1993a, 6). Sensorama generated city smells, wind sensation, and vibration as a participant sat on a motorcycle and went on a simulated ride through Manhattan (Kalawsky 1993b, 19). Heilig's Sensorama had all the features of a VR system except that the route was fixed and the experience was not an interactive one (Gigante 1993a, 6).

Computer graphics pioneer Ivan Sutherland holds the distinction of being called the originator of modern-day virtual reality (5). Sutherland first proposed the use of stereographic head-mounted displays in 1968 and pioneered techniques for using computers to represent 2-D and 3-D images (Pimentel and Teixeira 32).

Myron Krueger used the term "artificial realities" to describe his experiments combining video systems and computers (Kalawsky 1993b, 25; Pimentel and Teixeira, 37). Krueger developed "a computer-controlled responsive environment" called Videoplace at the University of Connecticut in the mid 1970s (Jacobson 13; Shneiderman 224). He also created a desktop version of this environment called Videodesk. These installations introduced an animated creature called CRITTER and enabled participants to see themselves in projected images on a screen (Kalawsky 1993b, 25; Shneiderman 224).

Artist Vincent John Vincent and computer programmer Francis MacDougall developed the Mandala Virtual Reality System in the 1980s (Jacobson 31–32; Shneiderman 224). This system allowed individuals to make music, play, create visual art, and communicate in a computer-based environment.

Technical components underlying VR applications such as image generators and tracking devices originated in digital flight simulators that came into use for pilot training during the 1970s (Gigante 1993a, 5). A general telepresence device and a multisensory personal simulator were developed as part of NASA's VIEW (Virtual Interactive Environment Workstation) project in the 1980s (6–7).

Jaron Lanier, one of the founders of VPL Research, Inc., is credited with coining the expression "virtual reality" (Pimentel and Teixeira xv). Lanier used the term to distinguish between immersive environments he created and traditional computer simulations. Another founder of VPL Research, Inc., Thomas Zimmerman worked with Lanier in developing the popular VPL DataGlove (Jacobson 6–7).

VR initially expressed the idea of human presence in a computer generated space. During the 1980s, VR became associated with the settings of various computer and video games (Delaney 40–44). Although not VR in a strict sense, popular monitor-bound CD-ROM adventures such as *Myst* and *Seventh Guest* feature 3-D landscapes that can be explored.

VR prototypes developed in the 1980s, such as MIT Media Lab's *Aspen Movie Map* and Bank Street College of Education's *Palenque* project, were early hypertext systems produced for instructional use (Nielsen 68; Hamit 98). As with VR applications, "hypertext is well suited for open learning applications where the student is allowed freedom of action and encouraged to take the initiative" (Nielsen 68).

The word "cyberspace" was coined by science fiction author William Gibson in his 1985 novel *Neuromancer* (Pimentel and Teixeira xiii). The movie, *Lawnmower Man*, introduced the concept of virtual reality to the public in 1992 (Kalawsky 1993b, 346).

VR AND WAYS OF KNOWING

VR offers the potential to escape the actual world and visit mythical domains, unexplored territories, science fiction realms, and cartoonlands. Any topic or situation imaginable can be examined in a VR setting. In a virtual environment, a student pilot could fly at Kitty Hawk with the Wright Brothers; an English high school major could discover the art of poetry by writing "Ode to a Grecian Urn" with poet John Keats; a ninth grader could learn about exploration by helping Christopher Columbus steer the Santa Maria in the search for the New World; and a high school senior could perform the lead in a production of *Romeo and Juliet* staged in England at the Globe Theater during William Shakespeare's lifetime.

Predictions can be made that, with the maturation of VR technologies, traditional paths to knowledge will be turned upside down and inside out, and the typical paradigm of teacher/student interaction will be reengineered. With the incorporation of VR applications into the curriculum, educators will be able to diversify their teaching strategies to help young adults learn in accordance with their specific strengths. Their instructional roles in the learning process as facilitators and change agents will be enhanced.

With the deployment of VR applications in the classroom, young adults will learn subjects ranging from archaeology and history to physics and calculus more effectively. A school site will become an arena for virtual communication where all types of learning and knowing are possible. No longer bound by time or place, students will interact in virtual educational communities and experience new knowledge domains with peers, instructors, and experts around the globe.

A RATIONALE FOR VR IMPLEMENTATION IN THE SCHOOL ENVIRONMENT

Traditional education is based on knowledge acquisition in the classroom. Effective instruction depends on creating and implementing a curricular program that is responsive to the sensitivities and needs of individual learners. According to Bunderson and Inouye (285–286), factors contributing to poor student performance include overcrowded classrooms, a shortage of experienced teachers, limited opportunities for identifying resources that have the potential to provide learning opportunities, and insufficient time for monitoring and advising students on their progress.

As a consequence, computer technology is emerging as a key component in the teaching/learning process (287). Interest is at an all time high in developing strategies and techniques for incorporating computer technology into the classroom to maximize learner productivity, increase student academic and intellectual achievement, support lesson development, and facilitate teacher training.

VR is a promising intellectual tool for educational enrichment. VR educational applications designed for young adults can support different learning styles and reach multiple senses, thereby leading to the acquisition of specific academic competencies and job-related skills. The structure, content, and objectives of VR course modules and directions for accomplishing learning activities can be adapted to individual needs, thereby allowing young adults to move ahead into new material based on their temperaments, abilities, and preferences. In addition to supporting consistent quality course delivery and classroom programming, VR applications can also help at-risk adolescents improve their academic performance and attitudes toward learning.

THE VR CYCLE

A virtual environment incorporates auditory, tactile, visual, and olfactory cues; acoustic, atmospheric, and color impressions; and real-time graphics into a model of reality that communicates with the human senses. Through the use of appropriate tools and software, the move into this simulated environment is relatively easy (Kalawsky 1993b, 12–13). There are many avenues of entrance.

Imagine a high school senior in a media center putting on virtual gear such as a DataGlove and head-mounted display (HMD) unit to experience a virtual tour of Jerusalem in a computer generated simulation that features 3-D walk-throughs, fly-bys, animations, sound effects, music, and full-motion videos. The cycle begins when this student visits the Dome of the Rock, Al Aqsa Mosque, and the Church of the Holy Sepulchre in the Old City; observes religious services at the Western Wall; and then proceeds to the Knesset to participate in a political debate with Yitzhak Rabin on the peace process in the Middle East.

By using the DataGlove, the high school senior squeezes, grasps, and interacts with such objects or 3-D shapes as a rotating pyramid, a speaking sphinx, and a flying camel. Through the HMD, this student hears sounds such as a thump if a virtual object is dropped; smells smoke if a virtual object catches fire; and see images of his/her hand in the virtual environment that corresponds to an actual hand position (Hayward 18–20).

The high school senior becomes immersed in a virtual environment with the capability to control actions from within. This student can explore new horizons and move around freely by manipulating information in a computer just as he/she would manipulate objects in the actual environment (Hamit 5).

VR in distributed computer simulated environments is made possible through network services that link remote locations in real-time (Pimentel and Blau 60–63). With interfaces to the information superhighway, distance learning or teleducation programs could be created that support multimedia conferencing and enable learners to participate in simulated group problem solving activities using information from a variety of sources in formats that include text, graphics, audio, and video in virtual global classrooms.

In a virtual global classroom environment, a group of high school seniors in government classes in Chicago, Los Angeles, and Miami could take joint virtual field trips to New York City, London, Warsaw, Budapest, Singapore, and Stockholm to gain a cross cultural perspective on urban violence and develop scenarios, under the direction of a virtual teacher, for dealing with street crime. Young adults interested in law could explore issues related to gender bias and affirmative action in virtual courtroom settings. Adolescents in the inner city could participate in virtual beach picnics and virtual mountain climbing expeditions.

In a traditional classroom, control of the learning situation remains with the teacher (Bunderson and Inouye 309–312). In a traditional group setting, only one person can talk at a time. VR enables young adults to control the learning situation and move at their own pace. VR also supports group interaction and real-time collaboration. VR as an instructional medium can be motivating, educationally productive, and enjoyable. No longer is the young adult on the outside "looking in" as an observer (Mallen 265–268). With VR, the young adult becomes absorbed by another reality and immersed in the learning activity.

ISSUES RELATED TO VR DEPLOYMENT FOR YOUNG ADULTS

The accelerating popularity of VR techniques in games and videos generates concerns about how VR applications will be presented in the classroom. As we have already seen, VR has the potential to advance significantly the depth of the learning experience and a student's ability to control knowledge. For young adults, the process of learning and understanding information in a virtual environment involves physically, emotionally, visually, rationally, and imaginatively participating in simulated spontaneous and organized events (Pimentel and Teixeira 6–8).

Any new technology carries with it positive and negative potential. For example, nuclear technology creates the capacity for both energy independence and the destruction of civilization. Genetic engineering offers new opportunities for saving lives but also involves destructive risks. There is always the danger that a new technology will be implemented before its ethical implications have been explored. During World War II, the atomic bomb was dropped before anybody had a chance to consider the consequences of the action. The ability to prolong life by artificial means generates unresolved questions regarding the quality and quantity of life and the criteria by which one patient will be chosen over another to receive the benefit of certain medical techniques.

A fully immersive VR application is designed to make you feel as if you exist totally in a virtual world apart from a physical reality. We are concerned that violence in two dimensions can produce destructive behavior. What happens if violence is internalized in a behavioral situation virtually indistinguishable from reality? What will be the impact on an adolescent who instead of merely viewing an Arnold Schwarzenegger film such as *The Terminator* becomes the terminator in a VR simulation? What are the outcomes if VR game playing becomes a substitute for real life interaction? Consider the effect of a war simulation in which a young adult spends hours in a virtual battle bombing and shooting every virtual opponent in sight. Will these experiences lead to desensitization to the value of human life and anesthetize adolescents to disturbing consequences of actual shotgun blasts and serial killings? How will young adults make the distinction between fantasy and reality?

What is the emotional effect of experiencing simulations of a virtual plane crash, a virtual shark attack, a virtual forest fire, a virtual earthquake, or a virtual hurricane? If there is concern with what happens to the psyche of young adults by observing trauma, how do we protect them from the effects of virtually experiencing the trauma?

Imagine developing a virtual psychodrama demonstrating how people could have been moved by David Koresh in Waco, Texas or Jim Jones in Jonestown, Guyana, that causes a young adult to suffer an emotional breakdown. What happens if an educator implements a virtual demonstration on how it feels to be a drug user to an adolescent and subsequently induces a psychotic state? If a teacher places a young adult into a virtual situation in order to demonstrate how certain results were produced, the teacher must be trained to anticipate and deal with the consequences of that reality.

Any educational technique can be exploited for propaganda and ideological control. If this can be done with a book, imagine the potential dangers associated with the use of VR to introduce young adults to only one point of view on issues such as civil rights, poverty, and race relations.

What would happen if a young adult studies abortion through a VR presentation in which he/she becomes a fetus undergoing planned termination of a pregnancy? Consider the consequences if a course on the Holocaust is created with a VR demonstration in which the student becomes Hitler or a victim of a gas chamber. Think of the results of analyzing the situation in Rwanda with a VR application in which the student becomes a Hutu soldier stealing food, intimidating refugees, and slaughtering Tutsis during Rwanda's civil war. How would a VR simulation in which a student becomes Fidel Castro affect a student's perception of the massive exodus of Cuban refugees from the island?

How will young adults critically distinguish between accuracy and authenticity and bigotry, bias, and intolerance in a VR presentation? How will they know if the VR presentation is balanced, accurate, unbiased, impartial, and objective?

As noted by Schmitt (85–87), VR capabilities enable you to get inside information and ideas in ways not previously possible. In a totally immersive VR interactive experience, "the computer disappears and you become the ghost in the machine" (Pimentel and Teixeira 7).

VR presents an unexplored universe. The projected impact of VR is unknown and unpredictable. What kinds of reinforcement will students need for dealing effectively with a virtual application? What kinds of training and preparation will aid educators and librarians in monitoring and optimizing students' virtual experiences? Additional research is required to understand ways in which adolescents interact with VR environments, the effect of these environments on their performance, and types of problems that could occur from extensive VR use (Greenhouse and Julian 1994).

As educators and librarians, we have the ethical responsibility for determining the role VR will play in instructing and informing present and future generations of young adults. VR can lead to a revolution in teaching, learning, and research. An understanding of the capabilities, advantages, limitations, and dangers of VR will enhance our ability to handle challenges involved in the development and widespread use of VR applications.

ENABLING COMPONENTS FOR A VIRTUAL WORLD

According to Pimentel and Teixeira, "VR is a tool for enabling the user's immersion into a sensory-rich interactive experience" (66). This immersion is accomplished through a VR system that incorporates sensors or effectors, a reality engine or computer system, an application, and a VR database (Ellis 17–20; Latta and Oberg 23–26). A VR system enables a participant to move through a barrier of a computer screen and interact or travel in a virtual world (Pimentel and Teixeira 17–18).

Input and output sensors or effectors are appliances worn on or near the body to create a sense of presence in the virtual world (Latta and Oberg 23–26). Popular devices include the following:

- Instrumented glove such as the VPL DataGlove for controlling the virtual environment, manipulating virtual objects, and providing tactile simulation and force feedback (Gigante 1993b, 20).
- Wired clothing such as a bodysuit for the entire body (Larijani 44–45).
- Head-mounted display units for creating a sense of presence in the virtual setting.
- A VR vest such as the Interactor developed by Aura Systems Inc. in Cupertino, California (*Miami Herald* 6b). The Interactor vest vibrates to the sounds of television programs, radio, recorded music and video games and lets the user feel every shout, kick, punch, shot, or explosion.

The core of the VR system is the reality engine or computer system and associated external peripherals such as sound synthesizing equipment for generating binaural sound (Pimentel and Teixeira 67). The reality engine integrates feedback from sensors in a computer generated simulation to provide immersive experiences resembling those in an actual physical environment (Ellis 17–20; Pimentel and Teixeira 66–67).

As noted by Pimentel and Teixeira (67), a VR application is a software product delineating the structure, architecture, and dynamics of interaction between the participant and objects in the virtual world. For example, the application defines if the virtual setting is for flying spaceships or designing virtual homes, how actual or animated characters are controlled, and whether windows are open or shut.

The VR database includes information on such physical attributes of virtual objects as their color and shape. This information is processed by the application or software product to construct the virtual environment (67). Without VR objects, the virtual world would be stationary. Tracing technology is used to determine a VR object's orientation and position.

A VR system should facilitate delivery of high resolution,

well focused images to end users and the creation of scenes that provide the illusion of being in another location (Kalawsky 1993b, 77–78). Imagine using "a special pair of binoculars" so that "no matter where you look, the correct view of the virtual world is displayed" (Pimentel and Teixeira, 67).

While VR systems are becoming more sophisticated, the complexity of application development and limitations associated with the hardware infrastructure have restricted their current functionality. Problems associated with VR implementations such as fuzzy images, poor graphics, and time lags between user movement and system response time ruin the feeling of immersion. Head-mounted display units are cumbersome and uncomfortable. Participants using head gear sometimes suffer from lack of initiative, chronic fatigue, nausea, drowsiness, and/or irritability when they interact with a virtual world for an extended period of time (Greenhouse and Julian 1994). Although the VR industry is small, new products continue to emerge and the potential for VR development is unlimited.

WHAT ARE THE COSTS?

The price of a VR system varies with the quality of the installation (Pimentel and Teixeira 93–96). Research-based VR systems used inside aerospace facilities, commercial laboratories, and giant corporations for creating fully immersive experiences can cost millions of dollars. Desktop VR systems intended for industrial design and manufacturing applications such as the Sun Virtual Holographic Workstation developed by Sun Microsystems begin at $46,000. Homemade or "garage VR systems" developed by resourceful VR enthusiasts seeking to explore virtual worlds at an extremely fundamental and rudimentary level can start at $2,500 (Jacobson 33).

The price of VR software toolkits for creating customized immersive virtual worlds varies with the sophistication of the package. According to Pimentel and Teixeira (255–256), the following toolkits are available:[3]

- PROvision from Division, Ltd. PROvision is a C-language toolkit that costs between $50,000 and $200,000 depending on options selected. These options include a VPL Data-Glove and a stereo HMD. PROvision requires an Intel i860 customized computer platform.

- Microcosm from VPL Research, Inc. Featuring a DataGlove and an EyePhone and the accompanying software to animate a virtual world on a Macintosh platform, Microcosm sells for $75,000.
- WorldToolKit from Sense8 Corp. The WorldToolKit includes a C library of functions supporting interfaces to common VR devices and costs between $3,500 and $12,000. WorldToolKit operates on Sun and PC platforms.

Present-day VR components range in costs as well (Ribarsky et al. 10–12). As noted by Pimentel and Teixeira (256–260), the price of various devices for building virtual worlds is as follows:[4]

- The DataGlove from VPL Research, Inc. sells for $8,800.
- The HRX head-mounted display is available for $49,000.
- The Dexterous Hand Master from EXOS Inc. costs $15,000.
- A laser-based optical tracking system from Spatial Positioning Systems, Inc. is priced in the range of $50,000 to $70,000.

PLANNING FOR VR IN THE WORLD OF EDUCATION AND LIBRARIANSHIP

Presently, there is no clearcut solution for determining the ideal combination of VR tools, components, and software required to create cost-effective VR applications that can contribute to the enhancement of cognitive skills and scholarly achievement in the school and library. While the press is promoting future scenarios involving the use of top-of-the-line VR systems for simulating reality, present-day methods for creating an immersive interactive experience are costly, complex, and limited in terms of application and direct use.

What is our role as educators and information providers in the VR paradigm? How can we influence the planning and development of next generation VR systems and applications?

We should be aware of ongoing research associated with this dynamic and rapidly changing field. We cannot wait for vendors to promote VR packages that fail to satisfy requirements, specifications, and standards incorporated in our institutional missions, goals, and objectives. We should take a proactive role in identifying concepts, techniques, and approaches for designing effective VR products that objectively and impartially portray content, concepts, and issues explored in the school curriculum and associated readings. We should ensure that VR products purchased with public funds for library consumption are consistent with professional ethical guidelines as well.

We can acquire information from Internet FTP sites and participate in Internet USENET groups, forums, bulletin boards, and listservs to become familiar with recent VR developments and applications targeted for change.[5] A VR listserv specifically designed for educators and librarians can be established through joint participation of such organizations as the American Society for Information Science (ASIS), the American Library Association (ALA), Association of Library and Information Science Education (ALISE), and the Association for the Advancement of Computing in Education (AACE) to help educators and librarians share information, expertise, and skills.

Strategies and performance metrics for creating VR applications, assessing VR projects, and planning VR implementations can be determined during round table sessions at meetings of professional organizations and through electronic workshops on the Internet. Research on the implications of VR in the classroom and in the library can be presented at conferences sponsored by such professional groups as the Institute of Electrical and Electronics Engineers (IEEE) and the Association for Computing Machinery (ACM); in electronic deliberations and publications on the Internet; and in articles in professional and popular journals. The options are diverse and call for a new spirit of adventure in tackling a domain that on the surface appears to be intimidating.

THE VR INTERFACE

Virtual reality has been called "an advanced human-computer interface that simulates a realistic environment and allows participants to interact with it" (Latta and Oberg 23). The use of virtual objects or graphic representations to create virtual environments and virtual gear as interface devices for accessing these environments is gaining popularity as a way of making computers more accessible or user friendly. Metaphors such as walk-about, fly-through, and run-through reflect the quality and creativity associated with immersion in a virtual world and are expected to replace the standard "office desktop" metaphor in use for more than twenty years (Chorafas 281–284).

Because they eliminate the need to memorize confusing command sequences, GUIs (Graphical User Interfaces) such as pictures, icons, windows, and pop-up and pull-down menus are popular HCI (human-computer interaction) interfaces in the present-day computing environment (Shneiderman 251-254). A GUI can be activated with one or two key strokes or the click of a mouse button. Advances in GUI interfaces are reflected in such popular multimedia products as Microsoft's *Encarta* and *The New Grolier Multimedia Encyclopedia*.

In contrast to a GUI, a VR interface can involve sound, sight, and touch and its associated sensations of weight, motion, and temperature (Pimentel and Teixeira, 104–106). For instance, a user equipped with a head-mounted display unit, DataSuit, and DataGlove would no longer click a mouse button but instead reach out directly to turn a virtual knob in a virtual environment in the same way that a real one is turned in the real world (Kalawsky 1993b, 187–195).

VR interface devices based on the use of present-day VR enabling technologies are cumbersome and awkward. Would an interface to a word processing program or spreadsheet justify strapping on a helmet, putting on wired gloves and clothing, and waving a VR wand? Two-dimensional tasks such as cataloging a new serial or checking in an overdue library book do not require this complexity.

However, VR interfaces could enhance our capabilities in dealing with problems in an increasingly sophisticated technological society and facilitate the presentation of information in innovative formats to educate and entertain (346). For example, instead of reading about the original Olympics held at Katakalon in Greece from a standard multimedia encyclopedia description of the topic, an adolescent with dyslexia or attention deficit disorder could put on appropriate VR gear and fly into a computer simulation of the original Olympic stadium, mix with the crowds, and compete in virtual athletic events.

A VR interface allows the user to move seamlessly through a virtual environment, thereby stimulating creative thinking and problem-solving in the process. Consider the impact of using VR interfaces for constructing innovative and meaningful learning experiences such as the following:

- Being in a scene with Tom Sawyer in a Mark Twain novel about Huckleberry Finn.
- Doing research in real-time at the Library of Congress with President Abraham Lincoln.
- Participating in a civil rights march with Martin Luther King in Selma, Alabama.
- Conducting the New York Philharmonic Orchestra with Leonard Bernstein.
- Singing arias with Luciano Pavarotti at the Acropolis in Athens.
- Sculpting *David* with Michelangelo.
- Painting *Guernica* with Picasso.
- Deep sea diving with Jacques Cousteau.

No single interface will be appropriate for all users and all situations. Rather than making GUIs obsolete, VR interfaces can serve as complementary mechanisms for achieving information access not possible with other methods. User information needs and task requirements will play critical roles in determining which HCI techniques are most efficient.

NETWORKING CONSIDERATIONS

The construction of networked virtual environments can trace its origins to military training and simulation programs. SimNet was created by the US Army and Defense Advanced Research Projects Agency (DARPA) in the early 1980s to teach tank, helicopter, and aircraft personnel tactical maneuvers (McCarty et al. 49, Hamit 228). Another VR networking simulation, NSPNET was developed at the Naval Postgraduate School in Monterey, California. NSPNET is a 3-D visual simulation that displays vehicle movement in the air or on the ground in a virtual environment that has such environmental effects as haze and fog. The VR environment poses an array of challenges in terms of design, application, and implementation. High performance computers with such features as large capacity storage systems and fast processors are needed to facilitate both standalone and networked VR applications. For networked VR applications, connectivity, interoperability, high transmission rates, and fast access times are indispensable. Designing a network to handle VR requirements is a complicated task.

General steps in the initial phase of planning for a VR network include:

• Determining network goals and objectives that are consistent with budgetary limitations.
• Conducting a feasibility study to identify user needs and current equipment that can be used on the new VR network.
• Analyzing traffic volumes and characteristics to determine system capacity and performance specifications.
• Indicating the geographic scope of the network.
• Prioritizing requirements for current and future networked VR applications.
• Designing network configurations to ensure that response time meets the needs of each VR application.
• Developing a timetable for network implementation.
• Delineating guidelines for network maintenance, management, operations, security, and user training.
• Evaluating the advantages and limitations of building the network in-house and outsourcing network design and development for vendor bid.

An important evolving technology, ATM (Asynchronous Transfer Mode) or cell relay has the capability to support tremendous throughput generated by networked VR applications. ATM's transport technology is based on the use of fixed size packets called cells and can be used in local and wide area environments (Minoli and Keinath 113–121). ATM is the mechanism underlying the development of gigabit networks as well. ATM provides sufficient bandwidth for applications such as the following:

- Distance learning.
- Imaging.
- Multimedia conferencing.
- Multimedia messaging.
- Desktop videoconferencing.

Called the most significant technical innovation to come out of standardization work on the Broadband Integrated Services Digital Network (BISDN), ATM is the technology of choice for emerging BISDN networks and next generation local area networks (LANs) (117). When fully operational, BISDN will enable universal communications between any two subscribers in any combination of media. As an example, BISDN eventually will support information access and exchange in multiple media from multiple sources among virtual communities of educators, librarians, attorneys, engineers, scientists, and clergy worldwide. BISDN also will expedite the distribution of educational, training, and entertainment materials to the library, school, home, hospital, museum, or office on demand.

As pointed out by Durlach and Mavor, in the future, communication networks will transform virtual environments into shared virtual worlds (6). With broadband networks in place, entering a VR environment will be a means of going to school, work, or the library.

STANDARDS

The Committee on Virtual Reality Research and Development was established by the National Research Council in 1992. According to the Committee, the federal government should explore opportunities to facilitate development of standards in the VR arena to ensure compatibility of software, hardware, and networking technology (Greenhouse and Julian, 1994). Standards are critical for supporting technological compatibility and the creation of distributed VR applications enabling multiple participants to interact in multiple modes in real-time virtual simulations. The development of VR regulations and guidelines by federal agencies in concert with industry and academia can benefit

VR users, vendors, and developers (Durlach and Mavor 8).

Compression is vital in VR applications at the communications and storage levels. A tremendous amount of data is produced by video, image, and audio signals leading to difficulties in real-time transmission in the virtual environment (Papathomas et al. 143–148). Through compression techniques, the amount of space required to store and reproduce a video or an image is reduced, thereby resulting in faster access times to standalone and networked computer generated virtual simulations (Luther 143–146). International standards for image and video compression are currently being developed by such organizations as the ITU (International Telecommunications Union, formerly the CCITT) and International Organization for Standardization (ISO) and by hardware and software vendors.

As noted by Luther (159–169), key standards under consideration include:

- JPEG. Developed jointly by ISO and ITU, JPEG (Joint Photographic Experts Group) compression is used for still video and images; but it is rather slow for full-motion video.
- ITU-T Recommendation H.261 (p*64). H.261 (p*64) coding and decoding methods work well with full color, real-time motion video applications.
- ISO MPEG-2 and MPEG-4. These newer MPEG Motion Video Compression Standards are designed to support full-motion video.
- DVI. The DVI (Digital Video Interactive) encoding compression standard is a propriety one that is based on the use of special hardware developed by IBM and Intel. Ultimedia, IBM's multimedia platform, uses DVI hardware for handling video.

The use of video and audio in VR application environments is time dependent and requires time ordered presentation (Little 175). Synchronization refers to the task of coordinating frame sequences. For example, suppose an individual takes a virtual tour through Ephesus and detours from the prearranged itinerary to stop at the world famous library. Through the synchronization process, VR segments can be played out in a random order, thereby supporting such spontaneous user initiated operations as random access and browsing and enhancing VR system functionality.

A standard interchange format will also play an important role in the expansion of the VR application market. There are several formats under consideration for multimedia that are also relevant to VR development.

According to Buford and Brennan (327–333) and McCarty et al. (49–52), these formats include:

- QuickTime Movie File (QMF) Format. QMF is a multimedia extension for Macintosh platforms.
- Open Media Framework Interchange (OMFI). Approved by the Interactive Media Association, OMFI deals with representing time-based media such as audio and video.
- ISO Multimedia and Hypermedia Information Encoding Expert Group (MHEG). MHEG supports interactive media and real-time transfer over networks.
- IEEE Distributed Information Simulation (DIS) Standard. The IEEE DIS standard supports message exchange among dissimilar systems in a distributed simulation environment.

APPLICATIONS IN A VIRTUAL WORLD

Imaginative and practical VR applications range from armchair tours of other galaxies to distance learning. VR applications have been inspired by computer controlled flight simulators, artificial intelligence, robotics, and computer graphics. Developments in broadband networks are expected to support global virtual communities interacting simultaneously in shared virtual worlds.

VR techniques enable users to experience firsthand the constraints of actual environments. For example, as noted by Delaney (44–48), the Hubble Space Telescope Mission Trainer developed at Johnson Space Center in Houston allows astronauts and flight controllers to explore movement in open space around a simulated shuttle. A virtual prototype built by Caterpillar Cab permits designers to test drive new bulldozers. The Tower Operating Training System (TOTS) created by the Federal

Aviation Administration provides instruction to air traffic controllers. Simulated street crime scenes are used in training police officers for work in the field. Through deployment of these simulation techniques, adolescents with coordination problems could learn how to ride virtual bicycles, play virtual tennis, run a virtual marathon, climb a virtual tree, and take part in virtual karate competitions.

Participants in a virtual world depend on cues in addition to the visual to prohibit the violation of real world environmental constraints. For instance, auditory signals and tactile feedback warn individuals when some action in the real world is about to occur (Kalawsky 1993b, 75–80). This type of feedback could be helpful in alerting young adults to the dangers of speeding and drunk driving.

EDUCATION

The Responsive Workbench is a virtual working environment enabling participants to collaborate on problem solving tasks corresponding to actual work situations in settings ranging from an architect's office to an operating room (Krueger and Broehlich, 12–14). In the operating room application, a young adult could use a DataGlove to remove and examine a beating heart, a kidney, or a liver and pick up a bone and look at its joints. Consider the advantages of one day using the Responsive Workbench as a guidance tool in helping high school seniors determine career paths and professions.

The potential of VR for creating imaginative virtual worlds where it is safe to experiment and explore ideas, situations, and emotions is reflected in the Coyote World Project developed by Brenda Laurel in association with Rachel Strickland and the Banff Center for the Arts (Pimentel and Teixeira, 155–159). Designed to introduce young people to a world of myth and magic, this project involves the creation of a virtual world based on Native American folk tales and characters such as the bear, coyote, quail, fox, and antelope. According to Pimentel and Teixeira, Laurel, author of *Computers as Theater* and editor of *The Art of Human-Computer Interface Design*, believes that a virtual world should be "user delightful" not merely user friendly or functional (155). For Laurel, "the theory behind the Coyote World Project is that if you put people in a virtual world with enough enticing possibilities and things to play with and things that play with them, then the technology bumps us up into a new kind of media experience" (157). Imagine the benefits associated with using the Coyote World Project to establish channels of communication with young adults suffering from parental abuse, traumatized by date rape, or contemplating suicide.

LIBRARIES

As noted by von Wahlde and Schiller (43), "virtual library" is a metaphor for a networked library or library without walls. The term applies to the vision of a next generation library in which users have real-time universal access to global electronic information resources. For example, Nova Southeastern University (NSU) is implementing an advanced fiber optic network linking the university's law, graduate, and undergraduate libraries to local, national, and international networks. This process will ultimately support a variety of information services including electronic access to bibliographic holdings, full text documents, online journals, and multimedia Electronic Classrooms (ECRs). Plans are underway to link the NSU High School Media Center, a component of the NSU complex, to this virtual library paradigm as well.

VR applications in a virtual library could enable a young adult to navigate through simulated shelves of classic fiction titles, select *Treasure Island*, by master storyteller Robert Louis Stevenson, and then go directly into the text to accompany Jim Hawkins in virtual adventures with hero-villain Long John Silver. Other VR enhancements could include the ability to conduct virtual tours in libraries worldwide, hold virtual workshops, and collaborate on the production of electronic texts.

Developed by Sense8 and the Institute for Simulation and Training at the University of Central Florida in 1992, the WorkRoom is a networked VR application created with DOS-based PCs (Pimentel and Blau 60–63). The WorkRoom represents one of the first applications of a collaborative design system based on immersive VR technologies and real-time 3-D sound and voice processing.

The WorkRoom is an example of a general purpose simulation enabling the interaction of multiple participants in a virtual world. In the WorkRoom environment, two individuals can collaborate on selecting building blocks for construction of a virtual building (64). Consider the prospects of using The WorkRoom in a virtual library environment to foster the collaborative design of library buildings, OPACs, and systems for tracking serials, lost books, and interlibrary loan requests.

MEDICINE

The field of medicine uses VR in teaching and research. Advances in visualization techniques enable teams of diagnosticians, surgeons and practitioners to collaborate in shared virtual examination rooms.

As Larijani (79–82) points out, medical professionals can interact with a virtual patient, a computer generated multidimensional image created from picture slides taken from various angles of a real person's body. Interns can be trained under the direction of a team of surgeons in performing high risk surgical procedures in virtual operating rooms. A neurologist may one day use a whole body DataSuit to restore an illusion of motor experience to an adolescent injured in an automobile accident or team sport such as football.

ENTERTAINMENT

Virtual games and adventures are available at Blockbuster arcades in Fort Lauderdale, Disney World's Pleasure Island, the Foxwoods Casino complex in Connecticut, and the Luxor Hotel in Las Vegas (Delaney 46). Virtus Corporation's *WalkThrough* program is used to develop sets for films such as *The Abyss* and *The Firm*.

PSYCHOLOGY

VR has potential application in the treatment of stress and phobias (Whalley 273). By creating virtual anxiety provoking situations, clinicians could help a patient learn to control symptoms such as head pain and neck pain. However, considerable care must be exercised to obtain informed consents prior to introducing patients to virtual reality treatment procedures. Virtual reality applications may "distort reality testing in those for whom it is already impaired and limit freedom of choice in those who do not understand their basic freedoms" (285). The inclusion of persons whose insight or judgment may be impaired in VR clinical research studies has the potential both of harming participants and triggering claims of malpractice and patient abuse.

MUSEUMS

New York's Guggenheim Museum featured an exhibit called "Virtual Reality: An Emerging Medium" in the fall of 1993. At the exhibit, Carnegie-Mellon University's Studio for Creative Inquiry showcased "The Networked Virtual Art Museum: The Temple of Horus." This display consisted of the lobby of a virtual museum with an exhibit of a restored Temple of Horus. Statues and hieroglyphics functioned as tour guides relating myths and rituals about Ancient Egypt (Whitehouse 8–11). In a virtual museum setting, high school students could view any painting in a collection as a 3-D representation; access relevant audio, video, and textual information on their topics of interest; talk to the artist; and test what they have learned by painting a virtual portrait.

ARCHITECTURE AND DESIGN

Kitchen design firms in Japan allow clients to walk through virtual kitchens and simulate their usage. Architects simulate and walk through buildings they design prior to beginning construction (Schmitt 85–86). Additional examples of VR design-oriented simulations include virtual golf courses, virtual racetracks, virtual offices, and virtual airports. Gifted high school seniors could use VR design-oriented simulations to create virtual homes, schools, and libraries.

SCIENCE

Work is under way in enabling scientists to visualize astrophysical phenomena in an immersive virtual environment at the Electronic Visualization Laboratory (EVL) at the University of Illinois (Goldman and Roy 12–14). The Cave Automated Virtual Environment (CAVE) virtual reality theater serves as the framework for developing a package called Worm, after wormhole, a hypothetical stellar object. Worm operates in an archive mode involving playback of data from a simulation run at an earlier time and stored to disk.

The real-time mode enables the investigator to control the simulation running live on a remote supercomputer. Consider the impact of using a package such as Worm for teaching high school students about the Milky Way, the moons of Jupiter and Neptune, quasars and interacting galaxies, black holes, and asteroids.

MUSIC

As noted by Sturman and Zeltzer (38), interest in direct natural manipulation interfaces has led to the development of a Data-Glove enabling a conductor to lead a synthetic orchestra. The position of the hand is captured by the DataGlove and interpreted through a function table to determine such musical expressions as "dolce" and "crescendo." These commands are combined to control playback of flat prerecorded MIDI scores and add expressive results. At the MIT Media Lab, composer Tod Machover conducts hyperinstruments with the use of an EXOS Dexterous Hand Master. Imagine students majoring in music exploring topics such as music composition and scoring with these applications.

VR APPLICATION ASSESSMENT

VR applications are characterized by the incorporation of multimedia sources that are used to enrich the appearance of virtual worlds (Papathomas et al. 139–140). At the core of the VR application environment is the computer system or reality engine containing a database of the required virtual world (Pimentel and Teixeira 65).

Creating VR environments is a complex undertaking. The range of possibilities is unlimited. Design decisions involve the selection of multiple media elements; graphics, sound, and animation tools; user interfaces; tracking devices; media input and output components such as video recorders, microphones, and CD-ROM players; hardware platforms; internetworking mechanisms such as bridges, routers, hubs, and gateways; and appropriate software.

Questions such as the following can serve as a guide in assessment of current and projected VR applications:

- Are the contents of the application clearly stated and objectively presented?
- Does the application include online help and instructions?
- Are elements of the application such as motion video, graphics, text, and animated images clearly displayed?
- Can audio cues be understood?
- Can the user interface accommodate individual learner skills and preferences?
- Is the program consistent with institutional guidelines and objectives?
- Will the application improve task performance?
- Can our hardware configuration support the implementation?
- What kinds of virtual gear are necessary to run the application?
- What are the total costs involved?
- What are expected benefits and limitations?
- What kind of staff training is needed prior to implementation?
- Is support provided by the application developer?
- Who are the other users in our discipline currently implementing or planning to implement the application?

CONCLUSION

The field of VR is changing rapidly, resulting in competing applications and pathways to progress. As a result, VR applications can be built with varied equipment and products. The enabling technologies and standards that facilitate the development of VR systems are complex and varied. The network infrastructure for supporting distributed VR applications is still evolving.

Concern with the performance of component VR technologies and devices and potential roadblocks and hurdles in VR implementation, while important, should not overshadow the potential significance of VR (Machover and Tice 15–16; Durlach and Mavor 8–9). Carefully designed VR applications can result in the development of new paradigms in fields such as librarianship, education, music, entertainment, and medicine that promote effective learning, instruction, and research; stimulate user involvement and control; and culminate in the acquisition, retention, use, and dissemination of new knowledge. Many young adults are eager to step into these VR worlds, and we must insure that they have the most positive life-enhancing experiences there.

NOTES

1. These were some of the possibilities at ACM SIGGRAPH 1994, the 21st Conference on Computer Graphics and Interactive Techniques, which focused on virtual reality (VR) as one of its major themes.
2. In this chapter, the terms virtual reality and VR are used interchangeably.
3. For information on VR products and companies see Pimentel and Teixeira (254–278). For additional information on toolkits mentioned in this chapter, contact the vendors at the following addresses:

Division Ltd.
Quarry Road
Chipping, Sodbury
Bristol, England BS17 6AX
(44) 454 324527

Sense8 Corp.
4000 Bridgeway, Suite 101
Sausalito, California 94965
(801) 531-0559

VPL Research, Inc.
950 Tower Lane, 14th Floor
Foster City, California 94004
(415) 312-0200

4. For additional information on these devices, contact the vendors at the following addresses:

EXOS Inc.
8 Blanchard Road
Burlington, Massachusetts 01803
(617) 229-2075

Spatial Positioning Systems, Inc.
Innovation Center
1800 Kraft Drive
Blacksburg, Virginia 24060
(703) 231-3145

5. For additional information on electronic resources in the VR field, see Gradecki (283–319).

WORKS CITED

Bolas, Mark T. "Human Factors in the Design of an Immersive Display." *IEEE Computer Graphics and Applications* 14 (January 1994): 55–59.

Buford, John, F. Koegel, and Rita Brennan. "Multimedia Interchange." *Multimedia Systems*. Ed. John F. Koegel Buford. Reading: Addison-Wesley, 1994. 323–340.

Bunderson, C. Victor, and Dillon K. Inouye. "The Evolution of Computer-Aided Educational Delivery Systems." *Instructional Delivery Systems*. Ed. Robert M. Gagne. Hillsdale: Lawrence Erlbaum, 1987. 283–318.

Chorafas, Dimitris N. *Intelligent Multimedia Databases: From Object Orientation and Fuzzy Engineering to Intentional Database Structures.* Englewood Cliffs: Prentice, 1994.

Delaney, Ben. "Virtual Reality Lands the Job." *New Media* 4 (August 1994): 40–48.

Durlach, Nathaniel I., and Anne S. Mavor, eds. *Virtual Reality: Scientific and Technological Challenges.* Washington: National Academic P, 1994.

Ellis, Stephen R. "What Are Virtual Environments?" *IEEE Computer Graphics and Applications* 14 (January 1994): 17–22.

Gigante, M. A. "Virtual Reality: Definitions, History and Applications." *Virtual Reality Systems*. Ed. R. A. Earnshaw et al. San Diego: Academic P, 1993a. 3–14.

_____. "Virtual Reality: Enabling Technologies." *Virtual Reality Systems*. Ed. R. A. Earnshaw et al. San Diego: Academic P, 1993b. 15–25.

Goldman, Jon, and Trina M. Roy. "The Cosmic Worm." *IEEE Computer Graphics and Applications* 14 (July 1994): 12–14.

Gradecki, Joe. *The Virtual Reality Construction Kit.* New York: John Wiley, 1994.

Greenhouse, Cheryl, and Richard Julian. "Substantial Technology Gap

Exists Between What Is Virtual, What Is Reality." National Research Council News Release available on the WorldWide Web at *http://www.nas.edu*; via Gopher at *gopher.nas.edu*; and via FTP at *ftp.nas.edu/pub/*. September 19, 1994.

Hamit, Francis. *Virtual Reality and the Exploration of Cyberspace*. Carmel: Sams, 1993.

Hayward, Tom. *Adventures in Virtual Reality*. Carmel: Que, 1993.

Hodges, Matthew E., and Russell M. Sasnett. *Multimedia Computing. Case Studies from MIT Project Athena*. Reading: Addison-Wesley, 1993.

Jacobson, Linda. *Garage Virtual Reality*. Indianapolis: Sams, 1994.

Kalawsky, Roy S. "A Comprehensive Virtual Environment Laboratory Facility." *Virtual Reality Systems*. Ed. R. A. Earnshaw et al. San Diego: Academic P, 1993a. 77–89.

―――. *The Science of Virtual Reality and Virtual Environments: A Technical, Scientific and Engineering Reference on Virtual Environments*. Wokingham: Addison-Wesley, 1993b.

Krueger, Wolfgang, and Bernard Broehlich. "The Responsive Workbench." *IEEE Computer Graphics and Applications* 14 (May 1994): 12–14.

Larijani, L. Casey. *The Virtual Reality Primer*. New York: McGraw-Hill, 1994.

Latta, John N., and David J. Oberg. "A Conceptual Virtual Reality Model." *IEEE Computer Graphics and Applications* 14 (January 1994): 23–29.

Little, Thomas D. C. "Time-Based Media Representation and Delivery." *Multimedia Systems*. Ed. John F. Koegel Buford. Reading: Addison-Wesley, 1994. 175–200.

Luther, Arch C. "Digital Video and Image Compression." *Multimedia Systems*. Ed. John F. Koegel Buford. Reading: Addison-Wesley, 1994. 143–174.

Machover, Carl, and Steve E. Tice. "Virtual Reality." *IEEE Computer Applications and Graphics* 14 (January 1994): 15–16.

Mallen, G. L. "Back to the Cave—Cultural Perspectives on Virtual Reality." *Virtual Reality Systems*. Ed. R. A. Earnshaw et al. San Diego: Academic P, 1993. 265–272.

McCarty, W. Dean, Steven Sheasby, Philip Amburn, Martin R. Stytz, and Chip Switzer. "A Virtual Cockpit for a Distributed Interactive Simulation." *IEEE Computer Applications and Graphics* 14 (January 1994): 49–54.

Miami Herald. "The Newest Sensation." September 6, 1994. 6b.

Minoli, Daniel, and Robert Keinath. *Distributed Multimedia Through*

Broadband Communications. Boston: Artech, 1994.

Nielsen, Jakob. *Hypertext and Hypermedia.* Boston: Academic P, 1993.

Papathomas, M., C. Breiteneder, S. Gibbs, and V. deMey. "Synchronization in Virtual Worlds." *Virtual Worlds and Multimedia.* Ed. Nadia Magenat Thalmann et al. Chichester: John Wiley, 1993. 135–152.

Pimentel, Ken, and Brian Blau. "Teaching Your System to Share." *IEEE Computer Applications and Graphics* 14 (January 1994): 60–65.

Pimentel, Ken, and Kevin Teixeira. *Virtual Reality. Through the New Looking Glass.* New York: Windcrest/McGraw-Hill, 1993.

Ribarsky, William, Jay Bolter, Augusto Op den Bosch, and Ron van Teylingen. "Visualization and Analysis Using Virtual Reality." *IEEE Computer Graphics and Applications* 14 (January 1994): 10–12.

Rowley, Terry W. "Virtual Reality Products." *Virtual Reality Systems.* Ed. R. A. Earnshaw et al. San Diego: Academic P, 1993. 39–50.

Schmitt, G. "Virtual Reality in Architecture." *Virtual Worlds and Multimedia.* Ed. Nadia Magenat Thalmann et al. Chichester: John Wiley, 1993. 85–97.

Shneiderman, Ben. *Designing the User Interface: Strategies for Effective Human-Computer Interaction.* 2nd ed. Reading: Addison-Wesley, 1992.

Stone, R. J. "Virtual Reality: A Tool for Telepresence and Human Factors Research." *Virtual Reality Systems.* Ed. R. A. Earnshaw et al. San Diego: Academic P, 1993. 181–202.

Sturman, David J., and David Zeltzer. "A Survey of Glove-based Input." *IEEE Computer Graphics and Applications* 14 (January 1994): 30–39.

von Wahlde, Barbara, and Nancy Schiller. "Creating the Virtual Library: Strategic Issues." *The Virtual Library: Visions and Realities.* Ed. Laverna M. Saunders. Westport: Meckler, 1993. 15–46.

Whalley, L. J. "Ethical Issues in the Application of Virtual Reality to the Treatment of Mental Disorders." *Virtual Reality Systems.* Ed. R. A. Earnshaw et al. San Diego: Academic P, 1993. 273–287.

Whitehouse, Karen. "The Museum of the Future." *IEEE Computer Graphics and Applications* 14 (May 1994): 8–11.

Wodaski, Ron. *Virtual Reality Madness!* Carmel: Sams, 1993.

Index

457

Parr, Joyce, 223
Pascal, Francine, 3
Pass It On: African-American Poetry for Children, 257–258
Patchwork Quilt, The, 257
Paterson, Katherine, 124, 205
patriarchal, domination, 57; society, 91
Peck, Richard, 289, 296–297
Peck, Robert Newton, 211
peer influence, 290
People Could Fly, The, 231
People: No Different Flesh, The, 398
Pet Sematary, 7
Peterson, D. A., 188
Petticoat Rebel, 109–113
Phantom Tollbooth, The, 2
Phone Calls, 289
Phule's Company, 400
Phule's Paradise, 400
Pigman, The, 5, 198–200
Pigman's Legacy, The, 5
Pike, Christopher, 4
Pilgrimage: The Book of the People, 398
Pimentel, Ken, 427, 428, 429, 432, 435, 436–437, 438, 440, 446, 447–448, 450–451
Pinkney, Andrea Davis, 257
Pinkney, Brian, 257
Pinkney, Jerry, 256–257
Pipher, Mary, 61, 67–68, 87–88
Planet of the Apes, 403
Polacco, Patricia, 230, 258
Polster, Miriam F., 105, 112, 114, 117, 120–121, 122, 125, 127, 130
Pool of Fire, The, 400
"Positive Portraits of the Elderly in Realistic Fiction for Young Adults", 197–199
Postman, The, 394
Powers, Harriet, 236, 244
Preminger, Erik Lee, 11
Prime Suspect, 10, 12
Prisoner of my Desire, 8
Probably Still Nick Swansen, 190
Project Pendulum, 398
Protestant work ethic, 124, 125
Psion, 405
psyche, abilities, 403, adolescent, 186–187

"Psychological Development and Females' Sport Participation", 343
Psychology of Oppression, The, 49
punishment, emotional, 71–72, 76–77; physical, 70–74, 76–77, 81; strict, 62

✦ Q ✦

Qualey, Marsha, 175
Quick, Amanda, 8
QuickTime Movie File (QMF) format, 445
Quilting the World Over, 230
quilts: as medium, 221–249; as stories, 228–229
Quilts from Appalachia, 223, 238
Quilts in America, 224
Quilts of America, 229, 239
Quilts of Illusion, 238
Quindlen, Anna, 317, 343

✦ R ✦

Rag Coat, The, 242
Rahn, Suzanne, 104
Rainbow Jordan, 51, 57, 61, 62, 207
Ralston, Penny A., 194
Reader's Advisor, The, 389
Reclaiming Space, Revisioning the Body: The Quest for Gender-Sensitive Physical Education, 342
Red Mars, 401
Regan, Jennifer, 240
relationships, family, 91–101; peer, 137; sibling, 137
Remember Me, 4
Remove Protective Coating a Little at a Time, 198–199
Republic, 180
Rescue in Denmark, 143
Rescue of the Danish Jews: Moral Courage Under Stress, The, 138–139, 143, 146, 149
Resource Guide of Recommended Curricula and Textbooks, 375
Response Workbench, 446
Restaurant at the End of the Universe, The, 287, 308–309
Rettberg, Georgeann Eskievich, 345
Reuter, Bjarne, 136, 144, 150–151, 152,

About the Contributors

LINDA A. CATELLI is an associate professor at Queens College of the City University of New York and founder/director of a school-university partnership program entitled Project SCOPE. She was honored in 1990 by the American Association for Higher Education for pioneering work in school-college collaboration. She has been involved as an action researcher, staff developer, and curriculum innovator with school practitioners to institute change and holistic reform in K-12 and teacher education. She teaches graduate and undergraduate courses in education. She has written numerous articles and research papers and has spoken on a wide-range of topics in physical education as well as in general education.

LYNN COCKETT is a Ph.D. candidate at Rutgers University. A former young adult and children's librarian, she is currently vice president/president elect of the Children's Literature Council of Pennsylvania for whose journal she writes a regular column on young adult literature. She has published articles and reviews in *School Library Journal* and *Booklist* in addition to "Periodical Literature for African-American Young Adults: A Neglected Resource," in *African American Voices in Young Adult Literature: Tradition, Transition, Transformation* (Scarecrow Press, 1994).

CAROL JONES COLLINS is a Ph.D. candidate at Rutgers University. She is the middle school librarian at the Montclair Kimberley Academy in Montclair, New Jersey. She holds both an M.A. in human relations from New York University and an M.L.S. degree from Rutgers University. She has published in *Library Trends: Twentieth-Century Young Adult Writers* (St. James Press, 1994), and has contributed a chapter of *African-American Voices in Young Adult Literature: Tradition, Transition, Transformation* (Scarecrow Press, 1994).

KIMBERLY LEANNE COLLINS was a high school senior in Milburn High School in Milburn, New Jersey when she wrote her chapter for this book. She is now a freshman at Simmons College, Boston, Massachusetts.

KAREN TORON COOPER is a youth services/reference librarian at the Hopewell Branch of the Mercer County Library System. She has an M.L.S. from Rutgers University, a Ph.D. candidate in comparative literature from UCLA, and a teaching degree in English from Trenton State College. As a teaching fellow at UCLA, she taught Danish and world literature, and, as an adjunct at Trenton State, she taught a research paper course. In her current position, she especially enjoys expanding services for young adults through such programs as Book Buddies, Book Club, and outreach visits to the local schools. At home she enjoys the enthusiastic support of her husband Peter and her children Jessica and Glenn.

HILARY S. CREW is a Ph.D. candidate at Rutgers University, completing a dissertation on "The Daughter/Mother Relationship in Selected Young Adult Novels: A Narrative Analysis." She has written "Feminist Theories and the Voices of Mothers and Daughters in Selected African-American Literature for Young Adults," in *African American Voices in Young Adult Literature: Tradition, Transition, Transformation* (Scarecrow Press, 1994) and, with Jane Anne Hannigan, "A Feminist Paradigm for Library and Information Science" (*Wilson Library Bulletin*, 1993).

DAUGHTER/WOMAN is a children's librarian who holds a degree in English Literature from Cornell University and a M.L.S. from Rutgers University.

PAMELA E. GROVES was born in Kingston, Jamaica and moved to the United States at the age of eighteen. After earning her degree in special and elementary education, she educated her two children at home in Princeton, New Jersey. She holds a M.L.S. degree from Rutgers University.

JANET KLEINBERG is a school media specialist at Briarcliff Middle School in Mountain Lakes, New Jersey. She earned her master's degree in library service at Rutgers University. Her publications include "Periodical Literature for African-American Young Adults: A Neglected Resource," in *African American Voices in Young Adult Literature: Tradition, Transition, Transformation* (Scarecrow Press, 1994); and "The Youth's Companion: Precursor to Today's Magazines for Children," in *The Journal of the Children's Literature Council of Pennsylvania* (1994).

BONNIE KUNZEL is a young adult librarian at the New Brunswick Public Library. She holds her M.L.S. from Rutgers University. She loves to read and talk about books and has given a number of presentations on Best Books for Young Adults throughout New Jersey. She is a member of YALSA and has served on the ALA Best Books for Young Adults Committee. She reviews for VOYA. She is married and the mother of two children.

MARY K. LEWIS is a graduate of Cornell University and a current student in the School of Communication, Information and Library Studies, Rutgers University. She lives in Perth Amboy, New Jersey, with her husband and two children.

MARLYN KEMPER LITTMAN is a professor in the School of Computer and Information Sciences at Nova Southeastern University. She is the author of many publications in the field of telecommunications, computer networks, and emerging technologies, including *Networking: Choosing a LAN Path to Interconnection* (Scarecrow Press, 1987). She has presented papers on network security at the 16th National Online Meeting and at the 32nd Annual Symposium of Rutgers University. Her article "New Educational Paradigms Through ATM" appears in the *Proceedings of the 12th Annual International Conference on Technology and Education*. Her chapter on "Computer Networks as Facilitators for Learning" appears in *Ways of Knowing: Literature and the Intellectual Life of Children*, the companion volume to this text.

B. ELIZABETH MINA holds a M.L.S. from Rutgers University and works as a school media specialist in New Jersey. She has also worked as a newspaper reporter, technical writer in the computer industry, and classroom teacher. She holds a degree in education from Valparaiso University in Indiana.

FARRIS J. PARKER is a Vietnam veteran and holds a master's degree in painting and sculpture from Montclair State College and a M.L.S. from Rutgers University. He has exhibited his work in one man shows as well as with the Vietnam Veterans Arts Group at various settings, including Cork Gallery, Lincoln Center, and New York. He currently works with young people at the Montclair Public Library, New Jersey. He resides with his wife in Orange, New Jersey.

NANCY L. ROTH is an assistant professor in the School of Communication, Information and Library Studies at Rutgers University. Her research focuses on issues of policy and identity in health communication. She received her doctorate from the University of Texas.

TESS BECK STUHLMANN has enjoyed the company of young people all her life, through family services, creative workshops, nursery schools, classrooms, and scouting. A youth services librarian, she works at the Plainsboro Public Library, New Jersey, in both reference and the children's room. She is the mother of three, and lives with her husband Bob and their two youngest in Allentown, New Jersey.

KAY E. VANDERGRIFT is an associate professor, School of Communication, Information and Library Studies, Rutgers University. She is the author of many chapters, articles and papers in the professional literature. She has written several books, including *Child and Story: The Literary Connection* (Neal Schuman, 1980), *Children's Literature: Theory, Research, and Teaching* (Libraries Unlimited, 1990) and *Power Teaching: The Primary Role of the School Library Media Specialist* (American Library Association, 1994). She has also edited a number of books, among them, *Library Education and Leadership* (Scarecrow Press, 1990) and the forthcoming *Ways of Knowing: Literature and the Intellectual Life of Children* (Scarecrow Press, 1996). Her research focuses on applying feminist theories and reader-response literary theory to youth literature.